A PROFILE OF

Carbondale and Edwardsville

TWENTIETH-CENTURY

Edited by Jack Myers and David Wojahn

AMERICAN POETRY

SOUTHERN ILLINOIS UNIVERSITY PRESS

Copyright © 1991 by the Board of Trustees,
  Southern Illinois University
All rights reserved
Printed in the United States of America
Edited by Dan Gunter
Designed by David Ford
Production supervised by Natalia Nadraga
94 93 92 91   4 3 2 1

Library of Congress Cataloging-in-Publication Data

A Profile of twentieth-century American poetry / edited by Jack Myers
and David Wojahn
     p.   cm.
   Includes bibliographical references and index.
   1. American poetry—20th century—History and criticism.
I. Myers, Jack Elliott, 1941–. II. Wojahn, David, 1953–.
PS323.5.P76 1991
811'.509—dc20   90-39757
ISBN 0-8093-1348-0   CIP
ISBN 0-8093-1349-9 (pbk.)

Gertrude Stein, "A Red Hat," from *Tender Buttons*. Copyright 1946 by Random House,
  Inc. Reprinted from *Selected Writings of Gertrude Stein*, edited by Carl Van Vechten,
  by permission of Random House, Inc.
Permission to quote from other copyright sources appears in the Acknowledgments, pp.
  xiii–xv, which constitutes an extension of the copyright page.

The paper used in this publication meets the minimum requirements of American National
Standard for Information Sciences—Permanence of Paper for Printed Library Materials,
ANSI Z39.48-1984. ∞

CONTENTS

Preface   vii

Acknowledgments   xiii

1. Introduction: Recircuiting the American Past   1
   Ed Folsom

2. Modernism Comes to American Poetry: 1908–1920   25
   Roger Mitchell

3. Helmet of Fire: American Poetry in the 1920s   54
   Edward Hirsch

4. Utopocalypse: American Poetry in the 1930s   84
   Michael Heller

5. Constructing a New Stage: The Poetry of the 1940s   102
   Richard Jackson

6. The "Forbidden Planet" of Character: The Revolutions of the 1950s   131
   Mark Doty

7. A Quilt in Shades of Black: The Black Aesthetic in Twentieth-Century African American Poetry   158
   Timothy Seibles

8. American Poetry in the 1960s   190
   Leslie Ullman

9. The Demise of the "Delicate Prisons": The Women's Movement in Twentieth-Century American Poetry   224
   Kate Daniels

10.   American Poetry: 1970–1990   254
      Jonathan Holden

      Selected Bibliography   277

      Notes on Contributors   289

      Index   291

Preface

There is a surprising dearth of comprehensive critical histories on the full course of American poetry. Those that do exist and that are thought of as being definitive either argue their views through a seductive and ultimately forced umbrella thesis by which all products, principles, and practices of American poetry are to be judged, or focus on a relatively few major writers whose force and influence are said to grasp and represent the full sweep of American poetry. The remaining critical histories fall short of capturing the complex flux of our poetry by being too limited in range. What makes matters worse is that since the 1970s there has been an increasing tendency on the part of critics and scholars to abstract poetry from its cultural matrix—at times from meaning and common sense itself—in what seems to be an effort to raise criticism to an overelaborated art form in and of itself; in effect, to pull the very function of criticism further away from the knowledgeable reader's grasp toward an unintelligibility that would make the early reactions to Modernism's perceived obscurity appear mild.

In an effort to help restore an eclectic, comprehensive, and humanistic overview to American poetry, we, as editors, invited writers who are first and foremost working poets to create their own unique models of their assigned periods or topics, models written from their own sense of a cultural, historical, and craft aesthetic, ones which stem directly from their creative work. The only exception in this book, and we gratefully acknowledge it, is our inviting Ed Folsom, an articulate and original Whitman and early American scholar, to create an introductory overview of pre-twentieth-century American poetry, one which, it fortunately turns out, challenges the traditional critical view of that period.

Folsom's revisionist approach, which argues that our literary history be seen as a sort of palimpsest, gradually emerging layers of previously unacknowledged sources of the true American aesthetic and historical experience (in slave songs, Native American chants, the diaries of pioneer women, etc.), along with the already sanctioned body of poetry, reveals a leitmotif that is everywhere important throughout this volume—that of the continual interreflections among periods of upheaval, nascence, and coalescence and among the critical assessments unfolding in our history. The massive political shift to the Left that took place in the poetry of the thirties, as a reaction to early Modernism, rising poverty, and fascism, is paralleled in the later revolutionary shift toward the Left during the mid- to late-fifties by the Beats, Projectivists, Black Mountain, and New York schools of poetry that occurred as a reaction against High Modernism and the New Critics. The same shock late Victorian poetry was given by the vociferous arrival of the Imagists and Symbolist-influenced early Moderns in the teens and twenties is mirrored in the sixties by the advent of the Deep Imagist, Internationalist, and anti–Vietnam War poetries. And it would not be stretching a point to say that the decades of the forties and early fifties, a period of relative complacence and congealment, may find its aesthetic double in the late seventies and early eighties; and that the present and quite visible feminist and Native American movements may again be wresting poetry away from the academy toward the living tissue of American experience, just as revolutionaries such as Whitman, Dickinson, and Williams brought poetry back into the language and interests of their respective cultural periods.

But this implied historical reflexiveness is only one aspect of the essays that form this overview. The very problem of organizing the sometimes orderly, sometimes hopscotching series of literary events in American poetry became the first business at hand, and we, as editors, went about trying to create a structure that would coherently unite these historical materials within the format of a collection of original, critical essays.

It quickly became apparent, as we reviewed the history of twentieth-century poetry, that there is a loose but observable series of periodic demarcations into decades over the last sixty years. Our poetics seem to fall in line sensibly with changing world events in technology, politics, and economics and their concomitant changes in substance and sensibility. Harvey Gross, acknowledging this modern periodization into decades, calls it a "contracted millenarianism" due to "the enormous acceleration of the historical process" and our attendant anxiety about the future. Ultimately, in the light of a larger and more distanced historical perspective, it may prove to have been somewhat myopic of us to have neatly and arbitrarily sliced American poetics into periods roughly and interestingly equivalent to the periods of growth in a human lifespan; but for now, as a sketch toward a more voluminous, omniscient overview, this format seems both inherently appropriate to the work under discussion and the best possible organizing principle.

Besides establishing a format, the editors asked the contributors to consider the following concerns in their essays: (1) the ongoing chronological and historical nature of developments in American poetics; (2) the emergence of seminal creative and critical developments; and (3) the continuities and disruptions in the lines of aesthetic force and influence. Early on, it was also apparent that certain important topics of great social, political, and literary impact and consequence had also taken place, such as the new black poetry and the women's literary movement, and that these subjects could not be treated effectively within the confines of a chronological format, though they are also touched upon within the period essays. Thus, we have also included these two special-focus essays—on women's and African American poetry—as separate and distinct entities and have placed them near the periods to which they roughly correspond.

Beyond the requirements that the contributors create accessible, readable overviews, the essayists were left to their own devices in matters of perspective, writing style, thematic strategy, and the selection, organization, evaluation, and interpretation of materials. Arising from their research in these complex and intellectually demanding territories, the contributors have provided a rich and provocative mixture of objective reportage, incisive argumentative theses, ground-breaking visions, and ardent support for what was discovered during these historical forays. Thus, our most crucial editorial task was the initial selection of contributing essayists, writers who were chosen on the basis of their knowledge and interest in their assigned areas.

Admittedly, there will be a fashionable critical stance and hierarchy in current favor within any given period. Recently, for example, the reputations of Wallace Stevens and William Carlos Williams have taken precedence over that of T. S. Eliot, the most lionized modern poet of the first half of the twentieth century. Attendant to the decline in Eliot's stature, there has been a reevaluation, almost a dismissal, of views by the New Critics that held sway for forty years. Furthermore, there is a noticeable turning away in the eighties from the poetry of general social and political protest, a vibrant sort of advocacy of the feminist movement, an aroused suspicion of the New Academics, and a dissatisfaction or restlessness with poetry written in the Confessional, Surrealist, and Deep Image modes. The canon changes with the views of its most articulate opponents and revisionists; figures once deemed preeminent (Conrad Aiken, Vachel Lindsay, Archibald MacLeish, and Allen Tate, to name a few) disappear from anthologies, and the ongoing waxing and waning of reputations keeps pace with the changes in art. On the other hand, reevaluations often exhume "out-of-date" aesthetics: for example, as the New Critics once dismissed the work of the Romantics as being too emotive and self-indulgent, the theoreticians of Deconstruction have recently reinstated and argued for their value. The fashion of the eighties, in direct opposition to the time when iconoclastic poet/critics such as Ezra Pound, T. S. Eliot, Yvor Winters, and Allen Tate unified theory and practice, sees the once complementary roles of poet and critic diverging. While critics have increasingly specialized their views and language to the point of being understood only among themselves, poets have chosen either not to understand or to ignore what their critics are saying. Some would go so far as to say that in the nineties poetry is faced with the threat of becoming the handmaiden of various arcane schools of criticism which see the critical function as the reverse of the traditional role in which the critic selects, interprets, and evaluates the poetry texts at hand. Instead, poetry is in danger of becoming little more than an extension of theory. While this volume may argue at certain points for or against these leanings, the essays, as products of the age, will necessarily have the stamp of the age upon them.

The one unquestionable development in literature in this century is that American poetry has come of age. Ever since the advent of Modernism and its willful breaking of the formal and metrical hold exerted over it by English poetry, in form and idiom our poetry can no longer be considered merely an adjunct to English literature. There are other current experiments within this country and influences from abroad (Asia, Africa, Europe, and South America) that continue to shape a distinct American poetry within whose confines there is a great deal of controversy, regimentation, and experiment. In the 1990s, we can point to three specific, simultaneous developments underway: (1) the ongoing solidification of "mainstream," conversational poetry which in its narrative, lyric, and meditative modes focuses on the domestic concerns of the American middle class and promises a new accessibility and the possibility of larger audiences; (2) the abstract, self-referential poetry of both the Language and Continuum poets whose focus on the creative process itself, and on the functioning of mind and language, are reminiscent of earlier Cubist efforts by poets such as Gertrude Stein, in whose works chance association, playfulness, and an oxymoronic subjective-objectivity revealed new frontiers of consciousness despite the charges of "difficulty" and obscurity leveled against it; and (3) the revival of traditional forms and meter by the New Formalists, meant possibly as a warning that the experiments in poetry over the last thirty years have led us too far afield from the more traditional mnemonic elements and pleasures of our poetic heritage.

In economic terms, the diversity within our current poetry may quite possibly be ended by the recent and severe cutbacks in government funding of fellowships to individuals and grants to presses, universities, and nonprofit organizations and by the efforts of politicians who feel it incumbent upon themselves to act as watchdogs over the arts. Concomitantly, the new merger/takeover mentality of business has created conglomerate chain bookstores that are reluctant to stock slow-moving poetry books and whose volume profit margins are driving small bookstores out of business at an alarming rate. Although there has been a steady increase in the number of students attending college-based workshops in creative writing—due mainly to the sanctioning of the master of fine arts in creative writing as a terminal degree—the diminishing book market and obvious lack of interest on the part of large commercial presses to publish poetry (a 400 percent drop over the last thirty years), suggest that once more American poets and poetry may have to depend heavily upon small presses, journals, and university-sponsored efforts in order to be heard. Once again, the leitmotif of reflexiveness surfaces even in the business of poetry.

The question observers, critics, and practitioners of poetry are asking is what forces now at work will shape the decade ahead. Will the sheer number of serious poets practicing their craft today, a number which has never before been seen in literary history, make the poetry at the end of the century extremely exciting, as Jonathan Holden suggests in his essay included here, or numbingly mediocre? Is the current domination of Postmodernist mainstream, conversational poetry, a vestigial form which took forty years to come into its own, so formulaic and prosaic in its current canonized form that it has lost the freshness and flexibility that once made it seem so vital? Are the recent avant-garde experiments on both East and West coasts by the Language poets doomed to become a minor footnote in our literary history because of their art-for-art's-sake overspecialization? And is the New Formalism simply and finally the last gasp of the New Criticism, the last vestiges of the English hold over American poetry? Within the following essays, which track the history of American poetry which goes back over the last one hundred and fifty years, there are explicit and implied indications that those minorities whose lives have been torn through custom, ignorance, and malice from their cultural matrices may become the most vital force informing the future of our art. For as can be seen in even the most cursory review of any period in our poetry, the future belongs to those who have been made to struggle against the confines of tradition, a word whose very etymology derives from the word "surrender."

Acknowledgments

The editors would like to thank Southern Methodist University and, in particular, Susan Meyn, for help in the preparation of this manuscript.

Permission to quote from the following copyright sources is gratefully acknowledged:

Kate Daniels, "The Demise of the 'Delicate Prisons': The Women's Movement in Twentieth-Century American Poetry," first appeared in *Cimarron Review,* Summer 1990; reprinted by permission.

Selections from *The Palm at then End of the Mind: Selected Poems and a Play* by Wallace Stevens, edited by Holly Stevens. Reprinted by permission of Alfred A. Knopf Inc.

Selections from *The Gold Cell* and *The Dead and the Living* by Sharon Olds. Reprinted by permission of Alfred A. Knopf Inc.

Selections from "From My Window," by Charles Reznikoff, in *Poems 1918–1930,* vol. 1 of *The Complete Poems of Charles Reznikoff,* edited by Seamus Cooney. Santa Rosa, Calif.: Black Sparrow Press, 1976. Reprinted by permission of Black Sparrow Press.

Selections from "Dream Boogie," by Langston Hughes. Copyright 1951 by Langston Hughes; copyright renewed 1979 by George Houston Bass. Reprinted by permission of Harold Ober Associates, Inc.

"The Weary Blues" and "The Negro Speaks of Rivers," by Langston Hughes. Copyright 1926 by Alfred A. Knopf, Inc., and renewed 1954 by Langston Hughes. Reprinted from *Selected Poems of Langston Hughes* by permission of Alfred A. Knopf, Inc., and Harold Ober Associates, Inc.

Selections from "A Tuft of Flowers" and "Directive," by Robert Frost, in *The Poetry of Robert Frost,* edited by Edward Connery Lathem. Copyright 1934, 1947, © 1969 by Holt, Rinehart and Winston. Copyright © 1962 by Robert Frost. Copyright © 1975 by Lesley Frost

Ballantine. Reprinted by permission of Henry Holt and Company, Inc.

"Soup," from *Smoke and Steel*, copyright 1920 by Harcourt Brace Jovanovich, Inc., and renewed 1948 by Carl Sandburg; reprinted by permission of the publisher.

Excerpt from "The Metaphysical Poets," by T. S. Eliot, in *Selected Essays*, copyright 1950 by Harcourt Brace Jovanovich, Inc., and renewed 1978 by Esme Valerie Eliot; reprinted by permission of the publisher.

Excerpt from "Little Gidding," by T. S. Eliot, in *Four Quartets*, copyright 1943 by T. S. Eliot and renewed 1971 by Esme Valerie Eliot; reprinted by permission of Harcourt Brace Jovanovich, Inc.

Excerpts from "Aunt Helen" and "Morning at the Window," by T. S. Eliot, in *Collected Poems 1909–1962*, copyright 1936 by Harcourt Brace Jovanovich, Inc., and renewed 1964, 1963 by T. S. Eliot; reprinted by permission of the publisher.

Selection from "Way Out West," by LeRoi Jones, in *Preface to a 20 Volume Suicide Note;* copyright © 1961 by LeRoi Jones (Imamu Amiri Baraka); reprinted by permission of Sterling Lord Literistic, Inc.

Selections from *Personae: The Collected Shorter Poems*, by Ezra Pound. Copyright 1926 by Ezra Pound. Reprinted by permission of New Directions Publishing Corporation and Faber and Faber Ltd.

Selections from *The Cantos of Ezra Pound* reprinted by permission of New Directions Publishing Corporation and Faber and Faber Ltd.

Selections from *Collected Poems of H. D. 1912–1944*, copyright © 1982 by the Estate of Hilda Doolittle, reprinted by permission of New Directions Publishing Corporation.

Selections from *Selected Poems, The Collected Earlier Poems*, and *Imaginations*, by William Carlos Williams, reprinted by permission of New Directions Publishing Corporation.

"Lesson, Lesson" and selections from "The Mortician's Twelve-Year-Old Son," from *Killing Floor*, by Ai. Copyright © 1979 by Ai. Reprinted by permission of Houghton Mifflin Co.

Selections from "Pro Femina," copyright © 1963 by Carolyn Kizer. From *Knock upon Silence*, by Carolyn Kizer. Used by permission of Doubleday, a division of Bantam Doubleday Dell Publishing Group, Inc.

Selections from "The White House," by Claude McKay, in *The Selected*

Poems of Claude McKay. Copyright 1981; reprinted with the permission of Twayne Publishers, a division of G. K. Hall & Co., Boston.

Selections from "Recitative," by Hart Crane, in *The Complete Poems and Selected Letters and Prose of Hart Crane*, edited by Brom Weber (New York: Liveright, 1966). Reprinted by permission of Liveright Publishing Corp.

"First Fig," by Edna St. Vincent Millay. From *Collected Poems*, Harper & Row. Copyright 1922, 1950 by Edna St. Vincent Millay. Reprinted by permission of Elizabeth Barnet, Literary Executor.

"Along History," "Myth," "Rational Man," and selections from "The Speed of Darkness" and "To Enter That Rhythm Where the Self is Lost," by Muriel Rukeyser. From *The Collected Poems of Muriel Rukeyser*. New York: McGraw-Hill, 1978. Reprinted by permission of William L. Rukeyser.

The lines from "Shooting Script," "The Burning of Paper Instead of Children," "Incipience," and "Diving into the Wreck" and the complete poems, "Prospective Immigrants Please Note" and "A Valediction Forbidding Mourning," are reprinted from *The Fact of a Doorframe: Poems Selected and New, 1950–1984*, by Adrienne Rich, with the permission of the author and the publisher, W. W. Norton & Company, Inc. Copyright © 1984 by Adriene Rich. Copyright © 1975, 1978 by W. W. Norton & Company, Inc. Copyright © 1981 by Adrienne Rich.

A Profile of Twentieth-Century American Poetry

1

Introduction: Recircuiting the American Past

ED FOLSOM

My faith is the greatest of faiths and the least of faiths,
. . . .
Looking forth on pavement and land, or outside of pavement and land,
Belonging to the winders of the circuit of circuits.
One of that centripetal and centrifugal gang I turn and talk like a man leaving
    charges before a journey.

—Walt Whitman, "Song of Myself"

Writing poetic history is like winding a circuit of circuits. There is no end to the turns, to the variety of patterns that will still carry the charge, still move the energy safely from its source to its desired end. There are many versions of how American poetry wound its way to the twentieth century, and critics over the last two hundred years have written the story—have wound the circuit—of American poetry in countless ways. Poets once considered major have become minor; poets unknown in one generation have emerged as the most vital poets for another generation; poets once famous have become forgotten for generations only to re-emerge later as important figures. As the times change, as the writers of our literary histories change, our poets get rearranged in a multitude of designs. Like a kaleidoscope, the tradition regularly gets shaken up, and poets who are central to one design may well be peripheral to another. We usually view our own present as offering us some sort of privileged perspective on history, as if we know more now about ourselves than previous writers of histories knew about themselves; our judgments thus seem secure where the judgments made generations ago seem quaint and always suspect. We need to hold in mind Whitman's perception about the inevitable power and necessity of composting, of tearing down the current forms—of life, of language, of thought—so that new forms

1

can emerge. There is no composition without composting; in their roots, both words—"compose" and "compost"—mean the same: taking apart to put together. Incessant composting defines the way we compose our past and compose our relation to our past; the past is always changing, and our judgments are made to be decomposed so that the fertile compost can produce new life. This composition of our poetic history, the one you are about to read, is offered as matter for the cultural compost heap.

Whitman, in the quotation that opens this essay, urges a democratic rendering of tradition, a view of the past spacious enough and generous enough to include all possibilities—"the greatest of faiths and the least of faiths."[1] He knows that no single priest, be it a priest of religion or art or literary history, has the final answer. Our only hope is to move in and out, weave back and forth, listen, as we begin our journey, to Whitman's charge that we be open to vast possibilities. This is, after all, what Whitman's new democratic poetry is—the poetry of the open road, poetry that declines hierarchical discriminations, breaks from dead traditions, leads us to surprising details we have not been taught to see.

We might think of American poetry, then, as a vast fabric—a *textus*/textile/text—composed of many different kinds of threads, forming no overall design but rather countless discernible patterns, each available for the observer diligent enough to spot it. Some of the patterns are faded in out-of-print books, some nearly colorless in unpublished notebooks, some gaudy but finally uninteresting in their once-ostentatious popularity. But all the patterns were always there; we need to remember that, remember that our own histories have blinded us to what has always been there, remember that there are patterns and influences lost in the welter of threads that nonetheless are essential to holding the fabric together, as essential as the more familiar patterns that our eyes have been taught to see. There has always been a tradition of women poets in America, a tradition of black poets, a tradition of Native American poets, a tradition of folk poets; sometimes we need a microscope to trace the threads, but they are all there, part of the pattern. Our task in this volume is to trace the overall American pattern, to find its origins and its distinctly original weave.

When the first voyagers from Europe landed on what would come to be American shores, the major pattern-weaving tool they carried with them was their language.[2] American poetry may have begun, as William Carlos Williams suggests, with the cry of Columbus's sailors on sighting land, "Nuevo Mundo!" or with Columbus's own groping for words to describe the "beautiful thing" he had stumbled upon.[3] What those first explorers saw had to be reported; European words had to be attached to things that the languages had no experience of. So the early voyage journals are filled with analogies (America is like Eden) and definitions by negation (America is unlike anything in Spain or England or France). The voyagers met natives who spoke a bewildering assortment of languages unrelated to their own, and the first responses to the New World were linguistically frustrated ones: a failure of the languages brought by the voyagers (they didn't have the words or the syntax to absorb the things of the New World, a place that their languages could yield only as "new" or "foreign" or "strange"), an inability to use the native languages that had grown up in and evolved out of this landscape (languages that were attached in their very roots to things that to them were native and familiar). Eventually, many of the voyagers would become settlers and use their imported languages to impose familiarity on landscapes that seemed to resist it: one nineteenth-century traveler on the New York frontier scoffed at the mania of American schoolboys with their smattering of Latin and Greek for imposing "Albany," "Schenectady," "Ithaca," "Syracuse," and "Utica" onto the wilderness.[4] To name a land "New England" or "New York" was, as Whitman came to see, the very opposite of the attitude necessary to create an American poetry, a distinct and intense language that would look out away from "English" and look to the native languages and look to what had to be named and seek new words and new ways to say it.

American poetry, then, was doomed to be a hybrid, emerging from Old World languages and inherited forms and traditions, but seeking to stretch, challenge, and, when necessary, break those languages and forms and traditions in the service of a fresh way of seeing: a poetry that would grow out of the encounter of the English language with a place that the language had not emerged from and had no intrinsic relationship with, a poetry (and a language) that would someday no longer be English but could be called American. The phrase "American poetry" embodies, then, something of an oxymoron: "America"—the unnamed land, pure potential—melded with "poetry," the Old World concept, refined and formed over hundreds of years of European experience. From the beginning, those Europeans coming to live in the New World felt pulled both ways, to the East and to the West, to the European past and to the American future, to their European relatives whom they were no longer quite like and to the American natives who were something they would never be; they would never again rest easily in any place, would always be weaving back and forth between divergent traditions, philosophies, cosmologies, languages.

Because of this peculiar cleavage of language and place, the tradition of American poetry has always been deceptive. Oddly enough, to trace the most fertile origins of American poetry we must, for the most part, turn away from poetry—or at least what most of us think of as poetry—during the first two centuries of English occupation of this continent. We can now see that it was not the tradition of Puritan meditative poetry, not the tradition of witty and patriotic Federalist or anti-Federalist verse, not the attempt to write an epic poem based on old models about a new subject, not the genteel and imitative Fireside poets who still occupy vast unread spaces in our anthologies—none of these things was the seedbed of that teeming, diverse activity that came to be American poetry in the twentieth century. Distinct new poetry was being generated, but it was appearing in odd and surprising guises: in travel journals and slave narratives, in captivity narratives and personal diaries, in slave songs and workers' songs, and in angry political demonstrations. *There* is where American poetry was brewing. What initially appeared to be American poetry was really only colonial imitation of European poetry, writing about America in Old World forms. The breakthrough would finally come when literally a new language began to be spoken on this continent, one that swayed to different rhythms and cadences, that absorbed slang, dialect, and vocabulary from a vast array of sources, sources such as black music and domestic life on the frontier, or the language of German and Japanese immigrants. Ralph Waldo Emerson knew that America's great poetic project was to find a way to give voice to this "sloven continent." Even by the 1840s, he said, "We have yet had no genius in America, with tyrannous eye, which knew the value of our incomparable materials, and saw, in the barbarism and materialism of the times, another carnival of the same gods whose picture he so much admires in Homer." "America is a poem in our eyes," he said, anticipating Whitman, who would take literally the idea of "America" as the "greatest poem." Emerson began cataloguing what needed to be said, what our words still needed to find a way to express. "Our logrolling, our stumps and their politics, our fisheries, our Negroes, and Indians, our boasts, and our repudiations, the wrath of rogues, and the pusillanimity of honest men, the northern trade, the southern planting, the western clearing, Oregon, and Texas, are yet unsung." Our "ample geography," Emerson concludes, "dazzles the imagination, and it will not wait long for metres." And he didn't mean the old meters, seeing the New World through old and trained eyes, hearing it with ears tuned to past European accomplishments. He meant meters that would emerge from the open and raw response of a loosened language encountering a sloven continent. He knew, too, that his own training and predispositions would prevent him from being that poet, but when Whitman's *Leaves of Grass* came his way, he recognized the raw genius when he saw it.[5]

Any history, of course, tells us more about the time in which the history was written than about the time the history supposedly records, and that is doubly true of our literary histories, which so conveniently lift literature from the vast cultural web in which it is embedded and abstract literature from the wider history so that it appears clean and precise—the action of a small club of authors who are responding to each other, creating a literature out of a coterie of concerns at a safe remove from the earthier concerns that the rest of the culture is experiencing. These neat versions of our past blind us by teaching us how to see only selectively. Our conception of American poetry is constructed of the various selective versions of it that we have read, and so we have forgotten what American poetry is. American poetry is in large part made up of what we have forgotten, of what we as a culture no longer even remember we have forgotten.

Part of the problem in searching out how American poetry got to the twentieth century is that so many twentieth-century American poets write their poetry over texts that are not American. If for a moment we rule out the pervasive influence of Walt Whitman, we realize that relatively few American poets of this century sense that their work derives in any meaningful way from poetry written in America before 1900. Ezra Pound does not construct an American poetic history for himself, but rather is concerned with energizing the English language by echoing rhythms and images from Provençal, Chinese, Anglo-Saxon. H. D. builds her palimpsest over Greek and Egyptian layers. T. S. Eliot's layered past includes much of British literature and yawns open to Sanskrit. Wallace Stevens seems more rooted in a European Symbolist tradition than in American poetic history. Recent scholarship has attempted with varying degrees of success to suggest American backgrounds for these and other modern poets,[6] but their careers remain stubbornly unresponsive to a pattern of American influences.

There *are* American poets, though, who seek out an indigenous American tradition, a system of American roots. I would like to look briefly at how some of our twentieth-century poets have retrieved vitality from the American poetic tradition, how they have learned to talk back to the poets of our past in order to prepare their own ground. These poets help us trace some of the most direct circuits that guide the discoveries and insights of our past poets into the present. The poet who makes the most explicit challenge for American poets to ground themselves here, in this soil and in this tradition, is William Carlos Williams. *In the American Grain,* one of the finest books of American cultural criticism ever written, is Williams's attempt to find or, more precisely, to *construct* or to *invent* the ground of his being:

> It is an extraordinary phenomenon that Americans have lost the sense, being made up as we are, that what we are has its origin in what *the nation* in the past has been; that there is a source in AMERICA for everything we think or do; that morals affect the food and food the bone, and that, in fine, we have no conception at all of what is meant by moral, since we recognize no ground our own—and that this rudeness rests all upon the unstudied character of our beginnings; and that if we will not pay heed to our own affairs, we are nothing but an unconscious porkyard and oilhole for those, more able, who will fasten themselves upon us. . . . That unless everything that is, proclaim a ground on which it stand, it has no worth; and that what has been morally, aesthetically worth while in America has rested upon peculiar and discoverable ground.[7]

So Williams turns to charged encounters with the American continent— Red Eric, Columbus, Cortez, the Puritans, Daniel Boone, Père Sebastian Rasles, Sam Houston, and others—and wrests out a tradition, a spiritual genealogy, that yields Williams as an American poet, here in the present, grounded on this continent as opposed to the usual historical genealogy that lifts most of us off this continent and carries us off to Europe or Africa or Asia. Williams's "ground" is quirky, surprising, outrageous, but he doesn't offer it up as anything more than his ground; his challenge is for all of us to take the same plunge, to immerse ourselves in the history of words dealing with this place and construct a tradition that grounds us, naturally, here and now. It is a process that attaches us finally to the natives of this land and leaves us looking at them with awe: "The land! don't you feel it? Doesn't it make you want to go out and lift dead Indians tenderly from their graves, to steal from them—as if it must be clinging even to their corpses—some authenticity."[8]

Williams's homemade poetic ancestry turns out to be centered in Edgar Allan Poe, informed by Whitman, and measured in contradistinction to Emily Dickinson and to all things Puritan. Puritan writers are for

Williams the cold and unfertile center of American culture, who "praised a zero in themselves" and "were condemned to be without flower." Dickinson, for Williams, was as close as America got to "a true woman in flower," but she was "starving of passion in her father's garden," unable finally to touch ("NEVER to allow touch"), doomed to become the frail opposite of Jacataqua (the native woman who was open to touch, to mixture, to joining), so he rejects Dickinson and turns to Whitman, who, in Williams's view, buried himself in the fullness of this continent, who "had to come from under . . . and through a dead layer." Williams turns to Whitman as the model of how to tune poetry to the "American idiom," listening to Whitman's word choices, which signaled "a revolution in the language." But the surprising gesture in Williams's scheme is his turn to Poe, the poet who wrote *from* America instead of *about* it, who "burst through to expression of a reawakened genius of *place*," embodying the terror of the continent in his desperately rational forms.[9]

American poets since Williams have often taken up the challenge to define their own American grain, to wind their own circuits of American influence and response. And most of the self-created traditions are as idiosyncratic as Williams's; American poets have discovered a surprising range of origins as they look back to this country's poetry before the twentieth century began. And they have shown great inventiveness in accommodating those poets to their own purposes and needs. Hart Crane, around the same time that Williams was tracking his genealogy, forged attachments to Poe, Melville, Whitman, and Dickinson, a series of poetic progenitors who, in Crane's reading of them, taught him not only how to survive intense suffering, but how to wrest art out of that suffering, to turn his pain into a heightened language of victory.

All four poets make an appearance in Crane's *The Bridge,* his epic attempt to bridge a diminished present with a heroic past in order to unveil the vitality that must still be buried beneath the waste of the present moment. (Writing of this quest during a moment of despair, Crane mourned, "If only America were half as worthy today to be spoken of as Whitman spoke of it fifty years ago there might be something for me to say.")[10] Melville's poem "The Temeraire" (about the loss of splendor and the emergence of "a deadlier lore" of rivets and machines in Civil War sea battles) melds with Crane's embrace of the Civil War nurse Whitman, who in *his* Civil War poems wrested camaraderie out of the fratricidal destruction. Crane, reeling from the machine destruction of World War I, calls out for Whitman:

O Walt! . . . .
   . . . O, upward from the dead
Thou bringest tally, and a pact, new bound
Of living brotherhood!
   . . . Thou, pallid there as chalk,
Hast kept of wounds, O Mourner, all that sum
That then from Appomattox stretched to Somme!

From Dickinson, Crane learns the art of "transmuting silence with that stilly note / Of pain" that "Breaks us and saves, yes, breaks the heart, yet yields / That patience that is armour and that shields / Love from despair—when love foresees the end—" Later Crane would address Dickinson directly, absorbing from her a compressed and intense language riddled with dashes (on the page, his poetry often visually resembles Dickinson's) that turn phrases away from the syntax and into themselves:

You who desired so much—in vain to ask—
Yet fed your hunger like an endless task,
Dared dignify the labor, bless the quest—

Crane encounters and addresses the grim visage of Poe "swinging from the swollen strap" on the subway:

And why do I often meet your visage here,
Your eyes like agate lanterns—on and on
Below the toothpaste and the dandruff ads? . . .

And Death, aloft,—gigantically down
Probing through you—toward me, O evermore!

Crane meets Poe in a scene emblematic of the emptiness, waste, and triviality of modern-day America. As Poe for Williams transmuted a silent wilderness into an original literature, here Crane wants to transmute a waste-land present into an exalted song: Poe's ruin, his rejection by his society, both haunts and energizes Crane as he attempts to avoid the same, but risks repeating it nonetheless. Crane is not looking for poets of an original relationship with the wilderness as Williams was, but instead weaves his American poetic past from a group of poets he perceives to be emblematic of an ability to wrest art out of deprivation and death.[11]

We must be cautious not to rule out possible influences in our collective past, even (and especially) in those parts of the past that have been effectively silenced by our histories. When a poet like Donald Justice tells us that Trumbull Stickney and Frederick Goddard Tuckerman are vital parts of his poetic past, we begin to realize that our poets tend to look into odd and dusty corners. If we deafen ourselves to early poets who do not fit the patterns of our preferred structures we will not hear how fully twentieth-century poets are part of an American tradition.

These new circuits of American poetry that our poets wind help to jar loose canonical pronouncements and teach us of the politics of canon making. One of the most challenging and rigorous attempts to ground the poetic self in America, to construct a genealogy that yields that self fully in the present, has been undertaken by Adrienne Rich. She records a deeply conflicted sense of tradition as she discusses the "peculiar confusion" that a woman writer faces: "She goes to poetry or fiction looking for her way of being in the world, since she too has been putting words and images together; she is looking eagerly for guides, maps, possibilities; and over and over in the 'words masculine persuasive force' of literature she comes up against something that negates everything she is about: she meets the image of Woman in books written by men." The search for a woman's tradition that will give her a natural identity as a writer comes to be an act of survival for Rich, but it is never a simple discovery: "I read the older women poets with their peculiar keenness and ambivalence: Sappho, Christina Rossetti, Emily Dickinson, Elinor Wylie, Edna Millay, H. D. . . . But even in reading these women I was looking in them for the same things I had found in the poetry of men, because I wanted women poets to be the equals of men, and to be equal was still confused with sounding the same." Her own style, she finds, was "formed first by male poets," for they were the poets she was taught to read as an undergraduate.[12]

Like so many American women poets, Rich turns to literatures outside of America to find sustaining voices (there are, after all, more powerful female voices in British literature in the nineteenth century than in American literature of the same period, and the female tradition generally tends to be less nationalistic than the male tradition). But in two remarkable essays, "The Tensions of Anne Bradstreet" and "Vesuvius at Home: The Power of Emily Dickinson," Rich has begun grounding her poetic career in a distinctly American tradition, a tradition of women voicing their experience in resistance to a patriarchal society that is out to silence such voices. Rich finds significant resonance—"real parallels"— between her own life and Bradstreet's: both modeled their early work on male poets, both had learned to read in their father's library, both had experienced the ambivalent blessings of male critics, and both had struggled with being simultaneously an artist and a mother. Rich finds true origin, then, in this first American poet, "the first nondidactic American poet, the first to give an embodiment to American nature, the first in whom personal intention appears to precede Puritan dogma as an impulse to verse." Rich's admiration for Bradstreet allows her to feel an affectionate attachment to poetic experience on this continent extending back three hundred and fifty years: "To have written poems, the first good poems in America, while rearing eight children, lying frequently sick, keeping house at the edge of wilderness, was to have managed a poet's range and extension within confines as severe as any American poet has confronted."

Bradstreet helped Rich deal with and define her relationship to the male-centered concerns of American poetry: "Much has been written, by white American male writers, of the difficulties of creating 'great literature' at the edge of the wilderness, in a society without customs and traditions. Were the difficulties the same for women? Could women attempt the same solutions?" If American poetry, as the various "American Adam" readings of it suggest, is about entering a rugged, unnamed, New World and bringing forms of language to bear upon the wilderness to name it, to mate with and conquer the "Virgin Land," then where do women fit into the tradition? They are excluded if one must be an Adam in sexual conquest of a female landscape. Bradstreet brings the question into focus for Rich: "What has been the woman poet's relationship to nature, in a land where both women and nature have, from the first, been raped and exploited?" Rich enacts a radical rejection of the Adam–Virgin Land myth, refusing to be the fertile, sustaining field on which the male writes the national myths: "I am not the wheatfield / nor the virgin forest," Rich says in her revisionary poem "From an Old House in America," in which she creates the domestic countertradition that allows her to find just how "I am an American woman."[13]

Similarly, Rich enacts a retrieval of Dickinson from stifling male versions of her career (including Williams's version of her starving in her father's garden), seeking to approach her "in terms of her greatness rather than her littleness, the decisiveness of her choices instead of the surface oddities of her life or the romantic crises of her legend." Rich is out to reveal Dickinson as a full and spacious source for women writers in America: "I have been surprised at how narrowly her work, still, is known by women who are writing poetry, how much her legend has gotten in the way of her being repossessed, as a source and a foremother."[14]

Rich's unique American poetic tradition also finds a useful source in Whitman, "that poet, that American, who of all his brothers was most able to accept himself in his bisexual wholeness. For him, as for Dickinson, there is no Muse: only his Soul. Whitman's homoerotic poetry does not represent a flight from woman but a recognition of woman, and of the being in himself and in his beloved that is capable of tenderness, vulnerability, mutuality." Rich looks to lines in Whitman like

> I believe in you, my Soul, the other I am must not abase itself to you,
> And you must not be abased to the other . . .

and finds hopeful origins for "a new bisexuality in poetry written by men, which in claiming its own wholeness would be able to greet wholeness in woman with joy instead of dread."[15] For Rich, then, a Bradstreet/ Whitman/Dickinson lineage weaves out a poetic pattern of battle with the patriarchy, of rejection of orthodox obedience—whether that orthodoxy be religious, political, or aesthetic. It is a healthy and sustaining tradition that embeds Rich in a web of long-standing American concerns that have been blurred by our standard formulated sense of ourselves.

We could add many more examples of poets inventing their American poetic past, but these few will serve to suggest that the reconstructions continue, turning American poetry into a healthy compost heap of fertile possibilities. Poets are discarded, discovered, rediscovered; they are misread, reread, and read in contradictory ways. But surprising new poetry continues to crop up out of the heap. A variety of poets return to Emily Dickinson or to Walt Whitman, and each discovers a distinct Dickinson and a distinct Whitman, sometimes only remotely connected to the Dickinson and Whitman that another may discover. Sandra Gilbert's Dickinson is different from Rich's, for example, as Gilbert emphasizes the domestic qualities of Dickinson, and the ways Dickinson comes to use "the details of domesticity, as if they were not facts but metaphors, in order to recreate herself-and-her-life as a single, emblematic text, and often, indeed, as a sort of religious text—the ironic hagiography, say, of a New England Nun."[16]

Dickinson as foremother for many American poets now seems as likely and obvious an occurrence as Whitman's role as forefather for generations of American poets. Clearly, Dickinson will increasingly come to be the central source for more and more American poets. Her absorption into the active and fertile past for American poets has been slower than Whitman's, but that is because she has entered our poetry as a relative contemporary; it was not until the 1950s that we had anything approaching a complete and accurate text of her poetry, and the patronizing way her poetry was published after her death—grammar, rhyme, and punctuation "corrected" to the point of blunting the power and much of the originality of those poems that did appear, which were usually grouped into safe and traditional categories like "Love," "Nature," and "God"—prevented her from being seen as the rich and original poet she is. Generations of twentieth-century American poets grew up not able to find origins in her, for the Dickinson they knew seemed attenuated and small; Jane Cooper recalls how her own attempts to find a tradition for herself, to identify writers she could use "as steps toward" her "own growth," were blocked because Dickinson was so thoroughly removed from consideration: "since I knew only the bowdlerized, smoothed-over versions of her poems, it didn't occur to me how original she could be musically within those repeated New England hymn tunes."[17] Rich, Gilbert, and others are now in the active process of weaving Dickinson completely into our past, of discovering her multiple origins: "Wherever you take hold of her, she proliferates."[18]

Proliferation of possible selves describes what twentieth-century American poets have found when they look back to Walt Whitman as a source. For more than a hundred years American poets have talked back to Whitman in a surprising dialogue that in many ways has come to define American poetry.[19] The varied conversations have been loving, angry, exalted, prophetic, and disillusioned, but the important thing is that our poets have directly confronted Whitman again and again in essays and poems as they agree with him, reject him, accept him, revise him, question him, and affirm him. His direct encounter with his readers— "Listener up there! What have you to confide to me?"—and his challenge to future generations of poets, the "Poets to come!" who would "prove and define" all that Whitman had anticipated, stirred a direct response from his readers, from those poets of the future. Even late in the nineteenth century, poets who were trying in various ways to open the forms and rhythms and subjects of American poetry to new possibilities— Joaquin Miller, George Cabot Lodge, Hamlin Garland—addressed Whitman intensely as a kind of rough muse whose presence and example could energize their own language.

Whitman's whole poetic project can be seen as an attempt to initiate a living tradition of American poetry, to write the kind of poetry that would engender active response, that would produce poetry that would seek to subvert the authority of the past (including that of Whitman himself), would progress in a dialectic of disagreement and incessant revision. No poet worked as hard as Walt Whitman to initiate such an intense verbal reaction from his readers. The massive century-long record of how and why poets have talked back to him, have responded to his challenge, is proof of the importance and validity of his project. Whitman worked out a program for a radical new breed of reader, a reader who would make democracy possible, a reader who would undermine the author and his authority, learning in the process the solid Jacksonian virtues of distrusting all absolute authority and instead trusting the self. Walt Whitman saw himself not so much as a poet but rather as the *generator* of poetry: he believed it would be in the *encounter* with his work that poetry would occur, and this would be true for *any* reader, not just for poets who happened to read him. Whitman saw his poetry not as *meaning*, or as a container of meaning, but as the event in which or out of which meaning is made possible. Whitman as an author, uneasily cast by tradition in a position of authority, seldom was comfortable with conventional ways of treating readers; he was not interested in readers who succumbed easily to his authority, who settled back into the subservient role of being talked to, guided, and lectured. He wanted to create, to engender with his poetry, a new democratic reader—one who would wrestle his or her way to equality with any authority, one who would "resist much, obey little,"[20] one who would not be afraid to talk back, and in talking back actually to *create* the poem and re-create it with each new querulous reading—the meaning of the poem not handed to the reader from on high, but emerging anew out of each charged individual encounter with the poem.

This new relationship of reader and writer is what the 1855 preface to *Leaves of Grass* (and much of *Leaves* itself) is finally about:

> The message of great poets to each man and woman are, Come to us on equal terms, Only then can you understand us, We are no better than you, What we enclose you enclose, What we enjoy you may enjoy. . . . A great poem is for ages and ages in common and for all degrees and complexions and all departments and sects and for a woman as much as a man and a man as much as a woman. A great poem is no finish to a man or woman but rather a beginning. Has any one fancied he could sit at last under some due authority and rest satisfied with explanations and realize and be content and full? To no such terminus does the greatest poet bring . . . he brings neither cessation or sheltered fatness and ease. The touch of him tells in action.[21]

Equal terms, democratic leveling of reader and author, beginnings without finish (without "finish" in a double sense: with neither endings nor elegance), reading requiring action instead of ease, outdoor exercise instead of sheltered lethargy: Whitman initiates a poetry that releases the reader from the oppressive weight of tyrannical authority. No longer will readers "sit . . . under some due authority and rest satisfied." Emerson, too, bemoaned how "our reading is mendicant and sycophantic,"[22] and Whitman's project for a democratic American readership is an extension and intensification of Emerson's call for a self-reliant readership.

Whitman's most daring experiment—and all of *Leaves,* he said, was "a language experiment"—was this ongoing attempt to create a new kind of reader, to give his poetry the intimacy that would allow for a fertile and productive relationship between poet and reader, to give his poetry an abrasive edge on which readers could sharpen their wits and hone their reading skills, if they would get close enough to create the necessary friction. This would be no sterile aesthetic exercise; it was instead an experiment, Whitman believed, that was vital to the creation of democracy: to change our *reading* habits was to initiate the change in all our attitudes—to move from vestigial feudalistic relationships to true democratic ones, every soul discovering its poetic potential. Poets as diverse as Ezra Pound, Edgar Lee Masters, Witter Bynner, Carl Sandburg, Sherwood Anderson, Edwin Markham, Wallace Stevens, Langston Hughes, Muriel Rukeyser, Allen Ginsberg, Jack Kerouac, Richard Eberhart, Jonathan Williams, John Berryman, Denise Levertov, David Ignatow, James Wright, Theodore Roethke, Charles Olson, Robert Creeley, William Stafford, Theodore Weiss, Diane Wakoski, Robert Duncan, Louis Simpson, Galway Kinnell, Dave Smith, Joseph Bruchac, Larry Levis, Patricia Goedicke, Robert Bly, June Jordan, Erica Jong, and Judith Moffett—to name a random few—have all written poems or essays working out their various resistant relationships with one or another of the many Walt Whitmans: the quiet and intimate singer of songs of intense personal friendship, the Civil War dresser of wounds, the brash prophetic democratic prophet, the lonely singer by the swamp, the mystical guru of self-transcendence, the crafty old decrepit man. We have seen how Williams and Crane and Rich returned to him, reinventing him as they learned from him. Several Native American poets have found Whitman to be the one American poet who seems to incorporate native attitudes and respect for this continent. "There were," says Joseph Bruchac, "other voices which sang the rhythms of this continent's soil before Whitman. Yet it in no way belittles his accomplishment to say that he was only the first of those whose traditions stemmed from Europe to truly come to terms with the nature and the reality of the American earth, with its spirit of place."[23] Black poets find in him a remarkable sense of identification with the dispossessed. "Walt Whitman is the one white father," says June Jordan, "who shares the systematic disadvantages of his heterogeneous offspring trapped inside a closet that is, in reality, as huge as the continental spread of North and South America."[24]

Dickinson and Whitman have come to be expected sources, but they were not always considered so. We can continue to expect surprising returns in our poetry, as forgotten poets reemerge as fertile sources for new generations. Andrew Hudgins, a young poet, immersed himself in an ongoing dialogue with Sidney Lanier, not employing Lanier's extravagant theories of the unity of the laws of music and poetry, but imagining himself back into Lanier's life, writing the poems that Lanier himself suggested but never saw as the stuff of poetry. In Lanier, Hudgins finds a southern voice and a southern sensitivity—honed by Civil War experiences and general ill health—that energizes his own imaginings.[25] And the composting continues; a book of contemporary poets' tributes and responses to William Cullen Bryant has appeared.[26]

I have emphasized the vitality of Whitman and Dickinson as sources for twentieth-century poets. They clearly are the central figures, and their presence has been so strongly felt that sometimes critics cast all of American poetry into a configuration that sets up a Whitman tradition and a Dickinson tradition—an open form, public poetry unfolding out onto a shared and recognizable reality, versus a closed, private poetry infolding into an esoteric psychological reality.[27] The Whitman poetry became the poetry of the public road, the poetry of political concern, while the Dickinson poetry became the poetry of the private, intimate inscription. Whitman seemed to work toward a public language that would wield its power in public speech—he usually had his poems set in type before he worked on revising them—while Dickinson mined a private language, discovering a subversive power in her handsewn and handwritten fascicles: hers was a poetry that accreted power precisely because it was not published while she was writing. She moved further with herself and a few intimate friends as an audience than she would have with a nineteenth-century public responding to her poetry.

What this easy dichotomy ignores, though, is that Whitman and Dickinson are looked back to by our modern and contemporary poets because they share the remarkable quality of being original. Their originality is exactly what makes them origins for so many twentieth-century poets. They have come to be our two images of the poet who gains greatness by breaking from the past, by undermining orthodox powers, by forging a poetry that could not have been predicted. Until they began writing, they were quite literally unimaginable. And, while they are clearly very different kinds of poets, they are equally responsible for setting up a tradition in American poetry of *not* following tradition, a tradition of antitradition, of continually making it new.

Ezra Pound would challenge the twentieth century to "make it new," but Pound knew that Whitman was the first to bellow out the call; he was, as Pound said, the one "that broke the new wood," allowing the Modernists to settle into "a time for carving." Pound said this in a poem addressed to Whitman, with whom he felt he had to come to terms: "I make a pact with you, Walt Whitman, / I have detested you long enough." Pound is ready now to have "commerce" with Whitman ("Let there by commerce between us"), to admit some exchange across clearly demarcated boundaries.[28] The important point here is not the difference between the two poets—the distinctions are obvious enough—but the fact that Pound felt it necessary to haul Whitman's presence into a poem in 1913 and to publicly make his pact with him. For American poets at the beginning of this century, it was not clear just what poets in their past they could talk to. There was an American poetry—a strong and popular tradition represented by images of old and proper men such as Lowell and Longfellow, Holmes and Whittier, Bryant and even Emerson—but it was an American poetry the Moderns had to rebel against, a poetry whose appeal to foreign models and to a homegrown piety was clearly not going to be tenable as an ongoing energizing force. *That* was a circuit that had worn out, that no longer carried much of a charge.

This peculiarly American desire to start over, to form (in Emerson's terms) "an original relation to the universe,"[29] is part of what makes so many twentieth-century poets reticent about constructing a tradition as a backdrop for their work. To be an heir of Whitman or Dickinson is to "destroy the teacher" (as Whitman said any good student must do: "He most honors my style who learns under it to destroy the teacher"),[30] to relive the Columbus-moment of confronting an unnamed world with a language of useless forms and thus to be forced to invent a new style, a new language, that responds to the new experience. For many of our poets, American poetry is not the territory of talented technicians who subtly alter the tradition with their individual talent; it is instead the realm of the destructive and outrageous genius, whose poetic power is

in direct proportion to her or his ability to shock or puzzle an audience
that has come to expect something else.

The great instrument of shock, of course, was the English language
itself, a language suddenly becoming American. One of the paradoxes of
American poetry has been its desire to gouge a new native language out of
an inherited European one. Our poets' language, like any revolutionary
gesture, always looks to the past that it is divorcing itself from. Whitman's
conception of the English language as it turned itself American was of a
tenacious open structure that would absorb whatever it came into contact
with. He initiated a long battle in American literature, the battle for an
indigenous language, an American speech that would evolve out of the
English tongue, "English" inflected to deal with a new continent and a
new democratic experience. Whitman had a faith that "the English
language befriends the grand American expression . . . it is brawny
enough and limber and full enough." An absorptive language that had
already assimilated words and structures from a variety of European
languages, English had proven itself essentially democratic, open to new
words, to an endless piling up of synonyms, a voracious language that
never could have enough ways to say any one thing and so would welcome
native words, words from languages as yet unheard, made-up words,
words constructed from the collision of various languages. But the En-
glish language—brawny and malleable as it was—needed continually to
be challenged, expanded, tested; once it rested on its laurels, Whitman
knew, it would start to become a dead language. The fatal paralysis had
already set in when British versions of English were held up as models
for American writers. If, as Whitman believed, English was to become
"the medium that shall well nigh express the inexpressible,"[31] it would
have to be as wide-open and as absorptive as America itself, opening
its shores to alien languages, unglimpsed landscapes, and unimagined
experiences that would meld themselves into a distinctly American
speech. Whitman's 1855 preface to *Leaves of Grass*, along with much of
what Thoreau and Emerson wrote about the American language, served
writers in the second half of the nineteenth century as a kind of linguistic
Statue of Liberty, beacons for raw experience to enter in and gain voice.
They opened the way for a literature whose authors would no longer
have only English names—where Lowell, Melville, Whitman, and Bar-
low could mix with Dreiser, Stein, Zukovsky, and Ortiz.

The problem of defining how American poetry winds its way to the
twentieth century gets trickier when we realize that many of our contem-

porary poets find sources in an American past, but not in texts that we hear as poetry. Many of our poets hear poetry in things we have not categorized as poetry, and they find their poetry more energized by those patterns of language than by most of what was called poetry in the nineteenth century. Much of the critical enterprise of the last twenty-five years has been an effort to break down rigid genre hierarchies, and as we reconsider how American poetry got to the twentieth century, we should listen for poetry in the language of all the literature in our past, not just in those things that we have been taught are poems. Galway Kinnell has noted how "a good novel is filled with little poems," and he goes on to acknowledge how *Moby-Dick* is one of the great books of poetry in the American tradition: "I would say 50 percent of it is poetry. . . . Melville would have probably been the greatest poet in English except for Shakespeare, if he had learned how to write poetry. If he had become friends with Whitman, Whitman would have said: 'Listen, you don't have to bother with all that meter and rhyme—just write out these things.' And Melville would have written better poetry than anyone."[32] Melville's language was freed into more original and powerful rhythms in his novels than in his poetry, where he struggled to write in a "poetic" language after studying intensely what "poetry" was; when his language became most poetic, in *Moby-Dick,* he was probably unaware he was writing poetry.

And W. S. Merwin, when asked about his relation to an American tradition, made this observation: "I've suspected for a long time that an American poet's sympathy would tend to go either toward Whitman or toward Thoreau, not toward both." Whitman's "rhetorical insistence on an optimistic stance . . . as a world view and as a program for confronting existence" and his "cultural and what you might call specietal chauvinism" disturb Merwin, who instead finds his American origins in Thoreau, in his "recognition that the human can not exist independently in a natural void," admiring the way Thoreau "even in a paragraph takes his own perception and develops it into a deeper and deeper way of seeing something—the actual seeing in Thoreau is one of the things that draws me to him. I think that Thoreau saw in a way that nobody had quite seen before; it was American in that sense." In Thoreau's prose, Merwin finds an intensity of language that teaches him about poetry.[33]

It is arguable that most of the language from the American past that has inspired twentieth-century American poets has derived from things not traditionally defined as "poetry." Emerson's poetry, in much the same way as Thoreau's and Melville's, has not been nearly as influential on our poets as his prose has been: both in what he says in prose and in how he says it. We should recall that Whitman for many years did not view his own work as poetry, though he sometimes called the things he wrote "pomes"; he was trying his best to separate what he was writing from "poetry" as it was understood in the culture of the time—an activity still suffused with the sense of classical learning, of high culture, of poetic conventions, of virtuous and orthodox tradition. Whitman turned instead to oratory and journalism and street slang to construct his rhythms and language and forms, and his first readers did not recognize the product as poetry. "Poetry" went under such a radical redefinition in the second half of the nineteenth century in America that we need to look long and hard at any work written then and ask whether or not it's poetry, whether it then was or is now. One reason "poetry" seems to vanish in America after the Civil War—our classes in American Realism or the Gilded Age seldom include poets—is that the old definitions of poetry were no longer producing vital work, and the culture didn't bother to look for its new manifestations. The "barren" period in our poetic histories—from after the Civil War until the turn of the century, until Edwin Arlington Robinson and the Moderns—is ironically the period of the first great flourishing of women poets in our history. It may be, as Emily Stipes Watts has argued, that a "broad basis of women's verse" in the last half of the nineteenth century was particularly generative for women poets in the twentieth century: "Unlike the men, the poetic momentum of the women was carrying them naturally into the twentieth century."[34] And if we want to look to the origins of black poetry in America, we do not go to Phillis Wheatley, who sought in her elegant verse to show that a former slave could write "Poetry" in the orthodox sense; rather, we need to go to slave narratives and slave songs, to folk seculars and spirituals, where what would come to be recognized as poetry was getting written, often anonymously and/or communally, in surprising new forms that didn't even pretend to be "Poetry." If we look for the fertile source in an American past for poets like Nikki Giovanni, Don L. Lee, Ishmael Reed, June Jordan, and Lucille Clifton, do we hear it in lines like Wheatley's "Should you, my lord, while you pursue my song, / Wonder from whence my love of *Freedom* sprung, / Whence flow these wishes for the common good,"[35] or do we hear it in lines sung by generations, such as "Were you there, when they crucified my Lord? / Oh, sometimes, it causes me to tremble, tremble, tremble, / Were you there when they crucified my Lord?" or "Free at las', free at las', / I thank God I'm free at las'," or "Dis sun are hot, / Dis hoe are heavy, / Dis grass grow furder dan I can reach; / An' as I looks / At dis Cotton fiel', / I thinks I mus' 'a' been called to preach"—lines that capture the humor, faith, and tenacious desires of a people in an idiom that pushes the language beyond formality, beyond what it had said in the realms of polite poetry.[36]

In some ways, the emerging form of the slave narrative toward the mid-nineteenth century anticipated the basic form of what would come to be seen as some of the most essentially American poetry. All of American literature is a kind of slave narrative about escaping imprisoning conventions and foreign habits, about searching out one's true name and shucking off the given name, the name imposed by the master, about learning to write one's own name, about getting access to a power of language that had been denied by the cultural powers. In essential ways "Song of Myself" is a slave narrative. Early on in "Song of Myself," Whitman pauses to tell us:

> The runaway slave came to my house and stopt outside,
> I heard his motions crackling the twigs of the woodpile,
> Through the swung half-door of the kitchen I saw him limpsy and weak,
> And went where he sat on a log and led him in and assured him,
> And brought water and fill'd a tub for his sweated body and bruis'd feet,
> And gave him a room that enter'd from my own.

Later he invites the "heavy-lipp'd slave" to his "meal equally set" where "I will not have a single person slighted or left away," and even later, now knowing the slave and his story, identifies fully with him:

> I am the hounded slave, I wince at the bite of the dogs,
> Hell and despair are upon me, crack and again crack the marksmen.[37]

Whitman has used the slave narrative as a deep structure for the song of himself; at key points in his poem, the narrative of escape continues, and Whitman's identity with the "hounded slave" becomes an identity with all humanity, all trapped in enslaving and discriminating roles. To be American, for Whitman, is to enact the narrative of escape from that which enslaves you.

Just as we can hear slave escape narratives playing beneath Whitman's work, so can we hear Native American captivity narratives playing beneath the work of America's first poet, Anne Bradstreet. Anne Bradstreet was an accomplished poet, but we read her now not for her most accomplished and extended poems, her quaternions that move us through the four elements, the four monarchies, the four balanced sides of all her seventeenth-century English background. Had she written only those things, we would no longer hear poetry in her work. Where we hear the poetry now is in the more personal and haunting poems she wrote after her house burned down, after her imported library vanished along with the manuscripts of all her imitative poems. When she was cast back upon a few simple patterns and a few simple words to deal with the pain of loss—her grandchildren, her house (her concrete images of memory), her youth—she wrote what three centuries later we would still hear as poetry. And it is, in its own way, a captivity narrative as much as those ruder ones written by other women and men near her. For Bradstreet, the narrative was one in which she was trapped and taken away by a Puritan tribe that made her dress and act in strange ways, ways against which her "heart rose." She succumbed to those ways, but she never gave in easily, and she kept her rebellion alive in her poetry, poetry that traces the resistance she felt against all the imprisoning patriarchal structures of the Puritan theocracy—from the dominating masculine God who was beyond question, to the husband and father she loved obediently despite their odd ways, their anger and harsh judgment of Anne's sister and of Anne Hutchinson, women who dared to take upon themselves the responsibility of thinking, questioning, and speaking outside of the narrow domestic realm they were supposed to roam. Bradstreet knew it was dangerous to break barriers, so she wrote in accepted forms, and her poems snap shut with the expected safe orthodox solutions. But, like encoded messages sent out by prisoners who have to cry for help between the lines so that the guards will not suspect them, Bradstreet's poems embody her struggle in their modest but striking violations of form, in their surprising puns, in their stubborn "yet" phrases that affirm her own creative powers ("Yet being mine own"): the poems *say* orthodox things, finally, but the process of reading them reenacts her refusal to acquiesce to a God and to his ministers on earth who so blatantly turn away from the simple affections of this earth, of human relationships. Hers is a poetry of resistant affirmation, and it is something of that spirit that John Berryman was attracted to when he imagined his poetic tryst with her in his *Homage to Mistress Bradstreet* (1956), one of the first attempts by a twentieth-century poet to reach back to her as a source.[38]

Too often our narrow and enervated sense of the American poetic past had led us to devote our critical energies to rejecting what we have taught ourselves is there. What we need instead is to follow the example of poets such as Berryman and Rich who have taken the challenge to embrace what we have forgotten or never knew was there, to carry our own notions of what constitutes poetry back into the endless circuitry of writing in America in order to discover poems and poets that have been silenced through generations of reductive and contagious anthologies. What Whitman said of the American self is equally true of American poetry—it is large, it contains multitudes. If it contradicts itself, very well then; we must learn a poetics spacious enough to contain the contradictions. In opening ourselves to the huge possibilities that constitute what has been written on this continent, we will discover poetry hidden not only in the language that was struggling to imitate the traditions and forms that had been left behind or brought along, but also in language that was struggling to wrest an unnamed strangeness into the tenuous hold of words working in ways they never before had—English words, American words, words that could be renewed by touching them to a world of difference.

Notes

1. Whitman, *Leaves of Grass*, Comprehensive Reader's Edition, ed. Harold W. Blodgett and Sculley Bradley (New York: New York University Press, 1965), 78–79.

2. The best discussion of the complex interrelationship of land, experience, and naming among the discoverers, explorers, and settlers of the New World is Wayne Franklin's *Discoverers, Explorers, Settlers: The Diligent Writers of Early America* (Chicago: University of Chicago Press, 1979).

3. See Williams, "The Discovery of the Indies," in *In the American Grain* (New York: New Directions, 1956), 7–26.

4. Harriet Martineau, *Retrospect of Western Travel* (New York: Charles Lohman, 1838), 1:67.

5. Emerson, "The Poet," *Selected Writings of Ralph Waldo Emerson*, ed. William H. Gilman (New York: New American Library, 1965), 324.

6. Hugh Witemeyer discusses Pound's relationship with Whitman in "Clothing the American Adam: Pound's Tailoring of Walt Whitman," in *Ezra Pound Among the Poets*, ed. George Bornstein (Chicago: University of Chicago Press, 1984), 81–105; Cheryl Walker suggests some American origins for H. D. in *Nightingale's Burden*, Midland Books no. 301 (Bloomington: Indiana University Press, 1983), 143–49; Sydney Musgrove looks at Whitman's influence on Eliot in *T. S. Eliot and Walt Whitman* (Wellington: New Zealand University Press, 1952); and James E. Miller, Jr., examines similarities between Eliot's *Four Quartets* and "Song of Myself" in "Whitman and Eliot: The Poetry of Mysticism," *Southwest Review* 43 (Spring 1958): 113–23, one of a number of essays in the last

thirty years examining the interrelationship of these two poets; Diane Middlebrook makes a case for Whitman's influence on Stevens in *Walt Whitman and Wallace Stevens* (Ithaca, N.Y.: Cornell University Press, 1974).

7. Williams, *American Grain,* 109.

8. Ibid., 74.

9. Ibid., 61–62, 178–79; "The American Idiom," in *Interviews with William Carlos Williams,* ed. Linda Wagner (New York: New Directions, 1976), 101.

10. Crane, *The Complete Poems and Selected Letters of Hart Crane,* ed. Brom Weber (Garden City, N.Y.: Doubleday, Anchor, 1966), 274.

11. Ibid., 81, 93, 106, 110, 170.

12. Rich, *On Lies, Secrets, and Silence* (New York: Norton, 1979), 39.

13. Ibid., 21–22, 31–32; Rich, *Poems Selected and New, 1950–1974* (New York: Norton, 1975), 238–39.

14. Rich, *Lies,* 167.

15. Rich, "Poetry, Personality and Wholeness," *Field,* no. 7 (Fall 1972), 17–18.

16. Sandra Gilbert, "The Wayward Nun Beneath the Hill: Emily Dickinson and the Mysteries of Womanhood," in *Feminist Critics Read Emily Dickinson,* ed. Suzanne Juhasz (Bloomington: Indiana University Press, 1983), 23; *Emily's Bread* (New York: Norton, 1984), 103.

17. Jane Cooper, *Maps and Windows* (New York: Collier, 1974), 44.

18. Rich, *Lies,* 183.

19. This continuing conversation is the subject of Jim Perlman, Ed Folsom, and Dan Campion, eds., *Walt Whitman: The Measure of His Song* (Minneapolis: Holy Cow! Press, 1981); I develop the notion in my introductory essay to that volume, "Talking Back to Walt Whitman."

20. Whitman, *Leaves,* 9.

21. Ibid., 717, 727.

22. Emerson, "Self Reliance," in *Selected Writings,* 266.

23. Joseph Bruchac, "To Love the Earth: Some Thoughts on Walt Whitman," in *Walt Whitman,* 276.

24. June Jordan, "For the Sake of a People's Poetry: Walt Whitman and the Rest of Us," in *Walt Whitman,* 343.

25. See Andrew Hudgins, *Saints and Strangers* (Boston: Houghton Mifflin, 1985), 33–36; and *After the Lost War* (Boston: Houghton Mifflin, 1988).

26. Norbert Krapf, ed., *Under Open Sky: Poets on William Cullen Bryant,* (Roslyn, N.Y.: Stone House Press, 1986).

27. There are many studies that posit the Whitman/Dickinson split; of recent examinations, see Karl Keller, *The Only Kangaroo among the Beauty* (Baltimore: Johns Hopkins University Press, 1979); Albert Gelpi, *The Tenth Muse: The Psyche of the American Poet* (Cambridge: Harvard University Press, 1975); and John Lynen, *The Design of the Present: Essays on Time and Form in American Literature* (New Haven, Conn.: Yale University Press, 1969). Agnieszka Salska, in *Walt Whitman and Emily Dickinson: Poetry of the Central Consciousness* (Philadelphia: University of Pennsylvania Press, 1985), attempts to combat the notion of dichotomy and to find common ground between the two poets.

28. Pound, "A Pact," in *Personae* (New York: New Directions, 1971), 89.

29. Emerson, "Nature," in *Selected Writings,* 186.

30. Whitman, *Leaves,* 84.

31. Ibid., 728.

32. Kinnell, Interview, in *American Poetry Observed*, ed. Joe David Bellamy, (Urbana: University of Illinois Press, 1984), 140.

33. Merwin, Interview, in *Regions of Memory*, ed. Ed Folsom and Cary Nelson (Urbana: University of Illinois Press, 1987), 321–25.

34. Emily Stipes Watts, *The Poetry of American Women from 1632 to 1945* (Austin: University of Texas Press, 1977), 146–47.

35. Wheatley, "To the Right Honorable William, Earl of Dartmouth," in *The Poems of Phillis Wheatley*, ed. Julian D. Mason, Jr. (Chapel Hill: University of North Carolina Press, 1966), 34.

36. See, as an example of an anthology that emphasizes the "nonliterary" roots of black poetry, the collection of folk seculars and spirituals in Dudley Randall, ed., *The Black Poets* (Toronto: Bantam, 1971), 1–32.

37. Whitman, *Leaves*, 66.

38. Berryman, *Homage to Mistress Bradstreet and Other Poems* (New York: Noonday, 1968). As Alicia Ostriker points out, Berryman's famous homage is anything but a praisesong for Bradstreet's poetry: Berryman, in fact, dismisses the poetry and celebrates instead her personal staunchness as he attempts to seduce her across the centuries; see *Stealing the Language* (Boston: Beacon, 1986), 26–27.

2

Modernism Comes to American Poetry: 1908–1920

ROGER MITCHELL

It would be just as misleading to say that the decade 1910 to 1920 was the decade when Modernism reached the United States as it would be to say that it reached here because the two most prominent American poets of the time, Ezra Pound and T. S. Eliot, left the United States and went to London. But the coming of Modernism was the principal literary event of that time (indeed, it is likely to be the principal literary event of the century), and it was Pound and Eliot who were, for a time, its chief advocates and practitioners. William Carlos Williams, H. D., Marianne Moore, Gertrude Stein, and Wallace Stevens all contributed significantly to the development of Modernism in American poetry, but without the examples of Pound and Eliot, it is doubtful that their work would have had the shape and force it did.

Literary history is not an exact science, so it is no surprise that other developments took place at this time. Two of the most notable were the slow rise in reputation of Edwin Arlington Robinson and Robert Frost and the emergence of a school of free-verse Populist poets which included Carl Sandburg, Vachel Lindsay, and Edgar Lee Masters. These poets refined a native strain of verse, largely in the shadow of Walt Whitman, at a time when American poetry suddenly became international. The work of these poets was often grouped with Pound's and Eliot's, but it was almost entirely because they, too, wrote free verse. It was the "freed verse" that most clearly identified the new poetry to the puzzled reader, but as we know now—and as Pound and Eliot were quick to say then— the new poetry involved a great deal more than the simple abandonment of meter and rhyme. Eliot went so far as to say that the new poetry was not free at all. "No vers is libre," he said, "to the poet who wishes to write well."[1]

Still, this period brought a nonmetrical or irregular verse into being, and its lack of meter and regularity had much to do with the general attempt made at that time throughout the Western world and in all the arts to free aesthetics from premises that thinking people could no longer take seriously. It is because Sandburg, Lindsay, and Masters did not perceive the main intellectual currents of the time or did not grapple significantly with them that their work seems pale today. With Robinson and Frost, it is a different matter. Like Bartleby, they preferred not to—in this case, not to go along with the radical new aesthetics. They listened well, however, and heard what it was saying and in their own sly way spoke to it and to the issues it raised.

Literary history is not neatly divided into decades either, but there is a remarkable knot of energy at precisely this time which might convince the unwary reader that the normal lifespan of literary movements is about ten years. "The heroic era of Modernism in American literature,"[2] to use Eric Homberger's term, might be said to have begun in 1908 when Pound reached London, and ended, to indulge in a Modernist warping of time, in 1920 when Pound left London for France and in 1922 when Eliot published *The Waste Land* in the *Dial*.

"In or about December 1910," wrote Virginia Woolf, "human nature changed. . . . All human relations. . . shifted—those between masters and servants, husbands and wives, parents and children. And when human relations change there is at the same time a change in religion, conduct, politics, and literature."[3] One might argue about the precision of Woolf's reading of history, but there is no mistaking its general accuracy or her urgent sense that something radically new was needed if literature was to keep up with it. The most compelling thing in her statement is the sense it gives of radical social upheaval. The change in literature came not because of internal tinkerings with the machine of literature but because the ground on which all social institutions stood, literature among them, was beginning to tremble. The history of ideas and history itself coincided to produce one of the most volcanic cultural upheavals ever known.

The great disjunction felt at the end of the nineteenth century between art and reality—the condition which precipitated Modernism—is largely attributable to the huge success, if success is measured by wealth and world domination, of the Industrial Revolution. Those qualities which made it possible—hard work, inventiveness, confidence in progress and the future, faith in reason and science, and the almost unchallenged sense that business and industry represented the natural fulfillment of the human race and of God's will—seemed unassailable for a very long time.

Information filtered slowly through the heavy screen of middle-class culture and began suggesting that not all was well or even accurately described. For one thing, the dirt and poverty created by industrialism would not go away. In fact, it spread. Karl Marx, among others, suggested that industry created poverty intentionally for its proper and profitable functioning, a notion that challenged the industrialist's confidence that he was doing the Lord's will. Darwin did further damage, not only by discrediting the version of creation offered by Genesis and therefore the authority of Christianity itself, but also by telling us that we were descended from apes. In a word, we were animals and not some privileged creature halfway to being an angel. Freud's invention and investigations of the subconscious scandalized the Victorian mind by suggesting that if we were civilized—and he raised considerable doubts about that— we were so only because we suppressed our deepest natural desires, which were, at root, selfish and sexual. Freud further threatened the outward calm of Victorian life by suggesting that our real life was an inner and isolated life, not unlike dream, and not that thing we shared or tried to share with other people.

If we add to this picture the strong currents of relativism in philosophy at this time which undermined the validity of absolute truths, Nietzsche's announcement that God was dead, and Einstein's theory that relativity ruled even in the physical world, we can begin to see why people felt that the ground beneath them had begun to shift. The fixed, solid Newtonian world which underlay the culture of the Victorian middle class was breaking up. No poet could dream of announcing, as Browning had in 1841, "God's in his heaven—All's right with the world!"

As a general term, *Modernism* (or *Modernity*) evoked, and still evokes, the culture made by science and technology. Things that are modern are still those that are technologically advanced. But at some time during the first half of the nineteenth century, as Matei Calinescu says, a split occurred between "modernity as a stage in the history of Western civilization—a product of scientific and technological progress, of the industrial revolution . . . and modernity as an aesthetic concept. Since then the relations between the two modernities have been irreducibly hostile."[4] Modernism became, in Lionel Trilling's phrase, an "adversary position" to the culture of industrialism and imperial expansion. For this it drew on all earlier complaints, from the faint graceful laments of Goldsmith in "The Deserted Village" to the keening of James Thomson in "The City of Dreadful Night."

The "bourgeois idea of modernity," says Calinescu, coincides with the bourgeois system of values:

> The doctrine of progress, the confidence in the beneficial possibilities of science and technology, the concern with time (a *measurable* time, a time that can be bought and sold and therefore has, like any other commodity, a calculable equivalent in money), the cult of reason, and the ideal of freedom defined within the framework of an abstract humanism, but also the orientation toward pragmatism and the cult of action and success—all have been associated in various degrees with the battle for the modern and were kept alive and promoted as key values in the triumphant civilization established by the middle class. . . .
>
> The "other modernity," literary Modernism, was from its romantic beginnings inclined toward radical, anti-bourgeois attitudes. It was disgusted with the middle-class scale of values and expressed its disgust through the most diverse means, ranging from rebellion, anarchy, and apocalypticism, to aristocratic self-exile. So, more than its positive aspirations (which often have very little in common), what defines cultural modernity is its outright rejection of bourgeois modernity, its consuming negative passion.[5]

We will have to consider the implications of this "consuming negative passion," since it is an undeniable feature of Modernism; but at first, in Modernism's "heroic era," it would be fairer to say that the various assaults on cherished forms and beliefs were joyous discoveries as much as they were complaints. Realism of setting, portraiture, and dialogue had to be violated if the novel was going to mirror the "new" reality, psychological life, more convincingly. Free verse in poetry and overt abstraction in painting allowed a degree of individuality into art that seemed to reflect the nature of perception more accurately. Certainly these new techniques "attacked" existing ones, but there was more than simple iconoclasm behind them. The world was more complex than the Victorian middle class believed or wanted it to be. Poetry, to speak only of that, became, as Eliot was to say much later, an "intolerable wrestle with words and meanings":

> Older and more traditional definitions of poetry—the spontaneous overflow of powerful feeling, the best words in the best order—were impatiently dismissed. Obsessive attempts to say "the unsayable" made extreme demands on the mind's elasticity. Not only literature but all art of the period seemed to be intent on stretching the mind beyond the very limits of human understanding. Human nature was "elusive, indeterminate, multiple, often implausible, infinitely various and essentially irreducible."[6]

It is true that much poetry of the time simply attacked the Victorians for their obvious failings. Pound, for instance, sometimes posed as a true-hearted Romantic so that he could belabor his stuffy contemporaries, as in "Salutation":

> O generation of the thoroughly smug and thoroughly uncomfortable,
> I have seen fishermen picnicking in the sun,
> I have seen them with untidy families,
> I have seen their smiles full of teeth and heard ungainly laughter.
> And I am happier than you are,
> And they were happier than I am;
> And the fish swim in the lake and do not even own clothing.[7]

Pound did not always belabor the late Victorian and Edwardian upper middle classes. His Chinese translations can be read as oblique criticisms of the culture of imperial Britain, but the criticism is so roundabout—the frontier guards only remotely resemble British troops in the trenches in World War I—that what is most impressive about these poems is their freshness and naïveté, as in "The River Merchant's Wife: A Letter":

> While my hair was still cut straight across my forehead
> I played about the front gate, pulling flowers.
> You came by on bamboo stilts, playing horse,
> You walked about my seat, playing with blue plums.
> And we went on living in the village of Chokan:
> Two small people, without dislike or suspicion.[8]

Here were several kinds of newness. Though the verse was free, it had a pronounced monosyllabic rhythm; and though there were none of the conventional properties of poetry like metaphor and simile or the grand rhetorical display of the feeling self, there was quite obviously a luminous depth of feeling. Not since the time of Chaucer had such trust been put in fact, in the image chosen for itself and not as grist for the synthesizing imagination. Though Pound took more obvious steps in other poems toward a colloquial vigor of speech, a poem like "The River Merchant's Wife" sounds much like a person thinking aloud or writing her most private thoughts in a letter.

In "Fabliau of Florida," Wallace Stevens not only dabbled in the new free verse (he would later abandon it), but also in highly imaginative renderings of reality.

> Barque of phosphor
> On the palmy beach,
> Move outward into heaven,
> Into the alabasters

And night blues.
Foam and cloud are one.
Sultry moon-monsters
Are dissolving.
Fill your black hull
With white moonlight.
There will never be an end
To this droning of the surf.[9]

Most disturbing to a practical mentality in this poem would have been the almost willful relationship to reality. Those who looked for Florida in "Fabliau of Florida" were naturally disappointed. Nothing like this was being written at the time in English, except possibly by Gertrude Stein in *Tender Buttons* (1914). The virtue in Stevens's poem lay in the poetry itself, the willing suspension of reality in a thick imaginative medium. With the nature of reality itself in question, poets like Stevens turned to the only solid ground left in human affairs, individual perception.

H. D.'s well-known little poem "Oread" was used for years to classify, not to say calcify, her as an Imagist.

Whirl up, sea—
whirl your pointed pines,
splash your great pines
on our rocks,
hurl your green over us,
cover us with your pools of fir.[10]

"Oread" is not so much a poem that uses an image as it is a poem that is an image. It does not discuss or explain; it is purely representative. Since it also avoids the metronome of regular meter, it qualifies in several ways as a representative Imagist poem. More important is its Modernist and post-Romantic celebration of natural energy and of the mind's ability to create meaning metaphorically. Whatever the sea is, finally, it is called upon—in ecstatic tones—to dominate us. The power of the imagination rivals that of the sea.

William Carlos Williams took other risks with conventional notions of poetry. He not only trusted the unadorned image to reveal beauty and truth (his first poems were Keatsian imitations); he trusted unadorned reality itself. His famous poem "The Red Wheelbarrow" drew perhaps the greatest derision of all early Modernist poems, greater even than *The Waste Land*, because of what looked like its pointless ordinariness.

so much depends
upon

a red wheel
barrow

glazed with rain
water

beside the white
chickens.[11]

Williams made the most radical departure of all because he was willing
to turn his back on all existing ideas of culture and tradition, certainly
those invoked by his peers. If Emerson's essays made it possible for him
to find "an original relation to the universe" and an American version of
the world, and if Whitman's example led him to trust the simple, abun-
dant facts of that world, he did all of these things without donning the
robes of seer or bardic father-of-us-all. The red wheelbarrow was first of
all a red wheelbarrow, and it was right in front of us. "The Red Wheelbar-
row" makes us wonder what sort of world it would be if everything were
seen, as in some sense everything must exist, as clearly and inviolably
itself.

All of these poems were written between about 1913 and 1921 and
indicate the sense of exhilaration and discovery in what Frank Kermode
has called the period of "paleo-modernism." The new work was certainly
critical of existing attitudes, but in every case the old was swept aside so
that something new could be given room to grow. It was not criticism
for the sake of criticism, but criticism to make creation possible. Stein,
Williams, H. D., Stevens, and others were hardly seized by a "consuming
negative passion." Their careers, in fact, illustrate the opposite.

The negative passion was there, however. The years 1913 to 1921 are
roughly the years of what was known as the Great War. It was not difficult
for many to see a connection between this cataclysm and the dominant,
materialist values of Victorian and post-Victorian culture. The war was
essentially fought over the rise of German economic power and the
British resistance to it. Two empires struggled to hold, or increase their
hold, on the world's markets and resources. The Germans had developed
the most impressive scientific establishment of the time and were confi-
dent that life could be improved through the direct, forceful application
of scientific ideals. The virtues of the middle class—individual effort,
inventiveness, competitiveness, faith in progress and reason—all were

easily converted, by both sides, into the energy needed to fight a brutal and senseless war. Nothing caused a deeper questioning of the nature of human beings than their eagerness and efficiency in slaughtering one another, not the disappearance of the fixed Newtonian universe in physics, not the disappearance of moral absolutism, not the discovery of the subconscious, of human evolution, or of class warfare. Pound spoke more directly and savagely in "Hugh Selwyn Mauberley." The best of his generation died for "a botched civilization," for a few "broken statues" and "battered books."[12]

Side by side, then, with a Modernist exploration of the kinds and limits of perception stood a vision of anarchy and despair, made most vivid in works like *The Waste Land* and the novels of Franz Kafka. It is this vision that most seriously challenges the optimism of the scientific and bourgeois worldview, and it is this vision, this "consuming negative passion," that is customarily implied by the word "Modernism." The idea of the modern, as Irving Howe has said, is an idea of radical, not to say reactionary, isolation, a condition in which people feel themselves cut off from each other and from all systems of religion and philosophy.[13]

Oddly enough, this characterization of Modernism is fairly recent. For one thing, the word "Modernism" was not used in the years 1910 to 1920.[14] Many other words were used, but not "Modernism." For another, the gloomy connotations of the word came from critics and writers who were decidely on the Left: Howe, Georg Lukacs, Thomas Mann, David Caute, and others. Mann once said that modern literature cultivated "a sympathy for the abyss." The typical condition of Modernist literature became a cloying inwardness. With nothing else to cling to, the modern sensibility clings to itself. From such a perspective, the plunge inward in the stream-of-consciousness novel or in Abstract Expressionist painting is easily seen as an abandonment of the social world and an act of social irresponsibility. It does not matter to such critics that, for instance, Virginia Woolf allows us to know more about the inner workings of the female mind. Until recently, critics have not been able to see that as an advance in perception with responsible, not to say radically responsible, implications.

Howe says, further, that the Modernist dispenses with history and tries to live outside it. The typical Modernist implies that history is merely cyclical or, if headed in any direction, is headed toward some cataclysm. Pound believed, as his *Cantos* show, that history was a random succession of periods of enlightenment and darkness. Eliot ridiculed

Emerson's hopeful view of history in "Sweeney Erect." Stevens seemed unaware of history. Williams and H. D. had to invent their own eclectic versions of it. Perhaps these are assorted ways of giving up on history, but when Howe and Lukacs criticize writers for doing this, they do so as critics with a definite view of the way history works. History, to them, is progressive and scientific. Reason is at work in history, and to attack such a view or show an indifference to it is taken by them to be an evasion of the truth. A progressive politics requires a progressive and rational view of history as its foundation. Whether that view of history is truer than a view which says that the conditions of human existence are eternal and unchanging is finally a matter of belief.

Graham Hough has said, "For the most part . . . the poets have refused the great public mythologies of our time, and have evolved rival myths of their own, some grandiose and comprehensive, some esoteric and private, but none with any status in the world of organized scientific and historical knowledge by which the world conducts its business."[15] It would be wrong, however, finally to describe Modernist writers as some species of intellectual ostrich, lost in a Darwinian cul-de-sac of their own choosing or making, a view shared oddly enough by Marxist critics and the great bourgeois who were their targets. The pressures under which the Modernists wrote would have made any thinking person question "the world of organized scientific and historical knowledge by which the world conducts its business." More to the point, however, is that the Modernists opened up the world for us to see. They gave us strategies of perception and criticism which continue to be valid. They lit up the body of the world in ways we are still learning from. Not just reading or looking at or listening to, but learning from.

Edwin Arlington Robinson (1869–1935) began by writing fiction. His teachers in that art were European Naturalists like Zola. A case can be made, in fact, that Modernist poetry owes a large debt to the theories and techniques of nineteenth-century fiction. Robinson's poems, for instance, are almost always narratives. Even his sonnets are stories. Like Conrad and James, Robinson experimented with point of view. His famous poem "Richard Cory" is told from the point of view of a fellow citizen of Tilbury Town, a small town in Maine which Robinson invented, as many local colorists in fiction were doing at the end of the nineteenth century. The speaker, then, is as puzzled as the reader why Cory, who seemed to have every reason for being happy, should have committed suicide.

> . . . we thought that he was everything
> To make us wish that we were in his place.
>
> So on we worked and waited for the light,
> And went without the meat, and cursed the bread;
> And Richard Cory, one calm summer night,
> Went home and put a bullet through his head.[16]

Cory was wealthy, so the poem takes part in the general criticism of materialism in post-Romantic literature, a criticism which it handed on to the poets of Modernism.

Robinson's poetry begins the turn toward Modernism in two other important ways. He has a strong sense of the limits of human aspirations, something that was very strong in Naturalists like Zola and Conrad. As "Richard Cory" suggests, Robinson was skeptical of the power of human reason and of the ability of people to know their world and manage competently in it. Finally, and this may be Robinson's most significant contribution to twentieth-century poetry, he used the language of everyday speech. This was unusual, especially in Robinson's early years, the 1890s, when poets were still trying to write a pretty, musical poetry in the manner of Tennyson or Longfellow. Nobody went home and put a bullet through his head in the poetry of Ella Wheeler Wilcox or William Vaughn Moody. Robinson's language was too colloquial and direct for poetry at that time, though not for the novel. When the new poetry arrived in roughly 1912, the year that *Poetry* magazine was founded in Chicago by Harriet Monroe, Robinson's manner as a formalist was well established. He did not join the makers of free verse, so his poetry seemed to belong to an earlier time. But this was an illusion. His contributions to modern poetry and to American poetry in general have been considerable.

Robert Frost (1874–1963) lived long enough into the twentieth century to have been not only premodern in his literary leanings but vocally antimodern. Frost's rejection of the new poetry, which is mostly a rejection of free verse, is stated forcefully in his review of Robinson's *King Jasper* in 1935, shortly after Robinson's death. It is a succinct and witty definition of the new poetry by a disbeliever.

> It may come to the notice of posterity (and then again it may not) that this our age ran wild in the quest of new ways to be new. The one old way to be new no longer served. . . . Those tried were largely by subtraction—elimination. Poetry, for example, was tried without punctuation. It was tried without capital

letters. It was tried without metric frame on which to measure the rhythm. It was tried without any images but those to the eye; and a loud general intoning had to be kept up to cover the total loss of specific images to the ear. . . . It was tried without content under the trade name of poesie pure. It was tried without phrase, epigram, coherence, logic and consistency. It was tried without ability. . . . It was tried premature like the delicacy of unborn calf in Asia. It was tried without feeling or sentiment like murder for small pay in the underworld.[17]

As we shall see, it would be wrong to conclude from this witty defense of traditional poetry, as Frost almost seems to hope we might, that his poetry had nothing to do with Modernism.

Frost rarely wrote badly, but he wrote his best work in his first years. The decade 1910 to 1920 was his first and most productive, beginning with *A Boy's Will* in 1913. He was thirty-nine that year, so it is not too surprising that he was able to publish three more books in the next four years—*North of Boston* (1915), *Mountain Interval* (1916), and *A Way Out* (1917)—plus a *Selected Poems* in 1923.

Frost was born in California, so his decision to make himself into a New Hampshire farmer poet, at a time when the New Hampshire farmer was nearly a thing of the past and when the country was rapidly industrializing, resembles Thoreau's decision to live beside Walden Pond in a cabin of his own making. Frost had more than a little Emersonian self-reliance in him, in fact, as well as the typical Transcendentalist's dislike of materialism. He was hardly a Romantic, however. Like Robinson and a good many other writers of the late nineteenth century—Hardy, Housman, James Thomson, Conrad, Dreiser, Stephen Crane, to name a few—he was a religious skeptic and doubted the willingness or ability of human beings to care for one another. He may have disliked the formlessness of the new poetry, but he understood its spirit. His philosophic gloom and his antimaterialism are quite typical of what was later to be called Modernist writing.

A poem, said Frost, "begins in delight and ends in wisdom." It achieves a "momentary stay against confusion." Confusion, in other words, however that might be defined, was the norm, and delight was usually dispersed by thought or wisdom. *A Boy's Will* tries to capture "sheer morning gladness at the brim," but does so, as in "The Tuft of Flowers," by first dramatizing the isolation of human beings. "I went to turn the grass once after one / Who mowed it in the dew before the sun." The speaker never comes any closer to this "one," except to notice that he had spared a tuft of flowers in his mowing. He feels a "spirit kindred" to his own but never sees or meets the man. It is therefore both inspiriting and disspiriting to conclude:

And dreaming, as it were, [I] held brotherly speech
With one whose thought I had not hoped to reach.
"Men work together," I told him from the heart,
"Whether they work together or apart."[18]

From *North of Boston* on, Frost's poetry confronts this loneliness and isolation more convincingly. Like most Modernists, he sees much more silence than brotherly speech between people. The first poem in *North of Boston*, "Mending Wall," announces this clearly, but in "Death of the Hired Man," "Home Burial," "A Servant to Servants," "The Tear," and other poems, the picture of humans reduced almost to animal silence is unmistakable and vivid. "Mending Wall" manages to modify this Zolaesque Naturalism by letting an idealist and rationalist speak the poem. He tries to instruct his neighbor, but fails. Reason's arguments cannot alter the instincts and habits of the "old-stone savage armed." If the neighbor is a sort of prehistoric figure, riddled with superstition, he is also, as the speaker seems almost to learn, a man with wisdom that a rationalist would never understand. Frost, however, does not make the old farmer a noble savage, as an early Romantic writer might have, but he is writing at a time when artists like Picasso and Braque were beginning to realize that primitive peoples were capable of great art and that the primitive itself needed reexamination. There might indeed be something that doesn't love a wall, but is it some innate goodness in nature that hates to see divisions among people, as the speaker would seem to want to believe, or is it a natural indifference or perhaps even a malevolence that destroys human attempts at order and orderliness? Worse yet, are both conclusions true? In this and other poems, Frost raises large questions and points toward conceivable answers, but he can finally give no answer. Instead, he realizes a condition of paradox in a world where only the most crude and fleeting communication is possible. Later writers such as Lawrence or Joyce would use Freud to light up this darkness. Frost is content to present it to us in vivid, realistic detail.

   "This first poet I ever sat down with to talk about poetry," wrote Frost years later, "was Ezra Pound [1885–1972]. It was in London in 1913. The first poet we talked about, to the best of my recollection, was Edwin Arlington Robinson."[19] Several parables of modern American poetry meet in such a remark. First, Robert Frost was in London. Frost, in fact, spent several of his formative years in England. Second, he was talking with his fellow American, Ezra Pound, who by 1913 had made himself the most vocal force in a new movement in poetry, soon to be given names like Imagism, free verse, the New Intellectualism, and so on. Frost, of course, was not interested in any of it. Pound had gone to London because it was the cultural center of the English-speaking world. Frost had gone not to London, but to England, pastoral England, the country of Wordsworth. Pound and Frost met, however, and their talk went immediately to American poets and poetry, specifically to their near contemporary, Robinson, who was living the isolated life of the artist typical of America at that time, a life they were trying to avoid in the traditional manner by living abroad.

Ezra Pound was born in Idaho but grew up mostly in the Philadelphia area, where he met other poets of his generation like H. D., Marianne Moore, and William Carlos Williams. After college at Hamilton and a graduate degree in romance languages at the University of Pennsylvania, Pound took a job as a college professor. He was to last only six months at Wabash College, however, before the authorities dismissed him as a "Latin quarter type." He left the country immediately, in early 1908, and went to Venice where he published his first book, *A Lume Spento*. By September of that year he had moved to London, where he was to remain until late 1920.

It is hardly an accident that Pound's residence in London coincides almost exactly with the decade we are looking at, for no one person did more, or as much, to bring English-speaking literature into the contemporary world than Ezra Pound. He was not only instrumental in bringing Robert Frost to public attention, but it was through his efforts that writers like T. S. Eliot, James Joyce, Wyndham Lewis, H. D., William Carlos Williams, and others were brought into print. A flamboyant, determined polemicist for the "new" literature, Pound bullied and harassed editors into printing what he thought mattered, reviewed without a break for the whole time he was in London, and found time in all these activities to write some of the best poetry ever written in English. Chief among his literary labors was "persuading" Harriet Monroe that he should be foreign correspondent for the magazine *Poetry*, which she started in Chicago in 1912. Almost at once *Poetry* became the leading outlet for the new poetry. In his reviewing at this time, Pound made what nearly amounts to a systematic survey of the whole of culture, writing long series of reviews on music, art, drama, the literary press, classical translators, French literature, and many other aspects of world culture which he felt were relevant to the modern world. Pound was not content simply to be a poet. The condition of mind that would make significant poetry possible had to be created first. Editors, readers, writers, even politicians, needed to be convinced that the old world was dead and the old way of doing things outmoded.

Pound's reputation was quickly established by the publication, in London, of his third book, *Personae* (1909). It was published by Elkin Mathews, the "discoverer" of Yeats. In quick succession came *Exultations* (1909); *The Spirit of Romance* (1910), a treatise on the "pre-Renaissance literature of Latin Europe" and the first of his many studies of culture; *Provençal* (1910); *Canzoni* (1911); *Ripostes* (1912); *Cathay* (1915), his famous translations of Li Po; *Gaudier-Brzeska* (1916), a study of the sculpture of a friend killed in the war; *Lustra* (1916); *Pavannes and Divisions* (1918); *Instigations* (1920), a book of essays; *Hugh Selwyn Mauberley* (1920), his "farewell to London"; and *Umbra* (1920). In this period, too, he was chosen by Ernest Fenollosa's widow to edit her husband's papers, and he began writing his *Cantos*.

Most critics are now inclined to dismiss the importance of the Imagist movement to Ezra Pound's career. His reasons for separating himself from it are complicated, but the truest thing to say is that the movement quickly developed a recognizable and easily imitated style with limited goals. By the time Amy Lowell had begun editing her Imagist anthologies in 1915, Pound was disaffected. He told her that he could not trust any "democratized committee" to maintain the standards of "Imagisme," as he preferred to call it, namely, "hard light, clear edges."[20] During its moment, however, Imagism exactly reflected the values Pound wanted for his writing and for writing in general, and the quickness with which it was imitated and institutionalized shows how wide its influence was.

Imagist theory is based on a few scattered pronouncements arrived at in 1912 by a group in London that included Pound, F. S. Flint, H. D., T. E. Hulme, and a few others. These pronouncements were written down in separate, short essays by Flint and Pound and, through the latter's position as foreign correspondent for *Poetry*, published in that magazine's March 1913 issue. The three points of what is sometimes called "the Imagist credo" were (1) "Direct treatment of the 'thing' whether subjective or objective"; (2) "Use absolutely no word that does not contribute to the presentation"; and (3) "As regarding rhythm: to

compose in the sequence of the musical phrase, not in the sequence of
the metronome." Add to this Pound's definition of the image—"That
which presents an intellectual and emotional complex in an instant of
time"—and the rationale for a poetry unlike any known before in English
was complete. It would be a poetry that avoided talking about things;
that is to say, it would avoid intellectualizing and generalizing. Instead,
it would treat matters directly. Direct treatment meant "presentation,"
the thrusting of the reader into the middle of intellectual and emotional
complexes without signposts or comforting explanations.

Imagist poems were intensely visual, and since they had little or no
comment, they were often like photographs or still lifes in painting.
Pound was to summarize this side of Imagism by saying, "Go in fear of
abstraction." The avoidance of abstraction—or, to use another word,
explanation—and the presentational method brought poetry in line with
leading theories of prose fiction, notably the "dramatic method" de-
scribed by Henry James. This may be one of the reasons why the language
of poetry at this time took on a prose quality.

The main reason why poetic language changed, though, had to do with
the second and third points of the Imagist credo. No word was supposed
to be used in a poem if it had only musical or metrical value. That is to
say, all words in a poem were to be scrutinized carefully and, if not
needed, discarded. Pound was opposed to what he called the "slither"
of late-Victorian and Edwardian verse, the pretty musicality for which
Tennyson was well known. The Imagists were so anxious to get away
from that sort of thing that they did away with the "metronome" alto-
gether, that is, with conventional meter. In a single stroke, free verse
was born.

Verse was not to be free of music, however. It was not to be an oddly
aligned prose. The poet was to "compose in the sequence of the musical
phrase," a delightfully ambiguous definition which at least theoretically
allowed greater individuality to each poet and a greater range of musical
possibilities in the language. Pound, whose ear was uncommonly sensi-
tive and who was also well trained in meter, could create original move-
ments and rhythms. But even more important, Pound believed that the
image could speak more powerfully than any abstraction or explanation.

Another reason why Imagism did not hold Pound's attention for long
was that it was a literary movement with exclusively literary ambitions.
Pound wanted more than that. He wanted to reinvigorate culture and
restore it to what he regarded as its proper relationship with political,

social, and intellectual authority. In his view the British empire was unenlightened, and it was his hope to change that by creating an informed artistic intelligentsia which could then act, directly or indirectly, as the culture's eyes and conscience. Pound's later work and his later life make sense only if we see him trying to make what he called at the end of *The Cantos* a "paradiso terrestre." He was inevitably (and lamentably) drawn to leaders and forms of government which seemed to value the arts and were willing to use their authority, even despotically, to achieve the high aims of enlightened culture. He left England in December 1920 because that no longer seemed possible there, and in a very short time he had attached himself intellectually to Italian fascism in the belief that Mussolini cared for the arts. But that is a later story. Now we are concerned with the poetry Pound wrote under the double pressure of his high hopes and their defilement by World War I. In all of this poetry, though, we will hear, sometimes quietly, sometimes not, the committed cultural polemicist.

One of the ways Pound created authority for himself in doing this was to find and translate poetry from other cultures that had been in roughly the same straits as the British in his day. The poems in *Cathay* evoke the loneliness and sadness of people kept by war, business, or imperial affairs from the people and places they love. Pound resumed his attack by translation two years later when he published "Homage to Sextus Propertius." Imperial Rome in Propertius's day was at its ostentatious worst, and Propertius simply turned his back on it. Not in rueful silence, however. He scorned the reigning culture, contented himself with modest comfort, and flattered the ladies. Through Propertius, Pound made the case over and over that bad writing, bad ruling, and ostentation are related matters.

Pound's aesthetics were always divided. Like Propertius, he thought that an art which praised the state was a false art. But an art which removed itself entirely from public awareness was doomed. This is the chief premise of his brilliant sequence "Hugh Selwyn Mauberley," his "farewell to London." Though there is much Pound in him, Mauberley is finally an ineffectual aesthete and hedonist. In "Mauberley," Pound again tries to place the artist in a significant relationship to social and political reality, and he records in vivid detail the threats in English society to the artist who wished art to avoid "the social inconsequence." The breadth of denunciations in "Mauberley" brings us as close as any poem in English before *The Waste Land* to the Modernist vision, but in Pound's case, this moment would prove to be an excuse to embark on a distinctly non-Modernist course, namely, to rebuild the world.

T. S. Eliot (1888–1965) shared Pound's dismay over the state of culture in the prewar years. As a student of Irving Babbitt at Harvard, he developed a critical attitude toward any form of Romantic optimism. Human nature was inherently flawed to Eliot, and the despair and misery he went on to record in his poetry served only to define and strengthen his conviction that human beings needed the support of a coherent Christian culture to lend purpose to their lives. Like Pound, he sought to acquaint people with what he called "the immense panorama of futility and anarchy which is contemporary history."[21] Like Pound again, in the last years of his life he all but gave up poetry for cultural polemicizing.

Eliot was born in St. Louis and attended Milton Academy and Harvard College, where he graduated in 1909. He began graduate studies in philosophy right away, spent the year 1910–11 at the Sorbonne, returned to Harvard to finish his studies, and in 1914 went to England, where by gradual process he settled down, married, and became a British citizen. He had written poetry as a young man, seriously enough so that when he went to Paris he went there more to visit the home of the Symbolist movement than to attend the lectures of Henri Bergson. He did finish his philosophical studies, but when he arrived in London in 1914 he was already carrying "The Love Song of J. Alfred Prufrock" with him. He found his way to Pound, who that winter would act as Yeats's secretary, and Pound knew at once what he had stumbled on. He wrote Harriet Monroe on 30 September: "He is the only American I know of who has made what I can call adequate preparation for writing. He has actually trained himself *and* modernized himself *on his own.*"[22]

Between 1910 and 1920, Eliot published three books of poetry— *Prufrock and Other Observations* (1917), *Poems* (1919), and *Ara Vos Prec* (1920)—as well as two books of criticism, *Ezra Pound: His Metric and Poetry* (1917) and *The Sacred Wood: Essays on Poetry and Criticism* (1920). Like Pound, he would later be known as much for his criticism as for his poetry, but in his first years as a published writer, he was almost exclusively and most intensely a poet. Eliot was the most gifted poet of his generation, and he created not just new rhythms in the language but also landscapes and conflicts which had rarely been seen in English poetry. Whitman was the only other poet of the city in the

English language, but his was the city of the open democratic masses. Eliot's city came from Baudelaire by way of the Decadents, and the people he found there were either coarse or cruelly oversensitive. "The Love Song of J. Alfred Prufrock" is at once the most vivid rendering of the late-nineteenth-century aesthetic sensibility and its most damning criticism. It undoubtedly influenced the writing of Pound's "Hugh Selwyn Mauberley."

The surprising thing about Eliot was, as Pound said, that when he appeared in the literary world, he was mature and fully formed. For one thing, he had a coherent worldview. Significant life took part in the city, where people were divided into the dispirited, lifeless poor, the insensitive merchants, and those from the class Eliot knew best, the pale harbingers of taste and breeding. None of these people merits much praise or pity. Eliot had a power of objectivity that occasionally makes him seem, especially in the early poetry, almost misanthropic. The merchants and commercial people, when they appear, are dismissed quickly and contemptuously and, alas, sometimes with what feels like anti-Semitism: "And the Jew squats on the window sill, the owner, / Spawned in some estaminet of Antwerp." This is not social satire but something like loathing.

If we feel that Eliot renders the lower and middle classes with unfair exaggeration, the same is not true of the members of his own class. A whole way of life, which must have been very close to Eliot's, is quietly dismissed in "Cousin Nancy," "The Boston Evening Transcript," or "Aunt Helen," who

> . . . lived in a small house near a fashionable square
> Cared for by servants to the number of four.
> Now when she died there was silence in heaven
> And silence at her end of the street.[23]

In the family poems, the criticism is gentler, much closer to social satire. Occasionally, as in "Morning at the Window," Eliot's satirical guard comes down.

> The brown waves of fog toss up to me
> Twisted faces from the bottom of the street,
> And tear from a passer-by with muddy skirts
> An aimless smile that hovers in the air
> And vanishes along the level of the roofs.[24]

Suddenly we are in Eliot's unique territory, an imprecise but vivid realm of the subconscious where ethereal and sordid images mix freely to create an atmosphere of intense isolation and loneliness. One of the most modern aspects of Eliot's writing is this ability to objectify the subconscious. The technique of juxtaposing images in "Prufrock" may look as though it owes a debt to Imagist objectivity and concision, but Eliot reached that technique by way of French Symbolism and, of course, by patient attention to the workings of his own mind.

J. Alfred Prufrock is not just the speaker of one of Eliot's poems. He is the Representative Man of early Modernism. Shy, cultivated, oversensitive, sexually retarded (many have said impotent), ruminative, isolated, self-aware to the point of solipsism, as he says, "Am an attendant lord, one that will do / To swell a progress, start a scene or two."[25] Nothing revealed the Victorian upper classes in Western society more accurately, unless it was a novel by Henry James, and nothing better exposed the dreamy, insubstantial center of that consciousness than a half-dozen poems in Eliot's first book. The speakers of all these early poems are trapped inside their own excessive alertness. They look out on the world from deep inside some private cave of feeling, and though they see the world and themselves with unflattering exactness, they cannot or will not do anything about their dilemma and finally fall back on self-serving explanation. They quake before the world, and their only revenge is to be alert. After *Prufrock and Other Observations*, poetry started coming from the city and from the intellect. It could no longer stand comfortably on its old post-Romantic ground, ecstatic before the natural world.

Had H. D. (Hilda Doolittle, 1886–1961) died in the thirties, we would think of her as an interesting minor poet. As it is, she wrought a startling change in her work in the last decades of her life, and we now think of her as a major poet of this century. She published only one book, her first, *Sea Garden* (1916), in the decade 1910 to 1920, as well as two books of Greek poetry in translation. Growing up in the Philadelphia area, she met and fell in love with Ezra Pound, and though the episode is shrouded somewhat, she went to England in 1911 futilely thinking that she and Pound were to be married. At any rate she soon found herself among the Imagists. Her early poems, in fact, contain some of the most beautiful and characteristic poems of that short-lived literary movement. They are spare and almost purely presentative.

Whiter
than the crust
left by the tide,

we are stung by the hurled sand
and the broken shells.[26]

These early poems are also, as this fragment from "The Wind Sleepers"
suggests, breathless and urgent in a straightforwardly Romantic way.
They avoid the banalities of Romanticism, however, first by freeing
themselves of accentual-syllabic meter and second by relying almost
entirely on the image.

The most striking thing about H. D.'s early poetry is its almost com-
plete removal from the living world. Much of it evokes the culture of
ancient Greece. The poems are filled with the sea, sunlight, beaches,
and, as in "Huntress," vaguely mythological beings and an incipient
feminism.

Come, blunt your spear with us,
our pace is hot
and our bare heels
in the heel-prints—
we stand tense—do you see—
are you already beaten
by the chase?[27]

It is natural to ask why she should so severely limit her contact with
the real world, and the last poem in *Sea Garden* gives a plausible answer.
"Cities" refers to no city in particular, but it is clear that she is talking
about the modern city. The poem is spoken by a member of a "cell," a
small group of enlightened people who have taken upon themselves the
task of guarding some treasure of the past and preserving it for use or
discovery in the indeterminate future. By implication, of course, the
present is ugly and threatening.

And in these dark cells,
packed street after street,
souls live, hideous yet—
O disfigured, defaced,
with no trace of the beauty
men once held so light.[28]

Years later Eliot would call this act of preserving things of value in an
unsympathetic age "redeeming the time." The foreshadowing of Eliot
extends even to her using the word "waste" to describe the contemporary
world ("Though we wander about, / find no honey of flowers in this
waste"). She is not an imitator, but she, too, wanted to build what Pound
called a "paradiso terrestre," in the belief that the modern world was

contemptible and horrifying. As it turned out, her utopia was quite different from either Pound's or Eliot's, primarily because she was a woman. But, in her earliest work, she is imbued with something like a reformer's zeal. Imagism would have stifled such zeal, which is the main reason why no poet of consequence stayed an Imagist very long. Like the typical Modernist, she found this world insupportable, and her refusal to name it or even refer to it in her early poetry is perhaps the most radical act of any of these early Modernists.

William Carlos Williams's (1883–1963) first book, *Poems* (1909), was privately printed in his hometown, Rutherford, New Jersey. It was, for the most part, Keatsian imitations. He had gone straight from Horace Mann High School in New York City, in 1902, to the University of Pennsylvania Medical School. There he met Pound and H. D. He had already decided to be a poet by then, and whether because Keats had been a doctor or because he liked Keats's poetry, he labored over a long work in imitation of *Endymion*. Pound, at the time, was writing a sonnet a day.

The friendship between Pound and Williams was crucial to the latter because, through Pound's badgering, Williams was able to change his style completely in a short time. His second book, *The Tempers,* appeared in 1913, and his mature style was established—not perfected, but established. *Al Que Quiere* appeared in 1917 and a book of prose poems, *Kora in Hell: Improvisations,* in 1920. Williams became an Imagist, as it were, by mail. He stripped his language of generality and gush, abandoned the "metronome" of accentual-syllabic metrics (indeed, he went so far as to write prose poems), and schooled himself rigorously in objective writing, writing with as little comment as possible.

More important, Williams steeped himself in his given world. Nothing in Imagist aesthetics required the poet to describe what lay out the window, no matter what it might be, but Williams took the factual and visual implications of that aesthetic to its logical end. He made a virtue of what he called "the local." None of his expatriate friends and contemporaries—Pound, Eliot, and H. D.—was interested in such a thing. Those poets who did celebrate localities—Robinson, of Maine; Frost, of New Hampshire; Masters, of the rural Midwest; Sandburg, of Chicago—did so in the manner and under the influence of local-color Realism in fiction. Williams instead used Imagist techniques to bring his poetry closer to the realities of his place.

This meant two things. The focus of his attention was immediate and close:

> There's my things
> drying in the corner:
> that blue skirt
> joined to the grey shirt.[29]

And, as this excerpt from "Portrait of a Woman in Bed" shows, he would use a language that was as straightforward and unornamented as the things it described.

Williams came as close as anyone ever had to using the language of everyday speech for poetry, and it is his great contribution to American poetry to couple this aim with that of putting America, warts and all, into his poetry. This might make him sound like an American Kipling. Not so. He does not use American speech as a dialect. American speech, as he heard it, was his poetic language. It is useful to remember that Williams lived all his adult life in one house—9 Ridge Road, Rutherford, New Jersey—and, living close to New York City, he came into contact with dozens of writers, painters, and photographers who were trying to do what Emerson had urged in his "American Scholar" address, namely, forge an American consciousness and art. Williams would not become vocal and programmatic about America until the twenties, when he published *In the American Grain*, but the impulses were there in the teens. The Armory Show in New York introduced American audiences to the new post-Impressionist art, and it took place the same year *The Tempers* was published. Stieglitz was making photography into an art form. Painters like Sheeler, Demuth, Sloan, Marin, Luks, Bellows, and others were looking closely at American places and people. *Poetry* magazine was a year old in 1913. The *Little Review*, *Others*, and the *Dial* followed quickly. Williams was very close to all this activity.

By the time of *Al Que Quiere*, Williams had found his voice and his material. Some of Williams's best early poems are found in it: "Tract," "The Young Housewife," "Love Song," "El Hombre" (which Wallace Stevens put into his poem "Nuances of a Theme by Williams"), "Good Night," "Danse Russe," "Smell," and "Pastoral." At this point in his career, Williams joined most writers in trying to undo the stultifying effects of "the genteel tradition."

Gertrude Stein (1874–1946) continues to baffle critics, partly because her work is so varied, partly because it eludes comprehension, and partly because her poetry stands outside all traditions. She wrote poetry as though she had never read any, except Mother Goose. When Stein published her book of poems, *Tender Buttons*, in 1914, she had already published *Three Lives* (1909), a work of fiction which not only focused on the little-known lives of women, but did so through some of the first stream-of-consciousness narration ever written. Her next publication wasn't until 1922, when *Geography and Plays* appeared with a foreword by Sherwood Anderson. She wrote incessantly, however, and as the Yale edition of the *Unpublished Writings of Gertrude Stein* shows, she wrote more in the teens and twenties of what we would call—and what she sometimes herself called—poetry than at any other time in her life. Most of these poems are found in volume three of the unpublished writings, *Bee Time Vine and Other Pieces [1913–27]* (1953).

It is an exaggeration to say that Gertrude Stein stumbled into writing, but her serious writing did not start until 1903 at age twenty-nine, two years after she failed four courses at Johns Hopkins Medical School. By that time, she had traveled extensively and had settled in Paris. She quickly found her way, mostly as a buyer, into the world of post-Impressionist painting. She saw her first Cezannes in 1904, met Picasso in 1905, and a year later sat for him. No writer has ever been as much influenced by painting; and living when and where she did, that influence created distortions of perceptions and syntax which, almost a century later, keep much of her work startling and largely unread. In important respects, however, she is the perfect embodiment of experimental tendencies in Modernism.

Stein is one of her own best critics. Her monograph on Picasso was published in 1938, but it often obliquely explains what she was attempting in her writing. "In the nineteenth century painters discovered the need of always having a model in front of them, in the twentieth century they discovered that they must never look at a model. . . . The truth that the things seen with the eyes are the only real things, had lost its significance."[30] Similar realizations had helped make psychological portraiture necessary in fiction and in poetry had opened a door into Surrealism. In Stein's poetry, the effect was quite different. The pieces in *Tender Buttons*, for instance, which Virgil Thomson calls "still lives," were attempts to get away from the object. Stein said she wished "to describe a thing without mentioning it," as in "A Red Hat":

> A dark gray, a very dark gray, a quite dark gray is monstrous ordinarily, it is so monstrous because there is no red in it. If red is in everything it is not necessary. Is that not an argument for any use of it and even so is there any place that is better, is there any place that has so much stretched out.[31]

The abandonment of line and meter seems incidental. What delights or infuriates the reader is her indifference to logic, her incongruity and discontinuousness. Richard Bridgman calls these poems "explosively subjective."[32] Stein's word for it is the painter's word: abstraction. Or, as she calls it in *The Autobiography of Alice B. Toklas,* "disembodiedness."

> Gertrude Stein, in her work, has always been possessed by the intellectual passion for exactitude in the description of inner and outer reality. She has produced a simplification by this concentration, and as a result the destruction of associational emotion in poetry and prose. She knows that in beauty, music, decoration, the result of emotion should never be the cause of emotion nor should they be the material of poetry and prose. Nor should emotion itself be the cause of poetry or prose. They should consist of an exact reproduction of either an outer or an inner reality.[33]

Playfulness, or as she calls it, "simplification," is probably the most conspicuous quality in Stein's work. We can see at once why she would have described Ezra Pound as "a village explainer." "Lifting Belly," one of the unpublished poems and one of her most playful and delightful, seems to be built from dialogue. Virgil Thomson calls it a "hymn to the domestic affections," and through its incongruities and apparent switches from inner to outer reality and back again reveals a liveliness of mind quite comparable to that in Milton's "L'Allegro," Smart's "Jubilate Agno," or Blake's *Songs of Innocence.*

> Lifting belly. Are you. Lifting.
> Oh dear, I said I was tender, fierce and tender.
> Do it. What a splendid example of carelessness.
> It gives me a great deal of pleasure to say yes.
> Why do I always smile.
> I don't know.
> It pleases me.[34]

It continues for another fifty pages. Does it have a beginning, middle or end, or is it all these things together at once? As Stein said in *Picasso,* "As the twentieth century is a century which sees the earth as no one has ever seen it, the earth has a splendor that it never has had, and as everything destroys itself in the twentieth century and nothing continues, so then the twentieth century has a splendor which is its own."[35] Few people read Stein's poetry these days, except as it has been absorbed and transmuted in the work of Frank O'Hara, Kenneth Koch, Allen Ginsberg, John Ashbery, and, by extension, a good many of the poets of our time.

None of the other American poets of this time became as prominent as Robinson, Frost, Pound, Eliot, and Williams. Other poets were widely known and admired at the time, some more than the ones I've mentioned, but time has not been kind to Amy Lowell, John Hall Wheelock, John Gould Fletcher, Conrad Aiken, and Vachel Lindsay. Their work has faded, much of it, it seems, forever. The same is not true, however, of Edgar Lee Masters and Carl Sandburg, and some accounting of them needs to be made.

Masters and Sandburg had many things in common. They grew up in the Midwest, away from the eastern centers of culture, away even from Chicago and St. Louis. They grew up in the era of Agrarian and Populist politics which, of course, were strongest in the Midwest. Sandburg came from a family of recent immigrants. And—a fact that cannot be ignored—they were male. In their different ways, they wrote a poetry that was proudly regional, that was democratic and forward-looking, and that made an effort to appeal to the common man. In all these things, their poetry was opposed to the new Modernist work which was urban and international, aesthetically intricate, politically and socially conservative, and difficult to grasp. The one thing both parties had in common was that they tried to make room in their work for what might be described as a "male consciousness." Whitman might have provided an example to them, but whether he did or not, it seems quite certain that both parties wished to rescue poetry from its reputation, cultivated and flaunted by the English Aesthetes and Decadents, as effete and unmasculine. When Pound shouted in "Sestina: Altaforte," "Damn it all! all this our South stinks peace," or when Sandburg announced that Chicago was "stormy, husky, brawling, [the] City of the Big Shoulders," it was part of a half-enlightened attempt to broaden the base of poetry. Such a similarity was too slight, however, to overcome the basic differences between these two kinds of poetry. Masters and Sandburg were the willing children of Emerson and the writers of Realist fiction in America. They were still trying to create an authentic American literature, one tied not only to the place but to its political ideals as well, and it is their principal glory and chief drawback that they succeeded.

Spoon River Anthology (1915) has found a permanent place in American literature, and though the rest of Edgar Lee Masters's (1868–1950) writing is less compelling, he will be remembered for his portrayal of small-town midwestern America in the days of subsistence farming and puritanical repressions, before the coming of radio, television, or the automobile. The poems in *Spoon River Anthology*, which take the form of epitaphs, were written over a short period of time, in something like a frenzy, and yet they sparkle with colloquial vigor.

> I went to the dances at Chandlerville
> and played snap-out at Winchester.[36]

Irony plays a large role in these poems. The whole world for Lucinda Matlock lay between Chandlerville and Winchester, two small towns unknown to the rest of the world. Masters's epitaphs, of course, give everyone the chance, in death, finally to tell the truth of their lives. The bland pieties of the traditional epitaph are replaced by the sorrows, secrets, and small triumphs of ordinary life. "Judge Somers" complains from the grave:

> How does it happen, tell me,
> That I lie here unmarked, forgotten,
> While Chase Henry, the town drunkard,
> Has a marble block, topped by an urn . . . ?[37]

Most of Masters's people lived their lives in this one small town, and their deepest feelings and most extravagant longings rarely extended farther than the end of Main Street. Yet Masters was able to create people who are fresh, direct, and complete. They are profoundly innocent and easily hurt, and, as in Greek tragedy, their experience is, without their realizing it, that of people everywhere.

Carl Sandburg (1878–1967) is remembered best for his poem "Chicago." It was the title poem of his first book, *Chicago Poems* (1916), a book which revived the almost forgotten legacy of Walt Whitman. *Cornhuskers* followed in 1918 and *Smoke and Steel* in 1920. No one had taken such risks with slang and colloquial language, not even Whitman, and no poet had looked as hard or as sympathetically at the lives of immigrant farmers and factory workers. The agrarian peasants of Whitman's day were almost gone. Sandburg lived in the midst of the first great industrial expansion in the United States, when the exploitation of workers was thought to be simply the operation of Darwinian principles in the social world. Sandburg was part newspaperman, part political organizer in his early days, and in 1910 he became private secretary to Emil Seidel, the Socialist mayor of Milwaukee. This was two years before the Socialists polled 900,000 votes in a national election, the high-water mark of political socialism in this country. When Sandburg asked the newspaper cartoonists in "Halsted Street Car" to "Take your pencils /

And draw these faces,"[38] he was writing almost the way Eliot did in "The Preludes," the large difference being that he wrote in the language of the people he described and in the belief that their lives mattered.

Sandburg's work has not fared well among critics because it is too interested in its subject and not enough interested in the art and craft of making poems. At the same time, his poems show a remarkable honesty of perception and loyalty to his subject matter. His work makes clear how much is left out of our poetry, and his efforts to include the hoboes, millhands, farmers, pimps, whores, gamblers, and drifters of every description, not as exotic backdrop, but as human beings, will always earn him respect. Occasional poems flash brilliantly into our subconscious like the great photograph taken by a neighbor on his vacation. Here is "Soup" from *Smoke and Steel:*

> I saw a famous man eating soup.
> I say he was lifting a fat broth
> Into his mouth with a spoon.
> His name was in the newspapers that day
> Spelled out in tall black headlines
> And thousands of people were talking about him.
>   When I saw him,
> He sat bending his head over a plate
> Putting soup in his mouth with a spoon.[39]

Decades are not tidy, as I've said, so I will have to lump together here in a note some excellent poets, at least one and possibly two of whom are among the best American poets of this or any other century. E. E. Cummings (1894–1961), Robinson Jeffers (1887–1962), Marianne Moore (1887–1972), and Wallace Stevens (1879–1955) all published important work in the late teens. Moore published seventeen poems in 1915 alone in three of the most important magazines of that day, the *Egoist* (London), *Poetry,* and *Others.* Stevens began publishing his mature poems in 1914, including "Peter Quince at the Clavier" (*Others,* 1915), "Sunday Morning" (*Poetry,* 1915, five months after Eliot's "Prufrock" appeared there), and "Thirteen Ways of Looking at a Blackbird" (*Others,* 1917). Cummings relied almost exclusively on the *Harvard Monthly* until 1920, when he suddenly published twelve poems, an essay, and a review in the *Dial.* At any rate, Moore's first book, *Poems,* published in London by the Egoist Press, came out in 1921, Stevens's *Harmonium* (Knopf) in 1923, and Cummings's *Tulips and Chimneys* (Thomas Seltzer) in 1923. I have left them to be considered with the poets of the twenties.

Notes

1. T. S. Eliot, "Reflections on Vers Libre," *New Statesman* 8 (1917).
2. Eric Homberger, "Chicago and New York: Two Versions of American Modernism," in *Modernism 1890–1930,* ed. M. Bradbury and Jay MacFarlane (Harmondsworth, U.K.: Penguin, 1976), 159.
3. Woolf, "Mr. Bennett and Mrs. Brown," in *The Captain's Death Bed and Other Essays* (New York: Harcourt, 1973), 91–92. Originally published as "Character in Fiction," *Criterion*, July 1924, 409–30.
4. Matei Calinescu, *Faces of Modernity: Avante Garde, Decadence, Kitsch* (Bloomington: Indiana University Press, 1977), 41–42.
5. Ibid.
6. Jay McFarlane, "The Mind of Modernism," in *Modernism 1890–1930*, ed. Bradbury and MacFarlane, 72–81.
7. Pound, *Personae* (New York: New Directions, 1926), 85.
8. Ibid., 130.
9. Stevens, *The Palm at the End of the Mind: Selected Poems and a Play*, ed. Holly Stevens (New York: Random, Vintage, 1972), 46.
10. H. D., "Oread," in *The Norton Anthology of Modern Poetry*, ed. Richard Ellman and Robert O'Clair (New York: Norton, 1973), 73.
11. Williams, *Selected Poems*, ed. Randall Jarrell (New York: New Directions, 1963), 30.
12. Pound, *Personae*, 191.
13. Irving Howe, "The Idea of the Modern," in *The Idea of the Modern in Literature and the Arts*, ed. Irving Howe (New York: Horizon, 1967), 11–40.
14. See Calinescu, *Faces of Modernity*, for an excellent discussion of the history of concepts such as "the modern," "Modernity," and "Modernism."
15. Graham Hough, "The Modernist Lyric," in *Modernism: 1890–1930*, ed. Bradbury and MacFarlane, 318.
16. Robinson, *Collected Poems* (New York: Macmillan, 1937), 82.
17. Frost, *Robert Frost: Poetry and Prose*, ed. E. C. Lathem and Lawrence Thompson (New York: Holt, 1972), 346.
18. Frost, *Complete Poems* (New York: Holt, 1949) 31.
19. Frost, *Selected Prose*, ed. Hyde Cox and E. C. Lathem (New York: Holt, 1956), 64.
20. Pound, *The Letters of Ezra Pound 1907–1941*, ed. D. D. Paige (New York: Harcourt, 1950), 38.
21. Eliot, "Ulysses, Order, and Myth," in *Selected Prose*, ed. Frank Kermode (New York: Farrar, Straus and Giroux, 1975), 177.
22. Pound, *The Letters of Ezra Pound*, 40.
23. Eliot, *Collected Poems, 1909–1962* (London: Faber and Faber, 1963), 21.
24. Eliot, *The Complete Poems and Plays* (New York: Harcourt, 1952), 17.
25. Ibid., 16.
26. H. D., *Collected Poems of H. D.* (New York: Liveright, 1925), 18.
27. Ibid., 32.
28. Ibid., 59.

29. Williams, *The Collected Earlier Poems* (New York: New Directions, 1938), 150.

30. Stein, *Gertrude Stein's Picasso* (New York: Liveright, 1970), 3.

31. Stein, *Writings and Lectures: 1911–1945*, ed. Patricia Meyerowitz (London: Peter Owen, 1967), 158.

32. Bridgman, *Gertrude in Pieces* (New York: Oxford University Press, 1970), 104.

33. Stein, *The Autobiography of Alice B. Toklas* (New York: Harcourt, 1933), 259.

34. Stein, *Bee Time Vine and Other Pieces*, vol. 3 of *Unpublished Works of Gertrude Stein* (New Haven: Yale University Press, 1953), 67.

35. Stein, *Picasso*, 76.

36. Masters, *Spoon River Anthology* (New York: Macmillan, 1914), 229.

37. Ibid., 13.

38. Sandburg, *The Complete Poems* (New York: Harcourt, 1950), 6.

39. Ibid., 165.

3

Helmet of Fire: American Poetry in the 1920s

EDWARD HIRSCH

All my beautiful safe world blew up. . . .

> —F. Scott Fitzgerald, *Tender Is the Night*

The age demanded an image
Of its accelerated grimace. . . .

> —Ezra Pound, "Hugh Selwyn Mauberley"

The decade of the twenties rightfully begins in November 1918, at the end of fifty-two slaughterous months that changed the world forever. It is difficult to underestimate the impact of World War I on a generation that had been trained and prepared for one kind of world—one that in retrospect seems almost prelapsarian—and then discovered that it existed in another kind of world altogether. By the time the war began in 1914, the Modernist revolution was well underway, but the sordid experience and reality of modern warfare propelled that revolution forward in an unprecedented and violent way. Poets who wrote in the aftermath of the war could never again forget its particular horrors, how the so-called civilized world put on a modern helmet of fire. In this sense, as Francis Hope has stated, "All poetry written since 1918 is war poetry."[1] In particular, the poets who wrote between 1918 and 1929 (the year of the stock market crash and the beginning of the Great Depression that so radically altered American life) inherited a fallen world, a world changed by the experience and knowledge of trench warfare, the blood-drenched reality of murderous carnage, what Ezra Pound's seminal post-war poem, "Hugh Selwyn Mauberley" (1920), calls "wastage as never before" and

54

disillusions as never told in the old days,
hysterias, trench confessions,
laughter out of dead bellies.[2]

Pound's poem inaugurates the decade and sums up the Modernist poets' sense of a "botched civilization," their communal belief in the dramatic failure of modern life. In a crucial way the war years delivered the final death-blows to the nineteenth century.

Experience seemed more chaotic and disjunctive for most writers; consciousness, language, and writing itself seemed more problematic than in previous times.[3] These changes help to account for the grave crisis in poetry in the late teens and early twenties, the final overhaul of the genteel and fin de siècle tradition in American letters, the complex and sometimes adversarial relationship between writers and readers as well as for the notorious difficulty of much modern poetry which was fueled by, and indeed assaulted its audience with, images of fragmentation, discontinuity, and collapse, what in "Mauberley" is called "consciousness disjunct." In 1921, T. S. Eliot, who was deep in the throes of *The Waste Land* at the time, put the case for the fragmented and "difficult" text succinctly in what turned out to be one of the key critical essays of the decade, "The Metaphysical Poets": "We can only say that it appears likely that poets in our civilization, as it exists at present, must be difficult. Our civilization comprehends great variety and complexity, and this variety and complexity, playing upon a refined sensibility, must produce various and complex results. The poet must become more and more comprehensive, more allusive, more indirect, in order to force, to dislocate if necessary, language into his meaning."[4]

There was an explosive sense of tension and energy at the end of the war. The war years created a bottled-up and nearly hysterical intensity that for most writers soon yielded to a mood of postwar disillusionment and despair, a feeling of large moral and cultural decay. That pessimism was perhaps most total and vehement in the work of Robinson Jeffers, who, in the six books he published in the twenties, universalized it into a critique of all human behavior, civilization itself. In a more representative way, *The Waste Land* (1922)—with its sense of the unreal city and the walking dead, hysterical voices and fragmented experiences—was unquestionably the central summary text of generational despair over the decline of the West. In Archibald MacLeish's words, "*The Waste Land* provided the vocabulary of our understanding."[5] Eliot himself repeatedly insisted that he never intended the poem to express what

I. A. Richards called "the disillusionment of a generation," but nonetheless that was how it was understood by a large number of young writers. Almost immediately it became the central canonical text of the decade and, indeed, of Modernism itself, the single postwar poem to which all other poets responded in one way or another. Whereas most young American writers found in the poem a symbol answerable to their own pessimistic sense and even diagnosis of contemporary life, others like William Carlos Williams and Hart Crane disliked the negativism of the poem and felt betrayed by it. They believed it moved American poetry powerfully in the wrong direction, that the death of the old order could be a prelude to the birth of a new one, the beginning of what Crane in "The Wine Menagerie" calls "new thresholds, new anatomies!" But whatever their response to Eliot's radical poetic methodology, his strategy of juxtaposition and collage, his gloomy prognosis and nearly pathological anatomizing of the death of modern civilization, and whatever their political slant or persuasion, for all but the most naïve of writers the war and its aftermath problematized and finally punctured forever the American myth of progress and improvement. What Van Wyck Brooks called "the confident years" (1885–1915) were over.

The twenties was the decade when, as Frederick Hoffman pointed out, "All forms of rebellion, protest, satire and experiment . . . were admitted."[6] It was also an era when the most puritanical and the most expansive and liberated aspects of American culture came into dramatic conflict and confrontation. The repressive aspects of American culture can be symbolized by the Prohibition amendment (which took effect on 1 January 1920 and wasn't repealed until 1933) and the Red Scare (the intolerant, paranoid form of patriotism which peaked with the arrest of Sacco and Vanzetti in one of the most celebrated legal cases of the decade). Beginning with the general strike in Seattle, the country was also torn apart by some three thousand labor strikes which were broken one after the other, leaving a heritage of failure for organized labor in the twenties. So, too, there was a tremendous black migration to Northern cities after the war, a strong reaction of repressive violence by many whites and, consequently, for a complex of reasons, there were race riots in some twenty-five cities during the "red summer" of 1919. At the same time the great northern migration also helped to lay the foundations for the creative ferment which would become the Harlem Renaissance.[7]

After the war a deep change took place in black consciousness around the country. The writers of the Harlem Renaissance were inflamed with a fresh faith in blackness and a fervent racial pride, the symbol and gospel of the New Negro. Harlem emerged as the new cultural center of black life. The lyric outpouring and achievement of the bright firmament of Claude McCay, Countee Cullen, Jean Toomer, and Langston Hughes essentially grew out of the radical evolution and change in American black life between the war years and the Depression. In the twenties the writers of the Harlem Renaissance self-consciously forged a distinct black aesthetic—reinventing and rediscovering traditional folk forms and, simultaneously, inventing a new formal expression of black life. As Langston Hughes asserted in 1926, "We younger Negro artists who create now intend to express our individual dark-skinned selves without fear or shame."[8] The collective work of the Harlem Renaissance poets forever redefined black life in literature. It marked a major watershed in black and, consequently, in American literary history.[9]

The more expansive and liberated aspects of American culture in the twenties can be symbolized not only by a changing black consciousness, but also by political developments such as the national woman's suffrage movement (women at last received the right to vote in 1920) and, in social terms, what came to be called the Jazz Age, an era of flappers and flaming youth, changing sexual mores and moral standards, a new bohemianism. Edna St. Vincent Millay and E. E. Cummings were the poets who seemed to express this bohemian aspect of the era most effectively and representatively in their work. Despite their different poetic modes and sensibilities, both Millay and Cummings were romantic individualists who had gravitated to Greenwich Village as the unquestioned center of bohemia. (So, too, Gertrude Stein and the young men she called "the lost generation" helped establish Paris as the center of romantic expatriatism in the twenties.) Millay and Cummings were writing in revolt against social and sexual puritanism, an outdated moral code. "Let's live suddenly without thinking," Cummings asserted in one poem. As Millay wrote in what was perhaps the most widely quoted quatrain of the decade:

> My candle burns at both ends;
> > It will not last the night;
> But ah, my foes, and oh, my friends—
> > It gives a lovely light.[10]

Millay and Cummings were poets of extravagant feeling writing on behalf of a changing system of manners. Their work reflected a new ethic. Thus, for the younger generation the Jazz Age—which was also an Age of Dismay—was a liberating time. F. Scott Fitzgerald referred to it as "the greatest, gaudiest spree in history."[11]

It was also during the twenties that the reigning ethic of middle-class America became a kind of rampant consumerism. Wilsonian idealism died, and under the leadership of Harding and Coolidge the route to normalcy became the road to a new commercialism and economic prosperity accompanied by an acquisitive spirit of materialism. Most writers reacted violently against America's materialistic ethics and, in alienated distrust, American poetry turned increasingly inward and away from social action.

At the beginning of the decade, it was still possible for critics to argue that modern American poetry scarcely existed. In "The Literary Life," his contribution to *Civilization in the United States*, Van Wyck Brooks surveyed the history of American literature as a "very weak and sickly plant" that couldn't be expected to flourish in the decaying soil of American civilization. Critics everywhere were willing to echo Brooks's opinion that, in comparison to contemporary European literature, American literature "is indeed one long list of spiritual casualties. For it is not that the talent is wanting, but that somehow that talent fails to fulfill itself."[12] Ten years later that opinion was scarcely possible. The twenties witnessed what R. P. Blackmur called an extraordinary "explosion of talent" that did, in fact, fulfill itself. A renaissance took place which established American poetry once and for all, at home and abroad, at the center of twentieth-century poetry. By the end of the decade American poetry had been recast and re-created as High Modernism. One result was a literary canon practically unsurpassed in American poetry.

T. S. Eliot and Ezra Pound together created an American version of continental Modernism. Their work of the late teens and early twenties has a closer affinity to Wyndham Lewis's Vorticist paintings and James Joyce's *Ulysses* than it does to the New World imperatives and ingenuities of William Carlos Williams and Marianne Moore, Hart Crane and Wallace Stevens. By 1920 the two expatriate American poets who had done so much to extricate twentieth-century poetry from the vagaries of late-Victorian verse were intent on reestablishing the connection between a fragmentary and chaotic present and a harmonious European past. In his seminal essay, "Tradition and the Individual Talent" (1919), Eliot argues that the contemporary poet needs to write with a strong historical sense "not only of the pastness of the past, but of its presence," with the feeling "that the whole of the literature of Europe from Homer and within it the whole of the literature of his own country has a simultaneous existence and composes a simultaneous order."

Eliot's idea of historical continuity and coherence, his idealized version of the comprehensive "mind of Europe," placed American poetry firmly in a European context and tradition. (In 1933, Pound concurred that "Eliot and I are in agreement or 'belong to the same school of critics,' in so far as we both believe that existing works form a complete order which is changed by the introduction of the 'really new' work.")[13] As a corollary to his emphasis on the interrelationship between the individual poet and the preceding tradition, the avant-garde artist and the deep (as opposed to the recent) past, Eliot also argued for the depersonalization of poetry in his well-known formulation, "The progress of the artist is a continual self-sacrifice, a continual extinction of personality." The essays in Eliot's first critical book, *The Sacred Wood* (1920), emphasize traditionalism, impersonality, and a transcendental European authority. They ask the critic to focus on the poem itself rather than on the personality or emotions of the poet; they call for "analysis and comparison" in considering the poem as an object. Although Eliot himself never practiced the method of close analysis and systematic criticism that would derive from the work of I. A. Richards (*Practical Criticism*, 1926) and William Empson (*Seven Types of Ambiguity*, 1928), his focus on the work of art as an ontological object is the inaugural step in a critical method that would become formulated as New Criticism during the thirties.[14]

In the July 1932 issue of the *Criterion*, Pound looked back to the moment when he and Eliot decided that free verse had to be replaced by regular forms:

> That is to say, at a particular date in a particular room, two authors, neither engaged in picking the other's pocket, decided that the dilution of *vers libre*, Amygism, Lee Masterism, general floppiness had gone too far and that some counter-current needed to be set going . . . Remedy prescribed "Émaux et Camées" (or the Bay State Hymn Book). Rhyme and regular strophes.
>
> Results: Poems in Mr. Eliots *second* volume not contained in his first (*Prufrock, Egoist*, 1917), also "H. S. Mauberley."[15]

There are twelve new poems in Eliot's second volume, *Poems* (1920). Eliot wrote four of the poems in French under the influence of Corbière to get himself unlocked from a stagnant period, seven in quatrains derived from Gautier (though the ironic diction harks back to Laforgue and the violent wit is reminscent of Donne). The quatrains are allusive, chilly, condensed, witty. Their rigid structure emphasizes coherence and control, an idea of imposed order. George Williamson calls the quatrains "a temporary discipline rather than a lasting form," and, tellingly, the book's most important single poem, "Gerontion," is a free-verse dramatic monologue which stands in the line of "Prufrock" and as a prelude to *The Waste Land.*[16]

Ezra Pound called "Hugh Selwyn Mauberley: Life and Contacts" both "a farewell to London" and "a study in form, an attempt to condense the Jamesian novel."[17] It is the poem that marks the end of Pound's London days as well as the close of his early work. Thereafter he would become the poet of his evolving Modernist epic, *The Cantos.* One of the central themes of "Mauberley" is the overriding tyranny of modern life, the relentless pressure it exerts upon the individual. Mauberley's limited Paterian aesthetic can't satisfy the demands of the age, and the poem ends with his isolation and death. Thus the poem becomes an elegy not only for the character of Mauberley but also for the heritage of aestheticism. By 1920 Pound had already published a version of the first three cantos and had begun to work toward *A Draft of XVI Cantos* (1925). One of the ways he turned away from aestheticism was by embarking on an epic poem that would tell "the tale of the tribe." In formal terms, the chiseled quatrains of "Mauberley" derive from Pound's reading of Gautier as well as of Bion's *Adonis*, though the material is grafted together and presented through a series of abrupt cuts and shifts that give the feeling of a Modernist collage. Many of its formal devices—especially the way it radically changes ground, shifting perspective, juxtaposing fragments and languages, mixing classical allusions and contemporary events—also anticipate the method of *The Waste Land.*

The most important poem of our century (and also the most explicated one) began, in T. S. Eliot's own words, as "the relief of a personal . . . grouse against life."[18] Eliot had been collecting fragments and planning a long poem for years, but he finally managed to draft most of the poem which would eventually become *The Waste Land* in 1921 in a sanitorium at Lausanne where he was taking a rest cure. On one level, the poem recapitulates his tormented personal life over the previous ten years— his full-scale depression, his disastrous marriage to a woman both sickly and high-strung ("My nerves are bad tonight. Yes, bad. Stay with me," her stand-in says in the final poem), his sense of being enslaved to a job at Lloyds Bank, his own fear of psychosis, hypersensitivity to noise, indecisiveness, and suffering from "nerves." The poem arises out of what he once called "some rude unknown *psychic materials.*"[19] In a psychoanalytic sense, the poem—which one of his friends called "Tom's Autobiography"—represents the psychic disintegration and reconstitution of a self.[20] The writing itself became "these fragments I have shored against my ruin," a psychic as well as a religious journey from sin to revelation. At the same time, as Eliot acknowledged many years later in a piece about Virgil, "A poet may believe that he is expressing only his private experiences . . . yet for his readers what he has written may come to be the expression both of their own secret feelings and of the exultation or despair of a generation."[21] Eliot's own inner nightmare correlated to what others perceived as an outer social nightmare, and thus his spiritual autobiography simultaneously became an account of a collapsing postwar society.

The Waste Land is an open structure of fragments, a poem without a fixed center. It has no single interpretation or truth, no one narrator or narrative thread to hold it together. It disseminates the self. It contains scenes and vignettes from a wide variety of times and places: agitated scraps of conversations, parodies, intertextual allusions, unattributed and often broken quotations, a medley of radically shifting languages, a disturbing cacophony of voices. The result is a poem with the feeling of a nightmare. As the facsimile edition of *The Waste Land* now makes clear, the manuscript which Eliot originally brought to Pound was much more sprawling and chaotic than the final poem. Pound ruthlessly cut the poem from about a thousand lines to its final four hundred and thirty-three lines, deleted eight major sections, made dozens of minor changes, recommended against the title ("He Do the Police in Different Voices"), against using an epigraph from Conrad ("the horror! the horror!"), and against using "Gerontion" as a prelude to the poem. The author of "Mauberley" was more comfortable with the poetics of fragmentation and collage, and his severe cuts foregrounded the poem's wrenching dislocations and juxtapositions. The result is a poem which is rhetorically discontinuous.

Eliot's method of dislocating language suits the basic despairing tone and vision of the poem—the theme of a ruined postwar world. The backdrop of the poem is the "unreal city" of London and, beyond that, the larger collapse of two thousand years of European history. The people who inhabit the waste land are the walking dead. The philosophic principle animating the poem is solipsism, F. H. Bradley's idea that, as

Eliot says in a note to the poem, "the whole world for each is peculiar and private to that soul." Thus there is no genuine sharing of worlds—the experience of each person is "a circle closed on the outside." The medley of voices that inhabit *The Waste Land* never connect. The idea of a contemporary world without meaning or connection is also highlighted in Eliot's next major poem, a kind of epilogue to *The Waste Land*, "The Hollow Men" (1925).

The Waste Land first appeared, without notes, in the *Criterion* in 1922. (Eliot became the editor of the journal in 1923 and stayed on until the late thirties.) The title of the poem and what to many critics has seemed to be its controlling myth (the Grail legend) were late additions and impositions on the poem. In his essay on Joyce's *Ulysses*, "Ulysses, Order, and Myth," Eliot defined the mythical method as "a way of controlling, of ordering, of giving a shape and a significance to the immense panorama of futility and anarchy which is contemporary history."[22] Eliot saw his own experience as well as contemporary history as a vast chaos and anarchy. He projected his personal life onto history and sought a way to shape and order that chaos. Thus his conservative turn. By the end of the decade he had declared himself a classicist in literature, a royalist in politics, and an Anglo-Catholic in religion.[23]

The Modernism of the twenties took regional form in the work of three Southern poets—John Crowe Ransom, Allen Tate, and the young Robert Penn Warren, all of whom were associated with the Nashville Fugitives and helped to publish the literary magazine the *Fugitive* from 1922 to 1925. Of the sixteen poets in the Fugitive group, Ransom was the one significant writer who reached his full (and nearly complete) poetic development in the twenties.[24] Tate, the recognized champion of experimental Modernism in the group, developed many of his key ideas during the decade and published his first book, *Mr. Pope and Other Poems*, in 1928. During the decade, Warren established his basic poetic dualism, his tragic vision of the fall of man, his interest in irony as a reigning, inclusive poetic mode, and perhaps even his redemptive vision of language; but his major poetic work rightly belongs to later decades in American poetry.

In formal terms, the Fugitive poets began at the same place that Eliot and Pound had come to by the early twenties—with the sense that the free-verse revolution needed a countercurrent. Consequently, they worked within traditional forms. In their commitment to the historical past, their antiindustrialism, their hatred of abstraction, their diagnosis of what Tate called the "deep illness of the mind," dissociation of sensibility, their belief in what Ransom defined as the "antipathy between art and science," and their prevailing sense of the tragedy of modern man, the Fugitives also developed a brand of what might be called Traditionalist Modernism which was related to the cultural critiques leveled at modern civilization by Eliot and Pound.[25] At the same time their work grew directly out of their own native region. One might say that the American current of European Modernism took a strong, unexpected turn in the modern South.

The first issue of the *Fugitive* proclaimed that the phenomenon sometimes "known rather euphemistically as Southern Literature has expired" and that "*The Fugitive* flees from nothing faster than the high-caste Brahmins of the Old South."[26] The Fugitive poets began in rebellion against apologetic, official Southern literature, the "moonlight and magnolia" school of post–Civil War Southern poetry. Initially, they showed little interest in regional self-consciousness and self-definition. Their most common and persistent theme was the alienation of the artist from society, especially Southern society. But the South suffered a powerful economic and social shock after the end of the war as an essentially closed and static society increasingly opened up to industrialism and mass culture. As the twenties progressed, modern industrialism encroached further and further into traditional Southern culture. After the national attention and criticism directed at the South during the Scopes trial, the Fugitives began to rethink their ideas of the old South and how it might resist the spirit of technology and science as well as the onslaught of American materialism. They were already classicists in literature, traditionalists in religion—they also became regionalists. By the end of the decade they had turned into Agrarians, a movement which culminated in the manifesto *I'll Take My Stand* (1930). In that book, twelve Southern writers defended an agrarian economy and looked back nostalgically to a preindustrial, racially segregated, Christian South. In so doing they turned away from the progressivism of contemporary America and toward the conservatism of older European traditions.

John Crowe Ransom's first book, *Poems about God* (1919), consisted of poems which Randall Jarrell once described as "old-fashioned amateurishly direct jobs that remind you of the Longfellow-Whittier-Lowell section of your sixth-grade reader."[27] Ransom himself came to consider them apprentice work, and none survived into his later *Selected Poems*. They do indicate, however, the beginning of Ransom's furious war against abstractionism, his desire to knit up what he perceived to be the modern dissociation of reason from sensibility. Ransom's development as a poet was so rapid that in a few years he had discovered and mastered his mature style—with its formal elegance and technical skillfulness, its complex mix of dictions and tones, its wry wit and understatement, its cool surface and subtle use of irony—and written about a dozen or so nearly flawless lyrics. His two books *Chills and Fever* (1924) and *Two Gentlemen in Bonds* (1927) contain nearly all of the poems he wished to preserve. They represent his primary achievement in poetry. By the end of the decade Ransom had mainly stopped writing poetry and turned his attention to philosophical literary and social criticism.

The principal theme that runs through all of Ransom's work is our curious and tragic human doubleness, our divided natures and sensibilities. He once told Robert Penn Warren that he thought of man as an "oscillating mechanism," and for him Eliot's notion of the fragmented modern psyche was a psychological rather than a historical truth.[28] Ransom's poems chart a war of inner human tensions and oppositions—the split between body and soul, desire and need, illusion and reality, emotion and rational intellect. His most characteristic poems enact a theme of thwarted love or else dramatize and investigate the relentless inevitability of death and how we respond to it. The tragedy of Ransom's characters is their inability to accept their own duality, oscillating between extremes, paralyzed and tortured—as the equilibrists are—by opposing forces in their own natures. The only reconciliation they can find is in their own death. Despite his playfulness and wit, a Hardyesque fatalism runs through all of Ransom's poems.

Ransom's typical poetic strategy is to take a passionate subject and hold it up at a certain distance, creating a feeling of balance and tension, emotions held in check, fever and chills. He created a detached surface and linguistic tension by mixing a raw, colloquial, and informal speech with an archaic and elegant diction. And his central poetic mode was irony. He believed that irony was the most inclusive response to human duality and in 1924 praised it in *the Fugitive* as "the rarest of the states of mind, because it is the most inclusive; the whole mind has been active in arriving at it, both creation and criticism, both poetry and science."[29] Thus out of his own poetic practice and experience, his idea of the proper response to man's perception of his difference from nature, Ransom began to define the term that would be the foundation stone for New Criticism.

In the early twenties Allen Tate carried on what he called "an impertinent campaign on Eliot's behalf in the South." Tate's first book, *Mr. Pope and Other Poems*, combines a traditional formality with a Modernist subject matter and was heavily influenced by Eliot's *Poems*. His style is chiseled, concentrated, difficult. Tate arranged the poems under three categories, "Space," "Time," and "History," but they all deal with the same essential theme—the suffering of the modern citizen who must live in a world of bewildering complexity (with understanding divorced from reason) and under the dispensation of a scientific and technological age.

Tate's most important single poem, "Ode to the Confederate Dead," is a kind of Southern analogue to *The Waste Land*. As opposed to Ransom, who thought *The Waste Land* "seemed to bring to a head all the specifically modern errors," Tate defended the way Eliot's poem embraced "the entire range of consciousness" and impersonally dramatized the tragic situation of those who live in modern times.[30] Tate's "Ode" treats that situation in specifically Southern terms. The poem presents the symbolic dilemma of a man who has stopped at the gate of a Confederate graveyard. He is trapped in time, isolated, alone, self-conscious, caught between a heroic Civil War past, which is irrecoverable, and the chaotic, degenerate present. In his essay "Narcissus as Narcissus," Tate argues that "the poem is 'about' solipsism, a philosophical doctrine which says that we create the world in the act of perceiving it, or about Narcissism, or any other *ism* that denotes the failure of the human personality to function objectively in nature and society."[31] As the poem develops, it becomes a drama of "the cut-offness of the modern 'intellectual man' from the world." The situation of the speaker is symptomatic of the crisis of his region—the crisis of the Old and the New South after World War I. In its diagnosis of that historical situation, the "Ode" is an Agrarian poem. It universalizes from the situation of the South in the middle and late twenties to the larger condition of the modern world.

In the twenties William Carlos Williams and Marianne Moore helped to continue to create and define a Modernist poetry of the New World, a local, homemade American poetic. Their "experiments in composition" are akin to the typographical innovations of E. E. Cummings and the verbal portraits of Gertrude Stein as well as to the more minor free-verse experiments of Mina Loy, Alfred Kreymborg, and Walter Arensberg. Their urgent struggle to create an indigenous American poetry parallels the innovative prose experiments of the expatriates Hemingway and Fitzgerald in the twenties. They had an even stronger and more direct connection to the visual artists who clustered around the photographer Alfred Stieglitz's gallery, "291" (Marianne Moore called it "an American Acropolis"), especially John Marin, Marsden Hartley, Arthur Dove, Charles Demuth, and Charles Sheeler. Along with the cultural journalists Waldo Frank (*Our America*, 1919) and Paul Rosenfeld (*Port of New York*, 1924), these artists emphasized immediate visual experience and the need for establishing American values in art. Out of this milieu, surrounded by the call for the emancipation of American art and literature, Moore and Williams created a body of early work (*Observations* and *Spring and All* are its masterpieces) that stands as a direct alternative to Continental American Modernism.

Williams's response to *The Waste Land* is the most extreme example of the way two strains of American poetry diverged in the twenties. Williams wanted a poetry that was forward-looking and experimental, self-consciously rooted in American soil. Years later he recalled how he felt when *The Waste Land* first appeared:

> It wiped out our world as if an atom bomb had been dropped upon it and our brave sallies into the unknown were turned to dust.
> To me especially it struck like a sardonic bullet. I felt at once that it had set me back twenty years, and I'm sure it did. Critically Eliot returned us to the classroom just at the moment when I felt that we were on the point of an escape to matters much closer to the essence of a new art form itself—rooted in the locality which should give it fruit.[32]

The poetry which Williams wrote and sponsored in the twenties was directly posed against Eliot's version of Modernism.

Williams and Moore are poets of immanence, anti-Symbolists. For them meaning inheres primarily in the external world, and their poems accord to objects a life of their own. They featured and appraised objects (also animals and other people) in and of themselves, not for what they represented. Williams said of Moore, "To Miss Moore an apple remains an apple whether it be in Eden or the fruit bowl where it curls."[33] There is no depth of transcendence in their world, no secret, symbolic nature in things, no hidden correspondences to another world. So, too, for them words were fundamentally things in themselves, solid objects that match the particular things they name. Williams writes in *Spring and All*, "Of course it must be understood that writing deals with words and words only and that all discussions of it deal with single words and their associations in groups." At the same time words are themselves marked by "the shapes of men's lives in places."[34] Words are objects interacting in their own right which simultaneously name and parallel the local, external world. This dual sense of language is the beginning of an Objectivist aesthetic.

To render the external world accurately also meant to break radically with traditional ways of presenting and describing that world as well as with traditional or received forms of poetry. The goal was not loveliness but reality itself. This is the basic premise behind Williams's claim that "destruction and creation / are simultaneous."[35] "Poetry," Moore's most celebrated early poem, begins with the assertion

I, too, dislike it: there are things that are important
        beyond all this fiddle.
    Reading it, however, with a perfect contempt for it, one
        discovers in
    it after all, a place for the genuine.[36]

Moore and Williams are revolutionary poets in the way they destroy preexisting forms in order to create new ones.

Williams published three books of poems in the twenties: *Kora in Hell: Improvisations* (1920), *Sour Grapes* (1921), and *Spring and All* (1923). All are what Webster Schott terms "crisis books."[37] Written in white heat, their style is fervent, headlong, embattled, often obscure and contradictory, sometimes radiantly clear and luminous. They are also the key books of Williams's early career, for they contain the basic premises of his mature thought. They show him trying to create a platform for his evolving aesthetic in prose even as he embodied that aesthetic in some of his most memorable short poems.

Kora in Hell is a book of experimental prose poems, a culling of journal meditations which Williams jotted down as a kind of automatic writing every night for a year. Later he added comments and explanatory notes, many of them equally dense and obscure. The title refers to the legend of Spring captured and taken to Hades. As Williams recalled years later, "I thought of myself as Springtime and I felt I was on my way to Hell."[38] Inspired by Rimbaud's *Illuminations*, *Kora in Hell* is one of Williams's most puzzling, disjunctive, and surreal texts, a broken composition that continually defies rational logic and coherence. *Kora in Hell* is a text divided against itself, energetically trying to find an equilibrium, holding together two conflicting forces and impulses. On the one hand, the improvisations are impromptu and open-ended, asserting the freedom and primacy of the imagination. They are fueled by what J. Hillis Miller calls an "anarchistic rage to demolish everything, all logical or rational forms, all the continuities of history."[39] The destruction of received models and forms is necessary in order to clear a space for spontaneous thought to arise. On the other hand, Williams's aesthetic asserts the primacy of treating objects in the world directly. Thus his thought oscillates between process and the thing itself. Williams's poetic struggle involved finding an equilibrium between these opposing energies and polarities. "Between two contending forces there may at all times arrive that moment when the stress is equal on both sides so that with a great pushing a great stability results giving a picture of perfect rest."[40]

Spring and All (1923)—first published by Robert McAlmon's Contact Publishing Company—is an experimental weaving together of poems and prose manifestoes about poetry. It is, as Williams said, "a travesty on the idea" of typographical form.[41] Chapter headings are printed upside down, chapters are numbered in the wrong order. The poems are untitled. The prose combines violent indictments of contemporary civilization and impassioned pleas on behalf of the imagination. As *Kora in Hell* is a descent into winter and hell, so *Spring and All* is a difficult ascent into the radiance of spring and the temporal world. The underlying subject of the book is the hard necessity of creating "new forms, new names for experience." In this cause, the prose rails against the false values of a rootless, materialistic society and calls for the annhilation of old values and forms. Against this materialistic malaise Williams poses the compensating imagination: "To refine, to clarify, to intensify that eternal moment in which we alone live there is but a single force—the imagination."[42] There are poems of great visual accuracy and precision, lyrics in which familiar objects are clarified and presented in a fresh context, such as the red wheelbarrow upon which "so much depends" and the flowerpot "gay with rough moss" (11). The primary subject of the poems in *Spring and All* is the difficult struggle to be reborn. The introductory poem sounds the call for a new world, describes the way the plants, still dazed and "lifeless in appearance,"

> . . . enter the new world naked,
> cold, uncertain of all
> save that they enter. . . .[43]

Later they "grip down and begin to awaken." In these poems consciousness and the world permeate each other. Subject and object are fused, and oppositions disappear between the inner world of the self and the outer world of things. This is Williams's central post-Romantic breakthrough. All of his work in the next decades would build on the basic premises and fundamental achievement of *Spring and All.*[44]

Marianne Moore's first pamphlet of twenty-four poems, *Poems* (London: Egoist Press, 1921) was published without her knowledge at the instigation of her friends Bryer and H. D. Her first American book, *Observations* (1924), contained all but three of the poems in the original pamphlet and added some thirty-two others. For Moore, poems *were* observations. Her poems have an acute visual sense, motivated as if by a painter's eye and a biologist's curious scrutiny. To borrow one of her phrases, her observations have a "relentless accuracy." She is a precisionist meticulously rendering visual phenomena, and her policy of exact comparison and the perfect word serves the facticity of the world. Her poems consist of scrupulous, and many separate, acts of attention to small and otherwise unnoticed animals and things. It is, as Hugh Kenner says, "the poetic of the solitary observer" confronted by a mute world that "seems to want *describing.*"[45] Moore writes as if seeing things for the first time, defamiliarizing the natural world. Her descriptions of things-as-they-are stands as a corrective to the overhumanizing impulse to turn the world into a mirror for human beings. The testimony of the eye constitutes the basic premise of her ethics. In her early work both her morals (and all of her work has a moral inflection) and her ideas about things grow out of the primary ground of her Objectivist aesthetic.

Moore's poems are so clear and "objective," her individual words so concrete and singular, her descriptions so vivid and precise, that it is as if her language had been cleaned and held up to the light at a slight distance. Williams said of her language:

> With Miss Moore a word is a word most when it is separated out by science, treated with acid to remove the smudges, washed, dried, and placed right side up on a clean surface. Now one may say that this is a word. Now it may be used, and how?
>
> It may be used not to smear it again with thinking (the attachments of thought) but in such a way that it will remain scrupulously itself, clean perfect, unnicked beside other words in parade. There must be edges.[46]

Moore's elaborate syllabic patterns foreground the visual aspect of her work. The stanza, as opposed to the line, is her operative unit, and her characteristic poems are an arrangement of stanzas, each a formal replica of the previous one. "The Past Is the Present" concludes: "Ecstasy affords / the occasion and expediency determines the form."[47] Moore's expedient forms rely on the cadences of prose as well as the music of colloquial speech. They shun traditional effects, seem hammered out on a typewriter. The formal arrangement of her work gives the impression not so much of a thing *said* as of a thing *made*. Implicitly the poems stand as a corrective to the formless and shoddy in life and art.

Moore is particularly American in her belief in "accessibility to experience" ("New York") and her faith in locale, her aesthetic of the independent observer looking intently at the brute forces of nature. *Observations* also looks acutely and knowledgeably at "this grassless, linksless, languageless country in which letters are written / not in Spanish, not in Greek, not in Latin, not in shorthand, / but in plain American which cats and dogs can read!" ("England").[48]

Like Williams and Moore, E. E. Cummings was a poet of contact and immediacy, the present moment. A lesser poet than either—in an ultimate sense he altered no language but his own—he was nonetheless allied with them in a commitment to the new and experimental. In a way he combined the romantic bohemian sensibility of Millay with the restless formal experimentation of Williams. On the surface his style was aggressively and typographically innovative. Cummings was extreme in the way he fractured spelling and syntax and played with capitalization, lineation, and stanzaic divisions, creating his own eccentric mode of punctuation and spacing, sometimes breaking up the integrity of individual words themselves. He was a determined individualist who signed his name in the lower case and defined the self with a small *i*. A feeling of adolescent rebelliousness still clings to a large number of his typographical experiments, and often the language seems wrenched into new shapes rather than truly renovated. More profoundly, his aesthetic favored spontaneity, motion, speed, process over product. As he wrote in the foreword to *Is 5*, "If a poet is anybody, he is somebody to whom things made matter very little—somebody who is obsessed by Making."[49] His favorite modern poet was Pound—he was especially influenced by the satirical aspect of "Mauberley"—and indeed his poems often move with a Poundian sense of juxtaposition and collage. At the same time, the subject matter of many of Cummings's poems is the time-honored, circumscribed, and conventional subject matter of much traditional lyric poetry: love, death, and the changing of the seasons.

Cummings's first book, *The Enormous Room* (1922), a striking prose memoir of his experiences as a prisoner in France during the war, established him as one of the representative voices of freedom for the new postwar generation. So did his first four books of poems—the work which defined his lifelong preoccupations as well as his basic stylistic method—all of which were published in the twenties: *Tulips and Chimneys* (1923), *XLI* and *&* (both in 1925), and *Is 5* (1926). The book *&*, more than any other, established him as a poet of erotic love just as his next book, *Is 5*, established him as a satirist who staunchly condemned America's moral corruption.

The central oppositions of *Tulips and Chimneys* defined the basic terms that would animate much of Cummings's work to come: the country against the city, the spontaneous against the planned, the organic against the lifeless, the natural against the artificial, the individual against the crowd, the beautiful against the ugly, the emotions against the rational intellect. His oppositions were forceful, elementary, reductive. Always he spoke up for the spontaneity of feeling—the new, the irreverent, the unselfconscious—and sang in celebration of love and the individual self. There may be what R. P. Blackmur called "a sentimental denial of the intelligence" in his work, but he also had an imagination which John Dos Passos called "essentially extemporaneous."[50] His best work gave a sense of freedom and buoyancy to the struggle to create an innovative, indigenous, process-oriented American poetry in the twenties.

A few years before *The Waste Land* appeared, Robert Frost wrote to Hamlin Garland, "I wonder if you think as I do it is time for consolidating our resources a little against outside influences on our literature and particularly against those among us who would like nothing better than to help us lose our identity."[51] Frost's two books in the twenties—*New Hampshire* (1923) and *West-Running Brook* (1928)—are a consolidating of resources, a strong affirmation of his local identity. For several years after he returned to New Hampshire in 1915, Frost made a renewed effort to insert himself into the tradition of New England regional literature. His most immediate precursor in that tradition was E. A. Robinson, who in the twenties was primarily engaged in a series of long, ultimately unsuccessful narrative poems. *New Hampshire* is one of Frost's most self-consciously regional books. It announces his commitment to the local, to "the need of being versed in country things," to a state which has "one of everything as in a showcase" ("New Hampshire"). The debilitating aspect of the regional tradition can be seen in the way Frost assumed the pose and role of the homiletic Yankee sage, acting not as an observer and analyst, as he had done in the great narrative poems of *North of Boston*, but as a patriotic spokesman for the region.

Against these editorializing tendencies one may pose such dark, playful, and compelling lyrics of the twenties as "Fire and Ice," "Dust of Snow," "Nothing Gold Can Stay," "To E. T.," "Stopping by Woods on a Snowy Evening," "To Earthward," and "Not to Keep" (from *New Hampshire*) and "Spring Pools," "The Freedom of the Moon," and "Acquainted with the Night" (from *West-Running Brook*), as well as the major dramatic dialogues "The Witch of Coos" and "West-Running Brook." These poems enact genuine dilemmas and contraries, confrontations with nothingness, playful differences in perspective, dark tensions, conflicts, and interactions between the inner self and the outer world. They seem spoken by a person in a scene or setting, and they register the colloquial nuances of a speaking voice played off against the rhythms of a traditional metric. As Frost said in the preface to his one-act play, *A Way Out* (1929), "Everything written is as good as it is dramatic."[52]

One of the central subjects of Frost's lyrics in the twenties is the longing for absorption or escape from the self against the desire to maintain the boundaries and integrity of that self. The full burden of loneliness is expressed in "Acquainted with the Night," in which the speaker, who walks away from home and town and is not called back by any one, is surrounded by an isolating darkness. Frost's acquaintance with the desolations of night and the gloom of consciousness closely parallels Stevens's understanding of the "mind of winter," the termless terms of nature, in "The Snow Man." The desire to escape consciousness and find peace in oblivion is at the center of Frost's well-known lyric "Stopping by Woods on a Snowy Evening," in which the speaker turns away from the lure of the woods' annihilating beauty and back to the world of human bonds and contracts. This is Frost's characteristic move, the mind pressing back against the desolations of reality. The self is most exposed and present in Frost's middle work when he is testing its limits (as in "To Earthward") or playing with its various perceptions (as in "The Freedom of the Moon"). Ultimately, he refuses to give the mind up to its own transcendental urges.[53]

In addition to the international Modernism of Pound and Eliot and the indigenous Modernism of Moore and Williams, the romanticism of Wallace Stevens, Hart Crane, and, to a much lesser degree, Archibald MacLeish stands as a third powerful tradition to emerge in American poetry in the twenties. In radically different ways, Stevens and Crane reconciled the demands of being both Modernist and Romantic poets. In the process they re-created an American visionary poetic, and their work directly relates to and extends the Anglo-American Romantic tradition—the work of Blake, Wordworth, Keats, and Shelley in England, and Emerson, Whitman, Melville, and Dickinson in America. Stevens's claim that "the whole effort of the imagination is toward the production of the romantic" and even that "the imagination is the romantic" is one of the motivating premises of their explicitly Modernist poetic.[54] Stevens and Crane questioned and refigured the problem and validity of belief in a faithless age. They are post-Symbolist poets of great verbal energy and extravagance, an exultant language and lavish music, who sought "a new order of consciousness" (Crane) and "a new knowledge of reality" (Stevens). Theirs is the psychology of American Adamic poets in a relativist time, alone before the brute forces of nature, trusting their own inner experiences, accepting the burden of examining their own individual states of consciousness and reporting on the evidence. Their poems attempt to move beyond the isolating negations of *The Waste Land*, to pass beyond the poetics of irony and alienation and, through the saving compensatory powers of the imagination, to reconcile self and world, imagination and reality. In his last major poem, "The Broken Tower," Crane writes: "And so it was I entered the broken world / To trace the visionary company of love."[55] These lines encapsulate the central redemptive struggle of the late-Romantic poet in a Modernist era.

Stevens entered the broken world with the fundamental premise of Modernism—that God and the gods are dead. The poems in *Harmonium* (1923, 1931) begin with the idea of the death of the gods and meditate on the unsponsored world we live in without them. A relentless skepticism became the basis for Stevens's radical humanism, his belief that the modern poet must rediscover the earth. In the essay "Imagination as Value" he wrote, "The great poems of heaven and hell have been written and the great poem of the earth remains to be written."[56] Stevens's own goal was to write that earthly poem. He came to believe in the imagination, the gaiety of language he defined as poetry, as the consoling force in a world bereft of certainty: "After one has abandoned a belief in god, poetry is that essence which takes its place as life's redemption."[57] The refusal to accept the consolations of orthodox Christianity or of any revealed religion is the subject of Stevens's first major poem of earth, "Sunday Morning." It was through his aestheticism and sensibility, the mind turning to the world of sensations and the splendors of its own productions rather than to the certainties of false belief, that Stevens traced the visionary company.

In *Harmonium* Stevens expresses a strong determination to be true to one's own inner experiences and sensations. Many of his poems record a world of exquisitely changing surfaces and appearances, things moving rapidly in the external flux of experience. Such lyrics as "Thirteen Ways of Looking at a Blackbird," "Six Significant Landscapes," "Metaphors of a Magnifico," and "Sea Surface Full of Clouds" are a collection of sensations, naturalistic notes of the eye recording natural phenomena. At the same time they track the interrelationship between mind and landscape, the solitary consciousness reacting to an external and wholly separate world which cannot be known apart from our awareness of it. Poems of appearance are also poems of perception. The self, too, is an unstable, fluctuating element in a world of flux. "The Comedian as the Letter C" asks, "Can one man think one thing and think it long? / Can one man be one thing and be it long?"[58] The implicit answer: no. Stevens's skeptical intelligence refused to rest in any single certainty or explanation of the world.

For Stevens, the imagination acts as a way to order a constantly changing and chaotic world. It takes the place of empty heaven. In the parable "Anecdote of the Jar," the speaker places a jar in Tennessee and the jar organizes the "slovenly wilderness": "The wilderness rose up to it, / And sprawled around, no longer wild."[59] Thus the human artifact, emblem of the imagination, structures everything around it. The mind transforms the place, creating order out of wilderness. At the same time the mind doesn't create a single unchanging or "true" world, but only versions of that world. Every new jar, every new combination of words also creates a new window, a fresh revelation about reality itself. This helps to account for the range of tones in *Harmonium*—from the verbal gaudiness of "Bantams in Pine Woods" and "The Emperor of Ice Cream" to the solemn musings of "The Snow Man" and "Sunday Morning." In a way all of Stevens's poems about the relationship between imagination and reality are also justifications of poetry. *Harmonium* was the first major testament in his lifelong romantic struggle to "live in the world but outside of existing conceptions of it."[60]

The sole collection of lyrics that Hart Crane published in his lifetime, *White Buildings* (1926) is a thickly textured and radiant record of his quest to transcend the spirit of negation and become a poet of joy, a seer testifying to the reality of the absolute. As he suggested in "General Aims and Theories," Crane emulated his precursors Rimbaud and Blake and tried to see *through* and not *with* the eye, to use the real world as a springboard for what Blake called "innocence" and he called "absolute beauty," seeking a higher consciousness and transcendental realm, "moments of eternity."[61] His poems often descend into a depth of horror or squalor out of which a grail of light suddenly radiates:

> Look steadily—how the wind feasts and spins
> The brain's disk shivered against lust. Then watch
> While darkness, like an ape's face, falls away,
> And gradually white buildings answer day.[62]

One of the principal dramas in all of Crane's work is the attempt to reconcile the rival claims of the actual and the ideal, the sensuous and spiritual worlds.

There are twenty-eight poems in *White Buildings*, all but two of them written between 1920 and 1925 when Crane forged his central aesthetic. Early poems such as "In Shadow," "Pastorale," and "My Grandmother's Love Letters" have a quasi-Imagist impressionism and a lyrical fragility. Crane was seeking a more charged language and more contemporary feeling in his poems, and by 1919 had turned toward Pound and Eliot for his poetic values and, through them, to the work of Laforgue and the Elizabethans. He confessed he read "Prufrock" and "Preludes" continually, and one sees Eliot's verbal hardness and ironic literary allusions in the quatrains of such early poems as "Praise for an Urn" and "Black Tambourine." He translated Laforgue's "Locutions des Pierrots," and in his most Laforgian poem, "Chaplinesque"—inspired by Chaplin's *The Kid*—he adapted the French poet's complex tone and wit in order to parallel the situation of the modern poet with that of the lonely, abused tramp of the movie. Crane was most lastingly influenced by "the vocabulary and blank verse of the Elizabethans" (in one of his letters he refers to his "Elizabethan fanaticism"), and his work often relies on a high rhetoric derived from reading Marlowe, Webster, and Donne.[63]

Crane's poems are "drunk with words." He was more interested in associational meanings than in ordinary logic and characteristically took unusual and highly connotative words and combined them in unexpected and musical ways. Reproved by the editor of *Poetry* for the difficult obscurity of his work, especially "At Melville's Tomb," he responded that his goal was to find "a logic of metaphor" beyond the boundaries of "so-called pure logic."[64] The principle of organizing a poem through the "emotional dynamics" of suddenly forced conjunctions correlates to the visionary subject and goal of the poems. Crane's verbal excess, his metaphorical and extralogical way of organizing a poem and, ultimately, his idealism, were attacked by such antiromantic critics as R. P. Blackmur, Yvor Winters, and his friend Allen Tate, although their pioneering essays helped to uncover the motivating romantic principles of Crane's poetic.[65]

Crane admired and imitated the way that Eliot's poems encompassed contemporary life, but after the publication of The *Waste Land* he began to think of his work as a positive alternative and direct counterstatement to Eliot. In a letter to Allen Tate, he declared: "In his own realm Eliot presents us with an absolute *impasse*, yet oddly enough, he can be utilized to lead us to, intelligently point to, other positions and 'pastures new.' Having absorbed him enough we can trust ourselves as never before, in the air or on the sea. I, for instance, would like to leave a few of his 'negations' behind me, risk the realm of the obvious more, in quest of new sensations, *humeurs*."[66] Six months later he emphasized his own "more positive, or (if [I] must put it so in a skeptical age) ecstatic goal . . . I feel that Eliot ignores certain spiritual events and possibilities as real and powerful now as, say, in the time of Blake. . . . After his perfection of death—nothing is possible in motion but a resurrection of some kind."[67]

"For the Marriage of Faustus and Helen" is the first fruit of Crane's attempt to break away from the poetry of negation. It is his first long poem, a direct precursor to *The Bridge* in its countering of pessimism and in its expression of a renewed hope in the American city. The poem employs Crane's own version of the mythical method, fusing the present with the past, paralleling contemporary life and ancient culture through the symbolism of Faustus (imaginative man) and Helen (ideal beauty). In a way Crane uses a reduced version of Eliot's method in order to "answer" *The Waste Land*, insisting—in a Blakean formulation—that we "Greet naively—yet intrepidly / New soothings, new amazements."[68] "Faustus and Helen" is the first poem in which Crane tries to absorb the influences of the modern era—jazz, electric light displays, advertising—and become a visionary poet of the Machine Age. As he wrote to Tate, "Let us invent an idiom for the proper transposition of jazz into words! Something clean, sparkling, elusive."[69] This transposition became his method of trying to move "beyond despair," showing "one inconspicuous, glowing orb of praise."

Crane's lyrical masterpiece "Voyages" is a coherent sequence or "suite" of six sea poems that he wrote between 1921 and 1925. His most personal poem, it traces a homosexual love affair with a young sailor, commonly designated as E. O., through the arc of elation, excitement, separation, betrayal, and loss. The final poem ends with the poet's solitary vision of ideal beauty. Crane's attempt to reconcile the erotic and the spiritual in love, indeed to comprehend the psychology of romantic love, is played out against the constant backdrop of the sea, which appears in the sequence as dangerous and threatening as well as "a great wink of eternity" and, finally, a source of visionary solace. Crane borrowed some of the sea imagery from the unpublished poems of Samuel Greenberg, who died in 1916 at the age of twenty-three; more profoundly, his poem is saturated with the arresting vocabulary and imagery of Melville's *Moby-Dick*. In "Voyages" Crane uses the sea to mirror and record the experience of love and its loss. His great subject is the precariousness of ecstasy in a phenomenal world and the necessary, doomed quest for spiritual wholeness. In the final lyric, the vision of Belle Isle and poetry itself become the compensation for the death of love: "It is the unbetrayable reply / Whose accent no farewell can know."[70]

The Bridge is a loosely joined sequence of fifteen poems that Crane wrote between 1923 and 1929. His original idea was to present the "Myth of America," a "mystical synthesis" of the American past, present, and future. His ambition was to become "a suitable Pindar for the dawn of the machine age," and he intended his poem as an "epic of modern consciousness," a full-scale reply to *The Waste Land* and a simultaneous embrace of contemporary life. Whitman acts as the presiding spirit of the poem, and Crane asserts a spiritual alliance with Whitman's large, transcendental vision of America. In the many years of writing his lyrical epic, however, he often suffered a wavering confidence about the spiritual worthiness of American life in an industrial and scientific era: "If only America were half as worthy today to be spoken of as Whitman spoke of it fifty years ago there might be something for me to say—not that Whitman received or required any tangible proof of his intimations, but that time has shown how increasingly lonely and ineffectual his confidence stands."[71] One of the underlying dramas of *The Bridge* is Crane's struggle to maintain his initial optimistic faith in the spiritual possibilities of America in the twenties. Along with such writers as Waldo Frank and Lewis Mumford, he sought to repudiate American materialism by finding a higher idealism in American culture. At the same time he read the development of American experience as analogous to the growth of spiritual consciousness.

The crucial fact and symbol of Crane's poem is Brooklyn Bridge itself.

To Crane the bridge not only connected Brooklyn to Manhattan, but also linked the past to the present, earth to heaven. It was a product of modern technology and science as well as a work of labor and art, a symbol of America's "constructive future" and "unique identity." Beyond its commercial and practical purposes, Crane also read it as a "harp and altar," a magnificent span between time and eternity, "terrific threshold of the prophet's pledge" ("Proem"), a sign of America's religious need to transcend the realm of ordinary experience in quest of ideal purity and permanence. Crane's different protagonists—Columbus in "Ave Maria," the poet/pilgrim in various guises and moods, whether contemplating Pocahontas and his own childhood (section 1), giving an account of American history (section 4), or riding and thinking about the subway as a modern hell (section 7)—are all versions of the American wanderer or prodigal in a restive search for America's lost patrimony.[72] The urgency and importance of this quest signal Crane's full visionary ambition. His most important poem stands as a record not so much of man's spiritual fulfillment as of his enormous spiritual desire and aspiration.

There were some compelling female lyricists in the twenties, all of them—in one way or another—Romantic poets. Elinor Wylie, Sara Teasdale, Edna St. Vincent Millay, Leonie Adams, and Louise Bogan (in her first two books) created a substantial body of lyric poetry that is essentially romantic in its procedures, its rhetoric, and its attitudes.[73] Their poems—many of them comparable to Elizabethan songs—assert the authority of the female self through musical lyrics of intense personal feeling. Their work belongs to the formal tradition of Anglo-American poetry and stands apart from the stylistic revolution in American poetry in the twentieth century. It also belongs to an alternative tradition of women's poetry.

Modernism precipitated two distinct styles of women's poetry that had divided clearly by the twenties.[74] One style was the innovative Modernism of such poets as Marianne Moore, Gertrude Stein, Amy Lowell, Mina Loy, and H. D. These poets were experimental in their methodologies. The female lyric poets, on the other hand, projected themselves more personally through a received poetic style and form. Their pared-down language and the direct way in which they treated their subjects were Modernist, but their work repudiated free verse and generally observed the conventions of the traditional nineteenth-century short poem. Their well-crafted lyrics have the colorings of Romantic poetry.

Wylie, Teasdale, Bogan, Adams, and, to a lesser extent, Millay were skilled metricists who embraced a poetics of closure and often wrote lyrics, ballads, odes, and sonnets. Their work is carefully wrought and has the formalist quality, as Moore said of Bogan, of "compactness compacted."[75] Each owes a large debt to the Metaphysical poets who were in ascendance in the early twenties, and each in her own way adapts a poetry of paradox and wit to a Romantic sensibility. Ultimately, they are poets of the expressive self, of a radical subjectivity committed to emotion. In Bogan's words, emotion is "the kernel which builds outward form from inward intensity."[76] Their neo-Romanticism was also a revolt against Victorian sentimentality, against false emotions and posturing, and against decorative ornamentation. There is a tension and conflict in their work between exuberant desire and romantic aspiration and the requirements of limited form, the demands of hardness, clarity, precision. Millay was the most florid and expansive of the poets, Bogan the most clipped and austere, but each expressed a deep longing for escape in strictly determined forms. Love is the circumscribed subject in most of their poetry—partially because the love poem was a form of discourse that included women in a way that the poetry of history did not include them. In these lyrics women are not idealized objects or muses, but motivating subjects: self-assertive, joyous, sometimes arrogant, singing of extreme emotional deprivation or thwarted passion, insisting, too, on physical passion and sensuality, the profound conflict between mind and body.

The traditional female lyricists of the twenties inherited a heritage of the divided self. Their poems enact a series of conflicts and unresolved contraries: passion against restraint, easy flow against containment, the outward suppression of the female personality in a male-dominated society against the inner desire for self-assertion and authorship. Often the need for self-expression and the desire for freedom from restrictive social roles is coded in terms of a timeless quest for spiritual loveliness and beauty. Inspired by Shelley and Christina Rosetti as well as by Donne and Jonson, their lyrics—especially the lyrics of Wylie and Teasdale—suggest a succession of strategies for fending off a hostile outside world and maintaining the fragile integrity of the individual self. Their Platonism and ecstatic love of beauty, their concern with ultimate themes, expresses a veiled personal and social need for autonomy. So, too, their poetry is visionary in its determined quest for an absolute truth to replace a lost god.

In their work in the twenties, Elinor Wylie, Sara Teasdale, and Louise Bogan, as well as Hart Crane and Wallace Stevens, showed themselves to be redemptive poets writing at perhaps an unredeemable time in American history. One of the romantic splendors of their poetry is its persistent spiritual aspiration in a world resistant and even hostile to that aspiration. And yet, as Wallace Stevens wrote, "After the final no there comes a yes / And on that yes the future world depends."[77]

Notes

1. Quoted in Paul Fussell, *The Great War and Modern Memory* (New York: Oxford University Press, 1975), 325.

2. Pound, *Personae* (New York: New Directions, 1971), 190.

3. Peter Faulkner, *Modernism* (London: Methuen, 1977), 14–15.

4. *Selected Prose of T. S. Eliot*, ed. Frank Kermode (New York: Harcourt and Farrar, 1975), 65.

5. Quoted in Gorham Munson, *The Awakening Twenties* (Baton Rouge: Louisiana State University Press, 1985), 291.

6. Frederick Hoffman, *The Twenties: American Writing in the Postwar Decade* (New York: Free Press, 1962), 441.

7. Geoffrey Perrett, *America in the Twenties* (New York: Simon and Schuster, 1982), 15–143.

8. Hughes, "The Negro Artist and the Racial Mountain," in *The Black Aesthetic*, ed. Addison Gayle, Jr. (Garden City, N.Y.: Doubleday, 1972), 172.

9. For a fuller discussion of the black movement, see Timothy Seibles, "A Quilt in Shades of Black: The Black Aesthetic in Twentieth-Century African-American Poetry," 158–90.

10. Cummings, *Poems 1923–1954* (New York: Harcourt, 1968), 121; Millay, *Collected Poems* (New York: Harper, 1956), 127.

11. Quoted in Malcolm Cowley, "Fitzgerald: The Romance of Money" (1956), in *F. Scott Fitzgerald: Modern Critical Views*, ed. Harold Bloom (New York: Chelsea, 1985), 53.

12. *Civilization in the United States*, ed. Harold Stearns (1922; rpt. Carbondale: Southern Illinois University Press, 1964), 181.

13. Pound, "Praefatio aut Tumulus Cimicius," *Active Anthology* (London: Faber and Faber, 1933), 9.

14. Bernard Bergonzi, *T. S. Eliot* (New York: Macmillan, 1972), 60.

15. Pound, "Harold Monro," *Criterion* 11, no. 45 (July 1932): 590.

16. Williamson, *A Reader's Guide to T. S. Eliot* (New York: Noonday, 1953), 89.

17. Pound, *Personae*, 185, and *The Letters of Ezra Pound, 1907–1941*, ed. D. D. Paige, (New York: Harcourt, 1950), 180.

18. Eliot, *The Waste Land: A Facsimile and Transcript of the Original Drafts Including the Annotations of Ezra Pound*, ed. Valerie Eliot (New York: Harcourt, 1971), 1.

19. Eliot, *On Poetry and Poets* (New York: Farrar, Straus and Giroux, 1957), 111.

20. Mary Hutchinson interpreted the poem as "Tom's Autobiography—A

Melancholy One," according to *The Diary of Virginia Woolf*, ed. Anne Olivier Bell (New York: Harcourt, 1978), 2:178. For a psychoanalytic reading of the poem, see Harry Trossman, "T. S. Eliot and *The Waste Land:* Psychopathological Antecendents and Transformations," *Archives of General Psychiatry* 30 (May 1974): 709–17, and Ronald Bush, *T. S. Eliot: A Study in Character and Style*, (New York: Oxford University Press, 1983), 68–69.

21. Eliot, "Virgil and the Christian World," in *On Poetry and Poets*, 137.

22. Eliot, *Selected Prose*, 177.

23. Eliot, *For Lancelot Andrewes: Essays on Style and Order* (Garden City, N.Y.: Doubleday, 1929), vii.

24. They are John Crowe Ransom, Allen Tate, Robert Penn Warren, Donald Davidson, Merrill Moore, Laura Riding, Walter Clyde Curry, Jesse Wills, Alec B. Stevenson, Sidney Hirsch, Stanley Johnson, William Yandell Elliott, William Frierson, Ridley Wills, James Frank, and Alfred Starr.

25. Tate, *Reason in Madness* (New York: Putnam's, 1941), ix; John Crowe Ranson, "Classical and Romantic," *Saturday Review of Literature* 6 (14 Sept. 1929): 125–27. See also Monroe Spears, *Dionysius and the City* (New York: Oxford University Press, 1970), 153–54.

26. Quoted in Louise Cowan, *The Fugitive Group: A Literary History* (Baton Rouge: Louisiana State University Press, 1959), 48.

27. Jarrell, "John Ransom's Poetry," *Sewanee Review* 56 (Summer 1948): 389.

28. Spears, *Dionysius and the City*, 154.

29. Quoted in *The Fugitive Poets*, ed. William Pratt (New York: Dutton, 1965), 27.

30. John M. Bradbury. *The Fugitives: A Critical Account* (Chapel Hill: University of North Carolina Press, 1958), 21–24.

31. Tate, *Reason in Madness*, 136.

32. Williams, *The Autobiography of William Carlos Williams* (New York: Random, 1951), 174.

33. Williams, *Imaginations*, ed. Webster Schott (New York: New Directions, 1970), 314–15.

34. Ibid., 145, 357.

35. Ibid., 127.

36. Moore, *The Complete Poems of Marianne Moore* (New York: Macmillan/Viking, 1967), 266.

37. Williams, *Imaginations*, xii.

38. Williams, *I Wanted to Write a Poem*, ed. Edith Heal (Boston: Beacon, 1958), 29.

39. Miller, *Poets of Reality* (New York: Atheneum, 1969), 338.

40. Williams, *Imaginations*, 32–33.

41. Williams, *I Wanted to Write a Poem*, 36.

42. Williams, *Imaginations*, 89.

43. Ibid., 95.

44. Miller, *Poets of Reality*, 287.

45. Kenner, *A Homemade World* (New York: Knopf, 1975), 92.

46. Williams, *Imaginations*, 316.

47. Moore, *Complete Poems*, 88.

48. Ibid., 46.

49. Cummings, *Poems 1923–1954,* 163.

50. Blackmur, "Notes on E. E. Cummings's Language" (1931), in *Critical Essays on E. E. Cummings,* ed. Gary Rotella (Boston: G.K. Hall, 1984), 107; John Dos Passos, *The Best Times* (New York: New American Library, 1966), 83.

51. Frost, *Selected Letters of Robert Frost,* ed. Lawrence Thompson (New York: Holt, 1964), 265–66.

52. Frost, *Selected Prose of Robert Frost,* ed. Hyde Cox and E. C. Lathem (New York: Collier, 1968), 13.

53. Frank Lentricchia, *Robert Frost: Modern Poetics and the Landscape of the Self* (Durham, N.C.: Duke University Press, 1975), 101–19; and Richard Poirier, *Robert Frost: The Work of Knowing* (New York: Oxford University Press, 1977), 173–225.

54. Stevens, *Opus Posthumous,* ed. Samuel French Morse (New York: Random, Vintage, 1982), 163.

55. Crane, *The Complete Poems and Selected Letters and Prose of Hart Crane,* ed. Brom Weber (Garden City, N.Y.: Doubleday, 1966), 193.

56. Stevens, *The Necessary Angel* (London: Faber and Faber, 1951), 142.

57. Stevens, *Opus Posthumous,* 158.

58. Stevens, *The Palm at the End of the Mind,* ed. Holly Stevens (New York: Random, Vintage, 1971), 71.

59. Ibid., 46.

60. Ibid., 164.

61. Crane, *Complete Poems,* 220–21.

62. Ibid., 25.

63. Crane, *The Letters of Hart Crane 1916–1932,* ed. Brom Weber (Berkeley: University of California Press, 1965), 71.

64. Crane, *Complete Poems,* 234–40.

65. Blackmur, "New Thresholds, New Anatomies," in *Form and Value in Modern Poetry* (Garden City, N.Y.: Doubleday, 1957), 269–86; Allen Tate, "Hart Crane" and "Crane: The Poet as Hero," in *Collected Essays* (Denver: Allan Swallow, 1959), 225–37, 528–32; Yvor Winters, "The Significance of *The Bridge* by Hart Crane, or What Are We to Think of Professor X?" in *In Defense of Reason* (Denver: Denver University Press, 1943), 575–603.

66. Crane, *Letters,* 90.

67. Ibid., 114–15.

68. Crane, *Complete Poems,* 30.

69. Crane, *Letters,* 89.

70. Crane, *Complete Poems,* 41.

71. Crane, *Letters,* 274, 305, 124, 129, 308.

72. R. W. B. Lewis, *The Poetry of Hart Crane* (Princeton: Princeton University Press, 1967), 219–45.

73. Elinor Wylie: *Nets to Catch the Wind* (1921), *Black Armour* (1923), *Trivial Breath* (1928), *Angels and Earthly Creatures* (1929). Sara Teasdale: *Flame and Shadow* (1920), *Dance of the Moon* (1926). Edna St. Vincent Millay: *A Few Figs from Thistles* (1920), *Second April* (1921), *The Harp-Weaver* (1923), *The Buck in the Snow* (1928). Leonie Adams: *Those Not Elect* (1925), *High Falcon* (1929). Louise Bogan: *Body of This Death* (1923), *Dark Summer* (1929).

74. Alicia Suskin Ostriker, *Stealing the Language: The Emergence of Women's Poetry in America* (Boston: Beacon, 1981) 44.

75. Marianne Moore, *Predilections* (New York: Viking, 1955), 130.

76. Quoted in Moore, *Predilections*, 130.

77. Stevens, *The Palm at the End of the Mind*, 190.

4

Utopocalypse: American
Poetry in the 1930s

MICHAEL HELLER

> Poetry which owes no man anything, owes nevertheless one debt—an image
> of the world in which men can again believe
>
> —Archibald MacLeish

No idea ever completely dies or, as we have seen, ever completely lives. The decade of 1930 to 1940, to the extent that what happened in the world of poetry reflected what was happening in the world at large, is a decade of birth songs and swan songs, of rising falls, of *dernier cris* each outlasting by a little bit their time. The pulsations and divagations in the art world and in the literary world are often counterpoints and rhythmic reinforcements to the drumbeats and, alas, the bootsteps of those times. The artistic revolutions of the first two decades, the period we now label Modernist, were clearly to color the activity of the thirties. By "Modernism" (the most vexed artistic notion of the twentieth century) I am referring not so much to a response to a particular world occasion "out there" as I am to the ongoing attempt to maintain art's primacy, to reanimate and indeed empower artistic activity as superior to, or at least coequal with, its rivals, science, economics, and philosophy, in generating worldviews. Thus, I mean Modernism as an activity, an ongoing engagement in producing permanent alterations in the way artists and writers go about their business. The question which animates the inner drama of the ten years leading up to World War II is whether or not, in this sense, the Modernist impulse would last.

That writers and poets were politicized in the thirties is, of course, a truism, but that the entire arena of literary activity, like much activity in the rest of the country, was suddenly bracketed by politics is less clear. Political consciousness did not necessarily supply labels which could be applied to certain writers; rather, an enormous amount of activity occurred among poets and writers which could not escape the political frame. And to the extent that politics settles into dogmatic states of mind, to a kind of social or psychological fixity, it wars with the evolutionary and even revolutionary nature of Modernism.

Political consciousness arises, it would seem, when processes previously unarticulated or taken for granted or labeled "natural" are no longer sufficient to meet social problems. The so-called natural order of things fails, and human beings begin to theorize and organize to solve or ameliorate conditions. If the communism of the thirties was to become a "god that failed," we must remember that it was preceded by at least two other failed gods, those of progress and money. Artists and writers at the beginning of the decade of the thirties were already waist-deep in the detritus of such natural and organic processes as "Progress" and laissez-faire economics. William Carlos Williams, according to his biographer Paul Mariani, had watched helplessly as the Black Tuesday crash of 1929 turned his stocks to wastepaper and destroyed forever hopes of full or partial retirement so that he could devote himself completely to his writing. Williams, Mariani writes, "had watched the age of unlimited progress tumble, the age of optimism to be replaced by what he [Williams] called 'bizarre derivations'. . . including suicide as the final economic solution!"[1]

As can be seen from Williams's observations, economic failure was only an aspect of an even more immense spiritual failure, a failure subliminally reflected in the art and writing of the period. Of the masterworks of poetry which appeared at the beginning of the thirties, none provides a better demonstration of how the failure was enacted than Hart Crane's *The Bridge*, a work teeming with optimism as it strained to reconcile the mythology of America with the new technological age. By contrast, Crane's later work, such as "The Broken Tower," with its "visionary company of love," thoroughly deconstructs the optimistic tonalities of *The Bridge*. "The Broken Tower" can be read as a minuscule reflector of Crane's epic, yet one suffused with an air of reflexive poignancy as it forsakes linguistic structural engineering and "builds, within, a tower that is not stone." Here Crane's poetry is no longer concerned with marvels of wire and steel (which he claimed "lend a myth to God") but with something beyond materialism, "the matrix of the heart."

Crane's death, presumed by all to be a suicide, was not only a personal tragedy for those who knew him but also, given the times and the critical reception of *The Bridge*, a totemic event. It signaled the failure of a kind of mystical adventure; Crane's poem was, if nothing else, inherently mythic and celebratory at a moment in time when history seemed to foreclose on the spirit, to present no future prospect but despair.

Crane's major work, and his death in 1932, affected other poets in a number of ways. His poetry and fate were a kind of Rorschach test from which one could draw any number of suggestive interpretations, their very variousness a function of the breakdown of any hegemonic view of the times. For Allen Tate, a close friend, Crane's fate was the passing of a last Romantic; Crane represented, in a sense, the poet without a society to sustain him.

The decade of the twenties had seen an increasing interest by writers in the politics of the Left. The examples of the Russian revolution, of socialist movements throughout Europe, and of labor unions in the United States had fired the literary as well as the political imagination. Still, the twenties were years of increasing economic well-being and of vast technological expansion, so politics seemed to many writers the realm of the ideologue. Criticism of the culture was more in the vein of Eliot's *The Waste Land,* an indictment of its materialism and lack of spirituality. In the twenties, the Modernist movement of Pound and Eliot (and here we must include Crane) was in one sense an attempt to find or create workable mythologies, not to refashion national economies but to arrest cultural decay. It required the crash and the Depression to make politics "take" in the literary community-at-large.

Daniel Aaron, in *Writers on the Left,* describes Malcolm Cowley's memories of the Depression decade. For Cowley, the times were a "capitalist nightmare" requiring a complete reorientation of what it meant to be a writer. "For one thing," Aaron tells us, "it meant the end of romantic dichotomies: art and life, intellectual and Philistine, poetry and science, contemplation and action, literature and propaganda."[2] Cowley was demanding a new art, one which would show, in his words, "the splendor and decay of capitalism and the growing self-awareness of the proletariat." The writer would be liberated from the "desperate feeling of solitude and uniqueness that had oppressed artists for the last two centuries."[3] Communities of the ideologically committed (as we shall see, there were groupings on both the Left and the Right) would replace those of the spiritually elect.

The political ferment intoxicated the arts; it led writers and poets into making defensive and often programmatic statements about their work and that of others. In a sense, this was only the final intensification of a certain kind of activity already licensed and undertaken by the Modernists: the furtherance of art by other means, namely manifestoes and proclamations, publicity and notoriety. In the thirties, however, it was no longer the furtherance of art but that of politics by art which became the central motif.

Writers on the Left such as Mike Gold, the poet and novelist, saw the writer not as a Shelleyan "unacknowledged legislator" but as a forthright, self-acknowledged partisan for the proletariat. By 1930, Gold was promoting what he called "Proletarian Realism" in literature, a realism which would spurn the "sickly sentimental subtleties of Bohemians" and deal with "the *real conflicts* of men." Every poem, novel, or drama, Gold insisted, "must have a social theme."[4] The major magazine of leftist writing, New Masses, was, according to Gold, the only journal prepared for the new politicized work. There were other magazines, however, whose titles—*Unrest, Anthology of Revolutionary Poetry, The Liberator*—tell as much about their contents as their printed pages do. Another focal point for writers was membership in one of the John Reed clubs, named after the correspondent John Reed, the model of the intellectual Communist activist who had visited Russia and had published poetry, criticism, and journalism in the two preceding decades.

Much of the poetry published in the early thirties by magazines such as New Masses, which were in open service of or in fidelity to leftist politics, is less than memorable. Often it was antiartistic, hard-boiled, socialist-realist pulp which played sentimentally to the "common" man. It came and went, drawing little attention from the literary critical community primarily because of the strident banners under which it was published but also because there was so little to say about it. Yet there were always some poets, such as Williams, Muriel Rukeyser, and Malcolm Cowley, who transcended the political contexts.

The cultural revolutions of the twenties and the early thirties bred counterreactions. It was not only left-wing politics but the zeitgeist itself that made many poets pull back, engendering in them a search for older or traditional values. This search often veered toward the reactionary. Among the Southern Fugitive poets, John Crowe Ransom was already arguing for the antebellum status quo, for the old plantation hierarchy with its "humane segregation." Ransom was at war not with the Depression or economic failure but with the entire technological spirit of the age and with the alienation and rootlessness it seemed to foster. "Religion," he wrote, "can hardly expect to flourish in an industrial society."

But that the so-called provinces need not necessarily be the home of a conservative politics or poetics was demonstrated in the example of Williams. For Williams, "the classic" was "the local fully realized, words marked by a place." The difference was in what kind of consciousness inhabited that place and what poetics were requisite to render it. Williams knew the tradition as well as anyone; that is, he was as familiar with the Metaphysicals as was Eliot, against whom he railed. But his daily life as a doctor brought him into direct engagement with all classes of people. He wanted a poetry which embraced, as he put it, "the speech of Polish mothers." This living speech was for him "the fountain of the line into which the pollutions of a poetic manner and inverted phrasing should never again be permitted to drain."[5] Williams seemed bent on abolishing the very ironic distance that poets such as Ransom and Tate needed to have in place. For him, the method was to follow out the unmediated life about him, to allow his perceptions free rein. At the same time, he was fully aware of how much of a *construction* the poem was. Williams was not the naïf or primitive he was often made out to be. Rather, his rubric of "no ideas but in things" and his insistence that "a poem was a machine made of words" were for him intentional markers or limits as to how "literary" or ironic he was going to allow himself to be against the evidence of his senses.

Both Robinson Jeffers and Pound, each in his own way, were in revolt against technocratic and democratic mass culture, a culture which had begun to emerge in the twenties with all the force of what the French would call a *mentalité*. The blurring of high art with popular art, the incursions into the stratifications of society, and the consequent leveling of the hierarchical cultural order were deeply disturbing to these poets.

Jeffers reviled the new state of affairs. For Jeffers, politics, salvation on earth, the whole ideological war of Right and Left, were execrable. Man, he claimed, as though washing his hands of the entire matter, was a "spectral episode" in the scheme of things. His views were misanthropic in the extreme, leading him to muse concerning mankind that "the unsocial birds are a greater race." In his poem "Margrave," Jeffers saw human consciousness itself as a kind of contagion, the rumor of which "has gone abroad in the world / the sane uninfected far-outer universes / flee it in a panic of escape as men flee the plague."[6]

Both Pound and Williams, nearing fifty in the mid-thirties, were the older generation of Modernists who meant the most to American poets at the time. But Modernism in the arts could never quite develop the kind of consciousness which would place the obviously political before the artistic. This is not to say that Modernist writers were apolitical but that they looked for the conditions favorable to art and artists as a basis for social action. Thus Pound, as he moved toward the Right, saw the matter of politics in an "aesthetic" way, as a part of his desire for a "paradiso terrestre." In 1931, he was writing in his inimitable fashion to Harriet Monroe of *Poetry* that "the intelligence of the nation [is] more important than the comfort or life of any one individual or the bodily life of a whole generation." For Pound, the artist was not simply another worker in the communal vineyards but a central organizer, a leader and a teacher. "I don't lay as much stock by teachin' the elder generation," he went on to Monroe, "as by teachin' the risin' and if one gang dies without learnin' there is always the next. Keep remindin' em that we ain't bolcheviks, but only the terrifyin' voice of civilization, kulchuh, refinement, aesthetic perception." For Pound, the civilized moments in history were those engineered by great men who not only patronized the arts but organized them along aesthetic-utopian lines. Thus, in a letter of this same period to John Drummond, he was advising, "Don't knock Mussolini, at least until you've weighed up the obstacles and necessities of the times. He will end up with Sigismundo and the men of order not with the pus-sacks and distroyers."[7]

Williams, meanwhile, sat nervously in the more or less democratic center of the political whirlpool, unwilling to cast his lot with ideologies or ideologues. He bemoaned the present state of letters. In 1930, he was writing in the magazine *Contact* that "there is no workable poetic form extant among us today." Williams, according to Mariani, insisted that poetry's first allegiance "was not to a political -ism but to words." More than anything else, the artist's truth would be seen in his relation to his materials. A priori restrictions, programs, and marching orders in the arts led, for Williams, to inevitable falsification and distortion. In his essay on Marianne Moore published in 1931, he felt moved to clarify his position: "There cannot be a proletarian art—even among savages. There is a proletarian taste. To have achieved an organization even of that is to have escaped it."[8] Williams's words here, probably without his being aware of it, penetrate to the dilemma faced by those writers who were as deeply committed to "making it new" as he and Pound were. As we shall see, among the Objectivist poets, the group most connected to Pound and Williams, which included poets such as George Oppen and Carl Rakosi, the confrontation between left-wing politics and the sense of art as formulated here by Williams was to be a devastating encounter.

In his essay of 1930, "American Poetry 1920–1930," Louis Zukofsky was writing of Williams that "no outside program has influenced his social awareness. It is the product of the singular creature living in society and expressing in spite of the numb terror around him, *the awareness which after awhile cannot help but be general.*"[9]

To create "an awareness" which "cannot help but be general" might well be a motto for what Zukofsky in 1930 saw in the work of the poets, Williams among them, whose poems he was gathering for an issue of *Poetry* magazine that Zukofsky would edit. This was the "Objectivist" issue of the magazine, so named because Harriet Monroe insisted that a group label be applied to Zukofsky's choices and that he write a covering essay explaining his selections. This label has adhered to the present to the poets in this group: to Zukofsky himself, George Oppen, Carl Rakosi, Charles Reznikoff, and Lorine Niedecker (who actually never appeared in the Objectivist issue of the magazine itself but who was allied with the group through her association with Zukofsky). The essay, entitled "An Objective," now stands as something of a landmark, one which defines not only an "objectivist" poetics but which offers a kind of honor code of writing which was keenly appropriate to the times. "The poet's form," Zukofsky wrote in "An Objective," "is never an imposition of history but the desirability of making order out of history as felt and conceived." The essay considered the making of poems from two interrelated terms, "sincerity" and "objectification." "In sincerity," Zukofsky wrote, "shapes appear concomitants of word combinations, precursors of . . . completed structures in sound. Writing occurs which is the detail not the mirage of seeing." "Objectification" was concerned with what Zukofsky called "rested totality . . . the apprehension satisfied completely as to the appearance of the art form as an object."[10]

Zukofsky was suggesting a poetics "faithful to a complex reality," as Hugh Kenner notes in "Oppen, Zukofsky, and the Poem and Lens," collected in *Literature at the Barricades: The American Writer in the*

1930s. This faithfulness marked off the Objectivist poets both from the ironists and from the idealists who called for, as Archibald MacLeish represented it, "an image of the world in which men can again believe." "The exacting Objectivist ambition," Kenner writes, "was to keep the poem open to the entire domain of fact, and simultaneously to keep it a thing made of words, which have their own laws." The facts were just the facts, neither too mundane nor too utopian for poetry. For Kenner, the Objectivist poem, like the photography of the period—one thinks of Walker Evans and Dorothea Lange—registers something new in representational art, an "indifference of the subject," a willingness to traffic without blinkers in the facticity of social reality.[11] Both the Objectivists and Williams, to the extent that he was a part of the group, made use of this principle which was, in effect, a reminder of the world's recalcitrance before the blandishments of art. The difficulties with factuality at its most extreme form can be found in Oppen's short book *Discrete Series,* which prefigures many of his later techniques in such lines as these "about" an automobile: "Closed car—closed in glass— / At the curb, / Unapplied and empty: / A thing among others."[12] An older lyricism—such as Crane might have imposed on the subject—is banished. A language having all the impoverishments of a new beginning refuses the romance as well as the hatreds of technology.

The Objectivist label was a loose one, yet it combined certain characteristically American features: a metaphysical bent, a language sufficiently sophisticated without the air of cosmopolitan ennui, and a desire for a Whitmanesque sweep. Oppen's stripped-down verse was not the only kind of response to Zukofsky's manifesto. The essay was broad enough to garner a large measure of allegiance without imposing a constrictive conformity on poets as different in style as Rakosi and Reznikoff. Rakosi, given to a more comic outlook on the times, could be both witty and Objectivist-spare in the same poem. He was fashioning a poetic stance which was at once existential, socially conscious, and shot through with humor. Reznikoff's language was the most "photographic" of the group. His poems, capturing New York urban life at its most quotidian, were made up of densely compacted images, drawn so sharply that their effect was aural and retinal at the same time: "From my window I could not see the moon, / and yet it was shining: / the yard among the houses— / snow upon it, an oblong in the darkness."[13]

The movement as a movement was short-lived; indeed, the term "Objectivist" was occluded from literary history by the welter of movements and poets which followed. Both Zukofsky and Reznikoff continued to write, but in obscurity, totally ignored by the academy which by the middle of the decade had begun to form the New Criticism.

Thus Zukofsky, even in the late thirties, was incorporating bits of Marx's prose into his major work, A, a poem some fifty years in the making. A, an epic not of heroes and quests but of one poet's attentiveness to language and to the leadings and strictures which words might impose, was as far removed as can be imagined from the "Proletarian Realism" of the left-leaning little magazines. Hugh Kenner has referred to it as the most hermetic poem in the language, and it was not until the 1960s, when the Objectivist poets resurfaced, that A was recognized as a masterpiece to be set alongside Williams's *Paterson* and Pound's *The Cantos.*

Meanwhile, first Oppen, then Rakosi a few years later, both under the sway of Marxist left-wing politics, stopped writing poetry. The sociopolitical moment, the poverty and suffering of the Depression as it affected the lives of these two poets, was overwhelming. Oppen, in one of a series of interviews with the Objectivist poets which L. S. Dembo published in *Contemporary Literature* in 1968, claimed that he was caught in "the dilemma of the 'thirties.' In a way I gave up poetry because of the pressures of what for the moment I'll call conscience."[14] Rakosi reported to Dembo in the same issue that he too was a casualty of Marxism: "I took very literally the basic Marxian ideas about literature being an instrument for social change, for expressing the needs and desires of large masses of people. And believing that, I couldn't write poetry, because the poetry that I could write could not achieve these ends."[15] One of the last "official" acts of the group was to form TO Publishers, which brought out books by Reznikoff and Rakosi and perhaps saved Williams from complete obscurity by publishing his *Collected Poems.* The book, with an introduction by Wallace Stevens (which much to Williams's chagrin labeled his work as "antipoetic"), brought some measure of notice to Williams at one of the lowest moments of his career.

What is most instructive about the example of the Objectivists is that in the ideological climate of the thirties there was no room for the "objectivity" which their work manifested. Two of the group's major poets had stopped believing in the social efficacy of their own work, in the efficacy of poetry itself. A unique strand of what we now call Modernism had nipped itself in the bud only to reappear in a more powerful and more mature form in the sixties—another period of great political

unrest—and, at that time, it entered permanently as a central element
of twentieth-century American poetry.

The left-leaning and/or Communist writers at the beginning of the
decade had deemed the Modernist tradition an insufficient vehicle for
bringing about social change. The American literary exiles of the twenties
(the "lost generation" which included Hemingway, Fitzgerald, Pound,
and Eliot, among others, who used the European avant-garde as their
model) had rejected mainstream American Realism and were contribut-
ing in their way to the evolving Modernist tradition. This tradition was
rejected by the politically committed writers in favor of a return to
something resembling the late-nineteenth-century Realism of Zola and
that of writers like Sherwood Anderson and Theodore Dreiser. The
Communist writer thought that history was on his side, that a depiction
of the life of the exploited worker coupled with a display of the proletarian
worker's noble virtues would engender a natural sentiment, if not a
sentimentality, in readers.

In poetry, the exemplary figure was Carl Sandburg, nominated by the
Left as a poet "of the people," though at times he could certainly be a
much more complex (and better) poet than his leftist enthusiasts might
have allowed. Oppen and Rakosi, it can be conjectured, had ceased
writing poetry rather than force themselves to write in the style of
Sandburg. Williams, closer to the Modernist mood than any other, was
ignored by most of the committed writers; if he seemed to display the
necessary Naturalism and even Populism when it came to subject matter,
he did not have the even more necessary touch of sentimentality when
it came to rendering "proletarian" life.

In the middle of thirties literary life were the liberals who were
repelled by both camps of Left and Right. Joseph Wood Krutch was
arguing that no writer could align himself with a political religion which
saw art as a weapon. Paul Rosenfeld accused artists of being swept up
into the "arms of dogma." He noted that Communists had a lot to say
about everything but were curiously silent on the meaning of culture,
the freedom of inquiry, and the conditions under which an artist ought
to be allowed to work.[16]

As early as 1932, a backlash had begun. The poet, labor organizer, and
journalist Joseph Freeman, one of the major figures in the Communist
movement and a coeditor with Gold of *New Masses*, insisted that the
magazine had to be made over. It was to forsake its crude propagandist

style and become something which "a trained mind could listen to with respect and intellectual profit."[17] William Phillips and Philip Rahv, both Communists at the time, were involved with the founding of the *Partisan Review*, which at first was the literary organ of the John Reed clubs.

Phillips and Rahv, however, were keenly aware of and valued the Modernist work done in the twenties. In an agreement with the editors of *New Masses*, it was decided that *Partisan Review* would be given to dealing with literary and critical matters. No single act of the thirties was more significant in rescuing a good part of the Modernist sensibility, fascist warts and all, from cultural oblivion. From the first, *Partisan Review* was engaged in, as Alan Wald writes in "Revolutionary Intellectuals" in *Literature at the Barricades*, a "campaign against mechanically applied Marxism." In this campaign, one of incorporating the Modernist advances in literature into the politically conscious writing of the thirties, even the reactionary Eliot could be enlisted. Rahv was to see "modern literature as essentially a dispute with the modern world," thus by nature political and worthy of support. The guiding light for the magazine in those years was Trotsky, the revolutionary who seemed most opposed to dogmatism in the arts. When, in the period of the Moscow purge trials, the magazine sided with Trotsky and rejected Stalinism, it was immediately attacked in the pages of *New Masses* and the *Daily Worker*. As Alan Wald reports, the purge trials in particular had the peculiar effect of leading writers back toward the stances which they had rejected and deplored; indeed, led them to the very position from which Modernism began, that of the "alienated intellectual."[18]

In the middle of the decade, poets were undergoing agonizing reappraisals, not only because of the clash of aesthetic traditions but because the Communists, through the two American Writers Congresses of the period (1935 and 1937), were consciously revealing their attempts at manipulating writers en masse. Hitler, who had assumed power in Germany in 1933, was an acknowledged presence in the psyches of American writers. For the American literary community, fragmented and strife-ridden as it was, the decline into barbarism of one of Europe's most advanced and enlightened nations was a traumatizing event; it heightened and sharpened the cry for some sort of literary activity on behalf of social usefulness if not on behalf of civilization itself. In this matter, as with so many others, the writing community was out of step with a mainly isolationist public, a public hostile not only to foreign affairs but to "foreign" art as represented by Modernist culture.

The ambivalence between High-Modernist art and the impulse to provide meaningful social commentary could be read in Zukofsky's poem "Mantis," published in *Poetry* in 1935. Zukofsky was bent on preserving High-Modernist energy and complexity within the poetic line; the music of the poem (in Zukofsky, often crabbed and gnomic) would be the very sound of sociopolitical contradiction. By contrast, Kenneth Rexroth, briefly aligned with the Objectivist group, was already producing a poetry which was at once politically aware and yet consummately readable. For Rexroth, the exemplary mode was that of the Chinese masters, Tu Fu in particular, which foregrounds human events against the spaciousness and grandeur of natural processes. This natural world, so powerfully evoked in Rexroth's work, is not a "moral" good or teacher (as in so much nature writing) but is instead a constant means of instigating a human world or occasion. In 1936 Muriel Rukeyser, near the beginning of her career, was also writing a poetry that could be embraced by other than party-liners. In "Time Exposure," from *Night-Music*, one could hear echoes of Eliot in the poem's concern with "the exposed spirit" in the suburbia of the bourgeois where one saw "down polished airways a purple dove descending." This was contrasted with the image of "factories" that "bellow mutilations, and we live needy still."[19]

The experiences of the two congresses, coupled with the reportage on the Moscow purge trials, was producing numerous schisms in the writing community partial to the Left. In the last few years of the decade, a general breakdown of the community occurred, followed quickly by an atmosphere of recriminations and mistrust. W. H. Auden (who, along with Stephen Spender, C. D. Lewis, and other young poets, belonged to a Marxist-oriented group of English poets), recently arrived from England, may have bracketed the moods of the politically weary American writers with the opening and closing lines of his poem "Journey to Iceland," first published in *Poetry* in 1937: "And the traveller hopes: let me be far from any / Physician. . . . Again the writer runs howling to his art."[20]

Not all poets of the time were running or howling. Marianne Moore and Elizabeth Bishop, in their poetry at least, stood firmly apart from the political storms, both writing some of their most significant poems. Wallace Stevens, like Bishop and Moore, was also doing some of his most important work, publishing poem after poem which seemed to rise not out of any contingent sociopolitical world but, as he would have surely claimed, out of the imagination itself. The mind in his poems was the supreme celebratory organ, transcending political bias or conditioning. For Stevens, less a "philosophical" poet than one who may be said to play with philosophical ideas, brute reality and the possibility of epistemological certainty occur only when a person has been disabused, made "ignorant" of philosophical encumbrances. Hence, in his work politics, and especially dogmatic politics, seem to represent psychological fixations, inhibiting rather than furthering the imagination.

Of course, much good writing existed which could have no effect on the immediate outlines of literary activity in the thirties simply because it remained submerged and ghettoized in this period. The poetry of black writers, of the ongoing Harlem Renaissance movement, was as invisible as Ralph Ellison's Invisible Man. Occasionally a poem of Langston Hughes would appear in a mainstream magazine such as *Poetry*, but there is almost nothing of Toomer, or Cullen, or the early Tolson. Minority writing of all sorts suffered, and it was not until the upheavals of the sixties that black, Hispanic, and Native American writing would begin to enter and transform white mainstream literary culture.

Williams, on the other hand, was running and howling, albeit in a roundabout manner. In the middle and late thirties, under Pound's influence, he flirted briefly with Major Douglas's theories of Social Credit economics. Both fascism and communism, however, were anathema to him; in a letter to Marianne Moore, he insisted, "I won't follow causes!" His reasons were complex: not only did he fear what an ideological commitment might do to any artist, but he also sensed the futility of such a commitment in the face of the general population's hostility to ideology in any form.

Zukofsky's relationship with Williams was at its strongest during this period. Zukofsky was not only Williams's confidant but also a correspondent-critic, editing Williams's work and suggesting changes in it, most of which Williams incorporated into his poems. Zukofsky, as active politically as ever, counseled Williams on his dealings with other magazines, in particular those of the Left. Williams was caught on the horns of his own dilemma, of trying to be accepted as a writer and yet at the same time trying to speak his piece. An anecdote involving Zukofsky, described in Mariani's biography, is revealing on this score. Williams received a questionnaire from *Partisan Review* asking him to comment on "Marxism in America." Zukofsky urged him to be careful in replying to this. But

Williams, having little literary reputation to lose anyway, wrote bluntly that "American tradition is completely opposed to Marxism. . . . Marxism is a static philosophy of a hundred years ago which has not kept up—as the democratic spirit has." Shortly, letters to the magazine were calling for sanctions against Williams.

Despite his combative distance from the ideological battles and his troubles, Williams was writing a number of brilliant poems, trenchant plunges of language into the atmospherics of the period. They were more "political," more meaningfully political, than the overt hackwork of the ideologues. Two poems in particular, "The Yachts" and "Perpetuum Mobile: The City," not only demonstrate Williams's magnificent use of Modernist technique, specifically the Imagism of the twenties and of Zukofsky's Objectivist influence, but they also convey a sense of the problem which lies at the heart of the Modernist impulse, the self-reflexive suspiciousness of obvious ideologies and traditions. For Williams, dogma was profoundly distasteful because it could never be squared with the unpredictable in man and nature. In "The Yachts," a stylistically atypical poem in Williams's oeuvre, the poet envisions the unpredictable on a number of levels: formal, social, and poetic. The poem, like Zukofsky's "Mantis," has its elements of regularity, namely the *terza rima* stanzaic form and the half-rhyme play in many of the line endings. But the form is an ironic contrast to the violent material of the poem, which contains a complex vision of the irrational forces at work in the world. The yachts of the poem are themselves sleek and fascinating engines that play with the natural forces of the wind and sea and over which men crawl "ant-like, solicitously grooming them." A sort of ideal mastery is implied until with violence the tables are turned and the yachts plow out of control through water which has become an ocean of human beings: "Bodies thrown recklessly in the way are cut aside. / It is a sea of faces about them in agony, in despair / until the horror of the race dawns staggering the mind."[21] Since it is the yachts themselves that overrun the people in the water, the poem seems less about humankind and nature than about the contemporary hubris implicated in the sociopolitical mechanisms which humankind has brought into being.

How to sum up the decade? As the thirties were drawing to a close, Apocalypse was no longer the theoretical possibility of abusive economic trends but was, with Europe at war, a tangible fact of existence. A few die-hard Marxists could analyze Hitler's rise as an aspect of the class struggle, but his racial and ideological policies could not be placed in any such rational framework. Thus, fewer and fewer writers and poets were associating themselves with the Communist party, or they were leaving it under the smart of its attempts to manipulate their work. The Nazi-Stalin defense pact of 1939 may be said to have been the final blow to the naïveté of the American Communist-inspired writer. The pact, which came as a complete surprise to American party officials, blew away the final cover on the Russian "experiment." The Party and its apparatus were now perceived as engaging in nothing less than a screen to disguise its own totalitarian self-interest in retaining power. Defections were massive, and for those who did not defect, their fate as writers seemed bleaker than ever. For the writers who remained loyal, the only sure or safe prospect was to become a party hack, equivalent on a minuscule scale to those writers in the official organizations of the Soviet Union; that is, to those who followed the line and toed the mark.

The more conservative writers such as the Southern Agrarians remained, in the late thirties, an influential group of poets, but this influence was not without its ambiguity. It is true that Tate, Ransom, and Warren in the thirties prepared the ground for the New Criticism and the hegemony which it exercised over the academy and its journals in the forties. But it seems that it is precisely in the academy that these poets remained, their work exhibiting a kind of museum-virtuosity which is, in the end, more used by the scholar and graduate student than by the practicing poet.

The end of the thirties also saw the emergence of new writers such as Delmore Schwartz, Kenneth Fearing, David Ignatow, Josephine Miles, Theodore Roethke, May Sarton, and many others who would form part of the central core of American poetry in the forties and fifties.

In addition to the painful disappointment with politics, the end of the decade produced another, more subtle, version of spiritual disillusionment such as had occurred at the end of the twenties. To glimpse this disillusionment, it is necessary to quickly scan the decade as a whole, to see the rising and falling arcs of aspiration and idealism.

Yeats could proclaim in 1933 in "Crazy Jane Speaks with the Bishop" that "nothing can be sole or whole / that has not been rent." Clearly, in the thirties, not only in America but in the world, society, culture, and the arts had been "rent" by loss of spirit, widespread economic depression, and the inability of governments to address local needs.

Society, like nature, abhors a vacuum, and the most obvious aspect of the beginning of the thirties had been the headlong speed with which people rushed to restore wholeness to culture. This activity had its own intoxicating effect, and the literary community was certainly more willing than the general public to imbibe from the activist cup. American artists and writers, not in spite of but *because* of the crash and the ensuing poverty and dislocation, had found for themselves some social role after years of isolation from the general public.

Yet the "high" of political action, even the turning away from radicalism to conservatism, had certain unforeseen consequences. Action seemed to nip in the bud the ongoing evolution of the arts that had begun in the early part of the century. Indeed, for many poets of the thirties, questions of poetic technique were placed in a holding pattern while the quest to solve, or to organize in order to solve, immediate social needs took precedence. As we have seen, for some, like Oppen and Rakosi, the desire to meet social needs meant abandoning poetry altogether.

In addition, immense psychological and cultural pressure was brought to bear on the writer who resisted social action. This pressure was not anything so simple as the urgings or condemnation of a group, or even the economic consequences of an action. In the thirties, the alternative to political and group identification, to partisan action in a cause, was an all-encompassing sense of uncertainty. This sense creates for the writer a disastrous climate, a kind of awful weather in the sea of humanity which is so unbearable at times that it drives one into any sort of port or shelter. Thus Howe observes of the thirties that it was a time when, all too easily, "talent betrayed itself to the wardens of authoritarianism."

Yet, as one examines the departures and the failures among American writers of the period, one is reminded of the remark of the recent Nobel laureate Elias Canetti that what marks the writer's duty to one's times is that in some profound way he or she is willing to stand *against* those times. This "stand," in retrospect, seems to have taken a number of forms. Among poets with already established reputations on the one hand (such as Frost, Stevens, or Moore, and the young Elizabeth Bishop for whom Moore was an exemplary figure), the stand meant placing oneself outside the whirling political storms. On the other hand, those who allowed themselves to have their "talent betrayed," as Howe puts it, can be read today only for period interest.

There is yet another form of writerly resistance, one closer to what Canetti means by standing against one's time. For the poet, it amounts to shaping the poetic instrument so that it is supple enough to confront the forces at work, not retreat from them, while at the same time preventing the poet from being overrun by them. The Modernist impulse, as we know, has many vices, not the least of which is its ready assent to a Fascist or authoritarian type of culture—such as Pound found in Mussolini's Italy, Yeats wished for in Ireland, and Eliot propagandized for in England—that appears to protect and honor the artist. Yet it must be remembered that what Modernism seeks is some notion of a "usable past" to marshal against a culture that seems inauthentic and oppressive. Hence, along with its vices, its reinvention of traditions, it can also develop great self-reflexivity and suspiciousness—indeed, develop a capacity to continually undermine its own presuppositions. It is this reflexivity and suspiciousness which allows us to speak of Modernism in evolutionary terms, terms which are ultimately at odds with the conservative traditions in the arts and, sometimes, at odds as well with the political sympathies of Modernists themselves.

Notes

1. Paul Mariani, *William Carlos Williams: A New World Naked* (New York: McGraw-Hill, 1981), 300.

2. Daniel Aaron, *Writers on the Left* (New York: Oxford University Press, 1977), 441.

3. Ibid.

4. Ibid., 208–11.

5. Mariani, *William Carlos Williams*, 330.

6. Jeffers, *Selected Poems* (New York: Random, 1938), 385.

7. Pound, *The Letters of Ezra Pound 1907–1940*, ed. D. D. Paige (New York: Harcourt, 1950), 237, 239.

8. Williams, *Selected Essays* (New York: New Directions, 1969), 127.

9. Zukofsky, *Prepositions: The Collected Critical Essays* (Berkeley: University of California Press, 1981), 151.

10. Ibid., 12, 13.

11. Hugh Kenner, *The Pound Era* (Berkeley: University of California Press, 1971), 163–64.

12. Oppen, *Collected Poems* (New York: New Directions, 1974), 14.

13. Reznikoff, *Poems 1918–1936*, vol. 1 of the *Complete Poems of Charles Reznikoff*, ed. Seamus Cooney (Santa Barbara: Black Sparrow Press, 1978), 108.

14. Dembo, "The 'Objectivist' Poet: Four Interviews," *Contemporary Literature* 10, no. 2 (Spring 1969): 174.

15. Ibid., 179.

16. Aaron, *Writers on the Left*, 253–54.

17. Ibid., 272.

18. Alan Wald, "Revolutionary Intellectuals," in *Literature at the Barricades:*

The American Writer in the 1930s, ed. Ralph F. Bogardus and Fred Hobson (Tuscaloosa: University of Alabama Press, 1982), 188, 201, 202–3.

19. Daryl Hine and Joseph Parisi, eds., *The Poetry Anthology* (Boston: Houghton Mifflin 1978), 166.

20. Ibid., 178.

21. Williams, *The Collected Earlier Poems* (New York: New Directions, 1951), 107.

5

Constructing A New Stage:
The Poetry of the 1940s

RICHARD JACKSON

Changing the Theater

"Poetry is nothing if not experiment in language," Wallace Stevens wrote to Delmore Schwartz in 1948, going on to explain that the experiment included "subjects and words."[1] As he said in his "An Ordinary Evening in New Haven," written the following year, poetry as a meditation on reality, on things and words and their shifting relationships, is "part of the never ending meditation, / Part of the question." These were not ideas new to Stevens, but influenced his poetry from the start. "Of Modern Poetry," from the beginning of the decade, is definitive in its description of what "the poem of the mind in the act of finding / What will suffice" must accomplish. In the past, in a world of supposed absolutes, "the scene was set; it repeated what was in the script." Now, however, "the theatre was changed." Modern poetry could no longer, after Einstein, Heisenberg, Heidegger, and other proponents of relativity, be purely referential, symbolic of a system of stable values. Rather,

> It has to be living, to learn the speech of the place
> It has to face the men of the time and to meet
> The women of the time. It has to think about war
> And it has to find what will suffice. It has
> To construct a new stage.[2]

So much of what was to become at issue is prophetically included here: the need for more colloquial language championed by Williams, Schwartz, and Frost, the emphasis on character championed by Jarrell and Lowell, the need to experiment as seen in Pound, Roethke, and Berryman; in short, a dialectic argument against the kind of symbolic poetry that Eliot, Tate, Ransom, and Winters, to name a few, had championed.

102

What many poets began to revolt against in the forties was succinctly described by Delmore Schwartz in his essay on Allen Tate (1940): "The symbol, being seen too much as idea, does not yield the images which would give a dramatic existence to the idea."[3] It is very telling that Schwartz uses the Stevensian metaphor of drama, for what was at stake was not really a question of belief, but of attitude, of openness, of the willingness to submit to poetic play. This is opposed to a notion of symbolism that needs clarification. In *Blindness and Insight,* Paul De-Man differentiates between "symbolism," which is a static reference to a world already known through an act of confirming a belief in the referent, and "allegory," which is more narrative, more oriented toward quest and discovery, and which dramatizes ideas while it rejects the absolutism buried in symbolism. Stevens himself, in "Effects of Analogy," published in the 1949 *Yale Review,* uses "analogy" in much the same way that DeMan uses "allegory"—a complex of shifting relations among author, narrator, world, and language, all constituting the "subject." Symbolism wishes to depose reality, as Donald Davie suggests in his book on Pound, and replace it with dogma: it is, he says, "an imperious, appropriating attitude towards the perceived world. When swans get into Yeats's verse, the swan loses all its swanliness except what it needs to symbolize something in the person who observes it."[4]

The point, then, was to deconstruct the language to *re-vision* the real, and then reconstruct it—"Make the language take really desperate leaps," as Roethke wrote in a notebook entry.[5] Even H. D., earlier a Symbolist sort of poet, wrote in her *Tribute to the Angels* (1944): "This is no rune or symbol," and "what I wanted to indicate was / a new phase."[6] In short, symbolic poetry had lost contact with what it had tried to symbolize. Schwartz put it best in "The Isolation of Modern Poetry" (1941): "the idiom of poetic style and the normal thought and speech of the community have been moving in opposite directions and have little or no relationship to each other."[7] The modern poet must be, as H. D. said in *The Walls Do Not Fall* (1942), a voyager without the Symbolists' aging maps, without the old stage.

Perhaps no one better exemplifies the dramatic voyage between imagination and reality than Stevens himself; in the forties, in particular, in *Parts of a World* (1942) and *Auroras of Autumn* (1950), he intensified the inquiry he had begun in *The Man with the Blue Guitar* (1937). "What is necessary is to recognize change as constant," he wrote to a friend in 1940: "Cross-reflections, modifications, counter-balances, complements, giving and taking are illimitable." Yet, as he would say in a 1948 letter, the important thing was "the attachment to real things" which nevertheless involves "abstraction." At the same time, poetry should be a "combat" with reality. Everything becomes metaphor, perspective, point of view—"So, say that final belief / Must be in a fiction," Stevens writes in the opening of "Asides on the Oboe."[8]

The notion of fictions is most thoroughly dramatized in the 1942 poem "Notes Toward a Supreme Fiction."[9] The headings for its three sections of ten poems, each in seven three-line stanzas of blank verse, give the thesis: "It Must Be Abstract," "It Must Change," and "It Must Give Pleasure." To be abstract—for Stevens goes back to the root of the word—is to take out the essence of the thing, to try to reach a beginning, an "early candor," or "what it is to be."

It is important to remember, as most critics have not, that Stevens's poems are always rooted in a reality in a way that links him with Williams and Frost. As he says in *Esthétique du Mal* (1945), one of his longest and finest poems, a meditation on the meaning, reality, and purpose of pain and suffering: "The greatest poverty is not to live / In a physical world." For Stevens, the greatest sin is "to hear only what one hears," to be "the lunatic of one idea / In a world of ideas."[10] One must not simply repeat the past and its symbols, but challenge them; not to do so, not to project a future, is to fail to come to grips with the world we "half-create, half perceive," in Wordsworth's phrase—and that is the source of pain. To do this, poetry would have to embrace as much as possible, which is perhaps why Stevens experimented with so many longer poems.

A good deal of what Stevens meant by the past "scene" was how that scene was described in criticism—"The Age of Criticism," Randall Jarrell had termed the period in the title of an essay. But the reconstruction of critical views and poetics was as much a revolt against an attitude as against a set of principles. Jarrell complains in a 1946 letter: "Several of my best friends have happened to become editors, and it seemed to me that their dogmatic convictions and idiosyncracies and general sectarian leanings hurt their work a lot." And Delmore Schwartz, along with Jarrell, one of the most perceptive critics of the age, reveals his agreement by the mere title of his 1947 essay, "The Literary Dictatorship of T. S. Eliot."[11] Schwartz had cogently pointed out that Eliot's judgments were really a matter of certain "preconceptions," and that, in addition, these supposed "universal" judgments were in fact "most influenced by his own poetic practice." The dictatorship that Schwartz perceives is one of tone and attitude, allowing subjective likes and dislikes, and theology, to pass under the guise of "objective" aesthetics.

Schwartz's criticism of Allen Tate's theories is best revealed in his 1941 letter to Tate himself concerning Tate's essays, *Reason in Madness:* "You seem most of the time to be using literature for the purpose of stating a general point of view and attacking a series of other positions which you lump together as positivism." He also accuses Tate of "misrepresentation" of his opponents' positions and simple "misunderstanding" of various philosophical ideas. Tate, to be sure, always claimed he was only an amateur at philosophy and almost always couched his misrepresentations in "if" clauses or other subjunctive constructions—a clever and often arrogant strategy that allowed him to divide black from white, carry black to an extreme, and thus save the day for white by default. Tate's imperialism on critical matters was really the issue. In 1945, Jarrell wrote to Lowell: "Allen's greatest fault is a defect of sympathy in the strict sense of the word, a lack of ability to identify himself with anything that is fundamentally non-Allen."[12]

Tate, for his part, was still fighting a quixotic battle against the forces of science and positivism, urbanization, relativism—all things he linked together in a vague mesh. It is surprising how much vagueness there is in this critic who hated it in others. He ends "Three Types of Poetry," for instance, with a refusal to define that type of poetry he would like to see against the naturalist and relativist he decries: "We may prepare our minds for its reception by the logical elimination of error. . . . Let us not argue about it. It is there for those who have eyes to see."[13] If that sounds like the Gospel of Mark it is because Tate's ultimate concern is with a mysterious and privileged "truth," a moral attitude only the elect can exercise; that is, what Allen Tate reveals.

The problem of mistaking religion and poetry or criticism was a difficult one, as I have been suggesting. For one, poets like Stevens or Williams ran the risk of being called relativists—an evil-sounding word in the realm of the general morality of the time—or hedonists, humanists, atheists. In this context, we can see why Tate slighted Keats because he lacked "an ordered symbolism through which we may know the common and the ideal reality in a single imaginative act." Keats was too sensual and agnostic a poet. By no means, though, was Tate as senselessly dogmatic as Yvor Winters, who even Tate knew "wants to see all the sense perceptions and feelings safely laid out in a logical order for progression, a laudable demand, but made at the risk of losing about half of the great poetry in the English language."[14] The phrase in commas highlights Tate's own conflicts—and perhaps accounts for the complexity of the man who would vote the 1949 Bollingen Prize for Pound, a poet whose ideas must have revolted him.

As Jarrell notes in "The Age of Criticism," critics such as Eliot, Tate, and Ransom, who were intent on judging works against the "classics," tended to suffocate poetry under a rigidly ideological interpretation of those classics; it wasn't the form but the values perpetrated by a Christian interpretation of classic texts that Eliot wanted to return to in "What Is a Classic?" (1944). And in the 1948 "Notes Towards the Definition of Culture," arguing for a cultured and cerebral poetry, Eliot links "culture and religion" as "different aspects" of the "same thing." Of course, religion means his version of Christianity as opposed to the "infidel." However, in "The Music of Poetry," from the same period, he focuses on the use of common speech and prose rhythm as values, though his conception of these differed, to say the least, from Williams's.

Perhaps the most complete critic of the hegemony of Eliot, Tate, and the others was William Carlos Williams, both in theory and practice. His essay "The Poem as Field of Action" (1947) contains the following seminal statement: "How can we accept Einstein's theory of relativity, affecting our very conception of the heavens about us of which poets write so much, without incorporating its essential fact—the relativity of measurements —into our own category of activity: the poem." For Williams, this meant finding a new language for poetry more closely linked to speech, and a new "structure" ("Imagism was not structured: that was the reason for its disappearance"), a new "measure." For Williams, "to destroy the past" was "precisely a service to tradition, . . . confirming and *enlarging* its application." What Williams finally hit on, during the latter part of the decade, was the three-step line, his most coherent attack on the "rigidity of the poetic foot." It is a line in three breaths or sections of variable length, perhaps hearkening back to Anglo-Saxon accentual verse. The hope for Williams here was a poetry that was large enough to be, as Heidegger would say, a "conversation," that would "listen to the language for the discoveries we hope to make," that would be open, expansive, large enough to include conflicting views on its stage. It would be a structure that was also a new subject, the poem as evolving process, showing its seams, its origins in its own sources.[15]

That form, of course, turned out to be *Paterson*, the poem that, conceived in the late thirties, occupied him for most of the forties. In *I*

Wanted to Write a Poem, Williams says, "Finally, I let form take care of itself; the colloquial language, my own language, set the pace."[16] The referentiality of the language in the poem, any symbolic associations it might have, is undercut by the reinscription of words from various sources; in the poem their referential base is dismantled and replaced by the evolving one of the poem. The script is rewritten. Paterson, a character in the poem, also stands for Williams's city in New Jersey, for the river there, the falls, the history stretching back to colonial times, and more—for Williams's evolving and sometimes conflicting attitudes toward all these within the poem itself.

One of the most famous sayings of the poem, repeated several times, is "no ideas but in things," itself a very abstract statement. But it needs the same sort of definition we gave Stevens's "abstract." In his *Autobiography,* Williams describes the "thing" in a holistic sense, drawing on his experiences as a doctor. As an object of the imagination, "It is an identifiable thing, and its chief characteristic is that it is sure, all of a piece and, as I have said, instant and perfect: it comes, it is there, and it vanishes."[17] The "thing" becomes analogous to the dramatic encounter between patient and doctor, characterized by both guilt (the past) and illumination (the present). What *Paterson* does, far more than the lyrics of *The Wedge* (1944) and *The Clouds* (1948), is attempt to totally remake the language, or to allow into the poem all forms of language. It is far more successful than Pound's *Cantos,* perhaps because of its insistence on the "thing"— the drama of common people, a variable but consistently heartfelt point of view.

Of course, not all the poets engaged in constructing a new stage to replace that of the New Critics were as confident as Stevens and Williams, who, to no worry of their own, built two opposite stages. Delmore Schwartz is a good example of a less secure though very brilliant poet. During the forties, and even later, Schwartz worried that he would not fulfill the promise of *In Dreams Begin Responsibilities* (1938). Schwartz's aim, as he wrote to a young poet, was like Williams's: "to get the kind of structure which would make reasonable and articulate and symmetrical the kind of international consciousness which keeps growing bigger all the time in the world.[18] As with Williams, the procedure was to develop a new "form-subject relationship," but Schwartz went to Hardy's *The Dynasts* for his model in the long autobiographical poem *Genesis.* Like the 1942 *Paris and Helen,* a farcical masque that has Paris telling Hector that anyone would do what he did for such a beauty as Helen, it reveals

Schwartz's sexual and Freudian orientation to the world. Favorably received by Richard Eberhart (though Auden wrote a long letter objecting to the theology) and a few others, *Genesis* is a Wordsworthian search by Hershey Green, clearly Schwartz himself. Self-analysis, philosophizing, lyricism—all are mixed here, and the poem reaches its best moments when the self-irony is most apparent.

The compassionate sense of what Wordsworth called "spots of time" is crucial to Schwartz's thinking: one must accept and embrace change, one must perceive the self's direction, and, as he showed in his criticism, preserve a generosity of spirit. The "spot of time" suggests also that Schwartz's main strength was lyrical; his strength was a sort of "vortex," as Pound called such a quality a few decades earlier, a dramatic-lyric vortex. Here is one of the significantly labeled "Present Moments" from his notebooks:

> I will observe present moments, he said, perhaps they
> Will give me a little happiness
> He always looked toward the particular fact, seeking
> To generalize from it.[19]

Those last two lines perhaps sum up the strategy for those poets who would revolt against the imperiousness of the New Critical dogma; they worked inductively rather than deductively, and if Schwartz, along with Stevens and Williams, could be any measure, they emphasized a largeness of spirit, a willingness to embrace more than what had been embraced, an ironic sense that their own vision was a version, a thing apart.

Learning the Speech of the Place, Facing the Men of the Time

Randall Jarrell, in "The Other Frost," was probably the first to point out the serious, complex thinking that went on in Robert Frost's poems: "No other living poet has written so well about the actions of ordinary men: his wonderful dramatic monologues or dramatic scenes come out of a knowledge of people that few poets have had, and they are written in a verse that uses, sometimes with absolute mastery, the rhythms of actual speech."[20] Frost, Jarrell knew, was not simply a nature poet but a manipulator of images that happen to be rural, like the poet's background, in an intellectual and emotional drama set within forms that ranged from the sonnet to blank verse. Frost was in many ways the paradigm for that group of poets who explored character and common speech perhaps more intensely than the other poets who revolted against New Criticism.

Jarrell also identified Frost's major themes, themes "of isolation, of extinction, of the final limitations of man."[21] So many of Frost's speakers, whether they are personae in monologues or stand in for the author, fight, as in "The Most of It" (A *Witness Tree*, 1942),[22] to remember, to consign, to keep (all favorite words of Frost) an order that continues to slip away and which they must continue to reinvent. The philosophical setting, then, is usually one of ambiguity. What happens, as with Stevens, is that reality and imagination intersect, though, while Stevens always keeps projecting toward the future, Frost is likely to cut in abruptly and end the poem suddenly with "and that was all," further enforcing the tenuousness of all projections.

Yvor Winters, in "Robert Frost; or, The Spiritual Drifter as Poet," could not understand the reason for ambiguity and dialectic; he wanted Frost to provide answers, the truth, absolutely. Frost's best answer occurs in *Steeple Bush*, a 1947 volume that, with the postwar times, is more oriented toward public issues than were earlier Frost books. In the poem "Directive," the narrator wishes us "back out of all this now too much for us, / Back in a time made simple by the loss / Of detail," but he goes on, paradoxically, to build the poem on a wealth of details from the glacial period to a timeless, mythic present. He is the narrator "who only has at heart your getting lost" because you have to be "lost enough to find yourself." The poem is earnest play, like much of Frost, a sort of wink in the face of "destination" and "destiny." The point of all this dialectic jostling is to create a past, and so a present, where we can "drink and be whole again beyond confusion," as the poem says in its enigmatic end. Of course, Frost, who loved puns, must have been aware that the poem also refers twice to "cellar holes" and to the quarry hole, empty spaces of the past our imagination must continue to fill; to be (w)hole is to be empty, to be lost is to be found—everything involves its opposite.[23]

What Jarrell—probably the most accurate evaluator of the decade—disliked about some of Frost's work was "an irresponsible conceit, an indifference to everything but himself."[24] It is not surprising, then, to find Jarrell's poetry, as dramatic and narrative as Frost's, almost always directed towards the world apart from the poet. One almost never hears Jarrell himself but rather characters, who live in average towns and cities or in a war zone, who go to public gardens, supermarkets, funeral homes, libraries, and who do average things like shop for detergent and worry about money, listen to the radio or hang the wash. Perhaps even more than Williams, Jarrell incorporated the everyday of our lives into his poems. But he does so within intensely Freudian and Proustian perspectives (he was a psychology major at Vanderbilt), sublimated and compensated, to use Freud's terms, to provide dramatic tension. And perhaps Jarrell's style, filled with more verbs and verbals than Frost's, reveals his more active and urgent vision.

In "90° North" (*Blood for a Stranger*, 1942), the speaker remembers his childhood dreams, sailing all night until he would find the North Pole. But there, his companions all frozen, facing a scene as blank as in Stevens's "The Snow Man," he discovers: "The world—my world spins on this final point / Of cold and wretchedness: all lines, all winds / End in this whirlpool I at last discover." What he finds, though, is that the pole, his world, his life, are all "meaningless." He ends the poem with a characteristically rhetorical push:

I see at last that all the knowledge
I wrung from the dark—that the darkness flung me—
Is worthless as ignorance: nothing comes from nothing,
The darkness from the darkness. Pain comes from the darkness
And we call it wisdom. It is pain.[25]

The imagination's value in describing and coming to grips with the world is at stake here, a conflict that Jarrell's characters will always struggle with in trying to overcome the imagination's selective view of the past.

This struggle, which defines the dramatic tension within the poems of all the poets discussed in this section, becomes more victorious as Jarrell's career progresses. In *Little Friend, Little Friend* (1945), and most of the poems of the forties, one answer is stoicism. In "Eighth Air Force" the character questions and requestions his own conclusions about the morality of killing in war, ending with a paraphrase of Pilate to Christ. A similar sort of questioning defines "Losses," the title poem from the 1948 volume where, having "burned / The cities we had learned about in school," the speaker, now dead, tries to figure out not just the meaning of his own life, but of war and its effects. Increasingly during this period, as Jarrell's poetic structures tend to loosen, he discovers other ways of defining the boundaries of form, the stage: repetition of lines, sometimes with slight changes to move the plot; repetition of key words; allusions to biblical and fairy tales; accidental rhyme; parallelisms of all sorts. Each device adds a certain dramatic intensity to poems that might be spoken by a swan, a dockworker, a falling parachutist, each point of view, each voice, providing the controlling perspective that the next poem, if not itself, is likely to question.

After the war Jarrell's poems became more philosophical and psychological in their dramas. A particularly productive year was 1948. The speaker in "The Orient Express" looks at and through a window, at surfaces and what is behind them: "Behind it—of all that was—was all," he says, but "behind everything there is always / The unknown unwanted life."[26] And "Moving," as the title suggests, counterpoints change and constancy, but through the eyes of a young girl. "A Quilt Pattern" begins with a young boy, sick, seeing an image of the Tree of Life in his quilt; tiring of his mother's stories, he falls asleep dreaming he is Hansel. In his dream a good self, a bad self, and an "Other," perhaps a superego, enact a psychological drama. The boy eats the house and his mother— all of which the bad self enjoys—and he is responsible for the Other being put in the furnace.[27] Jarrell's insights into the psychology of both the boy and the story are masterful, blending several perspectives that continually shift vantage point and expectations, ultimately questioning the validity of the speaker's own being. Jarrell will always be our best reminder, as he says in "The Age of Criticism," "that poems and stories are written by memory and desire, love and hatred, daydreams and nightmares—by a being and a brain," and his dialectic process will always remind us to eschew easy answers.[28]

Equally psychological in their orientation were the poems of Jarrell's friend John Berryman. If any single incident can be said to dominate a poet's life, then perhaps the suicide of John Berryman's father in 1926, just before the family moved to Gloucester, Massachusetts, was the dominating event of Berryman's life. In 1932, though, he entered Columbia University; after some difficulty he eventually graduated Phi Beta Kappa and, more important, came under the fatherly influence of Mark Van Doren. After traveling in Europe, where he met Yeats, Thomas, and Auden, each of whom had some influence, he began a colorful and sometimes troubled teaching career first at Wayne State, then at Harvard. There is always this sort of searching and wandering in Berryman's life and in his poems, evident equally in *Poems*, a chapbook from New Directions which appeared in 1942, and his first full collection, *The Dispossessed* (1948). The themes throughout his career were always related to loss of love, self, history, friends, society, sanity; faith and doubt, dream and madness are often the dialectic poles that the poems energetically dramatize.

Berryman's main poetic search in the forties was for a language that would suffice his very complex nature and concerns, a language that was simply unavailable in the Yeatsian or New Critical formulas. His progress in breaking from these, and it is almost a textbook movement, can be seen by comparing the 1940 poem "Winter Landscape"—an orthodox blank-verse portrait of three hunters as quiet in style and theme as the surface of the Brueghel landscape it echoes—with the 1948 poem "The Dispossessed." But Brueghel's quiet is only on the surface, and "Winter Landscape" mentions but does not explore several potentially disruptive images. However, the later poem is more expressively elliptical—it begins *in medias res*—allusive, complex, less neat in its metaphoric equations; it uses the detachment of a performance to describe the postwar alienation that so characterized intellectual thought throughout the decade. And there is always an unresolved ambivalence, here "the peachblow glory of the perishing sun."[29]

There is a sense, in these earlier poems, that Berryman, like so many poets, needs a larger format, and indeed in 1947 he had already completed most of the 115 poems that comprise the *Sonnets*, published much later, a thinly disguised autobiographical sequence about a violent and destructive love affair between a university poet and a Danish woman called "Lise." Set at Princeton, where Berryman also taught, the poem explores all the doubts and nightmares about the validity of the self's identity and its loves. He also began work on *Homage to Mistress Bradstreet,* a poem of fifty-seven stanzas which incorporates phrases, facts, and stylistic imitations from Bradstreet's writings and other sources interspersed with comments by her and the narrator. In this poem the leaps of thought which so characterize the later Berryman, and which are already beginning to emerge in the forties, are abundantly evident.

Robert Penn Warren presents a strange case; one of the original New Critics, he gradually broke with their practice. Jarrell wrote to Lowell that he thought it humorous to find people responding to Warren's poetry just after the publication of *Selected Poems, 1923–43.* For a long time after that Warren wrote only fiction and essays, but in a way, that became a schooling for the poems that he would begin to write with increasing success from the fifties to his death, becoming one of the major poets of the century. As Warren describes it, the poetry of the early forties served to break away from his earlier formal modes, and by the time of the colloquial long narrative in free verse, "The Ballad of Billie Potts," which Horace Gregory had condemned in the already stuffy *Sewanee Review,* Warren had abandoned that mode for a looser set of rhythms based on "rhythmical units" of phrase, syntax, and breath rather than meter.[30] The poems of the earlier period had begun with ideas or lines, but now, and especially after the fiction of the forties, narratives became the starting point. More than any of the other poets associated with the New Criticism—Tate, Winters, Ransom—Warren was always able to adapt, essentially because he thought and wrote poems inductively, taking his answers, and they are often very philosophic, as provisional and dramatic occasions, not dogma.

Another poet of the forties, with equal potential and with similar historical concerns, was Robert Lowell; Jarrell had ended his review of Robert Lowell's *Land of Unlikeliness* (1944) with the statement that "some of the best poems of the next years ought to he written by him," a sentence he repeated to show his prophecy come true in his review of *Lord Weary's Castle* (1947). Lowell's poems, Jarrell said, "understand the world as a sort of conflict of opposites."[31] This world included topics such as religion, nationalism, the military, sexuality, capitalism, fathers, propriety. According to Jarrell, the poems move either from the closed to the open or the open to the closed and are either liberating or confining to their persona. And the persona, the author himself, who is not finally able to be fully distinguished from the narrator, is probably the most important aspect of the poems, for Lowell's life, especially throughout the forties, was filled with unresolvable conflicts.

As Tate and Jarrell well knew, the early poems were promising though uneven; "The Protestant Dead in Boston" is clogged, more willed than inspired, though containing, as Lowell always did, the past and future in the present moment. Surviving, as so many poets were doing by now, by teaching whenever he could, Lowell produced the much heralded *Lord Weary's Castle.* Lowell's skill at producing unusual sound and rhythm effects—dazzling displays of assonance or alliteration, quick shifts in tone and perspective—are immediately evident in poems such as "The Quaker Graveyard in Nantucket," which confronts the problem of coming to terms with an elusive past that is yet needed to define the self.

In 1951 Lowell published *The Mills of the Kavanaughs,* which contained the long narrative-meditative title poem, in which a woman, with a Bible in her lap, faces the grave of her husband and reevaluates her life and love, not wanting to remain trapped by the past (the poem was begun in the forties). The volume also contains two other notable poems done in the forties—"Mother Marie Therese," a monologue in which the sister is able to balance past and present, religion and doubt; and "Falling Asleep over the Aeneid," in which a tension between realistic and mythologized versions of the self is also balanced, here by a fine, ironic self-consciousness on the part of the dreamer. The whole volume is important in Lowell's development because it shows, in the very period when he was losing control of his life, that he was able to use his poetry to regain control of it—eventually.

Gwendolyn Brooks was, like Lowell, much concerned with character studies, but unlike the early Lowell she was diverse in her prosody, composing in both free verse and traditional forms. For her, death was the central metaphor, experienced spiritually and physically, for individuals as well as for races. *A Street in Bronzeville* (1945) contains the sonnet sequence "Gay Chaps at the Bar," which in a dozen poems explores the utter lack of preparation the characters have to understand death, for they cannot read the signs around them. *Annie Allen* (1949), which won the Pulitzer Prize, is a more expansive and persistent sequence that traces an individual life in the basically narrative, understated manner of Brooks's poems of the forties. Here, too, death threatens from the beginning because it is so slickly packaged by the world outside the girl's control: "The dead wear capably their wry / Enameled emblems."[32] It would be almost two decades until Brooks completed her gradual break from the forms of the tradition, though here she had already begun to break in subject and language.

It might seem strange to end this section by referring to the work of Elizabeth Bishop, whose first volume, *North and South*, appeared in 1946 and who was then considered a descriptive, simply referential traditionalist. But in quiet poems usually as intellectually challenging as Stevens's and as much concerned with the speaker as Jarrell's, she was a leader in an unannounced move to displace the old poetry and theory. "The Map" sets up a counterplay between image and place, questioning in its short drama the epistemology of maps and finally of all reference systems. "Are they assigned, or can the countries pick their colors?" the speaker naïvely asks, reminding us of the drastic difference between symbol and thing.[33] "The Imaginary Iceberg" has a similar strategy, deliberately confusing an iceberg and a ship on a "shifting stage" where "the curtain / is light enough to rise on finest ropes / that airy twists of snow provide." And so she says: "This is a scene a sailor'd give his eyes for." Even a poem such as "The Fish," ending with Frostian suddenness, suggests not so much the physicality of the fish it so carefully describes as the elusiveness of it; we can know, but not hold for long, the physical world. "Little Exercise" proceeds by Stevensian hypothesis to qualify an imagined scene and its reality by each other.

One of her most striking poems, and here she fully undertakes a dismantling of simple referentiality, is "The Monument." Carefully described in great detail, the monument itself is impossible, or at least undecidable, uncertain. In fact, part of the monument is "wanting to be a monument." It denies perspective: "there is no 'far away' / And we are far away within the view." As with Stevens's supreme fictions, it is the process of thinking and feeling itself, but like Jarrell and Frost, and unlike Stevens, Bishop was able to find a colloquial speech to hold the heart and mind together in an intricate process of meditation. The dialectic of the poem, as in so many of her poems, is formed from the foibles of everyday characters whose reasoning, interpretations, and questions seem silly, but for which the poet has enough compassion, in the end, to praise.

Repeating What Was in the Script

If we are to truly understand what poets like Frost, Jarrell, and Bishop were working against, we must look at the poetry of the time that did not want to change the script—never mind the stage—but merely repeat it. This remains true for W. H. Auden, who had moved to America to find a new language and subject and who was moving into a third phase of his own development, a more religious but somewhat dramatic poetry influenced by Kierkegaard's sense of masks. Auden's language became more colloquial, especially from the 1940 "New Year's Letter" on, but his general structural mode remained the same. In a 1941 issue of *The Nation*, in the brief essay "A Note on Order," he argues that there is one set of laws for the cosmos and that individual laws of cultures must be manifestations—not variations—of this.[34] Of course, Auden had a far more copious vision in the practice of his own poetry than did poets such as Tate or Eliot. One of his best poems, not only of the decade but of his career, was "In Praise of Limestone," completed in 1948. Landscapes become symbols for ways of life, character traits—granite versus clay, for instance, the champions of stoic permanence against the molders of monuments. No description is going to account for the complex system the poem establishes, and Auden ironically recognizes the shortcoming of the system of equivalencies—that it can lead to static thinking: "Not to be left behind, not, please! to resemble / The beasts who repeat themselves, or a thing like water / Or stone whose conduct can be predicted."[35] It is the limestone landscape, more various in shape and style, that becomes the good here. We might say that such a landscape defines Auden's poetics, too. A master of numerous formats, Auden wrote several outstanding lyrics during the forties. "The Dark Years" is like Stevens's "Esthétique du Mal" in its search for a balance between good and evil that is meant to forestall pessimism. "At the Grave of Henry James" ends with a prayer to the "master of nuance and scruple," but it is a prayer notable for its compassion as well as Auden's characteristic self-irony.

Allen Tate was equally committed to preserving craft, though his vision was narrower than Auden's. R. P. Blackmur, in his analysis of Allen Tate's 1944 volume, *The Winter Sea*, says that Tate's use of a classical context that attempts to return to Virgil, Horace, and Dante, not simply adapt them to contemporary poetics, explains why Tate "can fight his lost cause as if there was money in it."[36] The lost cause is noble enough, the dignity of mankind, but the terms are hopelessly utopian, related to the Agrarian movement of the twenties and thirties which expressed a desire to return to a pastoral age which never existed in fact, only in idealized "histories." Earlier poems such as "Ode to the Confederate Dead" beautifully embodied such sympathies, while others such as "The Idiot," "The Wolves," and "The Mediterranean" embodied a "tension," as Tate used the word, between this desire and a dramatic-lyric account of what the world had degenerated into. The poems in *The Winter Sea*, however, lack the energy of the earlier poems.

T. S. Eliot's major work of the period—besides his poetic dramas— was a poem self-consciously structured to fit an idea, the *Four Quartets* (1935, 1940, 1941, 1942), about which only Schwartz expressed major reservations in public. Each quartet is divided into five parts, with varying sorts of rhythms in each: the first of each is usually a meditation on place, and the last four alternate between more lyrical and more didactic impulses. The aim, as he says in the last, *Little Gidding*, is "to apprehend / The point of intersection of the timeless / With time." Each poem blends religious, cultural, autobiographical, and historical events and references—the bombs in World War II, for instance—in a highly wrought symbolic frame. The four poems have a number of intricately woven symbols—the garden, the Incarnation, the Passion, the Cross, the elements (each of the four classical elements dominates a poem), a hospital (physical and spiritual), music, light, dance, a river—symbols that must be described as archetypal. By a musical progression, one symbol is introduced, then associated with others until the pattern is complete in a circular act of self-reflection. In lines like the following, the poem sounds a bit like Stevens, or even Frost's "Directive":

> We shall not cease from exploration
> And the end of all our exploring
> Will be to arrive where we started
> And know the place for the first time.[37]

But the aim is not a process of exploration; it is the end, for Eliot is our most teleological poet. To arrive at the end is to achieve a redemptive act, or rather, to report about the end is to reveal a sacred and symbolic world.

Metaphysicians in the Dark

A number of poets in the forties were concerned with developing a metaphysical context that would initiate change: their concerns with character, for instance, were more with types; their concern with language varied, from more traditional to more experimental, but always dealt with the ways language could hold ideas. In most of them some considerable traces of symbolic thinking remained, but they were far more aware of the arbitrariness of symbols—especially in a philosophical sense—than the New Critics were, for instance. Out of this group comes some of our strongest poets: Roethke, Pound, Rexroth, Kunitz, and Eberhart among them.

In a letter to William Carlos Williams in November 1942, two years after their first meeting, Theodore Roethke wrote, "You are my toughest mentor," foreshadowing perhaps the way Roethke's poems would increasingly be influenced by Williams, especially through his use of colloquial speech.[38] Roethke's first book, *Open House* (1941), shows the influence of Yeats, especially in its rhythms, an influence that would stay with Roethke for his whole life. In "Open House" he talks about a "language strict and pure," for instance.[39] Another poem, "Death Piece," uses very Dickinsonian rhythms—and it is primarily with rhythms, as his notebooks continually show, that he thinks. In "Epidermal Macabre," a

poem written in tetrameter that sounds a bit like accentual three-beat
lines, there is a hard, driving rhythm that suggests the need for expansion
that will lead to the longer poems and sequences.

It is precisely such a Williams-like direction that Roethke takes in his
second book, *The Lost Son and Other Poems* (1948). "I am nothing but
what I remember" and "I do not wish a sense of the past; only a sense of
the continuous," he had said in notebook entries from that time, and this
book enacts those statements.[40] *The Lost Son* is divided into four parts,
with poems of generally increasing length that outline the development
of a life from birth and infantile consciousness, through adolescence,
a discovery of self-consciousness, and finally into a retrospective and
projective adult vision. In the final section, the book suddenly opens up
with a sequence of four longish poems, including the title poem, each in
several sections of free verse that shows the range and associative struc-
ture of Whitman and the control of phrase and rhythm of Yeats. Corres-
ponding to that dichotomy, it is here, perhaps, that Roethke's true
strength as a dramatist of the mind, of the play between consciousness
and unconsciousness, emerges. "The Lost Son," for instance, confronts
the self's mortality, sinking into the abyss of the self ("I'm falling through
a dark swirl," he says towards the end). "The Long Alley" compares the
self to a plant in order to extricate for analysis the vegetative soul,
as Aristotle would call it. What is learned here is the self's ability to
regenerate—like a plant. "A Field of Light" is as visionary and spiritual
as the title sounds, and here the self takes consolation:

> To know that light falls and fills, often without our knowing,
> As an opaque vase fills to the brim from a quick pouring,
> Fills and trembles at the edge yet does not flow over,
> Still holding and feeding the stem of the contained flower.[41]

It is important in understanding Roethke's vision to realize that these
lines, from the last part of the poem, are gained by consciously returning
to the greenhouse world in the previous part: as with Blake, another
major influence, the way to the spiritual is always through—and with—
the physical. No degree of quotation, really, can give an adequate account
of the way Roethke can seem to vary rhythms spontaneously from one
section to another, from one part of a poem to another, sometimes from
line to line or phrase to phrase, but still within the copious and very
controlled overall rhythm of the book—and do all this while thinking
through some very complex psychological and philosophical problems.

It might be suggested that Roethke, more than anyone else of the age, found a new stage and played a whole range of dramas upon it.

Richard Eberhart, like John Berryman, was deeply influenced by the death of a parent, in this case the death of his mother from cancer when the poet was still an infant. In some ways this also may have contributed to his resistance to simple paraphrase in poems that seem on the surface easily paraphrasable, for, as he says in a recent poem, he wants to write a "meaningless poem" because "meaning ends in suffering." For Eberhart, poetry is a way of overcoming suffering and mortality and is based upon spiritual or metaphysical inspiration (see "Moment of Vision" in *Burr Oaks*, 1947). The actual poem, then, is a linguistic structure that puts things down, deductively, on paper. For him, the main themes are the impenetrable mystery of reality—which he can nonetheless appraise sometimes in a dogmatic manner—and the constant presence of death. These come together, of course, in an early poem like "The Groundhog." But they persist in poems like "A Meditation," from *Song and Idea* (1942), which is spoken in colloquial blank verse by a skull someone has picked up and which projects beyond human and mortal boundaries in a prophetic manner. A dualist and relativist, as he repeatedly calls himself, he likes to engage in poems that counterpoint two views. It is perhaps this dualistic sense of the world and the dialectic and saving power of poetry that Eberhart communicated to or confirmed in his young student at St. Mark's school, Robert Lowell.

Stanley Kunitz was influenced early on by Blake, Wordsworth, Coleridge, and Hopkins. For him, everything is a unity. "Open the Gates," from his *Passport to War* (1944), ends, "I stand on the terrible thresholds, and I see / The end and the beginning in each other's arms." Kunitz is a poet of terrible thresholds but terrible in the sense of the awe-inspiring and the terrifying—in other words, the sublime, as Samuel Johnson described it. At the threshold he witnesses the unity and the warring of elements. For him, the major problem was to avoid an easy language and form: "Language itself is a kind of resistance to the pure flow of self. The solution is to become one's language." That is, the poet must enter the rhythms, must grow, as Coleridge said, organically with the poem, and between poems. That is why, perhaps, Kunitz moved from pentameters in the twenties to tetrameters in the thirties and forties, and then in the forties started to rough up the meters before moving to three-beat lines and more pronounced accentual lines. He remarked in a *Paris*

Review interview in 1978 that pentameters tended to make his ideas fall into Renaissance modes of thinking.[42]

Passport to War itself is a dark book: literally, for there are many shadow and stain images, and psychologically, for it was, as he has often remarked, a time of deep trouble for him, and he almost gave up after four years of Medical Corps humiliation emptying bedpans, suffering pneumonia and scarlet fever, and of course, witnessing the effects of war. "Reflection by a Mailbox" describes a man waiting for an induction notice, trying not to make a "Pavlovian" response for himself and the culture; Kunitz's sense of unity also stems from a Jungian notion of a psychic community. This probably also accounts for the tremendous depression analyzed in "The Guilty Man": "when I kneeled, the dark kneeled down with me." And the macabre "The Fitting of the Mask" is a dreamlike search that concludes by putting on the mask of "the Self I hunted and knifed in dreams!" One of the most powerful is "Father and Son," in which the father implies any authority from which answers can be had; after a Blakean quest, the narrator finally gets the fleeing father to turn, asks him an essential question about the meaning of the world's horrors, about their own relationship, his own guilt "whirling between two wars," only to receive this response: "Among the turtles and the lilies he turned to me / The white ignorant hollow of his face."[43] After this volume, the same understanding, experimentation, and persistence, the very human response to the world, all allow Kunitz to solve some of these issues, though the quest for discovery about newer issues always remains unfinished. It is probably this aspect, besides his technical mastery, that made him such an influence on Roethke and James Wright.

Far more loose in her structures was Muriel Rukeyser, whose poems will be remembered for their Whitmanesque energy and inclusiveness. In fact, it is this very quality which William Carlos Williams saw in Pound and Rukeyser in his 1939 review in *The Nation* of her *US1*. One of her most characteristic poems is "Ajanta," from *Beast in View* (1944), a sort of Shelleyan quest, an "Alastor." For her, the "stage" upon which contemporary poetry and thought must be worked out is a symbolic cave—essentially the mind:

Space to the mind, the painted cave of dream.
This is not a womb, nothing but good emerges:
This is a stage, neither unreal nor real,
Where the walls are the world, the rocks and palaces
Stand on a borderland of blossoming ground.[44]

To enter the world is to enter the self's inner circles, to experience, as Whitman could, all the unpleasantries, the bestiality of mankind, the grossness of all things, but to make of them this "blossoming ground." Rukeyser's was precisely the sort of imaginative energy the world needed at this time. She ends the volume with a Blakean blending of qualities, a hope that freedom can be defined as a tolerance of "all the antagonists in the dance."[45] Like Stevens, she would construct a new stage, but it would be *entirely* an affair of the heart, though not, as Schwartz complained, to the discredit of intelligence. It would be a stage/cave whose language, in her usually long, copious lines, would focus on sequences of "moments" (one of her most common, and Wordsworthian, words); "I am haunted by interrupted acts," she says later in "Ajanta," and her many sequences—one set of elegies extends over two books—suggest the sort of space she needs, always expanding the cave.

Kenneth Rexroth's metaphysics were more formal than Rukeyser's, but he had a similar focus on instants of love. In many ways Rexroth is a good barometer for what happened to American poetry from the twenties to the sixties. His first poems, in the twenties, were Imagistic, then became more dissociated and "objective" in the thirties; in the forties he worked out a mode that emphasized philosophy while at the same time giving equal attention to the physical world. The poems became looser, more colloquial, and more direct. The process had become, as he described it in "Climbing Milestone Mountain, August 22, 1937," a political poem about Sacco and Vanzetti, very inductive: "A poem had been gathering in my mind, / Details of significance and rhythm, / The way poems do, but still lacking a focus."[46] "The Phoenix and the Tortoise," which he composed between 1940 and 1944 and which became the title poem of his 1944 volume, constitutes his answer to Eliot's *Four Quartets*, written at approximately the same time. Rexroth's poem alternates, as most of his poems do, philosophical and descriptive passages, and has as its subject "what survives and what perishes, / And how, of the fall of history / And waste of fact." The aim, then, is to find the "prime reality," and the poem reaches its climax not by a philosophical statement but by a dramatic event:

> My wife has been swimming in the breakers,
> She comes up the beach to meet me, nude,
> Sparkling with water, sighing high and clear
> Against the surf. The sun crosses
> The hills and fills her hair, as it lights

The moon and glorifies the sea
And deep in the empty mountains melts
The snow of Winter and the glaciers
Of ten thousand thousand years.[47]

Most of the central images and ideas of the poem appear here—sun and moon, light, speech, time and history—all melted, as the glaciers do, in a coherent and dramatic whole in ordinary but magical descriptive language.

Two poets often associated with Rexroth need mention. Kenneth Fearing wrote very long, loose lines, though often with internal rhyme, that were compatible with his desire to include all kinds of experience. "Higher Mathematics" is his version of Auden's "Unknown Citizen," and he has several poems on various types of characters—a doctor, a journalist. "Sherlock Spends a Day in the Country" (*Stranger at Coney Island*, 1948) is addressed to Dr. Watson and sees "signs" of an amazing number of types of societies, examining them to see what "conspiracies" and "conclusions" they reached, but "being careful to notice, as we go and return, the character and number of our own tracks in the snow."[48]

The other poet, Robinson Jeffers, presents special problems and illustrates, perhaps, the danger of the metaphysical mode: in typecasting characters, in trying to go beyond them, the poet may sometimes leave them behind, or, in Jeffers's case, turn against them. He ends "Their Beauty Has More Meaning," a description of a moonlit night at the oceanside, with his own sort of consolation—that the scene will last longer than humanity and that its "beauty has more meaning / Than the whole human race and the race of birds."[49] His "Original Sin" traces the origin of man's inherent evil to a Stone Age killing of a mammoth, where "happy hunters / Roasted their living meat slowly to death." It is perhaps his fidelity to the world of rocks and mountains that suggests a sense of form and language to him; his forms are loose, encompassing, nontraditional; in fact, they are perhaps meant to counter the tradition of poetry, and his language is direct and descriptive. Obviously, Jeffers's attention to "things" has none of the humanity that, say, Kenneth Rexroth shows.

Politically, the man who was accused of insensitivity, of course, was Ezra Pound. Pound had been a leader—from the early years of the century—in the fight against high culture and might be considered the most influential not so much for what he did, as for what he tried to do and for what he suggested could be done. His *Cantos LII–LXXI*, the John Adams cantos, had been published in 1940, showing his increasing disenchantment with the whole Western economic system. For Pound, most problems could be traced to this, as he says in his famous usury canto. In the forties, his broadcasts for Mussolini from Rome led to his humiliation in an American prison camp at Pisa. What was so important to Pound about the *Pisan Cantos* (1948), which won the Bollingen Prize, was their increased attention to detail—something he had not done since his early Imagist poems and the *Cathay* poems—but it is the nonhuman world of nature that he draws so close to. These *Pisan Cantos* are an attempt to come to grips with himself; as he says in the most pastoral of these poems,

> nothing matters but the quality
> of the affection—
> in the end—that has carved the trace in the mind.[50]

On the whole, though, they remain, as Tate observed even in praising them, incomprehensible—mixes of Chinese, several other languages, bits and pieces of brilliant language, all strung together to try to get at a universal experience of the times.

Very few things become symbolic in Pound's mode of thought; rather, they become Other, alien, absent—things the *Cantos* try to embrace. For Pound, any pieces and timbers of an ideal world must already exist out there if only we can construct the stage a different way. The problem was that it had become too big for one poet to see.

When such attempts to structure the world fail, the resort is to melancholy, a sense that the self is being persecuted. The *Cantos* are a history of one man's mind as it makes its own history of the world, reinventing language and interpreting facts as it needs them. It relies on three major principles: the "complex" (a vortex of the image and its myriad associations), the "cut" (a sense of the mind's rhythmic linking and undercutting), and the "ideogram" (the visual quality and texture of the verse). Probably the closest thing to a precedent for Pound's achievement here is Ovid's *Metamorposis:* for both, the past is here, now, around us, ready to be reshaped. This leads to the key to Pound's strength and weakness: the deconstruction of an imperious sense of history, mythology, and prosody, but at the expense of an almost disembodied voice and the supplementing of the supposed absence of civilization with a very singular vision that pretends to stand as a universal one.

For several decades H. D. had been searching for a metaphysical frame to fit her vision, moving gradually from the brief imagistic poems that were really, on closer examination, short mythic lyrics to the trilogy of long poems that she completed in the early forties. The first of these long poems, *The Walls Do Not Fall,* published in 1944 but completed in 1942, was a plea for peace through Freud's philosophy of breaking with the totalitarian father (Hitler, Mussolini, Stalin). It tries to ask the question, after the bombing of London which she lived through, "Why are we saved?" Filled with images of shells, walls, barriers of all sort (physical, cultural, spiritual), the answer comes when the spirit finally soars, sees an open sky.

The second poem, *Tribute to the Angels* (1945), is more esoteric, inspired by the Book of Revelation, and has seven angels who stand for seven states of being and also can be linked biographically with several characters in her rather full life. H. D. had seen the Nazis destroy the Christian symbolic base of Western culture, and she was determined to use her mythic impulses to construct a new one—a gesture similar to Pound's, who was an early influence she broke with in the thirties over fascism. The problem of the poem is partly to "invent" a "name" and thus create a reality to replace the ruins that were left after the first poem. The solution, though, is not just to name new symbols but to experience them as things.

> I do not want
> to talk about it,
> I want to minimize thought,
> concentrate on it
> till I shrink,
> dematerialize
> and am drawn into it.[51]

The attitude here recalls Jeffers and Eliot, even Williams, but the aim is not, as in Jeffers, a denial of the human, but rather an infusion of it with renewed, if sometimes vague, spirituality. *The Flowering of the Rod* (1944), the third poem, shows similar impulses but is more celebratory, using the confluence of the Virgin Mary and Mary Magdalene to suggest the reuniting of spiritual and physical. Written, as are all of these poems, in free-verse couplets, it shows H. D.'s method, which is not to focus on individuals but to make archetypes of them—almost, one is tempted to to say, case histories relying on a variety of mythic sources.[52]

A Wiry String, a Sudden Rightness

There were a number of poets in the forties who were in open revolt against the establishment or who were working subtly within it to change its stage; some of these, like Richard Wilbur and Robert Creeley, were new; others, like Cummings, were older. Kenneth Patchen championed a number of political causes, identifying the established system with traditional form, in poems often lacking in poetic power; but he also wrote a number of Shelleyan and Keatsian narratives of considerable range and some superb love poems, especially "Anna Karenina and the Lovesick River." In the forties, though, these poets never formalized a poetic, and several, such as Charles Olson, went off in unexpected directions. In Olson's case, it was a move from a lyric impulse with, say the Kingfisher poems of the forties, to the epic impulse of *The Maximus Poems*, begun in the fifties. It is easy, in retrospect, to categorize poets under various headings, as this essay does—and it is always to some extent a lie. Certainly it misrepresents the tenor of the times—a time of uncertainty in global politics and art, a time when no one really knew what the best poetry was, though many, as we have seen, claimed to write it, with varying degrees of imperiousness or humility.

In a letter to Robert Lowell in November 1947, Randall Jarrell wrote of Karl Shapiro: "I wonder if he's ever going to grow up any. And stop depending on Auden."[53] A more general problem, one senses from reading Jarrell, is that he objected to Shapiro's negative outlook; Shapiro, after all, was throughout his life in revolt against the "hi-cult" represented by Eliot, Yeats, Pound, Joyce, Lowell, and the academics, but he never quite found a substitute.

His strength, as seen in "mock" poems such as "Buick," from his first book, *Person, Place and Thing* (1940), is to create tough-minded and tough-worded poems that undercut established ideas of symbolic beauty. Sometimes it seems as if Shapiro had memorized the idea that Warren developed in his essay on Coleridge—the notion of "impure," roughed-up verse as being more dramatically interesting. Another stance of the book is a stoicism against a seemingly meaningless world, as evidenced in the much-anthologized "Auto Wreck." His next volume, *V Letter*, which won the Pulitzer Prize for 1945, also focuses on both the body as a "sign" of "senselessness and mud" ("The Leg") and "the soul's center where substance cannot dwell / And life flowers like music from a bell" ("The Interlude").[54] The title poem itself is a stoical letter from a young combatant to his lover, convincing her that their love and love in general will survive whatever befalls them.

With the publication of *Trial of a Poet* (1947), however, Shapiro had momentarily relaxed the thought and language that served him well. "The Southerner," for example, is an easy parody. But "The Dirty Word,"

a prose poem—he was to do several other very successful ones later on—
is a compelling allegorical, almost surreal, narrative; here Shapiro seems
to have made use of the freedom of the form to begin a new direction
with more colloquial poems. It is important to remember that Shapiro
was always very conscious of what he was doing, as his self-conscious and
Popean *Essay on Rime* (1945)—which pleased Williams—and his editing
stints at *Poetry* and *Prairie Schooner* attest.

One of the most well known poets of the century is E. E. Cummings,
whose experiments with language were legion. With the old unities
disintegrating he tended as a romantic idealist to want to cut himself off
from the world. But his language does not discover great things; rather,
it goes to local effects, with larger thematic issues left unattended except
on a very local level. His language is inadequate to deal with the big
issues; when he moves to larger issues it is through generalizations—
"anyone lived in a pretty how town," for example—as if there were no
way for the local and general to blend.[55] His approach is just the opposite
of that of a poet such as Rukeyser, for whom all is symbolically general.
In "what if a much of a which of a wind," he notes that "the single secret
will still be man" after any apocalyptic vision. But the problem of a
potential "nothing's only our hugest home" (in *1 × 1*, 1944) always lurks
in his work. Another poem, "love is more thicker than forget," uses a
simple strategy of relatively predictable comparisons.

Though far less experimental than Cummings, Robert Creeley is one
of the very few true experimenters in colloquial language that we have
had. Creeley's first published poem, by his own account in the preface
to his *Collected Poems*, is "Return." Following the example of Williams,
Zukofsky, and later Olson, whom he was introduced to by Williams,
Creeley's interest from the start has been in developing a music from
common speech, from an emphasis on the literal and direct, on the
"objective." The aim is to subvert literal and usual sense not by reworking
language from the outside, but by using line breaks and playful associa-
tions to see what subversions are inherent in words and syntax them-
selves. The early poems, and they are extant from 1945 on, often use
repetition of strategically important words lineated differently to suggest
a multiple music and meaning where only one was previously suspected.
Creeley's project, in sum, is one of disruptions, a way of dramatizing the
musical patterns of language he uncovers *within* language, a way of
building a new stage under the old one before the old one is fully torn

down. At this point in his career, the elaborate later theoretics of the issues had not yet emerged for him, but the practice had certainly begun.

Of all the poets in this group, perhaps the one who knew most what he was about during the forties was Richard Wilbur, and he will serve as a way to close off the decade. He balances a concern with objects with a desire for transcendence, quietly colloquial language with formal meter, vision with self-irony, symbol (as especially in the poems about art) with playful parody, the old script and some new parts for it. About Wilbur's *Ceremony and Other Poems* (1950), Randall Jarrell noted that the language "has a slight incongruity or 'offness' " that helps to rough up the otherwise clear, placid surfaces of the poems. He would have preferred something not quite so polished, but he is certainly perceptive in his description of a delicate effect. And we might add, as Wilbur has acknowledged in an interview, that the poems often jar by a sense of surprise at their endings. For example, "A Glance from the Bridge," after describing Boston and the Charles River, suddenly ends with a last glance at the river: "through the town the freshening water swirls / As if an ancient whore undid her gown / And showed a body almost like a girl's." And "Pity" describes a man's returning to a house or apartment to free a canary:

And he went back and climbed the stairs again,
Stepping across her body, freed the bird,
Which left its cage and out the window whirred
As a bad thought out of a cracked brain.

The focus on the bird and not the body emphasizes the horror, and our reaction is further underscored by the monosyllabic words in the metronome of the last line. There is only what can be described as a "sudden rightness"—to borrow Stevens's phrase—in this. And nearly all Wilbur's effects are this subtle—even the analysis of the pervasiveness of death in "Still, Citizen Sparrow." For Wilbur, "what's lightly hid is deepest understood."[56]

Wilbur's developing philosophy in the forties, and it parallels the development of so many poets of the decade, can be seen by comparing two poems. The first, "Objects," from *The Beautiful Changes and Other Poems* (1947), begins with map references, includes references to myth, and then returns by the middle of the poem to the physical world, but a world "where in every tangible tree / I see afloat among the leaves, all calm and curled, / The Cheshire smile which sets me fearfully free."[57] It is important to note that it is freedom, not adherence to abstract dogma, that is gained here. The other poem, "'A World Without Objects Is a Sensible Emptiness,' " plays with the quote—from the mystical Renaissance poet Thomas Traherne—to suggest the link between the two worlds of spirit and object. There is a slight shift between the poems toward the spiritual—a shift that will be later reversed—but in any development the poet stays towards the center.

The title poem, "The Beautiful Changes," plays on both the idea that beauty falters and that all change is itself beauty. It is in fact the lack of change, of progress, really—in worldviews and in poetry—that distresses him; surprise, in this context, takes on an almost definitive poetic and philosophic meaning. "The Eyes of an SS Officer" ends, "I ask my make-shift God of this / My opulent bric-a-brac earth to damn his eyes." For Wilbur, the Edgar Allan Poe scholar, the tension of poetry is represented by his own figure from his essay "The Genie in the Bottle": the tight form releases the moment of surprising discovery, and poetic vision is a way of "possessing" whatever world is released.[58]

In the forties the world each of the poets *possessed*—and that is as good a word as any for it—was a world more various than much of the criticism of the New Critics would have liked to see. But this, after all, was not an age of criticism but an age of new beginnings in poetry, the beginnings of a discovery of an American language and American themes which we are still working out in the ongoing drama to change the script, the actors, the theater itself. What the New Critics did not realize was that poetry was bigger than any theory—unless, as Stevens implied, one considered that the poem itself exemplified theory.

Notes

1. Stevens, *Selected Letters*, ed. Holly Stevens (New York: Knopf, 1977), 589.

2. Stevens, *The Palm at the End of the Mind*, ed. Holly Stevens (New York: Knopf, 1971), 331, 174–75.

3. Schwartz, *Selected Essays*, ed. Donald Dike and David Zucker (Chicago: University of Chicago Press, 1975), 163.

4. Donald Davie, *Ezra Pound: The Poet as Sculptor* (New York: Oxford University Press, 1974), 143.

5. David Wagoner, ed., *The Notebooks of Theodore Roethke* (Garden City, N.Y.: Doubleday, Anchor, 1964), 171.

6. H. D., *Collected Poems, 1912–1944*, ed. Louis Martz (New York: New Directions, 1983), 571.

7. Schwartz, *Selected Essays*, 10.

8. Stevens, *Letters*, 367, 601; Stevens, *Palm*, 187.

9. Stevens, *Palm*, 207–33.

10. Ibid., 262.

11. Mary Jarrell, ed., *Randall Jarrell's Letters* (Boston: Houghton Mifflin, 1985), 153; Schwartz, *Essays*, 312–31.

12. Schwartz, *Letters of Delmore Schwartz*, ed. Robert Phillips (Princeton: Ontario Review Press, 1984), 112; Jarrell, *Letters*, 132.

13. Tate, *Essays of Four Decades* (New York: Morrow, 1970), 196.

14. Ibid., 271, 230.

15. Williams, *Selected Essays of William Carlos Williams* (New York: New Directions, 1969), 281–85.

16. Williams, *I Wanted to Write a Poem* (New York: New Directions, 1967), 73.

17. Williams, *The Autobiography of William Carlos Williams* (New York: New Directions, 1967), 289.

18. Schwartz, *Letters*, 101.

19. James Atlas, *Delmore Schwartz: The Life of an American Poet* (New York: Harcourt, 1985), 181.

20. Jarrell, *Poetry and the Age* (New York: Random, Vintage, 1953), 30.

21. Ibid., 47.

22. *The Poetry of Robert Frost*, ed. E. C. Lathem (New York: Holt, 1969), 338.

23. Ibid., 377.

24. Jarrell, *Poetry and the Age*, 29.

25. Jarrell, *The Complete Poems* (New York: Farrar, Straus and Giroux, 1969), 113.

26. Ibid., 66.

27. Ibid., 57.

28. Jarrell, *Poetry and the Age*, 81.

29. Berryman, *Homage to Mistress Bradstreet and Other Poems* (New York: Noonday, 1968), 104.

30. Richard Jackson, *Acts of Mind* (Tuscaloosa: University of Alabama Press, 1983), 58.

31. Jarrell, *Poetry and the Age*, 198–99, 188.

32. Brooks, *Selected Poems* (New York: Harper, 1963), 26.

33. Bishop, *The Complete Poems, 1927–79* (New York: Farrar, Straus and Giroux, 1983), 4.

34. Auden, "A Note on Order," *The Nation* 152, no. 5 (Feb. 1941): 131–33.

35. Auden, *Collected Poems*, ed. Edward Mendelson (New York: Random, 1976), 414–15.

36. R. P. Blackmur, *Form and Value in Modern Poetry* (Garden City, N.Y.: Doubleday, Anchor, 1957), 329.

37. Eliot, *Collected Poems, 1909–1962* (New York: Harcourt, 1970), 198, 208.

38. Roethke, *Selected Letters* (Seattle: University of Washington Press, 1968), 101.

39. Roethke, *Selected Poems* (Garden City, N.Y.: Doubleday, 1966), 3.

130   Richard Jackson

40. David Wagoner, ed., *Straw for the Fire: From the Notebooks of Theodore Roethke, 1943–1963* (Garden City, N.Y.: Doubleday, 1974), 149, 166.

41. Roethke, *Selected Poems,* 67.

42. Kunitz, *The Poems of Stanley Kunitz, 1928–1978* (Boston: Atlantic–Little, Brown, 1978), 184; *Next to Last Things: New Poems and Essays* (Boston: Atlantic-Little, Brown, 1985), 95, 89.

43. Kunitz, *Poems of Stanley Kunitz,* 180, 182, 158.

44. Rukeyser, *The Collected Poems* (New York: Hill and Wang, 1978), 208.

45. Ibid., 260.

46. Rexroth, *The Collected Shorter Poems* (New York: New Directions, 1966), 64.

47. Rexroth, *The Collected Longer Poems* (New York: New Directions, 1968), 64, 91.

48. Fearing, *Stranger at Coney Island and Other Poems* (New York: Harcourt, 1948), 23.

49. Jeffers, *Selected Poems* (New York: Random, Vintage, 1963), 77.

50. Pound, *The Cantos* (New York: New Directions, 1970), 457.

51. H. D., *Collected Poems,* 555.

52. Ibid., 477.

53. Jarrell, *Letters,* 185.

54. Shapiro, *Collected Poems, 1940–1978* (New York: Random, 1978), 185.

55. Cummings, *Complete Poems 1913–1962* (New York: Harcourt, 1972), 515.

56. Wilbur, *The Poems of Richard Wilbur* (New York: Harcourt, Harvest, 1963), 144, 133, 167.

57. Ibid., 196.

58. Ibid., 182–83; Jackson, "Answering the Dark," in *Acts of Mind,* 141.

6

The "Forbidden Planet" of Character: The Revolutions of the 1950s

MARK DOTY

"Around the throne of God, where all the angels read perfectly, there are no critics—there is no need for them," Randall Jarrell declared in his essay "The Age of Criticism." "Critics exist simply to help us with works of art—isn't that true?"[1] Jarrell's question to the reader could only have become necessary in an era dominated by a critical mentality of another sort. By the beginning of the fifties, the stance of the once-radical New Criticism had become for its practitioners not a field of exploration but a kind of catechism, a set of principles to be rigidly enacted. The heirs of Pound had, in the space of thirty years, translated his cry of "Make it new" into "Make it explicable." As Max Baym summarized their position, "The New Critics recognized only structural tensions and their resolution within the literary work itself. The elements to be dealt with were diction, rhythm, metaphor . . . and texture. Life was, at best, a tangential consideration."[2] Examination and evaluation—not emotional or intellectual participation in the drama the poet has made by ordering experience in language—seemed the ends of academic poetry in the early fifties. John Crowe Ransom had spoken from an extreme of the New Critical perspective in 1941 when he asserted that "emotions themselves are fictions, and critical theory could not with a straight face have recourse to them."[3] If such a critical viewpoint came to dominate the composition of poems themselves, then it is not surprising that such a poetics should inevitably become moribund.

One can imagine the dilemma of a young poet seeking to craft a personal aesthetic in the face of such a codified, well-organized "club." "What confronted us in 1950," Robert Creeley has written, "was a closed system indeed, poems patterned upon exterior and traditionally accepted

131

models."[4] The grounds were set for a battle between the will toward authenticity, the need to speak from experience, and the will toward acceptance, the need to find a place within the tradition—a tradition which had, following Eliot's example, codified itself. The roles of poet and critic had become almost synonymous, one discipline mirroring the other, the work of the singer becoming not only to sing but to explicate his own songs. Even Allen Tate wrote that "our critics . . . have been perfecting an apparatus for 'explicating' poems (not a bad thing to do), innocent of the permanently larger ends of criticism." Though he would assert that the ground of modern poetry had been "trampled down to a flinty hardness" by critical surveying, his parenthetical assertion is revealing.[5] The desirability of an "apparatus" suggests that in the orderliness and formality of the New Critical approach there is something of the fifties' faith in science, in the power of scientific rationalism to bring order to the otherwise chaotic. Divorced from the daily, contained in its passions, rife with classical allusion, poetry had become redolent of the academy and the laboratory, not of the streets.

James E. B. Breslin has observed that "the fifties' domestication of modernism . . . ironically recreated the kind of literary predicament that had prompted modernity in the first place and so legitimized a new opening, a new revolt."[6] The motion of the fifties would be a decade's progress of rebellion, breaking the dominance of the formal mold with its mild ironies and modulated passions, and moving toward modes of including a greater variety of emotional and intellectual experience. This range of content suppressed by the formal constraints of the academics would seek its way upward, and the decade would see a multiplicity of innovations. Some writers linked to the New Critical tradition, notably Jarrell and Robert Penn Warren, would extend its boundaries through greater emotional depth and an emphasis on character. The work of the Beats would follow in the lineage of Whitman, their cultural pluralism and broad principles of inclusion unified by the incantatory line. The Black Mountain school would recast the poem, under the spiritual paternity of Pound and Williams, into an enactment of the process of perception. The New York school would playfully appropriate the compositional techniques of Abstract Expressionism, the icons and artifacts of pop culture, and a verbal wit that pushed at the limits of referentiality. Other poets, perhaps the group that would have the most impact on the developing American poetics of the next decade, would push at the limits of self-disclosure, reversing the New Critical emphasis on exclusion of the life of the poet; the "Confessionals" made direct use of the materials of experience, standing in exact opposition to the New Critical divorce of the poet and the poem.

Any division into firmly defined "schools" is finally a historian's artifice; the movements of the fifties overlapped and cross-fertilized one another to the point that any boundaries tend to blur and finally disappear. Where does one place, say, the later poems of Kenneth Patchen, or the poems of Elizabeth Bishop, passionate in their precision yet reticent in their passions? Both Wallace Stevens and William Carlos Williams were independently constructing their late, long poems, works which stand for both as their most challenging and, in some ways, most individual achievements; Marianne Moore likewise continued her alchemical, idiosyncratic work outside the confines of any "school." But the admittedly broad categories commonly used to identify the poetic currents of the fifties help to establish loci of change, points of origin for a dawning transformation. The canons which had ruled the art, translating Modernist theory into a code of correctness, would be challenged from various directions as the work of forging a new poetics began.

The American Way

That a sort of literary pluralism, a variety of reactions against the standard of academic verse, should characterize the fifties seems appropriate in light of the profound shifts in American culture that the decade held. The postwar boom produced a new economic security and with it technical innovation; both seemed to contribute to a new complacency, an American insularity. The generation who had participated in World War II could not easily return to the more coherent communities of the prewar years; economic expansion and the resultant drive for bigger, better, and newer would lead to the creation of the suburbs and to an increasingly transient nation, settling and resettling in areas around the country which grew more and more to resemble one another. There almost seemed to be a cultural imperative, after the chaos of the war and the resultant economic boom, to settle down, to create coherence and uniformity. No wonder, then, given the drive toward sameness, that Breslin can observe that "American poetry in the middle fifties resembled a peaceful public park on a pleasant summer Sunday afternoon."[7]

No force had greater impact in the growing homogeneity of American culture than one of the many technological innovations of the decade—

television. Never before had a culture spent its evenings collectively viewing images of itself. What began as novel entertainment became, by the end of the decade, the salient fixture of the American home, a small screen which gave the culture back to itself in a homogenizing and idealizing electronic mirror. Just as the cinema had affected the arts earlier in the century, so this far more inclusive and ever-present medium would make its impact with its immediacy, its rapid shifts in tone and image, and its assumption of intimacy between viewer and image. If the form of video would become a pervasive influence, then its content would be something to be reacted against: the glowing blue-and-gray screen seemed to engender a surety that all the world was the same, that lives were lived within the orderly realm of the hierarchical family. The neatly trimmed suburbs of the Cleavers and the Reeds became a new sort of American mythology, a depiction of our world as white, Protestant, and, above all, unquestioning. "These are the tranquilized fifties," Robert Lowell noted in "Memories of West Street and Lepke."[8] It was a complacency whose underside was terror, a horror of anything "other." The "red scare" would provide a metaphor for everything outside the sleep of the suburbs; the fear of communism created a necessary polarity which would reach its apotheosis in the absurdity of the McCarthy trials and the executions of Julius and Ethel Rosenberg. In his novel *The Public Burning*, Robert Coover employs as metaphor those cardboard glasses used for viewing films in the never-too-successful cinematic process of 3-D; a viewer stumbles out of a theater onto the New York streets, still wearing the red-and-blue plastic lenses, and sees through them the world split apart, divided into *them* and *us*—the forces of justice, sameness, and the domestic virtues on one side, the forces of anarchy, made flesh in the form of blacks, Jews, and homosexuals (all of them Communists or dupes), on the other. It is an irreconcilable polarity, and its consequences are damage—the overt oppression of those who represent the *other* and the more subtle oppression of those who belong to the dominant culture and are limited and defined by it. Just as the political climate reflected our doubts about the vaunted correctness of the American way, our other repressions surfaced elsewhere: thwarted sexual energy in the anarchic, urgent rhythms of rock and roll, our barely buried anxiety over the dangers of technological innovation in the lurid horror films of Hollywood. If the coy dilemmas of television's suburban families were our self-aggrandizing daydreams, then the movies chronicled our nightmares. Innumerable beasts were made horrific by the effects of radiation or scientific error. The Freudian *Forbidden Planet* portrayed what we repress as our greatest danger: voyagers in an unknown territory in outer space encounter "beasts from the id" which are projections of their own psyches. *Invasion of the Body Snatchers* portrayed the all-too-familiar transformation of human individuals into zombies without wills or ideals, shuffling servants of a force whose domination replaced the external control of totalitarianism with a profound limitation of individual possibilities. "The Republic summons Ike," Lowell concluded in his "Inauguration Day: January 1953," "the mausoleum in her heart."[9]

"Today many poets are driven to inventing private languages, or very narrow ones, because public speech has become heavily tainted with mass feeling," huffed Allen Tate,[10] and perhaps the ground-breaking volumes of poems of the fifties owe their existence to this very quality of being driven, the poets' imperative to discover a language for evoking experience that would take poetry out of its place in the quiet realms of the academy and make direct connection with the extraordinary pressures of the decade. Yet many of these poets would operate not by inventing a private language but by reinventing colloquial language, forging the rhythms of daily speech into the more urgent, essential music necessary to equal the personal and public events of the decade's "pressure of reality."[11] The work required was a construction—based upon available models and driven by the pressure of the need to include realms of experience (and thus ways of speaking about experience) previously denied—of a new sense of free-verse rhythms and the free-verse line. The heroes of *Forbidden Planet* triumphed, essentially, by choosing not to be afraid of themselves. It is oversimplifying, though not inaccurate, to suggest that the resuscitators of American poetry in the fifties undertook, to extraordinary success, a similar strategy. Whether it is Lowell's exacting and heartbreaking self-analysis or O'Hara's headlong exuberance and urbane wit that one examines, it is the distinctive stamp of character, of the presence of narrator as subject, which breathes new energy into the poetry of the fifties. New content would require new speech: what arose from the twin repressions of American culture in the fifties and the tired standards of New Criticism was the as-yet-unknown, the as-yet-unspoken, and this range of "disallowed" content turned out to produce not "beasts from the id" but a lively, various poetics capable of a sustainable music.

Opening the Way Out

Those poets who did not feel the need to break loose from convention in any radical way are perhaps best represented by Richard Wilbur, whose work of the fifties investigates, and often invigorates, traditional forms. An archetypal Apollonian, Wilbur values balance, formal harmony, the poem as the resolution of forces rather than the enactment of conflict between those forces. Traditional forms, with their inherent quality of resolution created by the fact that the form *itself* represents order without necessarily involving us in the making of that order, are thus his natural domain. In John Ciardi's *Mid-Century American Poets* (1950), Wilbur states that "the use of strict poetic forms, traditional or invented, is like the use of framing and composition in painting: both serve to limit the work of art, and to declare its artificiality: they say, 'this is not the world, but a pattern imposed upon the world or found in it.' "[12]

Just as the intent of the new painters of the decade would be to replace the notion of the painting as a finished act, an imposition of form, with the notion of works that were constructed of the struggle of their own process, the discovery of form, so American poetry would increasingly interest itself in "chaos." Lowell would describe this order in process, in accepting the National Book Award in 1960, as the "raw" rather than the "cooked." Wilbur advocated conceiving art as a window, rather than as a door; a window provides "a partial vision of a part of the world," whereas art seen as a door means that "the artist no longer perceives a wall between him and the world; the world becomes an extension of himself, and is deprived of its reality. . . . This is bad aesthetics—and incidentally, bad morals."[13] This conception of art as door, of the world reflected in art as one that is subject to the struggles of perception and the consequent imposition of character, is exactly what would fuel the essential aesthetic developments of the fifties.

The rebels of the decade would come to regard the fixed forms—and, more particularly, their use in combination with the conventional tactics of allusion, ironies, and avoidances—as morally vacuous. Wilbur clearly does not regard fixed forms as likewise having the potential to "deprive [the world] of its reality," but by eliminating the struggle toward order formalism is capable of doing exactly that. Particularly in *Things of This World* (1956), however, Wilbur's graceful poems would combine formal accomplishment and elegance with a celebratory engagement in the pleasures of experience. His joy ("Oh, let there be nothing on earth but laundry, / Nothing but rosy hands in the rising steam / And clear dances done in the sight of heaven") pleases, yet finally the poems' stasis and formal elegance deny us participation in the struggle to earn that triumphant poise.[14] To extend Wilbur's metaphor, a generation of poets would then find it necessary not only to open the windows but to break them, to widen them into doors, and the result would be a revisioning of the entire house.

But for one loosely defined group of poets, the challenge of the moment lay neither in pursuing the requirements of "academic" verse as exemplified by Wilbur's formal play nor in overthrowing those canons, but in extending the instrument to allow for idiosyncrasy, pushing at the boundaries of formal canons to make room for personal vision. For Randall Jarrell, the thrust of vision was toward character, the individual voice speaking in heightened moments or from the brink of transformation—a motion, prompted usually by grave suffering, toward the redemptive. The compassion of the poems included in his *Selected Poems* (1955) seems always directed toward those who suffer profound losses, whether it be a girl reading in a library who seems divorced from the living evidence of her culture which surrounds her, an English child whose father and sister have been lost in the war, or Jews or prisoners of war themselves lost in the wreckage of Europe. These characters suffer brutal losses which Jarrell's masterful use of voice captures in all their detail, and we most frequently encounter these characters in monologue, in moments when the accumulated pain wells up and the speaker attempts to create order, to strive toward something transformative in the recounting of the losses. The drama of these poems is thus the struggle for the identification of meaning which will make the pain experienced of value. In Jarrell the outcome of the struggle is never foreordained. The numbed child in "The Truth," who has forged a universe of denial to cope with the absurd losses of the war, can arrive at a return to connection with painful but necessary human truth ("And she said, 'Yes, he's dead, he's dead!' / And cried and cried; she *was* my mother, / She put her arms around me and we cried"). Similarly, in his "90° North," Jarrell is pulled back into the child-world, the territory toward which he is compelled by longing; as Karl Shapiro has noted, "His almost obsessive return to the great childhood myths is sometimes as painful as psychoanalysis." The children in these poems—whether they be contemporary fictions or the characters of fairy tales—seem always on the verge of, or in process of, metamorphosis; they are capable of making from brutality, from a violated sensibility, meaningful psychic order. "To the individual psyche," Stanley Kunitz has written, "[metamorphosis] is the way out of the cage." If transformation seems impossible for the adult, then the obsessive return to childhood in these poems becomes that much more luminous, that much more fraught with possibility.[15]

For Robert Penn Warren as well, the possibilities of character provided an extension of the limitations of current poetic modes in the early fifties. The rich and humane poems of *Promises*, written between 1954 and 1956, are often urgent addresses to the speaker's children, rich in allusion and surface texture but nonetheless emotionally urgent, compelled. The title's "promises" apply not only to the bond between father and child but to the connections between our collective ancestry and the present; the poet has spoken to his concern with contemporary "moral confusion" and the "world in which the individual is lost in his relation to society . . . in which man is a victim of abstraction and mechanism."[16] An examination of portraits of "Founding Fathers, Nineteenth-Century Style, Southeast U.S.A." leads Warren to note "those merciless eyes that now remark our own time's sad declension." "Some," he continues, "were given to study, read Greek in the Forest, and these / longed for an epic to their own deeds' right honor." Warren seems to be fulfilling this longing for an epic, but his historical poems glorify the past only in terms of our ancestors' courage, ambition, and grounding in their own desires, not their moral example; they have "nothing to tell us in our complexity of choices." We must "try to forgive them their defects, even their greatness."[17] The poet encourages us to refuse to sanctify the past even as we recognize the diminishment of the present.

Although the poems of Weldon Kees were not widely read until some time after Kees's disappearance and presumed suicide in 1955, they represent an essential contribution to the poetry of the decade. Whereas Warren could abstractly name "our own time's sad declension," Kees seemed to internalize it, to embody throughout his work, with remarkable consistency, a sense of both cultural sterility and reduction and individual hopelessness; even the most straightforward and reportorial of Kees's images are informed by a tone of bitterness ("Outside, white buildings yellow in the sun. / Outside, the birds circle continuously / Where trees are actual and take no holiday"). The theme of cultural decline is everywhere enacted; "Round" contrasts the enthusiasms of Marvell, the humanist Renan, and Cézanne with the immediate realm of experience confronting the speaker: "something in my head / Flaps like a worn-out blind. The soil / in which the ferns are dying needs more Vigoro." "The Umbrella" traces mythic and historical associations of umbrellas in Hindu, Buddhist, and Greek cultures; as the poem's catalogue of historical associations moves toward the present, it becomes increasingly compressed, increasingly random, until the umbrellas of the Victorians, having lost all religious associations, are seen as trimmed with "sequins, artificial flowers, ostrich feathers, / God knows what else." Kees's choice of verbs to evoke the present is revealing: "The sea is pitted with rain. Wind shakes the house. / Here from this window lashed with spray, I watch / a black umbrella, ripped apart and wrong side out, / Go lurching wildly down the beach." "Pitted," "shakes," "lashed," and "ripped" suggest the barely containable violence of the present moment, and the troubling motions of the ruined umbrella against the gray and motionless harbor stand in bleak opposition to the past in which human gestures invested the object with meaning. For Kees, meaning has been drained both from things and from human lives, and now the umbrella, that sad representative of the human intention to protect, goes "flapping and free, / Into the heart of the storm."[18] In his despair, the absolutism of his denial, Kees is in a sense the most contemporary of his contemporaries, the poet whose work most internalizes the conditions of post-Hiroshima society with its potential for the utter denial of all value.

Further Extensions

In 1950 Charles Olson published his essay "Projective Verse" and systematized an aesthetic rooted in the work of Pound and Williams. Olson's essay offered a new description of the free-verse line—which he saw as a unit of breath, a collection of syllables whose length and individual character were determined by the physiology of the speaker. The body, he asserted, must provide the "ground" for the form of verse ("This organism now our citadel never was cathedral, draughty tenement of soul . . . its power is bone muscle nerve blood"). If the form was to be shaped by breath, then the content of the poem arose from perception, from what entered the field of the writer's sensibility in the act of the composing process; "one perception must immediately and directly lead to a further perception," Olson insisted, quoting Edward Dahlberg. The act of perception was the key; rather than following any prescribed or received form, the poem Olson advocated must work in "open" form, finding its organic shape in the dynamic relation of breath and perception. "Form," Olson quoted Robert Creeley in a statement that was to become an essential credo, "is never more than an extension of content."[19]

In the late forties Olson—of Gloucester, Massachusetts, a town that would become the mythic and actual site of *The Maximus Poems*, an extended sequence which in *Canto*-like fashion juxtaposes bits of experience and meditation with historical and literary fragments—came to North Carolina's Black Mountain College, a short-lived institution which was to have a potent effect on the revolutions brewing in the arts in America. Innovators in poetry, painting, music, and dance—among them Robert Creeley and Robert Duncan, Franz Kline and Robert Rauschenberg, John Cage and Merce Cunningham—were active at Black Mountain as faculty or students. Olson and his colleagues hammered out the notion of "projective verse" or "open" or "organic" form—a notion which both addressed the work of Pound and Williams in retrospect and guided the work of poets who followed in Olson's lineage, particularly Robert Creeley, Robert Duncan, and Denise Levertov, though the notion of open form would have an even further impact on the continuing evolution of free verse in the sixties.

"Open form" stood in contrast to what Olson described as "that verse which print bred and which is pretty much what we have had, in English and American, and have still got, despite the work of Pound & Williams." Williams responded to Olson's dictums with enthusiasm, and Robert Creeley notes that "it was an excitement many of us shared." Creeley (and later Levertov) would elaborate upon and clarify Olson's pronouncements that "a poem is . . . a structure possessed of its own organization in turn derived from the circumstances of its making."[20] Structure, then, must arise from the content as it is perceived in the act of composition. There is a new reliance on spontaneity here, a new investigation which replaces fixed form with the idea of entering the field of the poem, creating the text as a sort of experience in itself whose form is determined by what will most embody that experience. Olson's long poems then, such as the *Maximus* sequence, work by means of complex juxtapositions of present and past, replicating or recording the speaker's field of perception.

Robert Creeley's work within the same conceptual framework led to radically different results, for Creeley's field of consciousness is focused, restricted to a particular incident or meditation, and the force of emotion which infuses his most powerful work seems absent in Olson. The operation of intellect, for Creeley, seems to lie almost entirely within the form itself, in the pattern of perception, and in his scrupulous attention to the perceiving mind and heart at work at the contemplation of compelling emotional issues. In the short, breath-determined lines of his poems of the fifties (collected in 1962 as *For Love*), Creeley hammers out an intense, rigorous aesthetic. Almost void of concrete objects, these poems somehow succeed in making feeling itself seem concrete; one feels as if one were eavesdropping, with the permission of the speaker, on an intimate address which gives one just enough information to feel included. Because we have come upon the speaker during a moment of great emotional intensity, we are able, through our seeming overhearing, to be present at a moment of tenderness, of revelation. These spare, barely furnished poems seem essential, representing not so much a distillation of experience and meditation as an utterance spoken carefully, almost haltingly, at times with great clarity and concentration.

Like Creeley, Denise Levertov would also expand upon and clarify Olson's poetics; it is ironic that the latter's principles, in their vagueness, provided fertile ground upon which younger poets might construct their own aesthetics. Levertov translated insistence on the breath as the measure of the line into a more complex system of lineation, regarding both the duration of breath and the instant of perception as the line's ingredients. Each line becomes an instant in a process of meditation, of feeling or observing; the poem thus enacts the experience about which it seeks to comment. In her three volumes of the fifties, *Here and Now*, *Overland to the Islands*, and *With Eyes at the Back of Our Heads*, Levertov moves away from stanzas defined by traditional patterns toward organic form whose lineation and stanza length are defined as acts of perception. In "Illustrious Ancestors" she describes her own ends:

> I would like to make,
> thinking some line still taut between me and them,
> poems direct as what the birds said,
> hard as a floor, sound as a bench,
> mysterious as the silence when the tailor
> would pause with his needle in the air.[21]

The image of actuality discovered within things, in subtle places, beneath the surface, is one which recurs: "I like to find / what's not found / at once, but lies / within something of another nature." James Wright noted that "the music of her verse . . . is spare, direct, measured more according to a voice speaking then a voice singing . . . such restraint allows her to speak . . . with inflections unmistakably her own."[22] Her music seems also to arise from engagement in daily events and perceptions; to return to Wilbur's metaphor, these poems are decidedly "doors." Each represents an act of perception which attempts to penetrate the perceived, which enacts the dynamic, inseparable relation of subject and object.

Shaking the Rafters

By the mid-fifties the West Coast, and particularly the San Francisco Bay area, where a rich cross-fertilization of influences had become a tradition, became a center of poetic activity dedicated to shaking the rafters of American poetry. This atmosphere was in no small part due to the influence of Kenneth Rexroth, a veteran of American Modernism who remained supportive throughout his life of innovations and experimentation in poetry. Rexroth's own work reflected a rich polyphony of influences: the directness of Imagism and of Oriental verse, of which he was a distinguished translator; his affectionate relationship with wilderness and attendant interest in the natural sciences; and his engagement with the economic and social analysis of leftist politics. His poems of the fifties continue his work in a short-lined, unornamented, directly stated lyric indebted both to his own translations of Tu Fu and to the early Pound. Though Rexroth experimented restlessly in longer forms and with forthrightly political poetry, it was the short lyric to which he would insistently return in poems characterized by their tenderness toward women loved, their awed affection for the natural world, and their insistent awareness of mortality. Richard Foster, writing in 1962, articulately summarized Rexroth's themes: "Love—the recognition of mortality, the turning of the seasons and the grand, silently commemorative drift of the constellations overhead, and the stepping forth into the full, intensely imagined reality of mortal persons, lover, wife, child and friend."[23]

The publication of Allen Ginsberg's *Howl* (1956) sounded a cry of rage, and in turn other cries of rage—or downright dismissals—were raised against it. Ginsberg announces himself, in the opening of the volume's title poem, as speaking for his compatriots, naming their collective condition of disaffection: "I saw the best minds of my generation, starving, hysterical, naked."[24] The title poem explicitly identifies itself as a lamentation for those most promising and most excluded from the "American ideal." In a long descriptive catalogue Ginsberg makes clear his contention that the finest have been driven, by what a critic called "the overwhelming pressures of conformity, competition, prestige and respectability," toward madness, dissipation, and the outraged enactments of the denied.[25] Not only is he exiled from the tranquilized suburbs by virtue of ethnicity, sexuality, political philosophy, and intellectual energy; he also cannot locate in the codified possibilities of American society a tenable way of living. Thus the speaker inhabits a sort of psychic inferno, a territory of the lost which underlies the flawless, bourgeois vision of American life. "He avoids nothing," William Carlos Williams wrote in his introduction to the volume, "but experiences it to the hilt. . . . Hold back the edges of your gowns, Ladies, we are going through hell." M. L. Rosenthal offered a more balanced appraisal: "Despite the danger that he will screech himself mute any moment now, he has brought a terrible psychological reality to the surface with enough originality to blast American verse a hair's breadth forward in the process."[26]

" 'Howl' lies," as Kenneth Rexroth observed, "in one of the oldest traditions, that of Hosea or the other, angry Minor Prophets of the Bible." The fault for the condition of Ginsberg's generation—and his own violated psychic state—thus lies with "Moloch," the embodiment of the State as evil, the demon of this world. But even in the "belly of Moloch" lies the possibility of transcendence. This tension between existential despair at the political and social conditions of the world and the prophetic optimism of vision would continue to inform all of Ginsberg's work. Transcendence is always possible, even in the shattered universe of *Howl*—through visionary experience, sex, or chemical transformation of the psyche through drugs: "flower of industry, / tough spiky ugly flower, /flower nonetheless, / with the form of the great yellow / Rose in your brain."[27] This excerpt from the concluding stanza of the final poem in the volume exemplifies Ginsberg's vision of the possibility of transcendence, a Neoplatonism in the tradition of Blake. The form of the poems in *Howl* is likewise Blakean and biblical; Ginsberg relied on parallel constructions and long incantatory lines which, like those of Whitman before him, take the form of the King James Bible as their model. Ginsberg fuses his Whitmanic apostrophes and catalogues with verbal play influenced by the prose of Jack Kerouac. It is a formal model which Ginsberg would employ to much greater emotional impact in his later *Kaddish* (1961), an equally ambitious poem which is finally more moving because of its greater intimacy of address.

Due in part to the poem's "obscenity trial" and resultant publicity, *Howl* became an important indicator of the changing climate in American poetry, an alarm sounding the decline of academic verse. If the poem was not taken seriously by many poets and critics—due to its bombastic, sprawling rhetoric, its spontaneous and chantlike form—then it at least offered a signal of a realm of possibility for powerful poetry to be constructed from "unmentionable" realms of experience. The poem would also, by virtue of its visibility and its radical loosening or re-visioning of formal design (which, Ginsberg said, echoing Olson, sprang "from a source deeper than the mind, that is to say, it came from the breathing and the belly and the lungs"),[28] serve as a rallying cry and focus to other poets in the loose nexus of artists who came to be known as the "Beats." Though the coherence of the group was at least in part created by the media (certainly a new phenomenon in American poetry: poets as somewhat scandalous news, interesting as much for their other activities as for their poetry), the group took the label to heart. "The word 'beat' originally meant poor, down and out, deadbeat . . . sleeping in subways. Now that the word is belonging officially it is being made to stretch to include people who . . . have a certain new gesture, or attitude, which I can only describe as a new *more*."[29] *More* seems an accurate term; the program of the Beats, like that of the Surrealists before them, was less a set of aesthetic principles than an embodiment of a philosophy of experience, a program of action. From existentialist philosophy, the Beats appropriated the replacement of given social, ethical, and religious codes with an emphasis on individual experience—or, to borrow the name of a magazine of the day, "the unspeakable visions of the individual." They yoked the existentialist sense of despair with a will to transcendence (thus their idolization of Whitman and Rimbaud and their linkage of the term "beat" with "beatitude") that found its vehicles in Oriental religion and meditational practices, in sheer verbal exuberance and in the visionary experiences of drugs, and in the rhythms and improvisations of progressive jazz.

Among the poets to emerge from the group was Lawrence Ferlinghetti, whose lively work, usually formally playful and alternating between celebration and despair (the latter particularly apparent in Ferlinghetti's frequent political poems), was collected in *A Coney Island of the Mind* (1958). Gregory Corso's *The Vestal Lady on Brattle* (1955) and *Gasoline* (1958) gathered exuberant, frequently comic poems held together by the vividness of the speaker's voice, an enthusiastic, energetic tone which rushes along declaiming jokes, condemnations, and praises. William Everson (Brother Antoninus) pursued an ecstatic Catholicism couched in long-lined celebrations of the natural world and the erotic; Lew Welch and others pursued the importation of Zen philosophy to American soil. This project was most successfully undertaken by probably the most significant of the poets to emerge from the group, Gary Snyder. Snyder's immersion in Zen philosophy and practice—he lived mainly in Japan from 1956 until 1964—coupled with his engagement with the poetics of Pound and Williams, resulted in a poetry at home in the natural world, presenting notions of human identity and place within the natural through experience, through "things." He regards the poet as facing "in two directions: to the world of people and language and society, and . . . to the nonhuman, nonverbal world, which is nature as nature is itself."[30] Though Snyder's work would come to public attention in the following decade with the publication of *Myths and Texts* (1960), it found its genesis in his involvement with the natural world of the West Coast, the poets working there, and Zen Buddhism's insistence on simplicity and direct accounts of experience.

A Blurring of Particulars

If San Francisco and the West Coast were one locus of activity, then New York was a generative point of another sort. The Beat poets sought expansiveness and freedom of form through a broadening of their principle of inclusion, both in poetics and in experience, under the tutelage of Whitman and Rimbaud. The poets centered in New York City pursued a course equally divergent from the mainstream, if quite different in character. Also advocating expansiveness and new formal dimensions, the poets who came to be known as the "New York school" sought a poetic milieu with the energy and freshness of the developments in the visual arts which surrounded them. The school's two most significant exponents of the fifties, Frank O'Hara and John Ashbery, were both art critics, and O'Hara was a staff member at the Museum of Modern Art. They found their models in a previous generation of poets who had been caught up in the revolutions in the visual arts, the explosion of Modernism: Pierre Reverdy and Guillaume Apollinaire. These poets shared a love for the new, the modern, the frothing detritus of popular culture and its icons and language. The New York poets also found heroes in Mayakovsky, with his brash assertions and commitment to being "of his time," and in the Dadaists, whose love of nonsense and spontaneity, the felicitous intervention of chance, marked their poems and collaborations between poets and visual artists.

Urbane, ironic, sometimes genuinely celebratory and often wildly funny, O'Hara would allow a realm of material and associations alien to academic verse to pour into his poems: the camp icons of movie stars of the twenties and thirties, the daily landscape of social activity in Manhattan, jazz music, telephone calls from friends; anything seemed ready material for inclusion into the particular order that the moment of composition would call for. Dadaist even in his approach to his own work, O'Hara composed huge numbers of poems with apparent spontaneity and ease; a friend estimates that his vast *Collected Poems* contains perhaps only a third of his work, which was often scribbled or typed quickly, stuffed in drawers or left about in stacks. This relaxed attitude toward preservation and collection results in a chronology of composition quite different from the dates of publication, but *Meditations in an Emergency* and the poems written throughout the late fifties comprise his finest work. "The Day Lady Died," "Steps," "A True Account of Talking to the Sun at Fire Island" (a brilliant re-visioning of Mayakovsky's poem on the same theme), and O'Hara's famous lament upon reading of the collapse of Lana Turner ("I have been to lots of parties / and acted perfectly disgraceful / but I never actually collapsed / Oh Lana Turner we love you get up") mark O'Hara at the height of his powers.[31] His language is often casual, relaxed in diction, yet it presses forward with a kind of breathless urgency, a will to celebrate the density and richness of experience—in all its refusal to be summed up, to marshal itself into an orderly vision—by including as much as possible. Many of these pieces have been labeled "I do this, I do that" poems; they report whole chunks of experience, days of walking, conversing, noticing, with careful specificity. Place-names and the names of friends and acquaintances abound; paradoxically, their inclusion seems to make the poems *more* universal, more available, convinced as we are by their artfully shaped controlling tone of the authenticity of the speaker's voice. The notion of contrasting and mutually influencing elements arranged on a surface—a key concept in Abstract Expressionism—is important in O'Hara's work. The poems seem, indeed, to spill one into the other, creating one immense canvas which displays in all its parts O'Hara's character engaged in all the business of living—alternately joyful, petulant, obtuse, tired, awed. The finest of his love poems—"Steps," for example, which concludes "oh god its wonderful / to get out of bed / and drink too much coffee / and smoke too many cigarettes / and love you so much"—disarm with their directness.[32] Their comic, carefully built quotidian contexts allow O'Hara to work with direct statement in an inimitable fashion, generating a current of emotion which rises above his camp humor, his exuberant ironies and mocking play.

The year 1956 saw the publication of John Ashbery's *Some Trees,* a Yale Younger Poets selection chosen by W. H. Auden. The title poem, an abstract, lovely lyric, demonstrates the kind of indirection which marks the volume, a blurring of particulars and pronouns, the result of which is to focus the reader on language itself. Poem after poem employs traditional and rather arcane forms—the sestina, the canzone, the pantoum—while avoiding referentiality; the result is that we see the form itself, a sort of historical relic, given a curious kind of life by no longer meaning what it once did. If we recall Wilbur's view that the fixed form reminds us that we are viewing a work of art, it becomes clear that *these* forms are here for entirely other purposes, perhaps epistemological ones: how does the poem construct a world? And what relation does that constructed instance bear to the world outside it? Are even the most conventional and accepted orders of reality, as usually contained in the poem of fixed form, finally as arbitrary as these constructs are? Where O'Hara is a poet of urgency and speed, language rushing by in the speaker's will to include and to tell everything, the Ashbery of *Some Trees* is laconic, reluctant to make assertions. "Our days put on such reticence," he notes dryly in the volume's title poem, "these accents seem their own defense," and the statement seems as self-referential, as much a comment on his own aesthetic as those asides that Ashbery will make in his later, mature poems of the seventies.[33] The times themselves, he suggests here, resist interpretation and meaning, and thus the poems speak for themselves—elliptical and suggestive objects, shaped by their references to the past, pushing toward the future with their abstracted, nonreferential surfaces.

Possibilities of the Self

The final group of poets to be examined within the context of the decade are those who staked out new territory for American poetry by envisioning and exploring the possibility of the self as narrator. To varying degrees, these poets opened private experience to scrutiny in their work, each creating a consistent persona who seemed increasingly naked and open to investigation. Whether or not their work was "confessional" is immaterial; they created themselves as *characters* within the poems, and usually as characters with consistent stances toward the world as defined by perceptions marked with the unmistakable stamp of individuality, idiosyncrasy, and style.

John Berryman's *Homage to Mistress Bradstreet* (1956) posited a dynamic relation between the poet-as-narrator and the seventeenth-century American poet Anne Bradstreet. Although Berryman did not like Bradstreet's conventional, doggedly Puritan verse, his poem comprises an act of passionate identification with her life. The poem's matter is not so much biographical as it is an imaginative reclamation of Bradstreet's times, involving the speaker—and the reader—intimately even in the sensations which accompany Bradstreet's pregnancy ("My world is strange / and merciful, ingrown months, / blessing a swelling trance") and the birth of her child ("I did it with my body! / One proud tug greens Heaven. Marvelous, / unforbidding Majesty"). Berryman begins by addressing his subject in the second person, but by the fourth of his fifty-seven stanzas Bradstreet speaks in the first person; the effect of this device is to heighten the sense, already nascent in the intensity of the poet's identification with her, that we are hearing a voice which lies somewhere between the twin personae, the "I" of the narrator and the "I" of Anne Bradstreet. The poem's odd syntactical constructions heighten its sense of otherness, as if the diction and syntax of the twentieth-century speaker and the seventeenth-century poet had merged: "Swell, imperious bells. I fly. / Mountainous, woman breaks and will not bend: / sways God nearby: anguish comes to an end."[34] This jarring, ultimately enriching syntax is musical and heavily textured, a kind of linguistic *impasto*. It anticipates the more extreme syntactical play of Berryman's later *Dream Songs*, though the fact that here these snarled, muscular sentences are in the service of a pair of merging voices, rather than the polyphony of the later work, makes them uniquely affecting.

Of the *Selected Poems, 1938–1958* which Stanley Kunitz published in the latter year, nearly a third was new work of the fifties. His work of the period is rigorously formal and richly allusive, and behind the contemporary scenes or incidents that the poems evoke the landscape of myth is always visible. Elms uprooted on a suburban lawn are seen as "amputated coils, / Raw Gorgons matted blind." The mythic dimension of experience is seen as both universal and ancient ("The spiral verb that weaves / Through the crystal of our lives, / Of myth and water made / And incoherent blood"); yet it is a mythology informed by the insights of psychoanalysis.[35] The poems are relentless in their self-investigation, informed by the poet's will to probe and to identify, to leave no matter of the heart unexamined. Thus, with the insistence of one returning to examine a wound or replaying the circumstances of an unresolved conflict, the poems circle around the nature of guilt, identify the anger and loss inherent in the experience of love, and obsessively investigate the poet's relationship with his father. It is a mark of the poems' contemporaneity, within their decade, that despite their carefully controlled formal designs they are enactments of the *process* of "coming to terms"; they resist easy resolutions, the consolations of distance and irony.

In reviewing Theodore Roethke's volume of collected work, *Words for the Wind* (1959), Delmore Schwartz described the essential nature of Roethke's method and matter: "These poems appear, at first glance, to be uncontrollable and subliminal outcries, the voices of roots, stones, leaves, logs, small birds; and they also resemble the songs in Shakespearian plays. . . . Roethke uses a variety of devices with the utmost cunning and craft to bring the unconsciousness to the surface of articulate expression."[36] For Roethke, boundaries between outer and inner dissolve; the natural world seems a vast landscape of the psyche, just as the voyage inward leads to natural things—roots, leaves, and flowers—as emblems of the recesses of the self. To travel either outward or inward is to encounter the self, and the voyage in either direction is fraught with the possibilities of transcendence, dissolution, or both:

In a dark wood I saw—
I saw my several selves
Come running from the leaves,
Lewd, tiny careless lives
That scuttled under stones,
Or broke, but would not go.[37]

Triune obsessions—nature as psychic landscape, love as a vehicle out of the limited self, and dancing as a metaphor for ecstatic being in the world—merge repeatedly, modifying one another, gaining heightened meaning through repetition in various contexts. The final stanza of "I Knew a Woman" seems to crystallize all three: "Let seed be grass, and grass turn into hay: / I'm martyr to a motion not my own; / What's freedom for? To know eternity. / . . . These old bones learn to live her wanton ways: / (I measure time by how a body sways)." Swaying, reeling, whirling, the body of the speaker (which we are always reminded is the vehicle or container of spirit) is always in motion, a dance which alternates between the ecstatic and the desperate. In the beautiful lyric "The Waking," from the 1953 volume of that title, the poet asserts, "We think by feeling. What is there to know? / I hear my being dance from ear to ear." But *Words for the Wind's* title poem, an epithalamion, concludes on a more ambiguous note: "And I dance round and round, / A fond and foolish man. / And see and suffer myself / In another being, at last."[38] If on one level the poem describes the joyful experience of love—emphatically made both physical and emotional in the metaphor of the circling dance—then on another it seems the narrative of a driven attempt to escape from the prison of self. There is a triumphant quality to "In another being, at last" which is made heartrending—even elegiac in the context of Roethke's life and work—since the will to enter another being besides the self can attain its desire only in a transitory dance.

It seems odd to include Elizabeth Bishop among this company of poets characterized by the opening of the private, the presentation of the self as character. And yet it is entirely accurate, for her poems bear, as much as those of any poet of her generation, the stamp of individual character, of an idiosyncratic perception which becomes both mode and subject of the poems. She combines the exactitude of a Marianne Moore with a compassion that lurks just behind her composure, her apparently off-hand, self-effacing voice. Ironically, in light of her reluctance to offer much in the way of autobiographical detail, we come to know a great deal about her by virtue of what she *chooses* to notice, and what she chooses to exclude. She is careful not to intrude between the reader and the thing under observation—be it an armadillo, a volume of engravings, or a seal to which she sang Baptist hymns—yet she is never absent, because the singular detail she observes and the language in which these details are presented create for us her character as speaker. It is a voice we immediately trust, responding to her exactness and her restless curiosity, her quality of remaining open to experience, even to epiphany, while she refuses hyperbole and doggedly pokes at the surface of the real. But we participate in the experiences this voice offers only to find that there is much more at stake than meets the eye, more emotion carefully contained, more uncertainty and self-questioning, than are at first apparent.

In 1955, the combined edition of her first book, *North and South*, and a new volume, *A Cold Spring*, earned Bishop the Pulitzer Prize. "Over

2000 Illustrations and a Complete Concordance," from the latter volume,
illustrates her method of generating meaning through the accumulation
of detail, of exactitude of observation leading inevitably to heightened
awareness of the situation of the observer. The speaker of the poem is
examining a nineteenth-century travel volume rich with illustrations.
She begins, "Thus should have been our travels: / serious, engravable,"
immediately establishing a "we" whose voyages have seemed less pur-
poseful, less worthy of preservation by an exacting art. The first-person
plural is then abandoned for twenty-nine lines of close examination of
the book itself. Despite its grandeur, the volume's "serious" travels are
described in terms which suggest the spiritual condition of the present-
day travelers; the Wonders of the World "are tired and a touch familiar,"
the fronds of the date palm "look like files" (a typical Bishop linking of
objects from disparate frames of reference), and the human figure is "far
gone in history or theology." At last the complex lines of the engravings
tire the eye of the viewer, just as the voyages have tired the travelers,
and they seem to disperse into "God's spreading fingerprint"; the context
of the image makes it seem more exhausted than transcendent, some-
thing immensely large and vague. Almost imperceptibly, the poem se-
gues from a description of the volume's illustrations to a catalogue of
sights seen by the travelers introduced in the poem's opening line.
Unlike the illustrations in the volume, this listing of sights is rich in color
and sound, but it is a jumble of the beautiful and the grotesque ("In
Mexico the dead man lay / in a blue arcade; the dead volcanoes / glistened
like Easter lilies"), the trivial and the terrible. A casually stated assertion
at the end of the catalogue shocks: "It was somewhere near there / I saw
what frightened me most of all." It is our first knowledge that the travel-
er's response to the hodgepodge of sights has been one of terror, and
what provokes the greatest terror is "a holy grave, not looking particularly
holy," which is full of dust. "Everything," the final stanza begins, "only
connected by 'and' and 'and.' " The crowded but finally exhausted and
sterile engravings, overwhelming in their number and detail, are linked
only by being contiguous; in the same way, the speaker's voyages seem
devoid of meaning, only an accumulation of detail, their implicit terror
made explicit in the image of the dusty grave which does not even contain
the prophet for whom it was dug; an amused guide looks on as if to mock
the viewer's expectations. Meaning is unavailable, mocked by the grave,
and this realization sends the speaker back to the book, wherein she
finds an image of the Nativity, a "family with pets" beside a sparkling

fire, that she wishes she and her traveling companion might have seen, and "looked and looked our infant sight away."[39] The doubled verb is insistent; the speaker would have chosen to look with all her heart at this image of promise and redemption rather than at the jumble of sights the world has provided, since the latter leads inevitably to the dusty irrelevance of a tomb unoccupied by its proper inhabitant. But even this image of the redemptive birth is entirely undercut; the Christian icon becomes "a family with pets" and thus a consolation that, even though the speaker would prefer it to the world she has seen, is entirely false.

When Randall Jarrell reviewed Robert Lowell's *Lord Weary's Castle*, he might have been describing Lowell's first volume of the fifties, *The Mills of the Kavanaughs*. He characterizes Lowell as "a dramatic poet: he presents people, their actions, their speeches . . . he does not present themes or generalizations but a world. . . . The 'personality' of the poet is usually not exploited." *Lord Weary's Castle* is saturated in Lowell's essential historical sense, what Jarrell called Lowell's "ambivalent knowledge of [his] damned kin."[40] The poems are informed by Lowell's passion for character; their urgency created by their obsessive meditation on death and decay and by the implication that the speakers are, indeed, "kin." They share in the dissolution of tradition, participate in an historical current leading inevitably into decline, the narrowing of possibility into loss and dissolution which will become Lowell's milieu. Though the thematic concerns of *The Mills of the Kavanaughs* are similar to those of Lowell's later work of the decade, the poems are rigidly formal, often tortuous in their syntax. Their real anticipation of what was to come lies in the careful creation of narrative personae whose voices control the reader's perception of their character, whose selection of images allows us to perceive their gestures and actions as metonymic and emblematic.

A similar use of character, metonymy, and emblematic gesture characterizes Lowell's seminal book of the fifties, *Life Studies* (1959), a volume indispensable to most of the poetry which followed it. The volume signaled to the coming generation of young poets the end of the domination of the New Critical perspective that the self and the poem are divorced, of the poem as artifact unto itself detached from the poet. It not only pointed the way toward an alternative to the domination of the High Modernists, but enacted that alternative successfully. As Marjorie Perloff has written of "Man and Wife," "it surely represents a reaction against Eliot's dictum that poetry is not the turning loose of emotion but an escape from emotion; it is a reaction against the autonomous, 'impersonal' symbolist mode of Eliot, Pound, Stevens, the early Auden, and of the Robert Lowell of *Lord Weary's Castle*—the mode that dominated the first half of our century." If Ginsberg's *Howl* had shaken the rafters of the acceptable, what M. L. Rosenthal had called Ginsberg's "screech" had made his work also easily dismissible. The formal grace of *Life Studies*, yoked with Lowell's depth of psychological insight and undeniable emotional power, could not be so easily disregarded.[41]

Jarrell had praised *Lord Weary's Castle* by noting that "the 'personality' of the poet is usually not exploited"; in the light of *Life Studies* the statement could not be more ironic, for the central feat of the volume is to establish the poet as character. M. L. Rosenthal would describe Confessional poetry as work in which "the private life of the poet himself, especially under stress of psychological crisis, becomes a major theme." But perhaps the essence of *Life Studies* lies in those elements which allow it to transcend mere "confession"; the poems do not document psychological crises so much as enact and embody them, placing the difficult events of the speaker's internal life in a specific cultural and historical context which it is the book's great labor to discover and to name. The speaker in the poems is consistent throughout, unlike the multiple narrators of Lowell's earlier work; if this is the creation of a persona much closer to the self, it is nonetheless a persona. As Lowell himself stated, "There's a good deal of tinkering with fact . . . the reader was to believe he was getting the *real* Robert Lowell."[42] His achievement, in the creation of self as the speaker of the poems, is to make us believe in the authority and actuality of the voice while artfully constructing the poem as dramatic monologue, rife with metonymy and metaphoric detail. The results of Lowell's careful creation of the self as persona are harrowing, not least because these poems refuse resolution. They may point to the cause of the smoldering losses of the present, but they offer no resolution, no possible outcome. This is decidedly not emotion recollected in tranquility, though it may be the sort of numbed tranquility created by Miltown; the force of recollection brings emotionally wrenching conditions to bear upon the present, unresolved, perhaps irresolvable. Lowell's motion toward a refusal of consolation, of easy resolution, is evident in two treatments of mortality, the first from the title poem of *The Mills*: "Why must we mistrust / ourselves with Death who takes the world on trust? / Although God's brother, and himself a god, Death whipped his horses through the startled sod."[43] In contrast, "Terminal Days at Beverly Farms" from *Life Studies* concludes: "Father's death was abrupt and unprotesting. / His vision was still twenty-twenty. / After a morning of anxious, repetitive smiling, / his last words to Mother were: / "I feel awful."[44] The latter example is a sort of catechism of rejections: of the consolations of redeeming the losses of the present through linking them either to classical allusions or to the promises of Catholicism, of the consolation of form to make of experience a beautiful and musical order. The insistent end-stopped lines, the details of the father's good vision and anxious smiling, seem to underline the speaker's sense of futility, and the last words come as no vision of an afterlife or eloquent address, but a mere notation of illness, a sort of metaphor for the death of a tradition.

Life Studies begins in dissolution, with a train journey in which the speaker enters Paris ("our black classic, breaking up / like killer kings on an Etruscan cup" [4]). The City of Light becomes yet another dissolving relic, moving through a sense of dissolution in the political realm ("Inauguration Day; January 1953"), in the social milieu ("A Mad Negro Soldier Confined at Munich"), and in the lives of four artists—Ford Madox Ford, Santayana, Delmore Schwartz, and Hart Crane. As if impelled to explain this phenomenon of cultural decay documented in the opening poems by examining the contexts of his own life, the poet turns to memory, to prose and poems which evoke fragments of childhood experience, placing the poet in the mandarin world of Boston's Beacon Hill, in what seem the dying days of a Puritan dynasty in which Lowell lives in "fogbound solitude" (65) and sees himself "as a young newt, / neurasthenic, scarlet / and wild in the wild coffee-colored water" (66). Lowell's use of a prose memoir is a radical gesture, and one which creates a specific context for the reading of the poems which follow it; the constraints of verse, one senses, would not have allowed him to provide so much narrative information which can inform our reading of the poems. "Prose is in many ways better off than poetry," Lowell said in an interview. "It's quite hard to think of a young poet who has the vitality, say, of Salinger or Saul Bellow. . . . I thought [poetry] was getting increasingly stifling. I couldn't get my experience into tight metrical forms."[45] The world Lowell evokes is one of stylish appearances which seem everywhere bordered by decay, in which sumac multiplies "like cancer / at their garden's border" (73). The speaker's parents move through an ineluctable process of diminishment; his father's death is "abrupt and unprotesting," his mother's grief portrayed as a temporary and superficial event characterized by the emotion we might bring to a trivial failure ("afraid / of living alone till eighty, / Mother mooned in a window, / as if she had strayed on a train / one stop past her destination" [76]). And in "Sailing Home from Rapallo," the speaker brings his mother's body home from Italy to the family cemetery, emblem of the family's long American tradition:

A fence of iron-spear hafts
black-bordered its mostly Colonial grave-sites.
The only "unhistoric" soul to come here
was father, now buried beneath his recent
unweathered pink-veined slice of marble. (77–78)

Mother's name is misspelled on her coffin; beside her ancestors whose "hewn inscriptions" have been given "a diamond edge" by the frost, her corpse lies wrapped in tinfoil like Italian candy, an absurd diminishment.

By 1960 American poetry had, in effect, been unfettered. A decade of revolution in the work of individuals and of small groups of poets widening their principles of inclusion had cleared the way for the generation of poets moving into their maturity in the early sixties to explore previously excluded aspects of the self and of experience. Robert Bly, in his journal the *Fifties,* was already calling for the liberation of verse from fixed forms, for attention to the important work of poets from Latin America and Europe previously unread in the States. An atmosphere of permission had been engendered in terms of experimentation with the possibilities of the free-verse line; the Black Mountain poets, in particular, had furthered an attention to the structural qualities of organic form which would allow the refinement of an increasingly subtle, increasingly flexible instrument throughout the decade to come. The New York poets had created a new latitude for play, for the creation of language-surfaces or textures which were in themselves as interesting as content. The Beats had created room within the canons of the contemporary poem for ecstasy. Snodgrass—in his influential *Heart's Needle*—and Lowell had opened the arena of private despair, for the bringing of individual experience of the most private sort into realm of poetry. What all these rebellions held in common was a notion of character as the prime differentiating force; it was the individual voice, the individual mode of perception enacted in language, which would provide the driving force for new American poetry, not critical codes or the demands of fixed forms. American poetry in 1950 had offered a prescribed set of "windows" onto experience; by 1960 American poets had not only embraced the notion of the poem as a door onto the world but had begun to create a diverse, radical architecture.

Notes

1. Jarrell, *Poetry and the Age* (New York: Knopf, 1953), 90.

2. Baym, *A History of Literary Aesthetics in America* (New York: Frederick Ungar, 1973), 244.

3. Ransom, *The New Criticism* (Norfolk, Conn.: New Directions, 1941), 72.

4. Creeley, "Introduction," in *Selected Writings of Charles Olson* (New York: New Directions, 1966), 6.

5. Tate, "Tension in Poetry," in *Essays of Four Decades* (Chicago: Swallow Press, 1968), 198.

6. Breslin, *From Modern to Contemporary: American Poetry 1945–1965* (Chicago: University of Chicago Press, 1984), 53.

7. Ibid., 250.

8. Lowell, *Selected Poems* (New York: Farrar, Straus and Giroux, 1976), 91.

9. Ibid., 57.

10. Tate, "Tension in Poetry," 57.

11. Wallace Stevens, *The Necessary Angel* (New York: Knopf, 1951), 22.

12. Ciardi, *Mid-Century American Poets* (New York: Twayne, 1950), 7.

13. Ibid., 7.

14. Wilbur, *Things of This World* (New York: Harcourt, 1956), 5.

15. Jarrell, *The Complete Poems* (New York: Farrar, Straus and Giroux, 1969), 196, 114; Shapiro, "The Shield of Achilles," *New York Times Book Review*, 13 March 1955, 4; Stanley Kunitz, Robert Lowell, Robert Penn Warren, and Peter Taylor, *Randall Jarrell, 1914–1965* (New York: Farrar, Straus and Giroux, 1980), 99–100.

16. Richard Ellman and Robert O'Clair, *The Norton Anthology of Modern Poetry* (New York: Norton, 1973), 682.

17. Warren, *Promises: Poems 1954–1956* (New York: Random, 1957), 39–41.

18. Kees, *Collected Poems* (Lincoln: University of Nebraska Press, 1975), 59, 100, 154–57.

19. Olson, *Selected Writings*, 14, 17, 16.

20. Creeley, quoted in Olson, *Selected Writings*, 6; Olson, *Selected Writings*, 7.

21. Levertov, *Collected Earlier Poems* (New York: New Directions, 1979), 78.

22. Levertov, *With Eyes at the Back of Our Heads* (New York: New Directions, 1959), 17; Wright, "The Few Poets of England and America: *The New American Poetry*," *Minnesota Review* 1–2 (Winter 1961): 252.

23. Foster, "The Voice of the Poet: Kenneth Rexroth," *Minnesota Review* 2–3 (Spring 1962): 378, 381.

24. Ginsberg, *Howl and Other Poems*, (San Francisco: City Lights, 1956), 9.

25. Thomas Merrill, *Allen Ginsberg* (New York: Twayne, 1969), 18.

26. Williams, "Introduction," in Ginsberg, *Howl*, 8; Rosenthal, review of *Howl*, *The Nation*, 23 February, 1957, 162.

27. Rexroth, *Assays* (New York: New Directions, 1961), 194; Ginsberg, *Howl*, 44.

28. Ginsberg, "The Art of Poetry VIII," *Paris Review* 37 (Spring 1961): 68.

29. Jack Kerouac, "The Origin of the Beat Generation," *Playboy*, June 1959, 32.

30. Quoted in David Kherdian, *Six San Francisco Poets* (Fresno: Giligia, 1967), 35.

31. O'Hara, *Collected Poems* (New York: Knopf, 1971), 449.

32. Ibid., 370.

33. Ashbery, *Some Trees* (New York: Corinth, 1970), 51.

34. Berryman, *Homage to Mistress Bradstreet* (New York: Farrar, Straus and Giroux, 1956), n.p.

35. Kunitz, *The Poetry of Stanley Kunitz, 1928–1978* (Boston: Little, Brown, 1979), 126, 146.

36. Schwartz, review of *Words for the Wind*, by Theodore Roethke, *Poetry*, June 1959, 203.

37. Roethke, *Collected Poems* (Garden City, N.Y.: Doubleday, 1966), 147.

38. Ibid., 127, 108, 126.

39. Bishop, *The Complete Poems* (New York: Farrar, Straus and Giroux, 1969), 65–67.

40. Jarrell, *Poetry and the Age*, 194.

41. Marjorie Perloff, *The Poetic Art of Robert Lowell* (Ithaca: Cornell University Press, 1973), 83; Rosenthal, *The Nation*, 162.

42. Rosenthal, *The New Poets: American and British Poetry since World War II* (New York: Oxford, 1967), 15; Lowell, Interview, in Malcolm Cowley, *Writers at Work: The Paris Review Interviews, Second Series* (New York: Viking, 1963), 349.

43. Lowell, *Lord Weary's Castle and The Mills of the Kavanaughs* (Cleveland, Ohio: World, 1966), 94.

44. Lowell, *Life Studies and For the Union Dead* (New York: Noonday, 1976), 74. Page references in text are to this edition.

45. Lowell, Interview, 346.

7

A Quilt in Shades of Black: The Black Aesthetic in Twentieth-Century African American Poetry

TIMOTHY SEIBLES

Insofar as self-esteem and self-concept determine the range of action and the boldness with which one acts, a culture is very similar to an individual. Just as a person without self-respect is destined to approach life halfheartedly, eyes fixed on the tops of the shoes, so too will members of an ill-defined culture most likely come to perceive themselves as less capable and less deserving than people who know who they are and who take pride in the events and traditions that have brought them to the present. Because of the plethora of physical and psychological barbarisms perpetrated against African Americans during three centuries of slavery and continuing not so subtly into the present, one of the primary concerns of black writers in the twentieth century has been the resurrection of dignity and self-worth among black people in this country. It is a matter of survival: if people are going to live in the teeth of adversity, they must love themselves enough to believe that their particular lease on the future is worth the effort required to continue struggling forward. Self-esteem is a natural consequence of knowing who you are and liking it, and, willingly or unwillingly, the writers of a particular culture teach that community to recognize, criticize, and, most importantly, to celebrate its truer "face," the portrait composed of all the essential aspects of that culture. By focusing their attention on the myriad features of their own community, black poets found themselves amidst a great sea of material as yet unexplored by (or actively ignored by) any American poet. In fact, until Paul Laurence Dunbar began publishing works in the late nineteenth century, even black American writers were inclined to avoid subjects directly relating to the experiences of black Americans. This was due in large part to a lack of interest among publishers and to the miseducation of these earlier poets whose writings often reflected the bigotry of the whites who had taught them history and literature.

When Dunbar began publishing poems in the mid-1890s, some of them featured phonetic spellings intended to approximate the sounds of what might be called "Slave English." With lines such as these from his poem "The Party,"

> All de folks fom fou' plantations was invited an' dey come,
> Dey come troopin' thick ez chillun when dey hyeahs a fife an' drum
> Evahbody dressed deir fines'— Heish yo' mouf an' git away,
> Ain't seen sich fancy dressin' sence las' quahtly meetin' day,[1]

Dunbar began shaping what has now come to be called a "black literary aesthetic," an aesthetic that embraces the full range of human creativity, but which makes a point of including the experiences of black Americans (as witnessed through their dreams, their rhythms, their physical appearances, their wisdom, their confusion, their anger) as distinct from those of their white counterparts. With both the standard and nonstandard English works of Dunbar providing substantial impetus, soon after the turn of the century black poets began in earnest to uncover and reconstruct the full countenance of black America, the face that had been defiled by white racism and denied a viable place in American society.

The Harlem Renaissance

If the variety and volume of contemporary black poetry can be likened to a literary forest, one could easily say that the few trees from which it sprang were planted and took hold in the ten or fifteen years immediately following World War I. During this period a great number of American blacks migrated to the industrialized North in search of the jobs and the justice that the South would seemingly never offer them. Of course, the racism which pervaded the Northern cities was almost indistinguishable from that which pervaded the Southern cities from which they fled; so black people once again found themselves, for the most part, poor and pressed into certain parts of town intended to "contain" their presence. One such area was Harlem, New York. It is difficult to say exactly why this period was such a fertile one for the black literary community and even more difficult to say why Harlem became home to many of the important writers of the time; but Harlem was indeed the Bethlehem of black literary revival, featuring the powerful voices of Claude McKay, Countee Cullen, James Weldon Johnson, and the man considered by most to be the heart of that movement, Langston Hughes.

In attempting to create and sustain a poetry deeply rooted in the real lives of American blacks, as opposed to a poetry that apologized for the black experience, the poets of the Harlem Renaissance faced a number of rather severe challenges. There was, quite naturally, the hydra of racist forces aligned against them—the white hydra that insisted they were not actually human and therefore could only mimic human thought and speech, that sang of a white God who sent a blond son as a savior, that insisted the only place for a black face was behind a plow or a broom. Even the whites who tried to rise above the bigotry of their own culture, who wanted to encourage the literary ambitions of African Americans, most often assumed that the goal of black writers was "to be as good as" white writers, was to produce works similar to those of whites in both content and style. There was also the inescapable self-doubt that resulted from the geographic and historical isolation of these Harlem voices. Having been grossly miseducated, they could not claim any intimate connection to African culture. They could not stand firmly, as though the Egyptian pyramids towered at their backs, and say, "We will create as the great Africans did before us," nor could they lay any serious claim to Shelley or Donne or Shakespeare. In many ways, these writers had to muster the courage and the genius to completely redefine, to invent, both themselves and the black American community. Otherwise, they would be doomed to echo the degrading idiocies popularized by the sociopolitical machinery of mainstream America. To begin this reconstruction of the African American face, these poets needed something akin to a new language; a new aesthetic demands new terms.

To minimize the chances for organized rebellion, the whites who controlled the plantations of the Old South seldom allowed their black slaves to gather in groups of more than three or four individuals, except on Sundays when they permitted them some crude form of church service. (It was assumed that as long as the slaves were partaking of the Bible and singing hymns for Jesus they could not be plotting against their masters.) As a result, these Sunday meetings became vital and dramatic settings for sharing sorrow and wisdom, for cultivating the hope that would solidify their resolve to survive the coming week. The style of oratory that evolved in the context of the "black church" was and remains a salient feature of the African American presence.

James Weldon Johnson drew the material for his most memorable poems from the rhythms and passionate language of black sermons. Although his first book of poetry, *Fifty Years and Other Poems*, was published in 1917, it was not until the release of *God's Trombones* in 1927 that the public saw Johnson's strongest work. In these lines from "Go Down Death (A Funeral Sermon)," he demonstrates consummate mastery of the diction, rhythmic nuance, and emotional grandeur characteristic of black preaching:

And Death took her up like a baby,
And she lay in his icy arms,
But she didn't feel no chill.
And Death began to ride again—
Up beyond the evening star,
Out beyond the morning star,
Into the glittering light of glory,
On to the Great White Throne,
And there he laid Sister Caroline
On the loving breast of Jesus.[2]

This poetry, like much of the poetry written by American blacks, is intended to be shared orally. The reasons for the development of this strong oral tradition are varied. Some believe it goes all the way back to the African tradition of the *griot*. In African communities griots were highly respected individuals who memorized intricate genealogies and village histories and passed them on orally. Each was a sort of poet-philosopher-historian who kept the wisdom of the people from being lost over time. A more immediate cause for the prevalence of this oral tradition is that during slavery it was a punishable offence to teach slaves to read and write. Therefore, the millions of blacks who suffered the ravages of bondage were completely dependent upon the spoken word, and even after the Emancipation Proclamation there were only limited opportunities for African Americans to become literate. Many of the first blacks to become literate were those early preachers who had been taught to read the Bible. This fact lends historical significance to Johnson's poetry, which remains a clear record of the importance of the black clergy as forerunners to those who would come to articulate the plight and needs of black people in more secular terms.

Of course, in fashioning a black poetry a good deal of borrowing from white poetry went on, especially where form was concerned. Jamaican-born Claude McKay, who immigrated to the United States as a young man, is best known for his proud and angry sonnets such as "The White House" from *Harlem Shadows*, released in 1922:

> Your door is shut against my tightened face,
> And I am sharp as steel with discontent;
> But I possess the courage and the grace
> To bear my anger proudly and unbent.
> The pavement slabs burn loose beneath my feet,
> A chafing savage, down the decent street;
> And passion rends my vitals as I pass,
> Where boldly shines your shuttered door of glass.
> Oh, I must search for wisdom every hour,
> Deep in my wrathful bosom sore and raw,
> And find in it the superhuman power
> To hold me to the letter of your law!
> Oh, I must keep my heart inviolate
> Against the potent poison of your hate.[3]

Another of McKay's powerful sonnets, "If We Must Die," was written in response to the increase in violence directed against blacks by the then-formidable Ku Klux Klan. In this poem the speaker champions an eye-for-an-eye approach to the problem of racial violence: "Like men we'll face the murderous, cowardly pack, / Pressed to the wall, dying, but fighting back!"[4]

Although McKay did not write exclusively in strict forms, his use of the sonnet, a European form, in discussing the predicaments of African Americans points to a number of ambiguities that the writers of the Harlem Renaissance were forced to confront. To complete the tasks set rather heavily before them, those of remaking the black American face and earning a respectable place in the larger scheme of American society for black people without shuffling apologetically toward "honorary white status" by imitating whites, these writers really did need something like a new language, but they knew only English and those bright variations featured in its black derivative. This meant that most of the poetry they studied in developing their skills as writers was written by whites. Therefore, it was inevitable that white literature would be significant in the shaping of the new black poetry. This was compounded by the fact that the vast majority of publishing houses were run by whites, not to mention the fact that the majority of those who could and would read poetry were white.

This problem of who would be publishing and reading their poetry, this problem of *audience*, affected the different Renaissance writers in

different ways. Some who believed, as Countee Cullen and Georgia
Douglas Johnson did, that poetry should be more universal than emblem-
atic of race, wrote with a biracial audience in mind. These writers were
as interested in proving black literary talent to whites as they were in
reaching black people. Others, most notably James Weldon Johnson and
Langston Hughes, were more committed to what is presently considered
a black aesthetic and thus focused on the muse of black culture.

Countee Cullen was cousin to Claude McKay in his fascination with
traditional English forms. His first book, *Color*, was released in 1925,
and although it was evident from his earliest works that Cullen was
determined to be a great poet, he was also tortured by the notion of
being a black artist in a world dominated ruthlessly by whites. In his well-
known meditative sonnet "Yet Do I Marvel," which features allusions to
Tantalus and Sisyphus, the speaker quizzically examines the actions of
God. Through the first twelve lines he repeatedly concludes, with some
effort, that God must know what He's doing, but in the last couplet he
is dumbfounded by God's having made "a poet black, and bid him sing!"[5]

Cullen was also among the first African American poets to write with
great passion (and sometimes confusion) about his relationship to Africa.
Knowing little about the land of his ancestors, he vacillated between the
belief that his African heritage was something about which to be proud,
as in these lines from the poem "Heritage,"

> What is Africa to me:
> Copper sun or scarlet sea,
> Jungle star or jungle track,
> Strong bronzed men, or regal black
> Women from whose loins I sprang
> When the birds of Eden sang?
> *One three centuries removed*
> *From the scenes his fathers loved,*
> *Spicy grove, cinnamon tree,*
> *What is Africa to me?*

and the belief, expressed in the same poem, that in some insidious way
his "hot jungle blood" would never quite allow him to be civilized, try
though he might to resist its "drumming":

> So I lie, who always hear,
> Though I cram against my ear
> Both my thumbs, and keep them there,
> Great drums throbbing through the air.
> So I lie, whose fount of pride,

Dear distress, and joy allied,
Is my somber flesh and skin,
With the dark blood crammed within
Like great pulsing tides of wine
That, I fear, must burst the fine
Channels of the chafing net
Where they surge and foam and fret.[6]

This conflict about who or what he was as an African American was symptomatic of the inner struggles of many American blacks in their search for an understanding of themselves that was different from the one offered by whites. Cullen's work as one of the initiators of "the dialogue with Africa" was extremely important in that it pointed toward the need for black people to embrace their ancestry as a first step toward embracing themselves.

Although he was never able to resolve this issue comfortably for himself, Cullen remained remarkably prolific, releasing two more collections of his poetry, *Copper Sun* and *The Ballad of the Brown Girl*, in 1927; in 1929 he released *The Black Christ*, which he wrote in France while on a Guggenheim fellowship. In "That Bright Chimeric Beast" from *The Black Christ*, Cullen articulates his faith in the poetic imagination, using a diction that offers no clue of his having grown up black in Harlem:

Bird of the deathless breast,
Fish of the frantic fin,
That bright chimeric beast
Flashing the argent skin,—
If beasts like these you'd harry,
Plumb then the poet's dream;
Make it your aviary,
Make it your wood and stream.

There only shall the swish
Be heard of the regal fish;
There like a golden knife
Dart the feet of the unicorn,
And there, death brought to life,
The dead bird be reborn.[7]

Georgia Douglas Johnson authored three books of poems during the Harlem Renaissance: *The Heart of a Woman* in 1918, *Bronze* in 1922, and *An Autumn Love Cycle* in 1928. Her poems usually featured formal metrical structures that were punctuated by end-rhymes. She is best remembered for her delicate and simple love lyrics such as "I Want to Die While You Love Me" from her first book. Only rarely did she address issues of race, but in the poem "Common Dust" she parodies the American obsession with keeping the races separate: "Can one then separate the dust, / Will mankind lie apart, / When life has settled back again / The same as from the start?"[8] Though she was the most prolific female writer of the Renaissance era, her works are often ignored by students of the period because their pastoral quality seems evocative of an earlier age.[9]

With the publication of his first book, a collection of poems called *The Weary Blues*, Langston Hughes embarked upon a literary career that would make him arguably the single most influential African American writer of the twentieth century. As its title suggests, his first book is shaped by his fascination with the blues, the musical form which Hughes had come to realize "embodied the classical black response to African experience in modern America." Blues music, at its core, is a vehicle for transforming misery, anger, and sorrow into a type of joy, a hope, a faith in the notion that "everything's gonna be alright—somehow"; and before the blues, the music of "Negro spirituals" served the same purpose. Hughes wanted a poetry that had a similar power, and in his quest brought a new verse form to English poetry. In examining the first half of the poem "The Weary Blues," the technical beauty of the lines is seen most clearly "when they are measured against the cadences of urban black speech . . . with its glissandos, arpeggios, and sudden stops"[10] that are clearly derivative of the rural Southern black dialect (which has at its phonetic roots some of the speech sounds of West Africa):

Droning a drowsy syncopated tune,
Rocking back and forth to a mellow croon,
    I heard a Negro play.
Down on Lenox Avenue the other night
By the pale dull pallor of an old gas light
    He did a lazy sway . . .
    He did a lazy sway . . .
To the tune o' those Weary Blues.
. . . .
In a deep song voice with a melancholy tone
I heard that Negro sing, that old piano moan—
    "Aint got nobody in all this world,
    Aint got nobody but ma self.
    I's gwine to quit ma frownin'
And put ma troubles on the shelf."[11]

Like most black poets of this century, Hughes perceived poetry not as some academic exercise intended as grist for fussy scholars and critics, but as a tool for restructuring the consciousness of society. He believed that the crisis of weak self-esteem in the black community as well as the ignorance and insensitivity that powered the harsh bigotry of the white community could be addressed and possibly corrected by a powerful poetry. In these lines from "The Negro Speaks of Rivers," the speaker of the poem meditates proudly upon African rivers as symbols of his ancestral origins, feeling his Africanness as a source of sublime power:

> I've known rivers ancient as the world and older than the flow
> of human blood in human veins.
>> My soul has grown deep like the rivers.
>> I bathed in the Euphrates when dawns were young.
>> I built my hut near the Congo and it lulled me to sleep.
>> I looked upon the Nile and raised the pyramids above it.[12]

In the poem "Mother to Son," a dramatic monologue, a mother exhorts her son—and by implication all black Americans—to keep trying, to keep striving toward a better day:

> So boy, don't you turn back.
> Don't you set down on the steps
> 'Cause you finds it's kinder hard.
> Don't you fall now—
> For I'se still goin', honey,
> I'se still climbin',
> And life for me ain't been no crystal stair.[13]

In these lines from the poem "I Dream a World," the speaker is certain of his humanity, but more wistful than strident in his plea for a socially just world:

> I dream a world where all
> Will know sweet freedom's way,
> Where greed no longer saps the soul
> Nor avarice blights our day.
> A world I dream where black or white,
> Whatever race you be,
> Will share the bounties of the earth
> And every man is free.[14]

Clearly this poem is intended as a call to wakefulness directed at the social conscience of white America, which Hughes is determined to prod toward acceptance of the notion that all people are equally human and, therefore, equally deserving of the fruits of this life.

Langston Hughes was fiercely proud of his black heritage—and utterly convinced that African Americans as African Americans, not honorary whites, would find a place of dignity in American society. He loved jazz, he loved ragtime, he loved blues, he loved the call and response ("A-men!") rhythms of the black church, he loved all things particular to the manner in which black Americans had sustained themselves during their time in the United States. There were those, however, who, though determined to succeed as Harlem Renaissance writers, had some sizable misgivings about cultivating a poetry that placed "too much emphasis on strictly Negro themes," as Countee Cullen said in discussing *The Weary Blues*. Cullen feared that the black authors of the time were becoming "racial artists instead of [universal] artists pure and simple," that they were setting "too definite a limit upon an already limited field."[15] Hughes responded to such criticism with what many consider the finest essay of his life, "The Negro Artist and the Racial Mountain," in which he states:

> Let the blare of Negro jazz bands and the bellowing voice of Bessie Smith singing Blues penetrate the closed ears of the colored near-intellectuals until they listen and perhaps understand. . . . We younger Negro artists who create now intend to express our individual dark-skinned selves without fear or shame. If white people are pleased we are glad. If they are not, it doesn't matter. We know we are beautiful. And ugly too. . . . If colored people are pleased we are glad. If they are not, their displeasure doesn't matter either. We build our temples for tomorrow, strong as we know how, and we stand on top of the mountain, free within ourselves.[16]

The mountain to which Hughes refers is the "urge within the race toward whiteness, this desire to pour racial individuality into the mold of American standardization, and be as little Negro and as much American as possible."[17] With this essay, his first book of poems, and his second book of verse, *Fine Clothes to the Jew* (1927), Hughes's place as the primary proponent of a black literary aesthetic in America was secured. His work, along with the great works of his contemporaries, provided an immense expanse of fertile ground from which the fine African American poets of the next two decades and beyond would spring.

The Thirties and Forties

It is difficult to determine exactly when the Harlem Renaissance came to an end, but within the first several years of the Depression it became evident that a noticeable amount of its momentum had been lost. Clearly, some of the interest in black writers shown by the white public and by

major publishing houses such as Harper and Row, Alfred A. Knopf, and
the Viking Press had had a faddish quality, and the fad had grown older
and lost some of its high luster. Black literary achievement was no longer
shocking. This meant, of course, that an important part of the battle was
won: African American writers had established themselves as a legitimate
cultural force. Their works were applauded and attacked by critics and
scholars of both races. Ironically, one by-product of this victory was a
generally diminished interest which, in conjunction with the nightmarish
economic situation, meant fewer book sales and, subsequently, fewer
publications. If a major press was going to take a loss, it would not do so
for the sake of black literature, which was still regarded by whites as
more ornamental than essential. Nonetheless, there was work to be
done, poetry to be written, as black Americans continued their struggle
for identity and social viability in the United States.

Sterling Brown made his entrance onto the American literary scene
with *Southern Road,* a book of balladic and blues-influenced poems
published in 1932. "The dominant note in Brown's poetry is provided by
his acute understanding of the tragic destiny that had been black people's
on American soil."[18] Although he had been born in Washington, D.C.,
and educated at Williams College and Harvard University, Brown spent
a great deal of time in the rural South, where he absorbed the folktales,
songs, and social perspectives of the blacks whom he believed lived a
life more closely connected to the ordeal of those African Americans who
had endured the ravages of slavery. He was somewhat suspicious of the
flashiness of Harlem (and cities in general), where he felt too much was
too easily "commercialized and prostituted."[19] In some ways, this makes
him the antithesis of Langston Hughes, whose poetry intently studied
urban black life. In these lines from the title poem of the volume, a
chain-gang worksong blues punctuated by the groan ("hunh") of a man
hard at work, it is easy to see the influence of Hughes, in terms of form,
and the presence of Dunbar, in terms of diction:

Swing dat hammer—hunh—
Steady, bo';
Swing dat hammer—hunh—
Steady, bo';
Ain't no rush, bebby,
Long ways to go . . .

Doubleshackled—hunh—
Guard behin';
Doubleshackled—hunh—

Guard behin';
Ball and chain, bebby,
On my min'.[20]

However, the bitter pessimism that pervades this and many other poems
by Sterling Brown is a distinct feature of his work. "In Brown's poetry,
the struggle of black against white appears not merely as an unequal
battle—this is in full conformity with reality—but as a conspiracy care-
fully plotted long before and the execution of which proceeds with all
the inexorable precision of a piece of clockwork." In the ballad "Old
Lem," a courageous black man is given a day to leave town after having
been "insubordinate" to a white man at the commissary; he ignores the
warning and is killed by a white mob that "came by tens."[21]

Given the indigence of the majority of African Americans in both the
rural and the urban setting of his day, it is not difficult to grasp the origins
of Brown's pessimism—especially when viewed against the backdrop of
the larger American society, a society that not only permitted the contin-
ual degradation of its black citizens but made it a mandate by limiting
their opportunities for education and employment and by embracing the
"whites only" signs and other implements that proclaimed the place of
black people as separate and lower than that of their blue-eyed counter-
parts. Nonetheless, Brown was able to write humorously in "When de
Saints Go Ma'chin' Home" that there "mought be another mansion for
white saints / A smaller one . . . not so gran' / As for the rest," and
with passionate optimism in "Strong Men," his lyrical exploration of the
continuing ascent from slavery that takes its title from Carl Sandburg's
line, "The strong men keep coming on":

They dragged you from the homeland,
They chained you in coffles,
They huddled you spoon-fashion in filthy hatches,
They sold you to give a few gentlemen ease.

They broke you in like oxen,
They scourged you,
They branded you,
They made your women breeders, . . .
You sang:
        Keep a-inchin' along
        Lak a po' inch worm . . .
You sang:
        Walk togedder, chillen,
        Dontcha git weary . . .
          The strong men keep a-comin' on
The strong men get stronger . . .[22]

Margaret Walker grew up in Birmingham, Alabama. Because of her deep ties to the South, the poetry of Sterling Brown was very important in shaping her earliest works, though she held Langston Hughes in high esteem as well. In 1942 her first book of poems, *For My People*, won the Yale Series of Younger Poets award. This collection contains a remarkable folk ballad called "Molly Means" which is both humorous and spooky, filled with all the fright of a good Halloween story. However, the most powerful device of this poem is its rhythm, which makes the poem move like a charged blues, a litany a voodoo priestess might use to tap into the mysterious force of the metaphysical: this is not a cadence based on a white European/American understanding of English prosody. In reading the opening stanza aloud, it is very difficult *not* to hear a pulse in the meter very similar to that which informs the rhythmic speech of contemporary rap music.

> Old Molly Means was a hag and a witch;
> Chile of the devil, the dark, and sitch.
> Her heavy hair hung thick in ropes
> And her blazing eyes was black as pitch.
> Imp at three and wench at 'leben
> She counted her husbands to the number seben.
>   O Molly, Molly, Molly Means
>   There goes the ghost of Molly Means.[23]

Although Walker, like Brown, was educated far from Southern black culture, it is clear that her aesthetic sensibilities were largely defined by her experience as an African American in the South.

Another of Margaret Walker's innovations was the introduction of the stanza-paragraph to black poetry. These stanzas resemble prose in that the individual lines travel from margin to margin with no regard for any particular meter; each line draws its significance from its relationship to the movement of the "paragraph" as a whole. In the title poem of the book, the speaker is a ranting oracle intent upon defining black Americans in terms of their sufferings and the small pleasures that allow them to endure. With this piece Walker has joined her voice to those others in the choir of poets determined to sing and sustain a proper face for black America. Note the sixth stanza:

> For my people thronging 47th Street in Chicago and Lenox Avenue in New York and Rampart Street in New Orleans, lost disinherited dispossessed and happy people filling the cabarets and taverns and other people's pockets needing bread and shoes and milk and land and money and something—something all our own.[24]

It would be inaccurate to suggest that it was the black poets exclusively who powered the evolution of a black aesthetic in literature. These poets were reacting to similar movements among black visual artists, black dancers, black novelists, and black social scientists, all of whom, like the poets, witnessed and shared the increasing agitation of the masses of black people who were steadily awakening to the need for a new understanding of both their predicament and themselves. However, it would be misleading also to imply that the development of a black aesthetic in literature (or in any other medium) proceeded with only one or two light skirmishes between the artists themselves. The differences that inspired the intellectual feuding between Langston Hughes and Countee Cullen gave rise to a good number of arguments along related lines. One of the most important debates centered on the question, Is black poetry, with its deliberate emphasis on black culture and the censuring of white America, art or propaganda? Influenced by the militant perspective of black social philosopher W. E. B. Dubois, Claude McKay declared, "All art is propaganda and ever must be."[25] McKay and others of a similar mind were convinced that, insofar as all art has some type of ax to grind, it is necessarily propaganda; the question of compatibility between the two is therefore absurd. In opposition to this perspective, Alain Locke, another distinguished proponent of the black awakening, wrote, "Art in the best sense is rooted in self-expression and . . . is self-contained. In our spiritual growth genius and talent must . . . choose art and put aside propaganda."[26] Later in the same essay, he seems to contradict himself by discussing the specific goals of black art as a vehicle for transforming the racial situation in American society.

The confusion seemed to center on the lack of a clear definition of an artist, and certainly no shared understanding of the black artist's relationship to society then existed. Then, just as now, many regarded an artist as someone whose work is governed by the enigmatic comings and goings of "inspiration." They perceived artists as individuals who appropriately stood outside of human society, whose poetry, music, sculpture, or other work transcended culture or reflected it in some utterly apolitical way—as a footprint in the sand reflects someone's having been in the desert. But most artists, like most people, find themselves inextricably bound to the cultural worlds they inhabit, and the products of their creative labors necessarily explore, explain, criticize, and celebrate this connection. These artists would be considered the spokespersons of their respective communities. In retrospect, it seems only logical that the majority of black American poets would find their niche in this latter category. Given the pathological treatment of the African American community, at what point, realistically, could black Americans—poets, priests, custodians, dentists, or soldiers—contemplate themselves as distinct from their color or race, particularly during the first half of the twentieth century? The conscious mind as well as the psychic substrata of a black American was awash with the sensations that race had prescribed in the context of American society. It would have required a substantial amount of misspent effort for a black writer to produce a body of work that ignored the plight of the black community, which was, in fact, *his or her own plight*. With all of this, the evolution of a black literary aesthetic was inevitable: the lashings of the racial predicament mandated a significant blurring of the boundaries between art and propaganda.

While Margaret Walker continued to enjoy praise for the poems of her prize-winning book, the ever-prolific Langston Hughes released *Shakespeare in Harlem*, also in 1942. Unquestionably a continuation of his earlier works, this book features a number of intimate studies of and dramatic monologues by urban black folks. One of the more memorable pieces in the collection is "Harlem Sweeties," a jubilant chronicling of the various beauty of African American women in which Hughes embraces the entire spectrum of skin tones made possible to black people through the mixing of races (much of it forced during slavery):

> Have you dug the spill
> Of Sugar Hill?
> Cast your gims
> On this sepia thrill:
> Brown sugar lassie,
> Caramel treat,
> Honey-gold baby
> Sweet enough to eat.[27]

It is significant that during a time when most African American women were not employed in glamorous professions, during a time when most were poor and less able to buy the fine dress, during a time when mainstream America's billboards and movies spotlighted only white "goddesses" in silks and satins, Hughes nonetheless croons of their deliciously attractive femininity.

In 1944 *Rendezvous with America*, Melvin B. Tolson's first book, was published. The most striking poem of the collection, "Dark Symphony,"

is a literary "symphony" in which each of its six movements elaborates
upon a loosely defined period of black American history. Tolson's use of
formal Italian pacing terminology throughout this poem is one of the
more obvious signs of the often subtle but ever-present influence of
white art on the works of African Americans. In the first movement,
"Allegro Moderato," the speaker heralds the death of Crispus Attucks, a
black man believed to be the first American casualty in the American
Revolution, who died "Before white Patrick Henry's bugle breath /
Uttered . . . / 'Yea, give me liberty, or give me death.' " In these lines
from the second movement, "Lento Grave" (meaning mournfully slow),
the speaker discusses the years leading up to the Civil War and the
emancipation of the slaves:

> The centuries-old pathos in our voices
> Saddens the great white world,
> And the wizardry of our dusky rhythms
> Conjures up shadow-shapes of ante-bellum years:
>
> Black slaves singing *One More River to Cross*
> In the torture tombs of slave ships,
> Black slaves singing *Steal Away to Jesus*
> In jungle swamps . . .
> Black slaves singing *Swing Low, Sweet Chariot*
> In cabins of death . . .[28]

The angst of the speaker is accented by the references to Negro spirituals,
which arose from the naked despair of those African Americans who were
born, grew old, and died as "property." In the fifth movement of the
poem, "Larghetto," a finger is pointed at the war machinery of whites
who, at that time, were making a wasteland of Europe:

> None in the Land can say
> To us black men Today:
> You send flame-gutting tanks, like swarms of flies,
> And plump a hell from dynamiting skies.
> You fill machine-gunned towns with rotting dead—
> A No Man's Land where children cry for bread.[29]

In the final movement, designated as a march ("Tempo Di Marcia"),
Tolson continues to articulate what must be, when considered in relation
to the various but strident optimism of most of the black poets that
preceded him, a poetics of hope:

Out of abysses of Illiteracy,
Through labyrinths of Lies,
Across wastelands of Disease . . .
We advance!

Out of dead-ends of Poverty,
Through wildernesses of Superstition,
Across barricades of Jim Crowism . . .
We advance!

With the Peoples of the World . . .
We advance![30]

It is also worth noting that, in addition to its symphonic structure, "Dark Symphony" features stanzas of differing lengths and shapes as well as a mixture of lines end-stopped by rhyming words and lines enjambed jaggedly to force irregularities in the meter. From this, it is evident that much of the experimentation (with regard to the strictures of form and the numerous possibilities of free verse) that was transforming the poetry of white America in the 1940s had not gone unnoticed by the black poets of the time.

It could be argued that Gwendolyn Brooks's voice rang more lyrically and beautifully than any other during the two decades immediately following the Harlem Renaissance. Her first volume of poetry, *A Street in Bronzeville*, hit the presses in 1945 as World War II was ending. Hers was a poetry of deep intimacies, isolations, sensitive studies of individual interiors. One of the more moving poems of this first collection is "When You Have Forgotten Sunday: The Love Story." In this poem a female speaker reminisces about a sweet love lost. Focusing on the poem's last section, where it seems one has stumbled upon an open letter that is private but irresistible to the eyes of a stranger, it is easy to see the lyrical and technical skill that Brooks has at her command. The section deftly recounts the fresh, high-spirited, and sensual pleasure of the lovers in their tryst, and then without missing a beat the passage softens in tone, using the metaphor of the lovers as bedclothes ("gently folded into each other"), to open onto the pure textural surface of a gentle but insistently ironic rhetoric in which the speaker points out the indelible quality of what at first might've seemed to them to be an ephemeral experience. Through this tonal and tactical glissando in recapitulating the tryst, the speaker both celebrates and scolds the letting go of it.[31] The sensual swim of Brooks's diction and syntax, the secret sharing implied by it, marks the beginnings of a break from the more "public" voices of the African American writers that preceded her.

Up to this point, most of the poetry written by black Americans spotlighted characters/speakers that resonated as symbols of the race, or symbols of the spirit that would sustain the race, or symbols of the suffering that black people have endured. In Langston Hughes's "Mother To Son," the mother is the embodiment of courage and encouragement. The speakers in Claude McKay's fiery sonnets are not livid with mere personal discontent but wield an anger powered by the frustration of the entire African American community. The man singing the chain-gang song in Sterling Brown's "Southern Road" is the personification of despair, that despair peculiar to black people living in the wake of slavery and in the presence of poorly disguised Jim Crow codes. But in Brooks's "The Mother" one senses a private guilt, a solitary torment, rather than a rallying cry. Similarly, "A Song in the Front Yard" examines the growing itch in a preadolescent girl for mischief "in the back yard now / And maybe down the alley." The child contemplates her mother's warnings about the fates of the bad children there—one "will grow up to be a bad woman"; another is destined for jail—but she nonetheless concludes:

> But I say it's fine. Honest, I do.
> And I'd like to be a bad woman, too,
> And wear the brave stockings of night-black lace.
> And strut down the streets with paint on my face.[32]

Surely, these are the simple, intimate ruminations of one little girl; she is not *every* black girl. There are those who have said that, because Brooks has not named the race of these characters or implied it in any exact way, these poems do not necessarily involve black people at all. To the contrary, it should be assumed that these figures are black, unless it is explicitly stated otherwise, because Gwendolyn Brooks is black—just as we assume unquestioningly that the speakers/characters who live in the works of, say, W. B. Yeats or Walt Whitman or Robert Frost are white, even though these writers seldom if ever specify race.

The efforts of black writers in the forties culminated with Brooks winning the Pulitzer Prize in 1950 for her collection *Annie Allen*. This work continues the delicate yet penetrating psychological portraiture of working-class black people that had its roots in her first book. Though, clearly, the flood of literary energy unleashed in the twenties had subsided somewhat, African American poets continued to produce powerful works that received both critical and, to some extent, popular acclaim. Unfortunately, the progress they had hoped to help effect in the larger social scheme lagged far behind their accomplishments in the artistic realm. Black Americans, on the whole, continued to be treated as second-class citizens—forced to ride in the backs of buses, denied entry to certain stores, offered inferior educational opportunities, turned away from the better jobs, and preyed upon by bigots on the police force and in the government.

The Fifties and Sixties: The Rise of the Revolutionists

In 1951 Langston Hughes published *Montage of a Dream Deferred*, a collage of rhyming and free-verse poems of varying lengths filled with folk wisdom, "hip talk," and a wide range of big-city, Harlemesque visions. Discussing the structure and strategy of this book-length extravaganza, Hughes wrote:

> In terms of current Afro-American popular music and the sources from which it has progressed—jazz, ragtime, swing, blues, boogie-woogie, and be-bop—this poem on contemporary Harlem, like be-bop, is marked by conflicting changes, sudden nuances, sharp and impudent interjections, broken rhythms, and passages sometimes in the manner of the jam session, sometimes the popular song, punctuated by riffs, runs, breaks, and the disc-tortions of the music of a community in transition.[33]

With this statement he heralds the rising significance of jazz as an influence on the poetics of black American writers. The jazz of Charlie "The Bird" Parker was blazing a new trail into the ears of America, and poets, black *and* white, wanted their works to wield some of this fresh force. These lines from "Dream Boogie," in the first section of the book, exemplify Hughes's use of jazz rhythms:

Good morning daddy!
Ain't you heard
The boogie-woogie rumble
Of a dream deferred?

Listen closely:
You'll hear their feet
Beating out and beating out a—

You think
It's a happy beat?

Listen to it closely:
Ain't you heard
something underneath
like a—
     What did I say?
. . . . .
       Hey, pop!
       Re-bop!
       Mop
              Y-e-a-h![34]

Here, Hughes celebrates jazz and related rhythms (most conspicuously in the first quatrain and in the last four lines) while simultaneously suggesting that jazz is quite possibly not as happy and carefree as it seems to be, that it is actually a new musical vehicle for anger, a new response to the frustration of living in a society that persists in "deferring the dream" shared by most blacks, that of a just America. By implication the same must be true of the poems in *Montage of a Dream Deferred*.

The Beat poets, who thrived in San Francisco and Greenwich Village later in the decade, were absolutely committed to the jazz aesthetic—so much so that many of them never committed their pieces to paper but rather composed spontaneously, performing their poems orally while being accompanied by the music in progressive night clubs. Just as the notes of a sax or trumpet solo vanish the instant after they're played, the often surreal, angry, ecstatic, cryptic, and sometimes silly poems of the Beats disappeared the moment after they were spoken. The Beats perceived themselves as jazz instruments whose notes were words. The Beat movement was biracial because the Beat community was too "hip" to be caught up in the idiocy of racism, which, in their eyes, reeked of the lifeless, fearful rigidity that typified the whole white, mainstream, "square" world. For mostly different reasons, the Beats, black and white, were fed up with America. Their attempt to embrace each other, sharing jazz as the members of a family (or race) share a bond of blood, was emblematic of the utopian vision that continued to inform the imaginations of most black writers of the period. The two best-known black Beat poets were Bob Kaufman on the West Coast and LeRoi Jones (Imamu Amiri Baraka) in Greenwich Village; their most important writing would begin early in the next decade in the aftermath of their association with the Beat movement.

In 1955 Rosa Parks refused to give up a seat in the front of a bus in Montgomery, Alabama. Had she not been black this would not have been of any importance, but she was black and was therefore arrested. The bus boycott that resulted from this began a series of events that would affect virtually every facet of American society insofar as race was concerned. In 1957 the first attempt to integrate the public schools of Little Rock, Arkansas, was thwarted by violence and threats of violence. Gwendolyn Brooks responded to the news with her poem "The Chicago 'Defender' Sends a Man to Little Rock," in which the reporter concludes that the racists of the town "are like people everywhere."[35] Poems like this one and Hughes's poems grumbling of a "dream deferred" could be viewed as prophetic with respect to the conflagration that would define the sixties.

With the release of *Preface to a Twenty Volume Suicide Note* in 1961, LeRoi Jones's break with the verse of the Beat scene became official. However, Jones approached the page with a self-absorbed expressionistic zeal that was obviously rooted in his Beat years. Clyde Taylor has written:

> The mark of LeRoi Jones' poetry is the mark of his personality on the printed page. He is the most personal so far of the Afro-American poets. For him poetry is the flow of being, the process of human electricity interacting with the weight of time, tapped and possibly trapped on paper. Feelings, impressions, moods, passions move unedited through a structure of shifting images. . . . Mostly his poems carry no argument, no extractable, paraphraseable statement. They operate prior to the pros and cons of rational, persuasive, political discourse. Even after several readings, one is likely to remember mainly a flavor, a distinct attitude of spirit, an insistent, very personal voice.[36]

If there is one distinct attitude that pervades *Preface* and his next book of poems, it is an attitude of seething unhappiness with regard to self and world. The speaker of Jones's poems is a tormented seeker, a black man who claws at his own mind and the reality that has "ruined" him. Unlike Gwendolyn Brooks's poetry, which invites a reader to take part in the personal discourse of the speaker, this poetry is often quite cryptic and unwelcoming. In reading it, one often feels like a spectator behind the glass of an operating room where a man is going through the first violent contractions of a psychological labor, the results of which will be a new language designed to bring to light a particular type of human agony. In these lines from "Way Out West," it is obvious that Jones does not intend to be didactic, at least not in the manner typical of most black poets before him:

There are unattractive wild ferns
outside the window

where the cats hide. They yowl
from there at nights. In heat
& bleeding on my tulips.

Steel bells, like the evil
unwashed Sphinx, towing in the twilight.
Childless old murderers, for centuries
with musty eyes.

I am distressed. Thinking
of the seasons, how they pass,
how I pass, my very youth, the
ripe sweat of my life; drained off . . .

Like giant rhesus monkeys;
picking their skulls,
with ingenious cruelty
sucking out the brains.[37]

At times, Jones's poetry is a quicksand of movement from thought to image, from observation to introspection. Even in looking outward, his eyes are turned drastically inward, and if the reader is to *learn* from this work he must first accept, to some extent, that Jones's search for a new terminology for disenfranchisement is, in fact, the reader's own.

What makes this poetry difficult is the same thing that makes it remarkable: Prior to Jones, black poets aimed their various sociopolitical complaints at whites and the specific injustices promoted by white bigotry; by contrast, Jones's antirationalism, his insistence upon writing a poetry that couldn't be "reduced" or explained (except as being *what it was*—just like jazz), denied not only the ascendancy but the fundamental validity of the "white reality" that seemed to worship reason and criticism and every facet of the scientific model while relegating the power of emotion and soul to the realm of things superfluous to life. By refusing to enter into the literary dialogue on standard white terms, LeRoi Jones, through his poetry, became a beacon to a new "blacker" reality, a reality more concerned with blues and beauty and the entire spectrum of human feeling than with order and machinery.

In *The Dead Lecturer* (1964) the color gray becomes an emblem of the coldness, the xenophobic rigidity of the white world with its big houses, blond-baby dolls, and Brooks Brothers suits. Jones, like Langston Hughes, was deeply aware of the "urge within black people toward whiteness," the tendency to perceive white people and white ways as somehow "naturally" better, as models to be imitated by all. He believed this urge was pervasive and insidious. How could it be otherwise? Throughout America the good life was presented with a white face—and with the rise of television as a consciousness-shaping tool this was truer than ever. He recognized this urge within himself and wrote to fight against it, and insofar as he felt himself losing the fight (which meant losing himself) he mistrusted and hated himself. In the last stanza of "I Substitute for the Dead Lecturer," the poem from which the book gets its title, Jones writes:

> For all these wan roads
> I am pushed to follow, are
> my own conceit. A simple muttering
> elegance, slipped in my head
> pressed on my soul is my heart's
> worth. And I am frightened
> that the flame of my sickness
> will burn off my face. And leave
> the bones, my stewed black skull,
> an empty cage of failure.[38]

His "sickness" is the urge toward whiteness which could destroy his (black) face, leaving him empty, a no one. Just as Langston Hughes suggested the parameters of a black aesthetic with his poems and, in particular, with his essay "The Negro Artist and the Racial Mountain," through the tumultuous introspections of his early poems LeRoi Jones illustrated that a black aesthetic, a system of creative perception through which African American visions are embraced and expanded, was clearly a psychological necessity for black citizens of the United States.

In 1965 New Directions published Bob Kaufman's first collection of poems, *Solitudes Crowded with Loneliness*. Many of the pieces in this book had been spontaneous creations performed on the Beat scene of San Francisco. Through the use of a tape recorder, they were written down and revised by Kaufman for publication. In contrast to Jones, Kaufman wrote a number of pastoral poems which featured a speaker at peace with, even delighted by, certain intervals of life. In "Cocoa Morning" he writes "Drummer, hummer, on the floor, / Dreaming of wild beats, softer still, / Yet free of violent city noise, / Please, sweet morning, / Stay here forever." As evidenced by these lines, the love of jazz which drew him to the Beat clubs of the fifties remains a part of his psyche. However, Bob Kaufman the iconoclast understood jazz as a weapon, too, as in these lines from "Battle Report":

One thousand saxophones infiltrate the city,
Each with a man inside, . . .

Ten waves of trombones approach the city
Under blue cover
Of late autumn's neoclassical clouds.

Five hundred bassmen, all string feet tall,
Beating it back to bass.

One hundred drummers, each a stick in each hand,
The delicate rumble of pianos, moving in.

At last, the secret code is flashed:
Now is the time, now is the time.

Attack: The sound of jazz.

The city falls.[39]

Here the fist is covered by the kid glove of humor, but it remains a fist, a threat. The "rumble of pianos" is more than mildly reminiscent of Hughes' "boogie-woogie rumble of a dream deferred." Something was terribly wrong in the cities and small towns of America. Although some minor progress pertaining to issues of race and social justice had been made (there had been the utopian gesture expressed in the biracial March on Washington in 1963), it was not nearly enough to stem the tide of desperation and anger that roared through the country after the assassination of Malcolm X in 1965. It seemed as if the invisible dam that had held the rage of black Americans for three hundred years suddenly gave way.

Forty years earlier black people were less sure of themselves—their place in America, their worthiness, and the meaning of their blackness. Because of this uncertainty, they were more willing to ask politely for justice and hope for the best. By the mid-sixties black was unequivocally beautiful, and African Americans, riding the momentum of the struggle for a true identity—begun, for the most part, in the twenties—lived by a new raging certitude and were ready to demand their rightful place in America, to take it by force if necessary. The civil rights movement continued to grow in force; "White Only" was fast becoming a thing of the past. Most of the poetry written by blacks during this period drew its power from the oral tradition of black literature; it was written to be spoken, shouted, and preached. Most poems were secular sermons, direct calls to social consciousness and action, with the "amen" response typical of the church congregation being replaced by the "right on" of the streetwise. As the community became angrier and more daring, the poetry became angrier and more daring; each mirrored and multiplied the passion and resolve of the other. In her poem "The True Import of Present Dialogue: Black vs. Negro," Nikki Giovanni asks:

Nigger
Can you kill . . .
Can a nigger kill
Can a nigger kill a honkie
Can a nigger kill the Man
Can you kill nigger
Huh? . . .
Can you kill the nigger
in you . . .
And free your black hands to
strangle . . .[40]

Don L. Lee, another of the revolutionist poets, well known for his fire-breathing readings, not only celebrated blackness but wrote a number of poems exhorting those African Americans who were hesitant to act against racism to change. Take these lines from "a poem to complement other poems":

change.
like if u were a match i wd light u into something
beautiful. change . . . change. i say into a realblack
righteous aim. like i don't play saxophone but that doesn't
mean i don't dig 'trane.
change . . .
change nigger: standing on the corner, thought him was
        cool. him still standing there. it's
        winter time, him cool.

change,
know the realenemy . . .
change: is u is or is u aint. change. now now
        change, for the better change.
        read a change. live a change. read a
        blackpoem.
        change. be the realpeople. . . .
know the realenemy. change. know the realenemy.
change . . .[41]

Here, Lee's work demonstrates the degree to which urban black dialect dominated the poetry of this new awakening. Standard English was regarded as "white English" by many and was consequently regarded as taboo among those who were most insistent about the need for a revolution in consciousness among blacks. It is also worth noting that, in the above lines, Lee uses the word "change" the way a jazz drummer might use a snare drum to accent or interrupt certain cadences or to emphasize the introduction of a new melody (idea).

During this period the black aesthetic existed as both sword and shield, intended to ward off or metaphorically kill all forces inimical to the rise of black Americans in their quest for self-love and self-empowerment, *black power*. In discussing this, Etheridge Knight wrote, "To accept the white aesthetic is to accept and validate a society that will not allow [blacks] to live. The black artist must create new forms and new values, . . . create a new history, new symbols, myths and legends (and purify old ones by fire)."[42] Of course, just as many of the poets of the Harlem Renaissance wrote with great longing and reverence about Africa, the revolutionists and other poets of the middle to late sixties and early seventies celebrated Africa, their true "Motherland," in their works. The main difference between the poets of the Harlem Renaissance and those of the Black Arts movement forty years later was that while the Harlem voices usually expressed an enduring faith in the essential goodness and corrigibility of American society, the poets of the latter era were all but convinced that the heart of white America was, in fact, a pit of vipers. This gave their works a decidedly separatist bent, in contrast to the works of the Renaissance poets that often pleaded with the conscience of America in the hope that she would mend her evil ways and embrace her black citizens.

An unfortunate by-product of the militancy that pervaded this period was the dismissal by most blacks—poets as well as nonpoets—of virtually all nonmilitant poetry. Not only were white writers shunned because of this attitude, but any black writer whose works explored subjects that were deemed unrelated to the "revolution" was cast away as well. (Probably the best-known African American writer to fall under attack for this reason was Robert Hayden.) Given this climate, poets felt obliged to censor themselves for fear of being labeled a "white man's poet." As a result, the bulk of the poetry written by black authors during this period had a relatively narrow focus, but with rampant police brutality, church bombings, several assassinations, and the Vietnam War forming the sociopolitical backdrop of the period, it is understandable that public anger and militant activism rather than various pastoral celebrations or more introspective self-studies would rule the words of the day.

The Seventies and Eighties: Cooling and Expanding

Eventually things quieted down. America had changed. It had not become a country divided between black and white separatists, nor had it become an integrated utopia. Segregation supported by law had come to an end, but many American hearts remained segregated, and in the work force black people often found themselves—as in the past—"the last hired and the first fired." What was different was the nearly ubiquitous pride that African Americans shared about *being black*, the spiritual stamina and physical grace that it implied. It is impossible to ascertain the degree to which the poetry of the black aesthetic was responsible for the dissemination of this feeling, but, inasmuch as it made the beauty, the yearning, and the visions of black people an exalted feature of the cultural buzz, one can rest assured its contribution was significant. Now it was time to move on. Although a penchant for social change had been and would continue to be an important aspect of the poetry of African Americans, this would no longer dictate the parameters of literary exploration as it had in the recent past.

In 1975 Michael Harper published *Nightmare Begins Responsibility*, which features intricate and jazz-referenced poems such as "Thereisatreemoreancientthaneden":

> Our mode is our jam session
> of tradition,
> past in this present moment
> articulated, blown through
> with endurance,
> an unreaching extended
> improvised love of past masters,
> instruments technically down:
>
> structured renderings reality
> our final war with self;
> rhetoric/parlance arena-word-consciousness:
> morality: man to man. [43]

Here one glimpses a mind in deep contemplation, not a poetry to be shouted but pored over and pondered.

In 1977 June Jordan published a collection of poems entitled *Passion*. Jordan had been influenced by feminist thinking, and a number of the pieces in this book reflect this background. "Case in Point" is a poem about a woman who had been raped twice, once by a white man and once by a black man. The speaker of the poem is responding to another woman who had denied that there was "a silence peculiar to the female." The speaker concludes that the silence of a woman being raped is exactly that silence. In that same collection, the poem "Newport Jazz Festival . . ." celebrates, among other things, a man singing:

> That man was singing
> Baby
> Baby if you come with me
> I'll make you my own Dairy Queen
> or if that's locked we'll find an all-night Jack-
> in-the-Box steak sandwich / fried onion rings
> blackcherry / strawberry / butterscotch shake
> blackcherry / strawberry / butterscotch
> *shake*[44]

This poem is surely meant to be read aloud or sung in the tradition of the blues poem initiated by Langston Hughes in the twenties.

Killing Floor (1979), the second book of poems by Ai (Florence Ai Ogawa) is a collection of brilliantly rendered persona poems. Ai's ability to bring to life characters, past and present, young and old, male and female, is simply unmatched by any poet, black or white. Her sense of detail and her mastery of the nuances of diction that bring a voice to life are evident in these lines from "The Mortician's Twelve-Year-Old Son":

> Lady, when you were alive
> I'd see you on the streets
> the long green dress with the velvet flower . . .
>
> Now the gas lamps half-light the table,
> washing the sheet that covers you with shadows . . .
>
> I lift the sheet, rub the mole on your cheek
> and it comes off black and oily on my hand.
> I bend over your breasts and sing,
> *love, sister, is just a kiss away.*
> I cover each nipple with my mouth.[45]

Although a number of the militant poets of the sixties were unable to make the artistic transition to the next period, Haki R. Madhubuti, formerly Don L. Lee, has remained prolific. His new African name, like

most of his poetry, reflects his ongoing, albeit quieter, fascination with
black people and the issues of the black community. In 1984 Third World
Press released *Earthquakes and Sun Rise Missions*, a collection of his
poems and essays. These lines from "Rainforest" constitute a love poem
to all black women:

> sweet knows honey & i know you.
> under salted water tides
> & running against polluted earth
> i've tried to be good to you woman
> tried to care beyond words . . .
> you are the original high & dream maker
> & true men do not try to limit you.
>
> listen woman black . . .[46]

The primary change in Madhubuti's work has been a softening in tone,
though his anger still finds a way into some of his poems, and much of
his writing remains didactic.

Cornelius Eady's *Victims of the Latest Dance Craze*, a collection of
poems that is, at various intervals, a jazz orchestra of sounds/rhythms, a
surrealist's eye feast, and a quiet place to think, was published in 1985.
Eady's work reflects a multicultural set of influences and has done a great
deal to stretch the parameters of the African American literary aesthetic.
In the title poem of the book he writes:

> Here is the world (what's left of it),
> in brilliant motion,
> The oil slick at the curb
> Danced into a thousand
> Splintered steps.
> The bag ladies toss off their
> Garments
> To reveal wings.
>
> "This dance you do," drawls the cop,
> "What do you call it?"
> We call it scalding the air.
> We call it dying with your
> Shoes on.
>
> And across the street
> The bodies of tramps
> Stumble
> In a sober language.[47]

In the final analysis, it is difficult to speak definitively about what possible forms and directions black American poetry may take in the future. In discussing the plight and the potential of African Americans, writer-philosopher Samuel Allen has written:

> The black poet is decisive in the task of striking from the disparate elements of the alienated African presence in the West the coin of a new awareness. It is, indeed, a fusion which is in the process of realization, yet the emphasis is necessarily upon the denied, but essential, sources of the black experience, rather than white Western influences. We are not heirs to the Greeks, but willy-nilly we inhabit in part this cultural terrain. The poet must simultaneously discover and create his authentic voice. He must find his way in the selective use of elements from these two bodies of tradition, the resolution of which must ultimately be felt as one, which must be cast in his likeness and according to his need.
>
> Black poetry will be, in a fuller sense, a poetry of self-discovery, . . . enabling us to know and to touch the wonder and the beauty, as well as the pain, of our common lot in this time and place. It is, ultimately, in its best expression, the task of the discovery of man, not in the sense of two thousand years of a xenophobic Western culture, . . . but in a more humanistic celebration of our own denied and particular experience.[48]

If American society continues to evolve in a healthy, culturally pluralistic way, then it is likely that black artists, the black aesthetic, will embrace more and more of the world's offerings because African Americans, like Asians and Europeans and Aborigines, are citizens of the world and, as such, are destined to share in and express its totality. If, on the other hand, whites insist on sustaining a virulent racism that allows them to treat other peoples as things, black people will sustain themselves with the same spiritual and physical tenacity that has allowed them to survive up to the present.

Notes

1. Dunbar, "The Party," *American Negro Poetry*, ed. Arna Bontemps, rev. ed. (New York: Hill and Wang, 1974), 9.
2. Johnson, "Go Down Death (A Funeral Sermon)," in *American Negro Poetry*, 4.
3. McKay, "The White House," in *American Negro Poetry*, 31–32.
4. McKay, "If We Must Die," in *American Negro Poetry*, 31.
5. Cullen, "Yet Do I Marvel," in *American Negro Poetry*, 88.
6. Cullen, "Heritage," in *American Negro Poetry*, 83–84.
7. Cullen, "That Bright Chimeric Beast," in *American Negro Poetry*, 87.
8. Johnson, "Common Dust," in *American Negro Poetry*, 20.

9. Darwin T. Turner, ed., *Black American Literature* (Columbus, Ohio: Merrill, 1970), 199.

10. Arnold Ampersad, "Langston Hughes," in *Voices and Visions: The Poet in America,* ed. Helen Vendler (New York: Random, 1987), 358, 374.

11. Hughes, "The Weary Blues," in *The Langston Hughes Reader* (New York: George Braziller, 1958), 87.

12. Hughes, "The Negro Speaks of Rivers," in *The Langston Hughes Reader*, 88.

13. Hughes, "Mother to Son," in *American Negro Poetry*, 67.

14. Hughes, "I Dream a World," in *American Negro Poetry*, 71.

15. Quoted in Ampersad, "Langston Hughes," 377.

16. Hughes, "The Negro Artist and the Racial Mountain," *The Nation* 122 (23 June 1926): 694.

17. Ibid., 693.

18. Jean Wagner, "Sterling Brown," in *Black Poets of the United States*, trans. Kenneth Douglas (Urbana: University of Illinois Press, 1973), 481.

19. Ibid., 477.

20. Brown, "Southern Road," in *The Forerunners: Black Poets in America,* ed. Woodie King, Jr. (Washington, D.C.: Howard University Press, 1975), 35.

21. Wagner, "Sterling Brown," 482; Brown, "Southern Road," 39.

22. Brown, "When de Saints Go Ma'chin' Home," in *American Negro Poetry*, 55; Brown, "Strong Men," in *The Poetry of Black America*, ed. Arnold Adoff (New York: Harper, 1973), 60–61.

23. Walker, "Molly Means," in *American Negro Poetry*, 130.

24. Ibid., 128.

25. Quoted in Jean Wagner, "The Negro Renaissance," in *Black Poets of the United States,* 170.

26. Ibid., 170.

27. Hughes, "Harlem Sweeties," in *Three Thousand Years of Black Poetry*, ed. Alan Lomax and Raoul Abdul (New York: Dodd, Mead, 1970), 33–34.

28. Tolson, "Dark Symphony," in *American Negro Poetry*, 38.

29. Ibid., 40.

30. Ibid., 41.

31. Brooks, "When You Have Forgotten Sunday: The Love Story," in *The Black Poets*, ed. Dudley Randall (New York: Bantam, 1971), 168–69.

32. Brooks, "A Song in the Front Yard," in *The Poetry of Black America*, 153.

33. Hughes, "Montage of a Dream Deferred," in *The Langston Hughes Reader*, 89.

34. Ibid., 89–90.

35. Brooks, "The Chicago 'Defender' Sends a Man to Little Rock," in *The Poetry of Black America*, 155–56.

36. Clyde Taylor, "Baraka as Poet," in *Modern Black Poets*, ed. Donald B. Gibson (Englewood Cliffs, N. J.: Prentice-Hall, 1973), 45.

37. Baraka [LeRoi Jones], "Way Out West," in *The Poetry of Black America*, 252–53.

38. Jones, *The Dead Lecturer* (New York: Grove, 1964), 37.

39. Kaufman, "Cocoa Morning," in *American Negro Poetry*, 187; Kaufman, "Battle Report," in *American Negro Poetry*, 189.

40. Giovanni, "The True Import of Present Dialogue: Black vs. Negro," in *The Black Poets*, 318.

41. Lee, "a poem to complement other poems," in *The Black Poets*, 300–302.

42. Quoted in Addison Gayle, Jr., "Introduction," in *The Forerunners*, xxii.

43. Harper, *Nightmare Begins Responsibility* (Urbana: University of Illinois Press, 1975), 94.

44. Jordan, *Passion*, reprinted in *Naming Our Destiny: New and Selected Poems* (New York: Thunder's Mouth Press, 1989), 80, 81–82.

45. Ai, *Killing Floor* (Boston: Houghton Mifflin, 1979), 9.

46. Madhubuti [Don L. Lee], *Earthquakes and Sun Rise Missions* (Chicago: Third World Press, 1984), 77.

47. Eady, *Victims of the Latest Dance Craze* (Chicago: Ommation Press, 1986), 3–4.

48. Samuel Allen, quoted in *The Forerunners*, 4.

8

American Poetry in the 1960s

LESLIE ULLMAN

Self as Frontier: Permission and Necessity

The intellectual and cultural climate at the end of the 1950s resembled a stew just put on to simmer, its flavors present but not yet blended, its ingredients still knocking against one another. Both the poetry scene and the culture at large were marked, on the one hand, by complacency and repression, expressed in varying degrees of zeal for spent traditions, and, on the other, by raw energy arising from new inventions, modes of thought, and styles of living which, in turn, had begun to open up compelling possibilities for self-exploration and expression. The culture's predilection for dichotomies, though not a necessarily true gauge of the options available to it, nevertheless created a kind of truth around itself; the sixties began in a spirit of polemic, its energies polarized between conservation and innovation, structure and anarchy, the known and the unknown.

The famous "war of the anthologies," in keeping with the spirit of the times, more or less defined the state of American poetry. *New Poets of England and America*, edited by Donald Hall, Robert Pack, and Louis Simpson, had appeared in 1958; it offered new writers under forty whose work best carried forward the tradition of formal, detached, and ironic poetry favored by the New Critics and the academic establishment. The fact that promising new poets of America were placed in a kind of aesthetic brotherhood with those of England reveals the basic assumptions held by this "camp": that the English tradition still provided major grist for American poetry, despite the impact of innovative American poets such as Whitman, Pound, and Williams; and that symmetry and restraint, as elements of style, could and very likely should govern content. The anthology generally was greeted with admiration but not with excitement. Its contributors obviously knew their business, but, with a few exceptions, they sounded very much alike in their restraint, their elegance, and their obvious concern with craftsmanship. James Dickey, who reviewed books articulately and with considerable influence throughout the late fifties and the sixties, labeled them "The School of Charm."[1] In 1960, however, Donald Allen's anthology, *The New American Poetry 1945–1960*, appeared on the scene to announce the arrival of a new, uniquely American verse descended from the Pound-Williams-Stevens generation, through more recent writers such as Kenneth Rexroth and Louis Zukofsky, and brought to fruition by the generation of poets associated with the four underground movements that had flourished, mostly on the East and West coasts, throughout the fifties: the Black Mountain Projectivists, the poets of the San Francisco Renaissance, the Beats, and the New York school. Their work was accompanied by statements on poetics by Charles Olson, Frank O'Hara, Lawrence Ferlinghetti, Michael McClure, and other contributors, all of whom either announced or implied an unconditional rejection of the aesthetic associated with academic poetry in favor of freer interaction between the poet's sensibilities and the content of the poem, allowing that content to create itself in adherence to its own laws.

The condition of the culture at large had a direct and understandable connection with the sudden popularity of these formerly avant-garde poetries. As the sixties got underway, remarkable economic growth and stability began to yield an unsettling plenitude of discoveries and improvements: jet travel, direct dialing, credit cards, oral contraceptives, space exploration, and the institutionalization of television which provided, among other things, the novelty of immediate and extensive news coverage.[2] Suddenly, historical events such as the Cuban missile crisis and four political assassinations were brought live or nearly live into living rooms, interchangeably with the evening's entertainment. As a result of all these developments, individuals were forced to undergo a quaking of the boundaries between self and world even as the stronghold of the self was being celebrated as intact, in a presumed and superficial manner, by the wealth of conveniences and opportunities being made available to the individual. In reality, any sensitive self was likely to feel divided in the presence of old rules and new choices, in the uncooked stew of the times, in the seductive pull of revolutionary thinking that touched upon every aspect of personal and political life. The world itself seemed to have grown much smaller and more complex. Time seemed to expand as a moment-by-moment construct without actually slowing. History no longer moved in its old, linear fashion but seemed to explode in layers of crisis and discovery. Thus, even before the Vietnam War pressed so many Americans to question their basic assumptions about themselves, the necessity to redefine some strong-hold within the self arose as a necessary response to the phenomenon of a changed reality. Forms of this response found expression in the burgeoning popularity of psychoanalysis and encounter groups, mind-expanding drugs, and sensationalistic forms of art, all of which sought to develop or emphasize the self, that construct of perception and consciousness, as the locus of experience and meaning. In the beam of all this attention, the phenomenon of self expanded before the American eye as a little known, hence explorable and expandable, entity—a legiti-mate frontier.

Although polarities in the early sixties have provided in this essay a convenient point of departure, they should not mark the last word about the poetry scene at the beginning of this crucial decade, when the brilliant energy of past and present innovators took hold once and for all and resulted in America's at last discovering itself through a poetry of its own. There was also a vast, reasonably tranquil middle ground where many "established" poets quietly were questioning and loosening the bonds of formalist demands. Adrienne Rich could have been speak-ing for a number of these poets when she explained in an introduction to a poetry reading in 1964 that the "perfection of order" had begun to grate against her increasing need to confront the fact that "experience is always greater and more unclassifiable than we give it credit for being" and that she now valued whatever might arise from her unconscious in order "to listen to more than the one voice of a single idea."[3] Elsewhere she compared writing in form to handling live, fiery material with "asbestos gloves." Galway Kinnell spoke of wanting to write without "scaffolding." Louis Simpson arrived at a point where form appeared to him as "a straitjacket." And in an article that appeared in *Commentary* in 1959, Barbara Gibbs and Francis Golffing observed that despite the persistent popularity of the small, self-sufficient, well-crafted poem, the poetry scene generally was being altered by poets' need to break the "tegument" of form, just as Navajo rug weavers left a "break" in their patterns, in order to "let the spirit in."[4] Thus were the fifties and early sixties marked by preparation, the small and large technical openings in poetic form. And the self rushed into those openings, releasing tremendous energy, as is now clear in retrospect, making the decade one of the most crucial in the history of North American poetry.

The Confessional Poets: Personal History as Medium

The Confessional movement in poetry served as a vital transition between the energies released by avant-garde poetry of the fifties, especially Ginsberg's Whitmanesque claims to total freedom of self-exploration and expression, and the quieter but pervasive loosening of the formalist aesthetic Gibbs and Golffing noted at the end of the fifties. Both Robert Lowell and John Berryman stand as crucial transitional figures of this movement, combining prodigious formal knowledge and skill with a kind of helplessness before the eruptions of the raw self, the flawed self, a self grappling with a congenital despair. The confessional force they released into their writing worked in direct opposition to the mannerly removal of poet as individual that had characterized the mainstream poetry offered in the Hall, Pack, and Simpson anthology, and it opened the way for public and critical acceptance of other, more exploratory and affirmative manifestations of self in the work of poets such as Adrienne Rich, James Dickey, and John Logan and in all the significant poetry movements in the sixties.

Lowell and Berryman were flanked by W. D. Snodgrass, Sylvia Plath, and Anne Sexton, all of whom had studied with Lowell at one time or another. Their work shares qualities which define Confessional poetry of the early sixties as a genre: a loosening if not a jettisoning of traditional aspects of prosody and form, aggressive candor, and direct confrontation with personal failure, emotional pain, and mental illness. Most of these poets also shared a tragic inability to redeem the self, in their personal lives, from the courageous but overwhelmingly painful process of self-confrontation they enacted in their poetry. Lowell succumbed to heart failure at the age of sixty-one after a long and debilitating struggle with mental illness, and Berryman, Plath, and Sexton committed suicide. Nevertheless, they left behind them a poetry that in itself is alive and liberating, fueled as it is by the will to explore, confront, and reveal.

The publication of Robert Lowell's *Life Studies* in 1959 heralded, after Ginsberg's *Howl*, a second and more solid beginning of this personal poetry. Earlier in the fifties, Lowell had been influenced by the idiosyncratically personal poems of his former student, W. D. Snodgrass, who seemed to him to travel successfully the thin line between sentimentality and dignified vulnerability. Snodgrass's own important volume, *Heart's Needle*, appeared around the same time as *Life Studies* and helped to launch Confessional poetry as a genre. Ultimately, however, the self-confrontation Snodgrass enacts is less extreme than Lowell's, cast more formally and more out of the "daily neuroses and everyday failures" of someone leading a more or less normal life, painful in a universal sense but not shocked or shaken by its own revelations.[5] In *Life Studies*, Lowell relinquishes religious faith, the illusions handed down by his lineage, and the familiar demands of the formalist aesthetic for the painful and perhaps seductive task of self-confrontation that became a popular undertaking throughout the culture as the sixties progressed. Coming at the end of a decade of cultural self-satisfaction marked by faith in science, God, and country, *Life Studies* broke new ground with its despairing yet elegant lucidity. It was followed by *For the Union Dead* in 1964, which continued to develop Lowell's stoicism and a finely balanced personal-historical perceptive, and then by the sonnetlike poems in *Notebook*, written between 1967 and 1968 and published in 1969, which he conceived of as a kind of journal, turning even more exclusively to the personal.

Where Lowell offers a self stripped of illusion and internal stability but not of dignity, John Berryman offers in the *Dream Songs*, which poured from him throughout the sixties, an outrageous self whose flaws are not only revealed but celebrated literally in "song." Berryman does not confront pain in order to transcend it or to reposition the self; rather, he creates a persona out of his pain, his unruly secrets, and the result is a picaresque hero riddled with lust and longing and an abrasive sort of integrity that makes him wear his life like a hair shirt. This persona is a multidimensional presence named Henry, Henry Pussycat, or Mister Bones, who talks to himself interchangeably in the first, second, or third person and ultimately reveals himself in all his dimensions as interchangeable with Berryman himself. Henry has, according to Berryman, "suffered an irreversible loss" (analogous to Berryman's father's suicide, which is thought to be the underlying cause of Berryman's obsessional relations with work and drink), hungers painfully after women, casts them aside, wrestles with his conscience (one of his many voices), and zigzags between being an outsider seeking acceptance inside and an insider seeking to be left alone. The first batch of Dream Songs appeared in the Pulitzer Prize-winning *77 Dream Songs* (1964) and the remainder in *His Toy, His Dream, His Rest* (1968); all were collected in *The Dream Songs*, published in 1969.

The self in Berryman's poems is less naked than it is in Lowell's, even though it is more aggressively neurotic, because it blossoms forth in language and syntax which break and remake old "rules" of form to produce a voice that is as much a brilliant performance as it is confession. Berryman was a first-rate scholar, steeped in the English poetic tradition and fluent with its forms; in the *Dream Songs* he draws from that tradition in his use of archaic syntactical inversions and other fragments of "high-style" speech reminiscent of the great English poets whose works he taught at Harvard and Princeton. He also retains a sonnetlike form in his consistent use in each Dream Song of three six-line stanzas and slant rhyme patterns. But he interweaves this with the blues beat of minstrel dialect, Henry in blackface, a soul voice that recasts all formal gestures into an idiosyncratic and unmistakably contemporary voice. One might think that Berryman's sleight-of-hand changes in dialect would clash with one another—arising as they do from a speaker whose very substance is conflict—but they rarely do. And the collective impact of all the Dream Songs, each of which reveals Henry in a different mood or dilemma and is not meant as an arrival, nevertheless is that of a long and skillfully orchestrated narrative poem that reinforces Henry's persona as memorable and cohesive in its very undoneness. This play of fragments and contradictions is characteristic of much experimental art and literature that emerged from "the underground" in the sixties, heralded by America's belated "discovery" of Surrealism and producing other aggressively original writers such as Donald Barthelme, whose satirical meshing of different states of consciousness and jargons in short stories parallels Berryman's innovations with poetic form. But Berryman's technical brilliance, influential as it was, facilitated a more significant advance in the treatment of self in poetry; *The Dream Songs* woo us to accept the impossible where self is concerned. John Bayley states that they offer no ideal but "the living ego as it has to be." He further notes that Berryman's creation of beautifully wrought poetry out of a chronically imperfect self is a particularly American undertaking.[6] By the authority vested in him by the power and caginess of his voice, Berryman manages to carry Ginsberg's enterprise a step further, demolishing the boundary between acceptable and unacceptable versions of self in poetry.

Both Sylvia Plath and Anne Sexton firmly grounded the Confessional movement in a more direct and intense use of the personal. They dealt straightforwardly, though in different ways and not exclusively, with their lives as women—the physical life of the body, the pull between that biological life and the mental life, the trickeries of love, the awesome or tyrannical presence of children, and the disturbing power still exerted by deceased parents. Both poets also dealt frankly with an attraction to death, a preoccupation which seems linked with extraordinary sensitivity and lack of defenses against the impact of daily observations and experience. In the work of both poets, this sensitivity took positive expression in dazzling and exact images, instant metaphorical fusions, and a prosody often stripped of all design save for the insistent beat of strongly felt direct statement. Their poetry conveys the tremendous pressure of an inner reality demanding expression. As a result, though neither poet consciously intended to speak out for womankind, Plath and Sexton broke ground for women writers and also expanded experiential territory for all writers by making female experience and sensibility not only viable but powerful subjects for poetry.

Of the two, Sylvia Plath is the most intense, the most disturbing. After her suicide in 1963 and the posthumous publication of her second volume, *Ariel,* she became both a cult figure and a respected member of the literary pantheon. Many of the poems in *Ariel* were written at the rate of three a day shortly before her death, and they consolidate opposing elements that had already begun to distinguish the work in her first book, *The Colossus* (1960): an almost ecstatic sensitivity that enlarges the outer world through disturbingly vivid but accurate images, and an overwhelming attraction to a release from that world to the purity of death. This attraction was a more central issue for her than it was for Sexton and seemed, in fact, the flame that fed both her life and her poetry. Her later poems especially play out a conflict that is universal in a certain sense but one that for Plath became pathological, ultimately resolvable only in death. From her autobiographical novel *The Bell Jar* (1963) and from the wealth of letters and journal material published after her death, it is clear that Plath's tragic self-absorption/self-exile had roots in her own self-defeating need to conform to—rather than transcend—a conventional world and set of expectations which offered meager outlets for her extraordinary energy and vision. Plath's poetry does not deal directly with these autobiographical facts but instead distorts them to render, with great emotional honesty, an inner atmosphere that literally consumed her in its compelling and terrible heat. Like Berryman, then, Sylvia Plath turned what might well have been pathetic neurosis into a poetry of great beauty and power. She offers a self in a state of jeopardy and awareness caught at exhilarating heights, poem by poem, before its final overload and plunge.

Anne Sexton's "confessions" relate less to a problematic self than to the self responding forcefully to the difficult business of living. Real circumstances generally are present as a backdrop or in the titles of her poems, and many of her revelations touch upon familiar "sins" such as abortion and adultery, the forebodings that surround early middle age, the poignant mixture of feelings aroused by the presence of growing children, and so on. This is not to say that Sexton settles for merely quotidian experience but that she plunges into familiar territory and intensifies it, renders it fresh and intimate. Like Plath, she longed for death and eventually took her own life, but her own experience of that sickness of spirit did not override other elements of her sensibility, such as a sometimes deadly wit and an ability to celebrate her body, her children, and the fiercely joyous side of a turbulent emotional life. Thus, although neurosis and suffering are present in her poems, they do not define, as they tend to do in Berryman and Plath's work, its range of experience and emotion. Sexton offered a more accessible presence than did the other two poets, and her work was enormously popular. Her first volume, *To Bedlam and Part Way Back*, appeared in 1960, followed by *All My Pretty Ones* (1962), *Live or Die* (1966), and *Love Poems* (1969).

The Projectivists: Body as Medium

The Projectivists preceded the Confessional poets in establishing and exploring personalized alternatives to Modernist aesthetics with the publication in 1950 of Olson's manifesto, "Projective Verse," and the consequent institutionalization of his theories at Black Mountain College and in the magazines *Black Mountain Review* and *Origin*. Olson sought to emphasize self as organism rather than as psychological construct and the body itself as a mediating system whose very acts of mediation between perception and communication provide both the form and content of poetry. Olson and the poets who worked this territory (Creeley, Levertov, Duncan, Snyder, Blackburn) comprised a major strain of the avant-garde throughout the fifties; in the sixties the Projectivists became part of the mainstream, with Olson's original, manifestolike tenets undergoing some softening, some expansion, in the prose writings of Denise Levertov.

Robert Creeley, who maintained an active dialogue with Olson and expanded the Projectivist aesthetic in several essays of his own, became known as a particularly ingenious and original practitioner of Olson's theories. In his poems, thought invents itself phrase by phrase—not in the orderly sentence-units of written thought but in the starts and stops, the rushes and slowings of the mind in the midst of its effort. His accomplishment is to re-create the *sensation* of thinking, in its moment, by transferring to the reader a kind of heightened or "stoned" awareness of the movements of his own mind. Creeley's poetry did not change significantly in the sixties, but it became very popular as the culture at large began to appreciate and explore heightened consciousness as a phenomenon in its own right, through drugs and rock music and, at a higher level, the provocations of other minimal forms, among them Abstract Expressionist painting and the atonal music of composers such as John Cage.

Where Creeley offers the sensations of thinking, Denise Levertov offers the sensations of perceiving, stressing the five senses as wellsprings and objects in the world as inexhaustible sources of nourishment for the poet. Her work in the late fifties dealt with the surfaces of ordinary objects; in the sixties it became increasingly visionary, probing those surfaces for the underlying energies, or powers, that generate language. This process began with her 1959 volume, *With Eyes at the Back of Our Heads*, and continued in *The Jacob's Ladder* (1961) and *O Taste and See: New Poems* (1964). The interplay between mind and objects became her focus, and in the process both the poet and the objects became luminous with presence, or meaning, revealed by what Levertov described as an "ecstasy of attention, a passion for the thing known."[7]

Like the other Projectivists, Levertov locates herself firmly in the body and the ordinary world, but she experiences her tenancy there more intensely, more omnivorously than does Olson with his academically objective approach or Creeley with his daringly pared-down one. For Levertov, experience is not just enacted in a poem but is "tasted for the first time."[8] Life is a "temple" before which "the poet stands open-mouthed." Where Olson uses the language of science, Levertov uses the language of awe. And like other poets who embraced those aspects of self and world which affirm the self in its moments of intense awareness (especially Bly, most theoretical of the group that celebrated the unexplored depths of consciousness and psyche), she became a strong force in establishing a poetry of protest. To be so vibrantly present in the world inevitably led her to disenchantment, indignation, recognition of "the now" as gone awry. As the decade wore on, her poems in *The Sorrow Dance* (1967), *Relearning the Alphabet* (1970), and *To Stay Alive* (1971) began to deal more with the experience of alienation, and they became more strident, although early in her transition she effectively navigated the fine line between the private and the political.

In the sixties Levertov also produced lectures and essays which expanded upon, and made more accessible, Olson's theories. "Some Notes on Organic Form," which she wrote in 1965, is a supple rendering of Olson's scientific terminology and manifestolike delivery, recasting the notion of form as an extension of content to form as a *revelation* of content, of breath-based rhythm to "rhythm of the inner voice," body as resonant organism to body as metaphorical entity. To the physical connotations of the word "organic" she added terms relating to the less definable but palpable phenomenon of that organism's inner life: "intuition," "feeling," and even "ecstasy."

Both Robert Duncan and Gary Snyder extended the original Projectivist tenets even further from their strictly Objectivist origins by seeking to establish organic poetry as more than an aesthetic of sensibility within a given moment—as an ultimate way of being, living, day to day. Levertov had moved in this direction to a point, embracing the world as contemporary Western culture knows it and seeing poetry as a way of worshipping, or celebrating, that world. Both Duncan and Snyder attempted, as Charles Altieri points out in an excellent discussion of their work, to use poetry "to transcend the realm of aesthetic questions" and discover beyond it "values capable of sustaining a religious faith." For Duncan, these values existed in "acts of reflection" incorporating a rediscovery of traditional Western myths; for Snyder they existed in "acts of attention" incorporating traditional Eastern values and sensibility which would lead to renewed, heightened involvement with the physical world and humanity's primitive ties with it.[9] Given the culture's burgeoning interest in Eastern religion, ecology, and communal living, Snyder gained by far the wider audience.

Well before the sixties culture welcomed such views as novel and then fashionable, Gary Snyder embraced a life of simplicity and closeness to nature as the antidote to the hazards of progress and civilization, but for the most part his work avoids such a stance. Through a sensual and inherently celebratory concreteness of attention, his poems suggest the natural world as an ultimate presence, a centering backdrop to centering acts. Snyder seems to center the self by removing the self, in keeping with his Buddhist background which also echoes the Projectivist view of self as an object among objects. In his poems the "I" repeatedly fuses with the phenomena of nature and daily tasks and often simply slips aside, leaving the reader with "things," as Altieri points out—with "concrete relations" implying the values of "a non-Western frame of mind without references to occult philosophy or a series of abstractions."[10] Thus, one finds in Snyder's poetry not an active promotion of utopian or transcendent alternatives to contemporary life, but simply the pulse of primitive, healing forces already inherent in our legacy as creatures of nature and members of a common tribe. Snyder did state his views directly, however, in a volume of essays entitled *Earth Household: Technical Notes and Queries to Fellow Dharma Revolutionaries*, which appeared in 1969. This work reflects the depth of his scholarly background, as well as his extensive experience as a laborer, traveler, and meditator, and at the more popular level it established Snyder as a kind of guru-spokesperson for those in favor of communal life, conservation of nature, Eastern religions, and transpersonal psychology.

Robert Duncan's energies were more erudite and classical than Snyder's, embracing the Western imagination as it manifests itself in Greek mythology, in Christianity, and in the work of writers who established the Romantic tradition of "form as Form, a spirit in itself."[11] A true Projectivist, however, Duncan regarded form as something to be discovered and enacted rather than as an expression of perfection in the classical sense; for him, many so-called closed and traditional works and patterns of thought which fell so firmly out of fashion in the sixties nevertheless held important resonance as allegories, as forms echoing and enacting energies fundamental to the human spirit and the workings of the universe. Bold as these assertions sound, Duncan expresses them with a combination of generosity and unassailable learnedness that makes them provocative and convincing, if not immediately accessible to the lay or casual reader. Duncan's influence was strongest on his peers Olson and Levertov, with whom he maintained active correspondence. And essays such as "From a Notebook," "Notes on the Meaning of Form," and "Towards an Open Universe" stand with Olson and Creeley's essays as important works ushering the Projectivist movement through the sixties.

The New York Poets: Experience as Medium

The New York school of poets had staked their claim away from the English tradition and developed their style by the mid-fifties, reflecting the influence of French Dada and Surrealist writers and the sensation-oriented visual and performing arts. Many of these poets, such as Frank O'Hara, John Ashbery, Bill Berkson, Peter Schjeldahl, and James Schuyler, wrote art criticism and collaborated with painters. Ashbery, Kenwood Elmslie, James Schuyler, and Kenneth Koch wrote plays. Many of them had lived in France and translated French poets. As a group they were more interested in art itself than in the discussion of art, tending to regard their poetry as part of the tremendous energy field of New York life, interwoven with all the arts that flourished there. In this respect they differed from the Projectivists, who also flourished underground in the fifties and became part of the mainstream in the sixties; whereas Olson, Creeley, and others taught and published manifestoes from their isolated home base at Black Mountain College, the New York poets simply inhabited, coped with, parodied, and spewed back the city. The one "manifesto" they produced was O'Hara's notorious antimanifesto "Personism," which he wrote as a joke in 1959, eschewing both "the abstract removal of the poet" and any self-conscious extension of self, including that of "personality." Instead, the "I" existed in their work as a central perceiving entity, really a filter, through which the multiple surfaces and movements of a cacophonous existence momentarily were fixed.

Continuing along the course it began in the fifties, New York poetry in the sixties was aggressively conversational, gossipy, irreverent toward overt acts of reflection, and whimsical in its use of apparently found images and bits of action from the immediate environment. O'Hara, Ashbery, Koch, and Schuyler, the most prominent figures at the end of the fifties, were joined in the sixties by Ron Padgett, Ted Berrigan, Ed Sanders (who was also leader of the hard-rock group The Fugs), Michael Benedikt, and others. Of these, Koch, O'Hara, and Ashbery were the most prolific and prominent.

Koch, attracted to the "incomprehensible excitement" he found in French poetry, incorporated that energy in his use of the comic and the absurd, producing a poetry of playful Surrealism which included some of the best parodies on poetics to come from the decade.[12] His works include *Permanently* (1960), *Thank You and Other Poems* (1962), and *The Pleasures of Peace* (1969). Koch also visited classes in the New York City public school system, where he experimented successfully with ways to teach children to write naturally and spontaneously. His ideas and a collection of poems written by the children appeared in *Wishes, Lies and Dreams: Teaching Children to Write Poetry* (1970), which helped launch the Poets-in-the-Schools programs in the early seventies.

Frank O'Hara and John Ashbery pushed the New York aesthetic into new territory by creating, in their different ways, poetic equivalents of the Abstract Expressionist art then being produced by Jackson Pollock, Robert Motherwell, Franz Kline, Willem de Kooning, and other groundbreaking artists whose work resulted in New York's rivaling Paris as the center of the art world. O'Hara and Ashbery stand out as the crucial figures of the New York group as it evolved in the sixties.

The work of both O'Hara and Ashbery illuminates the self in an urban environment devoid of natural law, that touchstone available to the Projectivists and the Deep Image poets, but bristling instead with an energy that threatened constantly to pull the self away from its center. The one constant available to them was experience, not as generative of meaning but briefly palpable, hence centering, at its moment of occurrence.

The work of Frank O'Hara uses New York City quite directly as the backdrop to his exertion of self as recipient and filter of bombarding energies; thus it takes on an immediate, documentary appeal as it reflects the New York art scene in the fifties and sixties, with its backdrop of Pop Art, Happenings, and the decadent aesthetics of Camp, all of which elevated and made colorful the trivial. *Lunch Poems* (1964), which O'Hara wrote literally as "ruminations" during his lunch hours, continues in the vein of his work of the late fifties, celebrating the vibrant urban world of surface and sensation even as it also suggests by the very frenzy of its pace that O'Hara is aware of how absurd this scene is and that it could well annihilate the self altogether unless met with a nervy sort of energy.

"Nerve" is what O'Hara recommends as the basis of self-expression in his essay "Personism," and here is where he coincides quite intentionally with Pollock, Motherwell, and other Abstract Expressionists who painted bold shapes and splashes which represented nothing outside themselves; that is, he viewed the gestures of making art as inseparable from the subject or impact of that art. Process, from its moment of conception to the natural diminishment of its own momentum, defined the work's form and content, aiming simply for a direct transfer of energy from artist to viewer or reader. Given the tidal-wave swell of fact, change, and possibility that characterized urban life in the sixties, O'Hara circumvented the dangers of losing the self by fixing the self in its responses, moment by moment, in the ever-shifting flow.

After the publication of *The Tennis Court Oath* in 1962 (his third book, followed by *Rivers and Mountains* in 1966 and *The Double Dream of Spring* in 1970), Ashbery's work became enormously controversial, generating critical discussions as impenetrable as the poems themselves. As his poems progress by means of sentence fragments, non sequiturs, and images that arise from no identifiable context, they force the reader away from a search for anchoring referents into the pure experience of language, or into undigested thought as it spills forth in language.

Most critics, trying gamely to navigate Ashbery on his own purely self-referential turf, have clutched at certain firm landmarks he sets out from time to time, the bits of direct statement which convey his aesthetic: that experience in its pure form is diffuse, random, and opaque; that language itself is pure experience; and that the nature of experience can be rendered precisely only through imprecision and distortion, in conjunction with what is remembered from prior experience and with what the experiencer (poet) leaves out. For Ashbery, distortion is a constant, a function of the mind's true work as a reacting organism. Thus, as O'Hara literally replays quotidian experience, Ashbery literally replays mental experience. And his poems suggest that the interaction between language and consciousness is so intimate a part of the self that its movements are still barely recognizable, that it is still a frontier.

Deep Imagists: The Subconscious as Medium

The Deep Imagist "school" of poetry, more than any of the others, proved to be both a watershed and catalyst for the diverse energies suddenly appearing in literature and the culture throughout the decade. It gave rise to a poetry whose characteristics recombined elements offered by other groups with a new energy source, Spanish Surrealism, to produce what two of its central apologists, George Lensing and Ronald Moran, define as a poetry of "the emotive imagination." The base element of this poetry is the image, and its "form" is a dreamlike rather than objectively recognizable progression of images whose aim is not to dismantle the reader's sense of self and the world but to startle one into quiet, unwilled acts of recognition. In this poetry, also known as Deep Image poetry (the term was first used by Robert Kelley in his essay "Notes on the Poetry of Deep Image," *Trobar* 2 [1961]), the poet's inner self and the outer world become landscapes described and fused by images that treat both as physical, yet associatively charged, phenomena.[13]

The self in these poems is a profoundly subjective presence whose state of mind, as enacted by a progression of significant but loosely connected images, leads to personal epiphany or emotion that is ultimately understood as interpersonal, reflecting a larger collective wisdom. In the best of these poems the poet's self brings writer and reader into a shared, exploratory state of mind and involves both in an associational journey to an open-ended sort of closure, a final image that feels like revelation yet leaves the participants feeling suspended and pleasantly provoked.

Although this "new" poetry historically is not so radical a departure, it marked a significant change in the approach taken by North American writers, critics, and readers to poetry in the twentieth century.[14] One of its most profound repercussions is a more direct and "poetic" sort of criticism that treats the poem as an experience rather than a statement, self-contained and self-referential, and the reader's experience of the poem as inseparable from the traditionally analytical act of "understanding." This new incorporation of self was echoed in developments other than poetry: the flagrant assertions of the journalist's presence in the New Journalism; the fusions between audience and performer in Happenings; the absurd, fragmented stories of Barthelme and others which nevertheless wooed the reader to reexperience the sensations of contemporary life; and finally a lucid intellectualism best exemplified by the criticism of Susan Sontag, who analyzed numerous aspects of sixties culture—Bergman's films, the role of "silence" in contemporary literature, Happenings, and Pop Art, to name just a few—by analyzing the dynamics of the attention paid them by their audience.

An even more important repercussion of this new poetry was its effect on a new generation of readers, which, in turn, enhanced the impact of poems produced by the variety of writers, the variety of "schools," throughout the decade. By highlighting the associative possibilities generated by well-chosen concrete imagery and insisting on the involvement of the reader in the poet's act of self-discovery, Deep Image poetry sensitized readers to a resonant and shareable subjectivity evident in much of the poetry being written within and outside the major movements by writers such as Adrienne Rich, Donald Justice, David Ignatow, John Logan, James Dickey, and Elizabeth Bishop.

The Deep Image movement, although it arose somewhat in response to the spirit of the decade, nevertheless came about largely through the singular energy of Robert Bly, who promoted it as an antidote to Modernist aesthetics. His and William Duffy's magazine the *Fifties*, which began in 1958 and soon became the *Sixties*, flourished throughout the decade as the showcase for writers they felt would steer contemporary American poetry in the direction it needed to go: inward, toward the underexplored regions of the psyche, by means of startling but rightly intuited images. The magazine also provided Bly with an arena for the impassioned, reductive, enormously provocative literary criticism for which he has become famous, a criticism that ranks intuition over rationalism and imagery over discourse as a means of penetrating, for a moment, the reader's unconscious.

If Bly's sense of mission inspired him even to dismiss things like Shakespeare and the entire formal English tradition with an overly theatrical sweep of the pen, it also made him recognize and offer to the public a new breed of North American poet for whom images were a mode of thought rather than skillfully crafted decoration. Some of these writers were James Wright, Galway Kinnell, W. S. Merwin, David Ignatow, Donald Hall, William Stafford, and Louis Simpson. He also produced and published translations of European and Latin American poets whose work, more than any other single factor, startled a younger generation of poets into recognizing the general direction they wanted to take. Especially influential were Bly's translations of German writers Gottfried Benn and Georg Trakl, Spanish writers Federico García Lorca and Antonio Machado, Peruvian writer César Vallejo, Chilean writer Pablo Neruda, French writers René Char and Paul Éluard, and numerous other nineteenth- and twentieth-century poets from Norway, Latin America, and other parts of Europe. All of these, Bly maintained, had "passed through surrealism" and as a result spoke from that fecund area of the subconscious, or collective unconscious, where spirituality resides. This spirituality, as Bly demonstrated both in his criticism and his own poetry, derives its force from the natural world, from silence and solitude, and equips the writer to surface and fully confront the complexities of modern life.

Like Olson and the Projectivists, Bly sought to explore the self in an area beyond that of ego, in an area that might offer "organic" truth of its own.[15] Whereas Olson mapped this territory using the body as a point of departure, Bly mapped it via the psyche, using ground broken by Freud and Jung to highlight the associative powers of the mind as it responds to resonant imagery and opens the self to depths that must be acknowledged despite the pressures from the culture and self-protective aspects of self to avoid them. Olson, he felt, stopped too short, treating the image simply as literal object. Yet much of the poetry produced in the sixties by Olson's adherents, especially that of Levertov, Snyder, and Creeley, did explore and reveal new depths of interaction between the self and the physical world, did address itself to nature and to perception in resonant ways, and Bly recognized this achievement by publishing and discussing at length their poetry in *The Sixties*. Indeed, another of the many repercussions of Bly's energetic revamping of the poetic imagination in America was the melting of boundaries between these two important movements, one of which was legitimately avant-garde in the fifties and one of which seemed an inevitable condensation of energies burgeoning anyway, throughout the culture, in the sixties. Ultimately, the two movements became even more closely aligned as they provided the major impetus to another unique and vital phenomenon in poetry of the sixties, the poetry of protest. By the time the Vietnam War had firmly entrenched itself in the national consciousness as morally untenable and out of control, both Bly and Levertov had forged, in their poetry and critical writings, links between inwardness and the outer world, the explorable self and the collective self, which legitimized "protest" as a necessary aesthetic in its own right and drew poets from diverse areas into its field of energy.

The Spanish Surrealist tradition contrasts with French Surrealism's aesthetic of deliberate derangement of the senses as it aims for a kind of rearrangement of the senses through images juxtaposed in such a way as to reveal their hidden affinities. This "softer" mode of Surrealism thus affirms, by challenging and then rewarding with some glimpse of the familiar, the sensibilities of the reader. Furthermore, its source is not chance but the release of strong emotion, and this grounding in emotion is what makes the flow of association feel somehow logical, despite the jolting combinations of images. Finally, and most important for Bly's purposes, the Spanish tradition offered poets of the sixties a means of grasping and transforming vital elements of modern life, through the poet's ability to descend into the subconscious and then rise to meet those elements from the depths of being. "Inwardness," Bly claimed in an important essay entitled "A Wrong Turning in American Poetry," was the alternative that the Latin American and European poets offered to the American imagination, which had allowed itself to be constrained by the Modernist tradition's myopic fixation on the outer world, the objective world.

The work of several poets in the sixties reflected this shift toward heightened consciousness via exploration of inner images, inner responses. Bly's work, of course, enacts quite clearly the states of mind he called for in American poetry, and many of his poems also echo the image constructs and pacing of images in the poetry he translated. With Bly, it is often difficult to tell who is echoing whom, but his work as a whole expresses such conviction and sense of celebration over a newly revealed state of mind that one cannot really doubt the authenticity of the experiences it enacts, even if that enactment becomes, after a time, insistent and formulaic. His first major book, *Silence in the Snowy Fields*, appeared in 1962. Most of its poems draw from the winter landscape of rural Minnesota and reveal the speaker in a brief, quiet moment of joy. They take place in solitude and benevolent darkness, two elements Bly feels to be important to a fruitful relation with the subconscious, and their images progress with the jolting yet supple movement which he so admired in poets like Pablo Neruda. *Light Around the Body* appeared in 1967, still reflecting Bly's mystical, at-one-with-self-and-nature predilections but adding to them a voice of protest: a condemnation of the public, rational modes of thinking which cut off the individual's access to the subconscious just as they have narrowed the sensibility of the entire society so that it acts brutally, out of ignorance, against others. Many poems in this volume speak in what Charles Altieri calls Bly's "satiric" mode, offering images that caricature the mentality of governments and armies and delineate them clearly as paternalistic, without spiritual resource.

The work of James Wright is thought by many to be the most genuine, most ground-breaking poetry to come directly from the Deep Image school. Wright met Bly when he moved to Minnesota in the late fifties, having published two books of poems cast in the current formal mode and knowing himself ready for a change. Other Deep Image-related writers, most notably Louis Simpson and Donald Hall, also turned away from formal poetry at about the same time and produced new work which expanded on the implications of Bly's theories; however, Wright's evolution, unlike theirs, took place directly within Bly's field of energy and undoubtedly influenced it as well. With Bly and William Duffy, he collaborated on a book of poems, *The Lion's Tail and Eyes: Poems Written Out of Laziness and Silence* (1962), and, most important, he collaborated with Bly to produce translations of Trakl, Vallejo, and Neruda, which appeared in *The Sixties* magazine and then in book form from the Sixties Press. The German Expressionist poetry of Trakl, classical Chinese poetry, and the Spanish Surrealists all can be seen as influences behind Wright's important third book, *The Branch Will Not Break*, which came out in 1963 and contains many landmark poems such as "Lying in a Hammock at William Duffy's Farm in Pine Island, Minnesota," "The Blessing," and "The Jewel." The power of these works lies in the crispness of their images, images drawn cleanly from the natural world, combined with Wright's evident willingness to lose himself in the associative process the poems generate, a process which can be felt as not crisp at all but somehow comprehensible. Whereas Bly's poems often assert their connections, assuming that the reader, like himself, is starting at the brink of an inward place, Wright must *find* his way inward, which he does helplessly yet gracefully, without apparent knowledge of where he will end up. His images thus become profoundly alive as the only clues he, as well as the reader, can hold on to as he progresses.

Another important aspect of Wright's work is its exploration of the American landscape, which went further than Bly's imagery drawn from the rural Midwest, to illuminate that bulk of drab, invisible lives around mill towns such as the one in which Wright grew up in Ohio, around railroad yards and cornfields that are neither rural nor urban, the undisclosed heart of the country. Wright drew naturally from the ambience of that landscape not through any sense of mission but because it was, for him, profoundly resonant with his own history. As a result, some poems in *The Branch Will Not Break* reflect a social consciousness born of compassion, longing, and a soft, underlying anguish which makes them darker than Bly's; this consciousness carries over to his next book, *Shall We Gather at the River*, which appeared in 1968. Wright's work, like that of many other poets working concurrently with the Deep Image movement, thus reopened America as a literal frontier for poets, a frontier which had been opened wide by Whitman and then overlooked in favor of a return to the English tradition.

Louis Simpson, another poet now associated with the poetry advocated by Bly, took it upon himself to deal more forcefully with a discovery of America in his work. But Simpson's relation both to his country and to Deep Image poetry arose more from his own interesting history and aesthetic predilections than from any conscious affinities with Bly, whose writings enlisted his interest but not his allegiance. Simpson grew up in Jamaica and did not even live in the United States or obtain citizenship until he was in his late teens, when he began his doctorate at Columbia University. He fought in World War II and became an ambivalent but passionate reader of Whitman. He taught for a time in California and found on that last Western frontier a frontier combination of natural beauty and spiritual deprivation which, along with his disappointment in the actual outcome of the industrial utopia Whitman had envisioned, eventually pressed him to explore the impoverished ethos beneath the busy facade of American life, especially as that life seemed to run itself aground in the suburbs. In the last of his three volumes written between 1940 and 1959, Simpson gradually began moving toward this exploration, in conjunction with a movement toward a more colloquial language and hallucinatory cast of image;[16] however, his work retained an essential reliance on regular forms and a tone of witty, intellectual understatement which had earned him a reputation as a skilled and elegant craftsman. *At the End of the Open Road,* which appeared in 1963 and won a Pulitzer Prize the next year, marked Simpson's real break from the confines of form into the shapes and rhythms of his own imaginative experience. This experience took him deeper into the image and deeper into America, especially its cities and suburbs, where people strove furiously for ease and had no sense of the power and the mythical reverberations inherent in the land and its history. Simpson's subsequent work in *Selected Poems* (1965) and later volumes continued to expand these explorations into his own Russian Jewish heritage and that of Native Americans. He continued to build his poems around the associative power of the image; however, unlike many Deep Image-related poets, he never broke away from a respect for and occasional use of form, nor did he jettison his educated and elegant tone. In this sense he stood slightly aside from the "movement," evolving naturally with it but never cutting himself off from the larger, historical body of American poetry.

The new aesthetic also manifested itself in the work of William Stafford, whose *Traveling Through the Dark* won the National Book Award in 1963, and in the Deep Image poems written by Donald Hall in the late sixties. But Hall's shift in aesthetic also manifested itself dramatically in his work as an anthologist and essayist. Having strongly supported formal, academic poetry as a coeditor of the 1958 edition of *New Poets of England and America,* along with Robert Pack and Louis Simpson, and having turned much of his critical attention to the new work of English poets in the second edition of that anthology, he then produced in 1962 a new anthology, *Contemporary American Poetry,* which marked a significant step in accommodating the diverse kinds of poetry that had been so polarized at the start of the sixties. From Allen's controversial list of poets in *The New American Poetry* Hall added Creeley, Snyder, Duncan, and Ashbery; Deep Imagists such as Bly, Stafford, and Wright; the more established Confessional writers; new work of Galway Kinnell and W. S. Merwin; formal poets such as Anthony Hecht, James Merrill, and Howard Nemerov; and prominent, independently exploratory writers such as Adrienne Rich, John Logan, and James Dickey. In his important introduction to the anthology he announced the end of the "orthodoxy" that for thirty years had "ruled American poetry" since the rise of Eliot and the New Critics. He advocated the coexistence of "all possibilities, even contradictory ones" as a new approach to the contemporary scene and ended with a description of a new kind of imagination making itself manifest, an imagination which has the "irrational" yet "quiet" and colloquial quality of language and the "profound subjectivity" that actually characterized Deep Image poetry, though Hall did not directly connect the two in his essay.[17] This anthology and its oft-quoted introduction marked a first step in a critical acknowledgment of the diverse poetries of the early sixties as consolidating themselves in a new way of addressing the self, the senses, and experience.

Soft Surrealism: Absence as Medium

From this point on it seems appropriate to blur some of the boundaries set up by the preceding discussions. The term *Soft Surrealism* is intended as elastic and open-ended, a descriptive rather than academic term to surround, quite loosely, the quality of imagination that defined itself in conjunction with the Deep Image movement and then simply became, as Paul Zweig points out in his essay "The New Surrealism," which describes the legacy of the sixties, "the language our poets speak." Many important sixties poets not identified with a particular movement or with Surrealism per se nevertheless wrote poems which arise from an appeal to the sort of imagination Bly and then others made accessible through translations. Mark Strand, one of the most prominent representatives of this legacy, simply described himself in an interview as "very much a part of a new international style that has a lot to do with plainness of diction, a certain reliance on surrealist techniques, a certain reliance on journalistic techniques, a strong narrative element." He could well have been speaking for any number of unwittingly Soft Surrealist poets— Diane Wakoski and David Ignatow, for example—whose work shaped the aesthetic embraced by the literary magazines and the flock of writing programs that arose throughout the country in the seventies.[18]

Galway Kinnell's first volume, *What a Kingdom It Was*, appeared in 1960, expressing the rich musicality that would characterize his later work and also an adherence to traditional form and Christian sensibility which he rechanneled in his subsequent explorations of the brutality and beauty of the natural world, the godlessness of the urban landscape, and the possibility of "saving" the self by losing the self to other forms of life, especially animal life, governed as it is by harsh natural law. Nature takes on a guttural, mythical presence in Kinnell's later books (*Flower Herding on Mount Monadnock* [1964] and *Body Rags* [1968]), its terrifying aspects illuminated but also made fiercely beautiful by the rich play of sound, the sheer lyricism of his voice. These qualities are highlighted in his famous long poem "The Bear," in which the dark vitality of death and the act of writing poetry are fused allegorically into his notion of salvation: the poet tracks a wounded bear, merging images of its weakening body with images of his own, until he finally reaches it, cuts it open, and climbs inside to be at once consumed and affirmed in its final, bloody struggle. The word "blood" appears frequently in Kinnell's work, as do images of fire, reflecting the self's effort to strip itself down as a physical object and perhaps be purified through death. However, this impulse is different from Plath's compulsion to annihilate the self; for Kinnell, death is more a sacrament, a final merging with a force that governs over and above the self's illusion of personality, separateness, or permanence to bring it closer to a primal, paradoxically religious, and hence fulfilling, reality.

Prior to the sixties, W. S. Merwin had worked successfully with form and conventional myth, earning himself a solid place in the literary establishment. In 1960 he published *The Drunk in the Furnace*, which marked a loosening in his style and a turning toward more personal material; in 1963 he published his dazzling *The Moving Target*, which marked his real arrival at an energetically surreal voice and sensibility. This was followed by his equally acclaimed *The Lice* in 1967 and then by *The Carrier of Ladders* in 1970, a collection which expressed a more anchored, less dizzying surrealist sensibility suggesting a partial resolution to the sense of furious quest, or homelessness, set up in the two preceding volumes. Merwin also worked actively as a translator throughout the sixties, navigating several languages and cultures to offer poems by Sebastian Chamfort, Antonio Porchia, Jean Follain, and Pablo Neruda, as well as classical texts such as *The Song of Roland* and *The Poem of the Cid*. Late in the sixties Merwin also began to write short prose pieces—really parablelike tales—the first collection of which appeared as *The Miner's Pale Children* in 1970. Merwin dealt less philosophically than Kinnell, but in a brilliantly dense and textural fashion, with the imminent presence of death and emptiness. In his work death is a less primal force, is perhaps more aptly termed "extinction,"[19] which suggests its nature as a condition or motif undermining every gesture made by the self and every signal received by the senses. Merwin's poems enact this undermining as they weave out a rich, palpable, but ultimately self-questioning play of images. The energy of these poems is unsettling but not nonsensical, as the images themselves create recognizable patterns and clusters that play opposites against one another to create a sense of shifting or suggested reality. Natural elements such as "air," "rain," and "shadow" interact with everyday objects such as "keys," "gloves," and "knives," subtracting from those objects their usual sense and solidity while still allowing them impact as concrete entities. The result is a dreamlike, often disembodied poetry which is nevertheless sensual and vivid. His speaker's presence as a self who dwells firmly in the senses paradoxically leads to a confrontation with a kind of absence enlarged to the proportions of myth. Merwin's quest is for "an abiding self," to quote Charles Altieri, that resides "not in its possessions but in that consciousness of what remains when all those possessions have been stripped away."[20]

Mark Strand, whose work began to appear late in the sixties, shares Merwin's obsession with self as absence, self stripped of possessions, and in this regard their names are often linked by critics. Unlike Merwin, however, Strand stands squarely in his poems as a particular rather than disembodied self, and he speaks with an almost dogged directness and clarity. The compelling ambiguity of his poems arises from his selection and arrangement of images, which seem straightforward and markedly visual but which also superimpose different time frames, settings, and fragments of narrative on one another to achieve the ambience of dream. Prior to poetry Strand studied painting, which probably accounts for the clarity of objects and surfaces in his poems even as those objects and surfaces are stripped away from the speaker to reveal an invisible self offering itself to the reader. "I empty myself of my life and my life remains," Strand says at the end of a litanylike poem called "The Remains," which is typical of much of his work in the sixties not only in its ending but in its incantatory use of repetition, its catalogue of possessions and attributes which do and do not belong to the speaker, and a faintly self-mocking tone which prevents its final self-cancelling line from sounding self-consciously gloomy. "Ironic surrealism" is the term Poulin uses in describing Strand's unique sensibility,[21] and this quality adds bite to his visually precise and lyrically rhythmic poetry. Strand's *Reasons for Moving* appeared in 1968, followed by *Darker* in 1970. Strand also edited the 1969 anthology *The Contemporary American Poets*, which sought, like Hall's earlier one, to accommodate the diversity and developments that now characterized the moved-and-shaken American poetry scene and to neutralize the sense of polarization that still echoed from earlier in the decade.

Steady Voices: The Formalists and the Expansional Poets

Joining in one category the formalist and expansional poets only superficially links two groups whose impacts, when viewed historically in relation to the sixties as a tumultuous period of change, were quite opposite. The small group of poets who continued to work successfully within the formalist tradition—Richard Wilbur, James Merrill, Anthony Hecht, William Meredith, Richard Howard, and Elizabeth Bishop—managed to preserve and validate the importance of form as an enduring and quietly liberating force in poetry. These writers thus provided ballast which is especially evident in retrospect, now that the colorful dust of the decade has settled. The poets in the second group—James Dickey, Adrienne Rich, John Logan, Alan Dugan, Richard Hugo, Muriel Rukeyser, and others—exhibited and fused qualities brought forward by the major movements, especially by the Confessional poets and the Deep Image school with all its offshoots; their impact was felt immediately as emblematic or representative of the spirit of the times as they incorporated and explored the phenomenon of self through exploration and expansion of the poet's personality.

The handful of formalist poets who persisted and succeeded did so because in various ways their work transcended the prejudices leveled against their aesthetic by the emerging avant-garde and because they understood form as more than mannerism or decoration. Richard Wilbur, thought by many to be the master craftsman among descendants of the New Critics, spoke of form as a stimulant, an energizing element, as it gave a writer "something to work for and against."[22] This comment implies emphasis on process rather than product and also an ingenious rather than unfettered use of self, both of which suggest that formalist concerns in the sixties, which might better be termed an appreciation for the bracing qualities of discipline, were not so opposed to the prevailing spirit after all.

James Merrill continued to write the rarefied, elegantly mannered poetry which had earned him a reputation, to quote a review by Richard Howard, as "the most decorative and glamor-clogged [poet] America had so far produced." However, as Howard also observed, Merrill's work in the sixties moved a little closer to self-confrontation as he began to turn away from the mediums of history, myth, and various personae to speak more directly from his own life. In the three volumes Merrill published in the sixties (*Water Street* [1962], *Nights and Days* [1966], and *The Fire Screen* [1969]), he also began to turn with some "humility" toward the contemplation of the natural world—as opposed to the embellished and witty ambience of the garden party and salon—and to loosen somewhat into the cadences of a poet talking out of pressure arising from within, rather than from desire to perform.[23]

Another representative of the true formalists, Anthony Hecht, produced in 1967 his acclaimed second book, *The Hard Hours*, which won a Pulitzer Prize. Although the book shared with its predecessor of thirteen years, *A Summoning of Stones*, a grounding in classical Western myth and sensibility as well as adherence to formal disciplines, it evidenced a dramatic opening in Hecht's sensibility toward an acceptance of change, pain, and disorder—elements which his skilled early poems had sought to exclude or gracefully overpower. Some of these newer poems draw from the landscape of Europe during or after World War II, reevoking through imagined scenes and personae the undisguisable horror of man's inhumanity toward man; this theme of violence or destructive change is echoed more quietly, is acknowledged with dignity, in other poems throughout the collection. Hecht's acceptance of strong emotion and his consequent enactment of difficult confrontations with unruly events and feelings partially accounts for the success of this volume so late in the decade; despite its "packaging," its elegance and restraint, *The Hard Hours* appealed to the sense of moral discomfort, even outrage, for which poets everywhere, in the aura of the Vietnam War, were beginning to seek and to find outlets.

Elizabeth Bishop continued in the sixties to write poems characterized by fine craft and a particularly keen and thorough use of the senses. Her use of strong, convincing imagery made her an inspiration to formalists and Surrealists alike, and many of her poems managed to convey openness and wonder, a sense of total engagement with an experience or witnessed scene, while maintaining graceful but firm technical control. Her third book, *Questions of Travel,* appeared in 1965, followed by *The Ballad of the Burglar of Babylon* in 1968 and then by *The Complete Poems* in 1969. In 1970, Bishop was awarded the National Book Award. Isabella Gardner published two volumes during the sixties, *The Looking Glass: New Poems* (1961) and *West of Childhood: Poems 1960–1965,* which expressed, both in subject and in a richness of language and rhythm, a strong sensual and sexual sensibility within deftly handled forms. And finally Carolyn Kizer, who published her first book, *The Ungrateful Garden,* in 1961, distinguished herself by dealing early on with both feminist and womanly concerns, doing so by means of considerable intelligence and a warm sense of humor that made her poetry emotionally forceful and revealing on behalf of women, yet sophisticated and ironic enough to save it from stridency or loss of apparent formal control. Her *Knock upon Silence* appeared in 1965, and her *New and Selected Poems* appeared in the early seventies.

The term "Expansional poets" comes from an essay published in the *Yale Review* in 1968 by Laurence Lieberman, entitled "The Expansional Poet: A Return to Personality," in which he discussed the work of John Berryman, William Stafford, and James Dickey as examples of fruitful confrontation with "the mystique of one's self" through the particularly risky, imaginative, or quietly centered exploration and exercise of the poet's personality. Rather than adhering to the Confessional poet's arena of literal biography, Lieberman maintained, the Expansional poet "plunges," via the imagination, "into an unfamiliar field of experience" which then becomes the poet's own, adding dimension to the self as well as the work. While this description could be applied to the work of several poets already discussed, it also provides a fairly accurate heading for other important, somewhat Confessional poets whose work seemed forcefully or subtly fueled by a tendency to explore many aspects of personal experience and thereby enlarge the poet's presence in the poem.[24]

The tendency toward growth and exploration was prefigured in the work of Randall Jarrell and Theodore Roethke, two poets who died around the middle of the decade and whose work had enormous influence on younger poets of the sixties and seventies. Before he was killed by a car in 1965, Jarrell published his widely acclaimed *Woman at the Washington Zoo: Poems and Translations* (1960) and *The Lost World: New Poems* (1965), which drew increasingly from his readings of Freud and German fairy tales to offer dark, psychologically insightful fables. *The Complete Poems* appeared posthumously in 1969. Theodore Roethke also set an example of personal quest through a poetry that sought union with natural forces, a transcendence of the opposite, oppressive awareness of the void which burdened him all his life. Roethke's whole-hearted engagement of self in this enterprise provided a vital precedent to most of the movements that arose in the sixties. His final volume, *The Far Field,* appeared in 1964, followed by the National Book Award, posthumously bestowed in 1965, and *The Collected Poems of Theodore Roethke* in 1966.

James Dickey enacted another kind of transformative energy, exuberant and almost self-consuming in its embrace of all forms of life, its forays into death and sexuality, and especially its imaginative propulsion that resulted in the poet's ability to enter the consciousness, or mythos, of other beings in the midst of such experience. Dickey's own experiences as a fighter pilot in World War II, a hunter, an athlete, and a Southerner with a Faulknerian sense of the primitive and the gothic all contributed to a voracious and flexible sensibility which earned him access to a variety of rather impossible incarnations: a half-human sheep child, a stewardess falling three miles from a plane, a captured soldier doing handstands moments before his execution, a firebomber lustily performing his work of annihilation. Between 1960 and 1970 Dickey produced six volumes, each more daring in its reach than the last and each remarkably persuasive in drawing the reader into its awesome transformations through the incantatory pull of its language, its rhythms, and its dark and luxuriant imagery. Dickey, in fact, expanded the self into animal and human personae so effectively and so aggressively throughout the decade that toward the end of it the public may have grown somewhat suspicious, or "chilled," to quote Richard Howard, by so much "renewal, transcendence, ecstasy"[25]—an attitude which probably had something to do with Dickey's somewhat ruthless and colorful behavior outside his poetry as public figure. The work itself remains a dazzling and vital landmark in the poetry of the decade.

In her third volume, *Snapshots of a Daughter-in-Law* (1963), Adrienne Rich began the long arc of her break from forms which had provided her, as has already been noted, with "asbestos gloves" for "[handling] materials

I couldn't pick up bare-handed."[26] Prior to the sixties, Rich had produced two well-praised books of gracefully made and intellectually impressive poetry, had received major awards, and had become a wife and typically busy mother who had time only to jot down fragments of thought; now, however, her innate attraction to powerful and untapped material, both in herself and her subject matter, led her to confront an essential sadness, loneliness, and disruption in family life and the more solitary life of the spirit, and also to acknowledge the impossibility of barricading those two relatively private realms from the public ones of war, sexual oppression, and civil violence. Without losing the essential musicality and graceful-ness that had made her a superb formalist, and without giving into shrillness, Rich managed to develop a strong political sensibility which she exercised first in the difficult personal area of sexuality and reconsid-eration of paths she had chosen. Her resultant changes, which are chroni-cled in the growth of the sensibility behind her poems in *Necessities of Life* (1966) and *Leaflets* (1969), and which reached partial fruition in *The Will to Change* (1971), led her to jettison old identities and emerge as a lesbian and feminist whose major message was not the superiority of those conditions but belief in the efficacy of, and willingness to undergo, whatever change is necessary for growth into the whole of the self.

Although Muriel Rukeyser was a long-time veteran of the poetry establishment by the time the sixties dismantled and rebuilt it to larger specifications, her work and sensibility grew with the times, perhaps because she had always been ahead of the times in her interest in social reform and her predilection for the world of the unconscious as generated through dream, eroticism, and fantasy. These two interests gave her work an authoritative, feminine energy, a sensibility that anchored itself in the trustworthy if not always comfortable external world and then traveled easily, with scarcely perceptible shifts in focus, to the mysterious inner world of associative thought and the ambience of myth. Her eighth collection, *Waterlily Fire: Poems 1935–1962*, appeared in 1962, and *The Speed of Darkness* followed in 1968. (For a fuller discussion of Rukeyser's work, see Kate Daniels's "The Demise of the 'Delicate Prisons': The Women's Movement in Twentieth-Century American Poetry," pp. 224–53.)

Richard Hugo and Alan Dugan published their major first books in 1961, both having reached their late thirties unpublished and having established themselves in nonliterary professions. Hugo's *A Run of Jacks* marked the beginning of a distinctive, powerfully naked poetry that he would continue to develop in *Death of the Kapowsin Tavern* (1965), *Good Luck in Cracked Italian* (1969), and on through his increasingly openhearted books in the seventies. Hugo's struggle throughout his poems as well as his life was with the self's own bent toward self-destructiveness, a struggle to which he managed to give stature by grounding his work in images of the bleak, often abandoned towns of the American Northwest and of Italian cities where he had spent time as a bombardier in World War II, places he used as conduits to his own inner life. As his sensibility matured, Hugo began to describe western landscapes and the imagined lives of their down-and-out inhabitants with a compelling, self-revealing intensity, letting his language mirror interchangeably the inner and outer worlds. In this manner he managed at once to render an overlooked but powerfully present American landscape and also to sing a long blues song of the self that, for the most part, transcended the maudlin.

Alan Dugan's first book, gruffly titled *Poems,* won the Yale Series of Younger Poets award, the Pulitzer Prize, and the National Book Award in the year of its publication. This was followed by *Poems 2* (1963), *Poems 3* (1967), and *Collected Poems* (1969). Dugan managed (as he has continued to do) to elevate abrasiveness into a generative poetic force. His speaking self is a trapped and somewhat self-punishing member of the glib commercial world, a drinker, a victim of the usual fantasies but too cynical to seek fulfillment, cynical about love but surreptitiously and sporadically seeking it anyway. He zeroes in on all this with a dry and direct self-mockery, seeking neither to elevate his "sufferings" nor to evoke the reader's identification with them; rather, he simply aims toward the truth in order to dispose of it as quickly and bluntly as possible. His poems are tight and astringent, perverse in content but offering pleasure in their fineness of wit and their emphatic movement.

Maxine Kumin's work, her first collection of which appeared as *Half-way* in 1961, was daring in its lack of psychic exploration, suffering, or self-scrutiny at a time when those qualities were desired and successfully applied by her contemporaries. Kumin's poems instead draw from a landscape that is legitimately hers, the relatively pleasant, upper-middle-class world of the gentleman farmer, a world of country labors and landscape, family and work, a world not ostensibly threatened by change or want. Yet many of her poems carry, through the power of contemplativeness and sensitivity to the physical world, a weight of their own in their penetrations of dream and death, the dark fantasies that add dimension to the interior life. At the same time, they express a willing and often humorous submission to the workings of nature, a force that arises from her work as accompaniment and nourishment to the life of the mind. Kumin's work ultimately demonstrates that such life of the mind, and its consequent expansionist effect on a poet's sensibility, takes place more as a function of character than circumstance, and that middle-class life is as reasonable a backdrop for this process as is any other. Kumin's second collection, *The Privilege,* appeared in 1965, followed by *The Nightmare Factory* in 1970. Kumin also wrote several books for children, three in collaboration with Anne Sexton.

Robert Hayden had been publishing his exceptionally well-crafted, well-researched poetry since 1940, but it wasn't until the appearance of his third book, *Selected Poems,* in 1966 that he transcended his former label as one of the better black poets to win overdue praise as a poet of rounded sensibility whose subjects often happened to be, but were not exclusively, issues relating to black history: the Baha'i faith, slavery, the Klan, and famous real and imaginary figures such as Frederick Douglass, Bessie Smith, and Aunt Jemima.[27] Whether dealing with the personal or historical, Hayden's work expresses a full range of emotion and empathy, rendering black history and experience at once accurately and as something shareable. His fourth volume, *Words in the Mourning Time,* appeared in 1970.

The bold, indignant, peppery work of Gwendolyn Brooks won her earlier acclaim, and it prefigured much of the protest poetry written by blacks in the sixties and seventies. However, her work was, and continued to be, warmer and more expansive and more revealing of existing conditions than that simply fueled by protest. Hers is a sensibility shaped by the urban ghetto, with its rank stairways and newspaper carpets, its invasions of gingerly do-good matrons from the rich suburbs, its "cool cats" strung tight with energy and hopelessness. A fierce sensuality underlies Brooks's work, evidenced by her supple use of adjectives, unhesitant handling of rough detail, equally direct handling of images or moments of tenderness, and her flair both for controlled, syncopated rhythm and its opposite, incantation that achieves resounding momentum. Over and above her revelations of life in hard places, Brooks offers through her own fierce vitality a sense of life, period. Indignation is her fuel, not her goal: thus, her work stands as a prime example of how a spirit of protest can lead away from the purely historical, the purely temporal, to true expansion of the personality as forged and shared through poetry. Brooks's *Selected Poems* appeared in 1963, followed by *In the Mecca* (1968), *Riot* (1969), and *Family Pictures* (1970).

Protest Poetry: The Imagination of Commitment

The clichéd word "protest," with its implied attitude of shrillness, changed in the sixties to convey something far more subtle and pervasive. Poulin's term the "imagination of commitment" better describes the force underlying a new poetry that fused art and social awareness, with varying degrees of success and great overall impact, in a manner unprecedented in the history of North American poetry.[28]

As has already been pointed out in discussions of the work of Lowell, Bly, Levertov, Stafford, and others, an underlying social consciousness arose quite naturally, from all directions, in tandem with an increasing awareness of the health or distress of the individual psyche. The imagination that led poets in all the major movements to explore and develop the stronghold of the self led them inevitably to perceive America as a still-unawakened "self," a collective psyche dangerously out of balance, and this awareness united many of them in an effort to produce and support a poetry of protest whose fundamental aim was not to destroy the establishment but to rethink it, heal it, render it more flexible and self-aware.

The work of Allen Ginsberg paved the way for this sensibility by claiming the right of the self to be what it has to be and write the poetry it has to write, as poets had done before; but Ginsberg also went a step further "to insist," as James F. Mersmann points out in his lucid and comprehensive book *Out of the Vietnam Vortex: A Study of Poets and Poetry Against the War*, "that these freedoms also extend immediately into all other realms of public and private life."[29] With the advent of the Vietnam War, other poets began to participate in a diagnosis of the nation's social and political psyche and to detect other symptoms: emphasis on masculine or empiricist impulses at the expense of feminine forces of nurturance and primitive mystery, with a consequent loss of touch with "the inner man" (Bly's term); resistance to the openness and changeability that promotes growth; blindness toward the future of humanity in the wake of present actions and convictions; unreason passing for reason; and a consequent distortion and misuse of language. In other words, all the qualities which poets in the late fifties and the sixties had begun to discover as aesthetically and spiritually valuable to the self and to a fully realized poetic found opposite expression in the phenomenon of the Vietnam War.

The focus of protest underwent an especially interesting change during this time. As exemplified by Ginsberg's poems, the Beats and the San Francisco poets in the fifties had protested against pejorative labels being given to things they felt to be natural to the life of the self; their emphatic references to sex and drugs and homosexuality, and their often incantatory use of four-letter words, were all designed to normalize these things, to forge outrageousness into acceptability. The fifties avant-garde thereby sought to expand the realm of "normal" behavior. Poets of the sixties reacted against an opposite condition, the government's tendency to regard acts of tremendous brutality and illogic as "normal" and "logical," and to confuse a baroquely self-justifying system of convictions with moral law. The world of Joseph Heller's *Catch-22* became more and more literal as American forces in Vietnam bombed entire villages in order to "save" them. The word "normal" began to take on terrifying connotations, and poets felt pressed to restore some clarity of vision, some sense of reason, before it was too late.

The poetry of the sixties thus yielded many expressions of protest, some aesthetically moving, some simplistic, some satirical, some bitter, some hopeful, and many touching on other ills, such as the limited rights of women and blacks.

A remarkable number of these poems written during the sixties have outlived their surrounding circumstances and have deservedly made their way into today's leading anthologies. This validation offers an appropriately "open-ended" closure, perhaps analogous to a final cooking-down, to a turbulent and complex decade. Beneath the indignation and argumentativeness so openly expressed by scores of American poets, there had developed an undercurrent of pure awareness, a sensibility hungering after benevolent change, a maturing which had begun with the self's efforts to celebrate and defend its territory and whose flowering manifested itself in a willingness to risk all it had gained. By the end of the decade, poets had begun to ground themselves firmly enough in their new awareness of self to be able to turn their attention outward again, not toward form and rebellion against forms, but toward language itself as inseparable from consciousness and conscience. As protest and the reasons for it gave way to other concerns, this new intimacy between the self and language remained, becoming the multifaceted and undeniable legacy of the 1960s.

Notes

1. Dickey, "In the Presence of Anthologies," in *Babel to Byzantium* (New York: Farrar, Straus and Giroux, 1968), 10.

2. Klinkowitz, *The American 1960's: Imaginative Acts in a Decade of Change* (Ames: Iowa State University Press, 1980), 6–7.

3. Gelpi, "Adrienne Rich: The Poetics of Change," in *American Poetry since 1960: Some Critical Perspectives,* ed. Robert B. Shaw (Chester Springs, Penn.: Dufour, 1974), 133.

4. Barbara Gibbs and Francis Golffing, "The Public Voice: Remarks on Poetry Today," *Commentary,* July 1959, 67.

5. A. Poulin, Jr., ed., *Contemporary American Poetry,* 4th ed. (Boston: Houghton Mifflin, 1985), 665.

6. Bayley, "On John Berryman," in *Contemporary Poetry in America: Essays and Interviews,* ed. Robert Boyers (New York: Schocken, 1974), 67–68.

7. Levertov, "Great Possessions, in *Poet in the World* (New York: New Directions, 1973), 97.

8. Ibid., 94.

9. Charles Altieri, *Enlarging the Temple: New Directions in American Poetry During the 1960s* (Lewisburg, Penn.: Bucknell University Press, 1979), 128, 129.

10. Ibid., 135.

11. Duncan, "From a Notebook," in *The Poetics of the New American Poetry,* ed. Donald Allen and Warren Tallman (New York: Grove, 1973), 186.

12. Poulin, *Contemporary American Poetry,* 544.

13. George S. Lensing and Ronald Moran, *Four Poets and the Emotive Imagination: Robert Bly, James Wright, Louis Simpson and William Stafford* (Baton Rouge: Louisiana State University Press, 1976).

14. Ibid., 5.

15. Altieri, *Englarging the Temple,* 18.

16. Lensing and Moran, *Four Poets,* 140.

17. Donald Hall, ed., *Contemporary American Poetry* (Baltimore: Penguin, 1962), 17, 24.

18. Paul Zweig, "The New Surrealism," in *Contemporary Poetry in America,* 329; "A Conversation with Mark Strand," in *American Poetry since 1960,* 195.

19. Poulin, *Contemporary American Poetry,* 647.

20. Altieri, *Enlarging the Temple,* 204.

21. Poulin, *Contemporary American Poetry,* 673.

22. John Briggs and Michael Newman, "Craft Interview with Richard Wilbur," in *The Craft of Poetry: Interviews from the New York Quarterly* (Garden City, N.Y.: Doubleday, 1974), 184.

23. Howard, *Alone with America,* enl. ed. (New York: Atheneum, 1980), 407, 396, 400.

24. Lieberman, *Unassigned Frequencies: American Poetry in Review* (Urbana: University of Illinois Press, 1977), 263–71, 118.

25. Howard, *Alone with America*, 118.

26. Stuart Friebert and David Young, eds., *The Longman Anthology of Contemporary Poetry* (New York: Longman, 1983), 360.

27. Friebert and Young, *The Longman Anthology*, p. 65.

28. Poulin, *Contemporary American Poetry*, 697.

29. Mersmann, *Out of the Vietnam Vortex: A Study of Poets and Poetry Against the Vietnam War* (Lawrence: University Press of Kansas, 1974), 132.

9

The Demise of the "Delicate Prisons": The Women's Movement in Twentieth-Century American Poetry

KATE DANIELS

If there is one poet who can be considered a predecessor—or matri-arch—of the women's movement in twentieth-century American poetry, it is Muriel Rukeyser. Born in New York City in 1913, she published her first book, *Theory of Flight*, in 1935, when she was only twenty-one, a mere "girl," as the critics kept reminding each other even as they mar-veled at a new and provocative poetry. Rukeyser's first book was a signal work not only for herself but for succeeding generations of American women poets who took its central metaphor of aerodynamics to heart: "Believe that your presences are strong," she wrote in the long and complex title poem, "O be convinced without formula or rhyme / or any dogma; use yourselves : be : fly. / Believe that we bloom upon this stalk of time."

Although the poems in *Theory of Flight* were not launched under the specific aegis of "feminism"—in 1935, a term that still primarily reverberated with connotations of the fight for suffrage—they were nev-ertheless full of portents of the feminist direction Rukeyser's work would take during the next half-century. Her poems, from beginning to end, celebrate the lives of women as artists, as workers, as political activists, as mothers and daughters and wives. Nevertheless, one could not say— utilizing an archaic terminology still extant in the thirties when she began publishing her work—that Rukeyser wrote a purely "feminine" poetry, for part of the excitement that attended the publication of her early work was the way in which she brought her female consciousness to bear on experiences that had always been considered off-limits for women writ-ers. She refused to be confined within the narrow, nineteenth-century romantic/lyric tradition of women's verse that still dominated the national consciousness when she began to publish her work. And she was never tortured, as some of her contemporaries were, by whether or not her work dealt with "appropriate" female subject matter or utilized the female poet's alleged gift for the lyric. Although many readers were startled by the "unfeminine" nature of her early poems, at least one perceptive critic greeted this new poetry by a woman with relief. Compared to other women writers, observed Willard Maas, Rukeyser's approach was "fresh and vital, and her poems happily lack the restricted metaphysical concern with a feminine world decorated with trees and flowers and inhabited by birds on wing—a characteristic peculiar to the verse of women of the last decade."[1]

Over a period of almost fifty years, from the publication of *Theory of Flight* in 1935 until her death in 1980, shortly after the publication of her collected poems, Rukeyser created a remarkable body of work that continually inspired passionate response from women readers for reasons that were often unapparent to male critics (particularly to those associated with the New Criticism of the forties and fifties, a number of whom attacked her work viciously and in an inappropriately personal manner).[2] What makes Rukeyser such an inspiring figure was her adamant refusal to relinquish any part of her femaleness even as she repudiated society's ideas about what females were and what they should do. Her task was never to be "as good as a man" or "equal" to a man; from the beginning, she had a strong and innate sense of the power and worth of women. She insisted on her right to write her poems about mothers and children, domestic dramas, and romantic love just as she insisted on her right to bring hydroelectric power projects, the trial of the Scottsboro Boys, and the Spanish Civil War into her work.[3]

Nevertheless, it was not only the liberated subject matter of her poetry or its feminist legitimizing impulses that attracted women readers to her work. Her highly individualistic and organic sense of form and the freedom she felt to improvise upon or even to totally reject the received forms of English-language poetry found great favor with twentieth-century women who were beginning to poke their heads out of the literary pigeonhole they had historically inhabited. From the very beginning of her career, Rukeyser was preoccupied with ways in which traditional poetic forms could be refashioned or revised to express more mimetically her concerns with female experience (particularly female sexuality), political leftism, and urban life. In search of this, she experimented with montage and documentary techniques, stream-of-consciousness narration, and the prose poem; before her first collection ever appeared, she had created an idiosyncratic system of spacing and punctuation that she absolutely insisted upon. (During the sixties, frustrated by proofreaders, typesetters, and editors who persisted in standardizing the punctuation of her poems, she had a rubber stamp produced that read "PLEASE BELIEVE THE PUNCTUATION." She stamped this polite request in red ink all around the margins of all her manuscripts.)

Rukeyser's ideas about form were not always easy to follow. What intrigued her was a nonlinear, inclusive verse form that held greater possibilities, she felt, for recreating some of the physical imperatives that lay at the base of her own urge to poetic expression and that related to the gender-specific nature of her life as a woman. "I write from the body, a female body," she often said.[4] And in 1962, she articulated this belief unforgettably in "To Enter That Rhythm Where the Self Is Lost":

> To enter that rhythm where the self is lost,
> where breathing : heartbeat : and the subtle music
> of their relation make our dance, and hasten
> us to the moment when all things become
> magic, another possibility.
> That blind moment, midnight, when all sight
> begins and the dance itself is all our breath,
> and we ourselves the moment of life and death. (303)

Muriel Rukeyser was one of the most prolific writers of our century, and her poetic corpus is huge; her collected poems run to more than five hundred pages, and in addition she published translations, children's books, short stories, plays, a novel, and two biographies. Her subject matter and her formal approaches suggest the ambitious and restless nature of her genius, for they change, sometimes radically, from poem to poem. Within the pages of her collected poems, published in 1978, slightly more than a year before she died, one can find sonnets, ballads, elegies, poetic sequences, dramatic poems, a verse play, a full-length poetic biography, free verse, light verse. There are pieces that have been variously classified by the critics as Social Realist, Marxist, Jungian, feminist. Side by side, scenes from classical mythology, the streets of New York City, the squalor of miners' camp towns in Depression-era West Virginia, the dramatic landscapes of northern California, and the marvelous Ajanta caves of India coexist. Thus, any suggestion that an accurate assessment of the nature and range of her work can be made

within the confines of any methodology or thematic summary is ludi-
crous. Still, at the risk of being reductive and of not giving full credit to
a remarkable body of work, it *is* possible to isolate several specifically
feminist themes and subjects that characterized Rukeyser's work
throughout her career and that caused her work to be highly regarded
by the women's movement of the sixties and seventies. These include
the pain of a lost female history and subsequent efforts to retrieve and
articulate it; the documentation of gender-specific female experience;
the celebration and affirmation of a new woman-identified consciousness;
a strong impulse toward pacifism and nonviolence that is explicitly related
to the life-giving powers of the female; and, finally, the exploration of
androgyny. These recurring themes in Rukeyser's work became particu-
larly important to many of the women poets who followed her and
who regarded her work and the example of her life as instrumental in
facilitating a greater acceptance of the female voice in literature. The
importance of Rukeyser to the contemporary women's movement is
suggested by the fact that several of the first feminist anthologies of
literature by women borrowed their titles or epigraphs from her work or
bore an introduction that she had written. The title of *No More Masks!*
an anthology of poetry published in 1973, referred back to her poem
"The Poem as Mask" (1968), which explored the notion of female myths
of identity (such as those inherited from Greek mythology) and rejected
the use of unexamined, male-inscribed versions of the received myths.
*The World Split Open: Four Centuries of Women Poets in England and
America*, published in 1974, also took its title from Rukeyser's "Käthe
Kollwitz" (1968).[5]

Some examples from Rukeyser's poetry throughout the fifty years of
her career will illustrate the early feminist themes within her own work
and suggest through example, perhaps, the profound meaning and pecu-
liar relevance younger women writers and feminist activists have located
in her work.

The pain of a lost female history. Rukeyser had an early awareness of
the absence of female voices from literary history, and when she was
only sixteen years old, in 1930, she wrote a tongue-in-cheek poem,
"Ballad of the Missing Lines," in which she suggested that our entire
view of history might be radically different if we had had access to Eve's
and Helen's versions of their well-known stories, along with Adam's and
Paris's.[6] Her published poetry is full of this awareness, and from her very
first book she set herself the task of restoring to the literature the women's

voices that had been left out. Although she was never reluctant to celebrate the lives and achievements of men (both of her biographies and a number of her long portrait poems she called "Lives" took men as their subjects),[7] she could be sarcastic and ironic on occasion about the ways in which men have convinced both men and women that it is only men's histories and men's lives that are significant, as in "Along History" from 1973:

> Along history, forever
>   some woman dancing,
>   making shapes on the air;
>   forever a man
>   riding a good horse,
>   sitting the dark horse well,
>   his penis erect with
>   fantasy (503)

The documentation of gender-specific female experience. Rukeyser wrote many poems that dealt matter-of-factly and unsentimentally with the corporeal aspects of female existence. She wrote repeatedly of pregnancy and childbirth; she wrote of menstruation, of sex and sexual desire, of nursing, of masturbation and orgasm. In many cases, she was the first American woman poet to break the silences that had surrounded women's own expression of their sexuality in literature. Still, it was not an inevitable, biologically based femininity that she embraced; her poems argue for a full range of experience for women that will take them beyond the nursery worlds and "interminable girlhoods" they have historically inhabited (218). Rukeyser herself led a life of extraordinarily committed (and sometimes life-threatening) political activism, and in another section of "Letter to the Front" she warns against the solipsistic dangers of motherhood that can turn women, who create the world through giving birth, away from it. She felt strongly that women's lives, though deeply enhanced by motherhood, extended far beyond the confines of the nursery world.

In attempting to bring female sexuality within the range of literary expression, she found, like many of the younger women writers who followed her, that it was often necessary to work with traditionally "unpoetic" language in order to overcome powerful cultural taboos and sexual stereotyping and get to the point. In "The Speed of Darkness" (1968), she wrote:

Whoever despises the clitoris despises the penis
Whoever despises the penis despises the cunt
Whoever despises the cunt despises the life of the child.

Resurrection music,   silence,   and surf. (484)

In 1948, her "Nine Poems for the Unborn Child" documented her own dangerous pregnancy, which she undertook alone, without the support either of marriage or of the welfare system that single mothers benefit from today. The poem was remarkably successful in suggesting not only the various physiological symptoms and bizarre physical changes of pregnancy, but also in communicating the extraordinary psychic experience of pregnancy, which is at once specifically and narcissistically personal and overwhelmingly public and historical, linking the pregnant woman with all of history and the survival of the species.

The celebration and affirmation of a new, woman-identified consciousness. From her early poems where she sought a voice that was authentic and capable of transmitting the specifics of female experience—"I want to speak in my voice! / I want to speak in my real voice!" she demanded in "Suicide Blues" in 1944 —to her final poems which sometimes dealt with real issues (like male-inscribed language) confronted by the contemporary women's movement, Rukeyser explored joyously and often with humor the transforming possibilities of feminist conscience and consciousness. The following poem, "Myth," exemplifies her exploration of male-inscribed language:

Long afterward, Oedipus, old and blinded, walked the
roads. He smelled a familiar smell. It was the
Sphinx. Oedipus said, "I want to ask one question.
Why didn't I recognize my mother?" "You gave the
wrong answer," said the Sphinx. "But that was what
made everything possible," said Oedipus.   "No," she
said. "When I asked, What walks on four legs in the
morning, two at noon, and three in the evening, you
answered, Man. You didn't say anything about woman."
"When you say Man," said Oedipus, "you included women
too. Everyone knows that."   She said, "That's what
you think." (498)

She held a deep and reverent belief in women's capacity for love and nonviolence, and although she did not believe that these qualities were *not* present in men, she clearly felt that, as far as history was concerned, it was women who had been on the side of life more often than on the side of death. The unexplored potential of female solidarity and the breaking of centuries of silence imposed on women by patriarchal systems excited her, and she envisioned in numerous poems the revolutionary effect of the liberation of women. Perhaps her most famous expression of this occurred in the third section of her well-known long poem "Käthe Kollwitz" (1968), whose extraordinary, concluding couplet became a slogan of the contemporary women's movement:

> What would happen if one woman told the truth about her life?
> The world would split open (482)

A strong impulse toward pacifism and nonviolence specifically related to the life-giving powers of women. Rukeyser often spoke of herself as having been "born into war" (she was born six months before World War I erupted in Europe), and some of her earliest poems document the deforming influence of the mass-media images of death, dismemberment, and destruction that are a by-product of modern war. She felt strongly that such precocious awareness of the aggressive, bloodthirsty side of human nature inhibited the mind's natural, optimistic tendency to make generative metaphors of experience. Although World War I had concluded by the time she entered grade school, another international conflict was brewing when she left college in 1932. She affiliated herself rather openly with the Communist party throughout the thirties, editing and publishing in their cultural organs. Many facets of Marxism appealed strongly to her—the abolishment of capitalism and hierarchical bourgeois society, the fraternal spirit and communal sense of the Communists' mission—but she could not go along with the Party's implacable acceptance of the inevitability of violence and warfare in achieving the revolution. She envisioned a nonviolent revolution accomplished by the spiritual and political solidarity of millions, informed by the power of a liberated female consciousness, and she expressed this from the beginning through metaphors and tropes that were laden with a female sense of procreation. "Split by a tendril of revolt / stone cedes to blossom everywhere," she wrote in "City of Monuments" in 1935 (50). By the time World War II began, she had articulated clearly her position of passionate pacifism. During the sixties, when the country was embroiled in the war in Vietnam, she became an active participant in the antiwar movement, an involvement that culminated in a visit to Hanoi in 1972, with Denise Levertov, as an invited representative of the American peace movement.

Many of the poems from Rukeyser's final volumes of poetry—*The Speed of Darkness* (1968), *Breaking Open* (1973), and *The Gates* (1976)—concern themselves with the expression of her opposition to war and with her belief in the transformative powers of individually enacted nonviolence. In "Waking this Morning" (1973), she speaks of herself as "a violent woman in the violent day" who "will try to be nonviolent / one more day" (491). And in "Rational Man," a section of the long poem "Breaking Open" (1973), she produced a piece that was both profoundly eloquent and profoundly disturbing. It is worth remarking that although Rukeyser had by this time begun her explorations of male-inscribed and male-signifying language, she declined to attribute any of the atrocities she described in the poem to women. "Rational man" is the object of her meditation:

> The marker at Auschwitz
> The scientist torturing male genitals
> The learned scientists, they torture female genitals
> The 3-year-old girl, what she did to her kitten
> The collar made of leather for drowning a man in his chair
> The scatter-bomb with the nails that drive into the brain
> The thread through the young man's splendid penis
> The babies in flames.   The thrust
> Infected reptile dead in the live wombs of girls
> We did not know we were insane.
> We did not know we are insane.
> We say to them   :   you are insane
> Anything you can imagine
>   on punishable drugs, or calm and young
>   with a fever of 105, or on your knees,
>   with the world of Hanoi bombed
>   with the legless boy in Bach Mai
>   with the sons of many torn by man
> Rational man has done.

> Mercy, Lord.   On every living life. (533)

The exploration of androgyny. From an early age, Rukeyser was exploring through her work the sex roles available to her and attempting to create a poetic language that would bring together the female and male possibilities inherent in human experience. In this, her life imitated her art, for, although she had experienced a "conventional" heterosexual adolescence (experimenting with boys in the boathouse at the country club), she soon found exclusive sexual liasons with men ultimately unfulfilling—both physically and emotionally. Although perhaps her most committed relationships were with women, she was involved with numerous men throughout her life, was once married for a brief time, and bore a child. Her feminist politics were adamantly not those of sexual separatism, and the whole impulse of her work is an androgynous one: her concern was to liberate female power and consciousness and integrate them with the male principle for the mutual benefit of both men and women.

Although she said many times that she wrote to break out of imposed silences and to overcome destructive sexual stereotypes, Rukeyser found it difficult—perhaps because of deeply ingrained post-Victorian generational mores—to speak directly of her sexual love for women. Like many other twentieth-century women writers, she often obscured that portion of her narrative by using non-gender-specific pronouns. As she grew older, perhaps empowered by the openness of the feminist dialogue about lesbianism and new social mores that were (relatively speaking) more accepting of alternative lifestyles, Rukeyser began to approach the subject of her own bisexuality somewhat more directly, as in this excerpt from "Käthe Kollwitz":

> She said: "As a matter of fact
> I believe
>
>   that bisexuality
> is almost   a necessary factor
> in artistic production; at any rate,
> the tinge of masculinity within me
> helped me
>
>   in my work."

In 1911, two years before Muriel Rukeyser was born, Sara Teasdale (1884–1933), one of the most celebrated women poets of the generation that preceded Rukeyser's, had expressed the prevailing attitudes of American society about that "damned mob of scribbling women" (as Nathaniel Hawthorne had even earlier characterized American women writers): "A woman ought not to write. Somehow it is indelicate and unbecoming. She ought to imitate the female birds, who are silent—or if she sings no one ought to hear her music until she is dead."[8] Fortunately for the history of our literature, Rukeyser was as uninclined to follow

Teasdale's advice as she was incapable of suppressing her genius for poetic expression.

"Why does a woman write a poem?" Rukeyser often asked. She never faltered in her belief that (at least during her historical moment in time) women wrote to break out of silence, to overcome weakness, to escape invisibility. Her own strong constitution and indomitable will enabled her to prepare the way for a younger generation of women poets who would follow her: more radical and less disposed to give men the benefit of the doubt.

By the middle of the century, when Adrienne Rich (born 1929) entered Radcliffe College, Muriel Rukeyser had cleared a considerable amount of ground for women writers, even though she had accomplished this at great cost to her own reputation with the critics. Her work suffered countless attacks from critics (almost always male) who could not understand the nontraditional form of her poetry and who would not credit a poetic endeavor that was identifiably female and that was often irreverent—or happily deaf—to the demand for conformity to the male literary tradition.

One might consider that the pioneering work Rukeyser had done in legitimizing the presence of female voices and female experience in literature by 1950 would have made it easier for a new generation of women writers who were clamoring to get their voices on record. This was not initially the case, however, for Adrienne Rich, trapped in the powerful "feminine mystique" of the fifties and pressured by postwar attitudes that sought to reassert the primacy of male experience and privilege in a society that had undergone a noticeable "femininization" during the war years.[9] Rich's early task, like that of all talented "girls" in the fifties, was, as one critic has pointed out, to prove that she was as good, as smart, and as capable as a man.[10] This she set out to do immediately by perfecting an early command of the male literary tradition. Her first published poetry, which found great favor with the male critical establishment, was highly formal and recognizably imitative of several of the male contemporary "masters": W. H. Auden, Robert Lowell, and Robert Frost. When Auden himself selected her first volume, *A Change of World*, for the Yale Series of Younger Poets in 1951, he described the virtues of her poems in a language that was full of unspoken allusions to sexual stereotypes, that did not, in fact, seem to have changed much at all since Muriel Rukeyser published *her* first book:

> Miss Rich, who is, I understand, twenty-one years old, displays a modesty not
> so common at that age, which disclaims any extraordinary vision, and a love
> for her medium. . . . [Poems] are analogous to persons; the poems a reader
> will encounter in this book are neatly and modestly dressed, speak quietly but
> do not mumble, respect their elders but are not cowed by them, and do not
> tell fibs.[11]

Undeterred by such backhanded flattery, Rich continued to explore the
possibilities of formal rhyme and meter in her second collection, *The
Diamond Cutters and Other Poems*, which she published in 1955. The
poems in this volume, as in her first, are decorous, graceful, and conven-
tionally "feminine," and for this she was once again richly rewarded,
receiving the Ridgley Torrence Award from the Poetry Society of
America and high marks from the critics for poems like "Love in the
Museum":

> But art requires a distance: let me be
> Always the connoisseur of your perfection.
> Stay where the spaces of the gallery
> Flow calm between your pose and my inspection
> Lest one imperfect gesture make demands
> As troubling as the touch of human hands.[12]

The poem's final line came to greater meaning: in the same year that
The Diamond Cutters was published, Rich, who had married in 1953,
gave birth to her first child. Within four years, she had borne two more
children and was mired in the demands of domestic life and childrearing.
Poetic silence descended. She did not publish another volume of poems
until 1963, when her children were of school age. The intervening years
were, as she has stated on many occasions, full of "pain" which she
seemed "to be feeling most of the time." Isolated in motherhood and in
the fifties' overwhelmingly sexist expectations of women, she found her-
self in an entirely different kind of female community from that of Rad-
cliffe College, where she had lived an imaginatively expansive and liber-
ating life, awash in brilliance and intellectual energy. Suddenly, only a
few years later and still living in Cambridge, Massachusetts, she found
herself in strikingly different female company, part of a group of "restless,
educated women [who] sat on benches with baby strollers, half-stunned
. . . by the middle class American social expectations of the 1950's." The
sense of waste—not only her own, but of all women—began to bear upon
her with increasing urgency, and by the time she began to publish poems

again in 1963, she had become another person. "The experience of motherhood was eventually to radicalize me," she has said.[13]

During the long period of silence, Rich had been profoundly influenced by the writings of Simone de Beauvoir and James Baldwin, and it was their language and their arguments that convinced her that political and social inequities need not be accepted with a Promethean sense of inevitability. She had, from the beginning, displayed a strong responsiveness to the past and a clear sense of history; a number of her early poems had cast a penetrating, though calm, eye on the past. Now, with the new analytic tools that Baldwin and de Beauvoir provided her, she began groping toward a poetic language that would express her personal frustration of the preceding decade and her rapidly growing awareness of the oppression of women and the overwhelming institutionalization of patriarchy. Rarely has a poet's career mirrored so faithfully the political and social course of a generation, and the new poems that appeared in *Snapshots of a Daughter-in-Law: Poems 1954–1962*, as personal as they were in tone, spoke not only for Rich's own birth of consciousness but for the nation's as well, as the civil rights movement moved to its full power. "Prospective Immigrants Please Note" is a powerful example of that parallel:

Either you will
go through this door
or you will not go through.

If you go through
there is always the risk
of remembering your name.

Things look at you doubly
and you must look back
and let them happen.

If you do not go through
it is possible
to live worthily

to maintain your attitudes
to hold your position
to die bravely

but much will blind you,
much will evade you,
at what cost who knows?

The door itself
makes no promises.
It is only a door.[14]

As the country, embroiled in the birth of a new consciousness, strug-
gled with the civil rights movement and the broad social changes that
occurred in its wake, Rich, too, struggled with the responsibilities her
own rebirth entailed: from the dutiful daughter of the early poems to
political activist of the late sixties to radical lesbian feminist of the sevent-
ies. As her awareness expanded and her political commitment intensi-
fied, so did the poems, and by 1971, when she published *The Will to
Change: Poems 1968–1970*, the form of her work had undergone a revi-
sion as radical as its content. She articulated quite straightforwardly her
apprehension that the language available to her was not her own and
could never be her own; it was, as she said, the "Oppressor's language,"
just one more product of partriarchy, and it was, perhaps, just this
realization that empowered her to overthrow the last vestiges of her
allegiance to traditional poetic form and narrative. Although her poems
had been slowly but surely deconstructing themselves formally since
1963, when she had first raised the voice of her new feminist conscious-
ness and found the received poetic forms incapable of expressing it, now
the poetry exploded on the page. No longer polite, respectful, modest,
quiet, or without vision, Rich strove furiously and angrily to overcome the
limitations of her own necessarily male-inscribed mind and the history of
women in a male-dominated society. From the mysterious and por-
tentous monostichs of "Shooting Script":

We were bound on the wheel of an endless conversation
Inside this shell, a tide waiting for someone to enter.
A monologue waiting for you to interrupt it.
A man wading into the surf. The dialogue of the rock with the breaker.

to the autobiographical and "found poem" sections of "The Burning of
Paper Instead of Children":

*People suffer highly in poverty and it takes dignity and intelligence to overcome
this suffering. Some of the suffering are: a child did not had dinner last night:
a child steal because he did not have money to but it: to hear a mother say he
do not have money to buy food for her children and to see a child without
cloth it will make tears in your eyes.* [Written by a student of Rich's]

. . .

I am composing on the typewriter late at night, thinking of today. How well
we all spoke. A language is a map of our failures. Frederick Douglass wrote
an English purer than Milton's. People suffered highly in poverty. There are
methods but we do not use them. Joan, who could not read, spoke some
peasant form of French. Some of the suffering are: it is hard to tell the truth;
this is America; I cannot touch you now. In America we have only the present
tense. I am in danger. You are in danger. The burning of a book arouses no
sensation in me. I know it hurts to burn. There are flames of napalm in
Catonsville, Maryland. I know it hurts to burn. The typewriter is overheated,
my mouth is burning. I cannot touch you and this is the oppressor's language.

to the fragmented narrative and interrupted grammar of "A Valediction
Forbidding Mourning":

My swirling wants. Your frozen lips.
The grammar turned and attacked me.

Themes, written under duress,
Emptiness of the notations.

They gave me a drug that slowed the healing of the wounds.

I want you to see this before I leave:
the experience of repetition as death
the failure of criticism to locate the pain
the poster in the bus that said:
my bleeding is under control.

A red plant in a cemetery of plastic wreaths.
A last attempt: the language is a dialect called metaphor.

These images go unglossed: hair, glacier, flashlight.
When I think of a landscape I am thinking of a time.
When I talk of taking a trip I mean forever.
I could say: those mountains have a meaning
but further than that I could not say.

To do something very common, in my own way.

the poems testified to Rich's transformation.[15] In 1973, at the height of
the contemporary feminist movement, Rich won another prestigious
literary award: the National Book Award for her seventh volume, *Diving
into the Wreck: Poems 1971–1972.* This time, however, the prize was
not a reward for conformity, modesty, and femininity, for the volume
was, in essence, a poetic manifesto of the women's movement. The all
but uncontainable anger that Rich displayed in poems like "The Ninth
Symphony of Beethoven Understood at Last as a Sexual Message,"

"Rape," "Waking in the Dark," and "Trying to Talk with a Man" spoke for an entire generation of women who, for the first time in history, found themselves in possession of political and economic power sufficient to overcome the suppression of their message by antagonistic forces in society. The contemporary feminist movement saw itself and its concern reflected in the angry and impassioned poems of *Diving into the Wreck*, such as this from "Incipience":

> Nothing can be done
> but by inches. I write out my life
> hour by hour, word by word
> gazing into the anger of old women on the bus
> numbering the striations
> of air inside the ice cube
> imagining the existence
> of something uncreated
> this poem
> our lives[16]

In the years since *Diving into the Wreck* was published, Rich has elucidated with great care her position as a lesbian, a feminist, and a political activist in volumes of poetry and prose that continue to be more intellectually provocative and formally innovative than almost anything else being produced in the world today. In her recent volumes of poetry (*Twenty-One Love Poems* [1976], *The Dream of a Common Language* [1978], *A Wild Patience Has Taken Me This Far* (1981), and *Your Native Land, Your Life* [1986]), she has addressed herself repeatedly to certain topics that can be connected specifically with the contemporary feminist movement, among them the oppression of women, violence against women, heterosexism, feminist self-determinism, female eros, and the rediscovery of feminist history.[17] Although the topical nature of some of this work has led it to be embraced by an audience that is larger and less exclusively "literary" than is usual for American poetry, it is undoubtedly her raging search for a new form and a new language in which to express herself that has been most compelling and most meaningful to younger women poets who look to her example. Although Rich may now appear to be possessed of an indomitable courage and a determination that have always been hers, she, like Muriel Rukeyser, was clearly a pioneer, waging an early, lonely fight against a critical establishment that was threatened by the angry voice and rebellious spirit of her work. When she abandoned the polite and modest "feminine" tone of her first two books for a more feminist voice during the early sixties, she encountered a wave of resistance and hostility that affected her deeply. "It took me a long time not to hear those voices internally whenever I picked up my pen," she has said.[18] By the end of the sixties, the feminist movement had coalesced into a community and a political entity that obviously empowered her. Since then, she has created a fearless body of work that has been and continues to be enormously important to younger women writers fortunate enough to have been born in an era more populous with female literary role models than that into which Rich herself was born.

For anyone familiar with the recent women's "movement" in American poetry, the ideas, subjects, and approaches contained within the poetry of Muriel Rukeyser and Adrienne Rich are recognizable as the main issues around which the debate has centered.[19] One can, however, question the whole idea of a women's literary "movement." Although we may more easily agree on the historical fact of a woman-centered, feminist social and political movement, and on the creation of a critical orientation and practice known as feminist theory, it is more difficult to ascertain the outlines of an actual contemporary literary movement, practiced by a large number of consenting women poets under the banner of feminism. Part of this has to do with the way in which writers and critics who have interested themselves in the subject have defined themselves by their strong aversion to canonical ways of thinking, often linking those with precisely the attitudes and hierarchical thought of patriarchy that have been responsible for the exclusion of women's voices from documented literary history. Thus, the very politics of "inclusion" that feminist thinkers and critics have propounded has often made it difficult to identify or recognize the boundaries—or even the existence of boundaries—of the material or movement under examination. Adding to this difficulty are extreme definitions of "feminism"—both left and right—that have tended to create turf battles, diverting attention from the endeavor as an entity and focusing it on specific, highly politicized issues.

Literary critics, often the arbiters of such matters, have been unable to agree among themselves upon the existence or nonexistence of an identifiable women's movement in contemporary poetry. Poet and critic Alicia Ostriker, author of the important study *Stealing the Language: The Emergence of Women's Poetry in America* (1986), believes that at the "grassroots level . . . a woman's movement exists in poetry as in society at large." Her book goes a long way toward documenting the claim that she makes.[20] By contrast, Helen Vendler, the powerful Harvard professor and critic of contemporary poetry, has refused consistently to consider the notion of "women's poetry" on the grounds that "no lived reality is so easily characterized." And although she finds it easy enough to imagine the formative influences of nationality—"Every poet is in the end only one sort of poet—a poet of the native language," she has said— she has spoken repeatedly against any gender-specific readings of poetry and has written, with obvious repugnance, of "woman" poets and of "vulgarly feminist" interpretations of recent poems by women (Vendler's quotes). In spite of this, Vendler has found herself pressed, in reviewing Adrienne Rich's work, to make the kind of gender-specific remarks that she professes elsewhere to find beneath the consideration of the "properly aesthetic criticism" that she claims to practice:

> It is true of all literary voices that they have had fewer women than men practioners. But in the case of the voice Rich uses, the disparity arises not solely from the relative numbers of male and female writers. Rather, it is used chiefly, as many women writers have said, by the existence of a competing voice, one thought more "suitable" for women than this voice of Protestant personal and public drama, command, and reprobation. The competing choice is the one that Dickinson, Moore, Bishop, Sexton, and Plath repudiated as strongly as Rich repudiates it. It is the voice of girlishness, erotic pining, winsome coyness, religious submissiveness, and sentimental motherhood, the voice of the nineteenth-century woman poet.[21]

Somewhere between these two positions (paradoxically enough, considering the amount of ground-breaking work they have done in formulating both a feminist literary aesthetic and a feminist critical approach) lies the work of Sandra Gilbert and Susan Gubar, who have dedicated themselves for the past twenty years to the rediscovery and documenting of an ancient "female literary tradition" and who published one of the first collections of critical essays on women poets undertaken from a feminist theoretical perspective, *Shakespeare's Sister's: Feminist Essays on Women Poets* (1979).[22] As far as contemporary literature is concerned, Gilbert and Gubar observe much less of an organized movement than does Alicia Ostriker, but much more feminist consciousness among women writers than does Helen Vendler:

> Whether they defined themselves as feminists or not, women writers between 1940 and 1984 wrote out of a double consciousness: on the one hand, a

newly intense awareness of their role as female artists who had inherited an increasingly great tradition, and, on the other hand, a newly protective sense of their vulnerability as women who inhabited a culture hostile to female ambition and haunted by eroticized images of women.[23]

Women poets themselves have often exhibited frustratingly ambivalent attitudes toward their own work when considered within the context of gender. This ambivalence is not surprising given the social and psychic obstacles women have historically had to overcome in order to write.

Louise Bogan (1897–1970), one of the century's most extraordinary lyric poets, was well-known for her hatred of and cruelty to other women writers. Although she occupied a position of great influence as the poetry reviewer for the *New Yorker* magazine from 1931 until 1968, she rarely championed or celebrated the work of other women, preferring to focus her keen critical eye on the work of men. Like Sara Teasdale earlier in the century, Bogan found herself in an impossible situation. Convinced of the inferiority of women and the thinness of female experience (as far as literary subject matter was concerned), and both awed by and terrified of the corpus of work by men, she still had to reckon with the fact of her own genius and her own quite undeniable femaleness. Cutting herself off from the possibilities of a female literary tradition for fear that her work would not be taken seriously by the critics—a quite rational fear—she found herself thrown back on a male tradition that only frustrated her with its unwillingness to accommodate itself to the particular nature of poetry by women and the axiomatic principles of its critical approach that maintained that women were incapable of writing profound or important poetry. Still, while she found herself quite openly expressing her envy of male poets and the tradition that supported their efforts, she found it impossible to conceive of any tradition—or any possibilities—other than that, and she spent much of her life in the grip of creative stasis that allowed her to go neither forward to develop her gifts nor backward to connect with an earlier female tradition that might have helped her understand some of the source of her frustration and her inability to articulate fully and fearlessly the lyric forces that moved within her.[24]

This kind of identification with male power structures by women writers of genius such as Bogan has presented problems for younger women writers who turn to the poets of the past looking for encouragement and models—not just for literature, but for life. Not only have aspiring women writers encountered the general anxiety of influence one experiences when first confronting the great examples and overwhelming expanse of the literature that has preceded them, but they have had to reckon with the strongly negative response of our society to women's ambition and then, sometimes, with even more negative responses from some of the few women writers who have managed, against the odds, to raise their voices and have them heard. While, as a poet and a woman, one wants to claim the remarkable work of women writers like Bogan and Sylvia Plath, the undeniably self-destructive and antifeminist impulses within each that disparage female achievement can create intense ambivalence in women writers about affiliating themselves with their literary foremothers. It can seem far too dangerous.

Elizabeth Bishop (1911–1979), surely one of the finest and most memorable poets of recent times, is a perfect example of the double bind in which women writers can find themselves. Although the example of her accomplishments and the work itself have both been profoundly meaningful to young women writers, she refused without exception to publish her work in anthologies of women writers. "I didn't think about it very seriously," she said in 1977, "but I felt it was a lot of nonsense, separating the sexes. I suppose this feeling came from feminist principles stronger than I was aware of."[25] Given the abhorrence with which Bishop viewed the description that was so often bestowed upon her by reverential male critics, "the best woman poet of her generation," her assessment of her own feminism seems somewhat unexamined at best, and disingenuous at worst.

The scale of extremes represented by the conservative, closemouthed feminism of Elizabeth Bishop on one end and the radical lesbian feminism of Adrienne Rich on the other continues to define the parameters of the situation for women poets today and suggests some of the reasons for the tentative nature of these comments on the existence or nonexistence of a contemporary women's movement in poetry. Granted that such a "movement" does exist, or has existed, or exists intermittently, the amount of literature that might be examined is quite overwhelming. For the purposes of this essay, then, the definition of feminism shall be, admittedly, a conservative—and in the terms of the feminist debate itself, an exclusive—one that occupies much of the space between the extreme definitions alluded to earlier. The recent poetry considered in the remainder of this essay will be considered feminist, or a product of the woman's movement in literature, if it is written by a woman who has published the majority of her work since 1960 and if it exhibits specific acknowledgment of gender that is connected with an explicit or implicit political awareness of the patriarchial orientation of the Western world and the ways in which this has affected the experience of women.

In our time, we are fortunate to enjoy a wide array of poetry by American women that is available both within the mainstream publishing industry and within a flourishing small-press community that was nourished by the grassroots political movements of the sixties and seventies. The feminist movement in particular engendered the founding of a number of publishing ventures in the seventies that were specifically devoted to the work of women writers and critics. The Feminist Press, the Alice James Poetry Collective, Persephone Press, Women in Literature, Inc., Kitchen Table: Women of Color Press, Crossing Press, and Sinister Wisdom Books are only a few of the many small presses that have devoted themselves in recent years to the publication of work by and about women.[26]

Of course, it is obvious that there was not always such an interested market for work by women, and many of the contemporary poets who have had the most success in incorporating "female" subject matter in their work began, like Adrienne Rich, by adhering to the formal poetic styles of an earlier era that were more acceptable to (and more likely to be accepted for publication by) the mainstream publishing industry.

Carolyn Kizer (born 1925), who published her first book in 1961, adopted an elegant, highly formal technical style in her early poems that was greatly admired by the critics. As she matured and as the social and political changes of the sixties facilitated a greater acceptance of free verse and alternative subject matter, Kizer's central concern with the female creative principle—a concern which culminated with the publication in 1984 of *Yin*, which was awarded the Pulitzer Prize for poetry— rose more to the surface of her poems.[27] In *Knock upon Silence* (1965), Kizer created one of the major poems identified with the feminist movement, "Pro Femina":

I suppose they [women of letters] reacted from an earlier womanly
    modesty
When too many girls were scabs to their stricken sisterhood,
Impugning our sex to stay in good with the men,
Commencing their insecure bluster. How they must have swaggered
When women themselves indorsed their own inferiority!

Vestals, vassals and vessels, rolled into several,
They took notes in rolling syllabics, in careful journals,
Aiming to please a posterity that despises them.
But we'll always have traitors who swear that a woman surrenders
Her Supreme Function, by equating Art with aggression
And failure with Femininity. Still, it's just as unfair
To equate Art with Femininity, like a prettily-packaged commodity
When we are the custodians of the world's best-kept secret:
Merely the private lives of one-half of humanity. [28]

Like Kizer, Maxine Kumin (born 1925) published her first collection of poetry, *Halfway*, in 1961. [29] Where Kizer often chooses to distance herself from some of the angrier emotions of her work through the devices of satire, parody, and irony, Kumin has chosen another route, creating poems that are noted for their affirmative spirit, their authenticity, and their unobtrusive formal devices. Much of her work has documented the pastoral life she leads in New England and, through an examination of her own personal history, the many absurd ways in which girl children are reared in our culture. Her work has almost always been more indirect in its political implications than other, more obviously feminist women writers of her generation (like Rich and Kizer). Nevertheless, this has not prevented her from documenting women's struggle for psychic survival in a culture that would keep them enfeebled, frail, and "feminine."

The feminist conflict for black women writers has been more pronounced. If every female writer finds herself, as I have suggested, in a double bind of perplexity about the nature of female genius in a profoundly male-dominated society, how much more complicated is that bind for women writers of color who find themselves at every turn confronted by the deforming pressures of racism?

Gwendolyn Brooks (born 1917) was the first American black woman poet to achieve national prominence and a significant critical reputation. Like most other women writers of her generation, Brooks achieved this by conforming to white male poetic models—a task she mastered well enough to win the Pulitzer Prize for poetry in 1950 for her second collection, *Annie Allen*. [30] Her early work, mannered and characterized by wordplay and a beautifully complex linguistic structure, was never consciously "black" or "female," she has said, although her subject matter has most often been the lives of those in black communities, particularly women. Her well-known poem, "The Mother," lyrically yet unblinkingly focuses on and addresses women who have had to undergo, by necessity, the tragedy of abortion and its haunting aftereffects. The poem is not meant to be a moral condemnation; rather it deals with one of Brooks's leitmotifs, the relentlessness of memory. Through a series of presentationally wrought, rhymed lines, the poem projects scenes that the grieving mother will imagine yet will never have the opportunity to live out because of the irreversible fact of abortion. At the end of the poem, the speaker ordains in a tone ambivalently mixed by implacability and bittersweetness the paradoxical situation of the mother: "You will never leave them, controlling your luscious sigh,/ Return for a snack of them, with gobbling mother-eye."[31] In 1967, under pressure from younger black writers who were reconceptualizing the responsibilities of black writers in the midst of the civil rights movement, Brooks underwent a change of heart that resulted in a radical formal revision of her poetry. Since then, although she has declined to define herself specifically as a feminist, she has worked in free form, consciously utilizing black speech patterns, and has moved consistently toward a position of greater political clarity, as in "Primer for Blacks" (1981):

Blackness
stretches over the land.
Blackness—
the black of it,
the rust-red of it,
the milk and cream of it,
the tan and yellow-tan of it,
the deep-brown middle-brown high-brown of it,
the "olive" and ochre of it—
Blackness
marches on.

The huge, the pungent object of our prime out-ride
to Comprehend,
to salute and to Love the fact that we are Black,
which is our "ultimate Reality,"
which is the lone ground
from which our meaningful metamorphosis,
from which our prosperous staccato,
group or individual, can rise.[32]

Among younger women writers of color, the poet Ai (born 1947) has, perhaps, expressed most directly the nature of the problem faced by black women writers in a white, patriarchal society. Part Japanese, Native American, and black, Ai, like Gwendolyn Brooks, has found it difficult to identify directly with feminist issues. Her mixed heritage has complicated for her the already intense demands made by gender and race on the formation of personal identity: describing herself as "one-half Japanese, one-eighth Choctaw, one-fourth black, and one-sixteenth Irish," she has said that she doesn't "feel black," and has responded to some feminist criticism of her poems (for writing too often from a male point of view in persona poems) by saying, "Whoever wants to speak in my poems is allowed to speak, regardless of sex, race, creed, or color. . . . I don't want to be catalogued and my characters don't want to be catalogued and my poems don't want to be catalogued. If a poet's work isn't universal, then what good is it?"[33] Despite her protestations, Ai has written some of the most powerful and convincing of all recent poems on issues that arise directly from the suppression of women in our society, as in "Lesson, Lesson" from *Killing Floor* (1973):

> I draw a circle on a paper bag
> with the only crayon you've ever had
> and hold it above the cot.
> You laugh. So the sun ain't green.
> You not supposed to know yet.
> Just pretend maybe won't be
> another little gimme-fill-my-belly
> next year while you out in the fields.
> Hear me. You imagine real good
> because your daddy a hammer.
> Hard-time nail in his pants.
> He feel wood beneath him,
> he got to drive it home.[34]

Audre Lorde (born 1934) has taken on an even greater burden of expression in her work. As a black feminist and lesbian, Lorde's task has been to express the specifics of her life as a "Black lesbian feminist socialist mother of two, including one boy, and a member of an inter-racial couple" to a society that is highly invested in keeping those who live such alternative life-styles as marginalized and invisible as possible.[35] While Lorde's strident demand for accountability (her own and others') and her personal intensity have led her to examine discrimination and hostility from the obvious (male and heterosexist) quarters, they have also brought her face to face with the personal pain of the "particular resonances of heterosexism and homophobia among Black women" themselves.[36] With a passion that fuels both tenderness and anger, Lorde has, like her friend Adrienne Rich, created a body of work that is remarkably courageous and dedicated to claiming new territories for women writers.

While the explicit lesbian content of some of her poems has, predictably, made some readers uncomfortable, it is difficult to understand the objection of any reader to poems of such beauty as "Love Poem," from *The New York Head Shop and Museum* (1975):

> And I knew when I entered her I was
> high wind in her forests hollow
> fingers whispering sound
> honey flowed
> from the split cups
> impaled on a lance of tongues
> on the tips of her breast on her navel
> and my breath
> howling into her entrances
> through lungs of pain.[37]

It is Alice Walker (born 1944) whose work has generated, perhaps, the most controversy (in part due to the extraordinary popular success of her novel *The Color Purple* [1982]) about the race-specific issues facing black feminist writers today.[38] Walker's focus on the empowering nature of a reclaimed black matrilineage and her insistence on the importance of female communities for black women today has enraged some black male writers who have seen her celebration of black women as a turning away from the possibilities of a fully realized and fully empowered black society comprised of both men and women. The furious dialogue her work has generated between black men and women has been further provoked by the fact that Walker has never been reluctant to point out misogyny or sexism wherever she has seen it—among white *or* black men. Thus, she has sometimes been seen as a traitor to her race through her allegiance to her sex, and numbers of her poems have spoken to this conflict, if not always directly, then with an implicit awareness of the ways in which the collective claims of an embattled race can frequently collide with the individual's will to self-expression, as in this excerpt from "On Stripping Bark from Myself":

> My struggle was always against
> an inner darkness: i carry within myself
> the only known keys
> to my death—to unlock life, or close it shut
> forever. A woman who loves wood grains, the color yellow
> and the sun, I am happy to fight
> all outside murderers as I see I must.[39]

Among feminist political activists today, the question is often asked: what has happened to the younger generation of women? Why are they so content to rest on the achievements of the past? Why are they so apathetic? It is obvious that in spite of the many significant changes brought about by the feminist movement, American society has not yet been transformed radically enough to allow passage of the Equal Rights Amendment—a document that really requires no more than admission of the fact that women are equal to men under the law. Thus far, Americans have not yet been able even to *say* that men and women are equal. Thus, to an older generation of politically active feminists, it often seems strange that younger women display relatively little interest in continuing the struggle that began twenty years ago. Society, of course, could not maintain itself if it were continually involved in the upheavals and protests of counterculture movements like the recent feminist movement. After the revolution must come a period of rest and replenishment; new spokespersons must be found; new goals articulated once the impact of newly enacted societal changes has been fully made and clearly understood. Perhaps it is in such a period that we now live. If it is less exciting than that of fifteen or twenty years earlier, it is also in many ways more comfortable, particularly for younger women writers, who now have a plethora of female literary models before them and a highly visible and widely respected body of criticism and theory to support and invigorate their efforts.

Thus, it is not surprising to find a generation of younger writers who accept, most often without comment, the larger, more liberated worlds they have inherited through the efforts of those women writers who have preceded them. A number of younger women poets such as Marilyn Hacker, Olga Broumas, and Jane Miller have found it possible to write of lesbian existence without didactic straining, without necessarily positioning their work in a politicized context, and without encountering ghettoization in the marketplace.[40] Hacker in particular has created an interesting, highly formal body of work that details joyously and explicitly the details of lesbian lives in fixed forms such as sonnet crowns. Other poets—for instance, Molly Peacock, Mary Jo Salter, Katha Pollitt, and many others—who write more or less in line with a formal tradition recognizable from an earlier, prefeminist age nevertheless enjoy a greater acceptance of their work and a greater consciousness of the value of female experience in the articulation of human experience overall than they would have only thirty years ago. Peacock, for instance, published an entire book of brief, rhymed poems, *Raw Heaven*, in 1984, encountering no apparent difficulties in expanding the ancient sonnet to accommodate her many highly mannered, elegant poems describing female experience, as in "Smell," which is about menstruation.[41] The title poem of Salter's most recent book, *The Unfinished Painting*, which was awarded the 1988 Lamont Prize by the Academy of American Poets, documents her mother's inability to satisfactorily bring to fruition her gift for painting: a subject that—while it is never addressed in gender-specific terms in the poem—is one of the most compelling and painful issues confronted by feminist theorists and historians who must account for the silences of women in all the arts.[42]

The work of Sharon Olds is perhaps most representative of a contemporary, less radical generation of women writers who enjoy a new freedom of expression in their work. Although Olds is aware that the freedom she has assumed to write not only honestly but explicitly of her life as a woman was bought with the efforts of women poets who preceded her (a debt she has acknowledged openly to Muriel Rukeyser in both poems and prose), she has not found it necessary to identify herself publicly as a feminist or to link her work with either a political or literary movement.[43] Her three books of poetry—*Satan Says* (1980), *The Dead and the Living* (1984), and *The Gold Cell* (1987)—have inspired women through their graphic depictions of heterosexual lovemaking and through Olds's diligent exploration of the sexual and emotional abuse of children by parents.[44] This is from "What If God":

> And what if God had been watching when my mother
> came into my bed? What would He have done when her
> long adult body rolled on me like a
> tongue of lava from the top of the mountain and the
> tears jumped from her ducts like hot rocks and my
> bed shook with the tremors of the magma and the
> deep cracking of my nature across— (*The Gold Cell*, 25)

Male readers and critics, however, have sometimes found themselves quite uncomfortable at being "undressed" in the pages of Olds's poetry in a way that is reminiscent of the centuries-old tradition of undressing women for the gratification of male readers. She writes in "First Sex":

> I knew little, and what I knew
> I did not believe—they had lied to me
> so many times, so I just took it as it
> came, his naked body on the sheet,

the tiny hairs curling on his legs like
fine, gold shells, his sex
harder and harder under my palm
and yet not hard as a rock his face cocked
back in terror, the sweat
jumping out of his pores like sudden
trails from the tiny little snails when his knees
locked with little clicks and under my
hand he gathered and shook and the actual
flood like milk came out of his body. (*The Gold Cell*, 50)

Nevertheless, it is not something as simple as reverse sexism that Olds
practices, for, as a number of critics have pointed out, her embrace of
heterosexuality and her quite unabashed delight in her sexual experi-
ences with men are not merely another version of male-inscribed sexual
attitudes toward women.[45] It is a true sexual equality that Olds depicts
in her poems, with each of the partners active agents of desire and will,
both devoted to the creation of a mutual pleasure that diminishes neither.
It enriches each, as in this from "Love in Blood Time":

The large hard bud of your sex in my mouth,
the dark petals of my sex in your mouth,
I could feel death going farther and farther away,
forgetting me, losing my address, his
palm forgetting the curve of my cheek in his hand.
Then when we lay in the small glow of the
lamp and I saw your lower lip
glazed with light like liquid fire
I looked at you and I tell you I knew you were God
and I was God and we lay in our bed
on the dark cloud. (*The Gold Cell*, 62)

One particularly astute contemporary male poet has spoken of the way
in which Olds's poetry challenges, over and over, the damaging claims
that Freudian psychoanalysis has made on the consciousnesses of both
men and women. "What I really like about Sharon Olds' poetry," he has
said, "is that it tells Freud to fuck off."[46] Perhaps this is an appropriate
place to end this essay, which has, it is hoped, documented some of the
successes of recent American women writers in extending the poetic
expressions of their lives beyond the tiny world inscribed by the theory
of penis envy. If there is one poem in our recent literary history that
expresses precisely the desire of women to overcome damaging sexual
stereotypes, it is Olds's tender, hilarious, and highly ironic "The Con-
noisseuse of Slugs," from *The Dead and the Living* (51). Accept it with the

compliments of all women writers who see their freedom of expression as empowering to both men and women and who envision a world in which we may come together not only with a new equality but with a new harmony and an exquisite satisfaction:

When I was a connoisseuse of slugs
I would part the ivy leaves, and look for the
naked jelly of those gold bodies,
translucent strangers glistening along the
stones, slowly, their gelatinous bodies
at my mercy. Made mostly of water, they would shrivel
to nothing if they were sprinkled with salt,
but I was not interested in that. What I liked
was to draw aside the ivy, breathe the
odor of the wall, and stand there in silence
until the slug forgot I was there
and sent its antennae up out of its
head, the glimmering umber horns
rising like telescopes, until finally the
sensitive knobs would pop out the ends,
delicate and intimate. Years later,
when I first saw a naked man,
I gasped with pleasure to see that quiet
mystery reenacted, the slow
elegant being coming out of hiding and
gleaming in the dark air, eager and so
trusting you could weep.

Notes

1. Willard Maas, review of *Theory of Flight*, by Muriel Rukeyser, *New York Herald-Tribune Books*, 19 January 1936, 7.

2. See, for example, Weldon Kees, "Miss Rukeyser's Marine Poem," *Partisan Review* 9 (November–December 1942): 540; and Randall Jarrell, review of *The Green Wave*, by Muriel Rukeyser, *Nation* 166 (8 May 1948): 512–13.

3. See, for example, "Theory of Flight," "Mediterranean," "The Book of the Dead," and "Letter to the Front," in *The Collected Poems of Muriel Rukeyser* (New York: McGraw-Hill, 1978). Page references in text are to this edition.

4. Quoted in Jane Elizabeth Crutis, "*The Woman Writer Confronts Traditional Mythology and Psychology*" (Ph.D. diss., University of Wisconsin, 1981), 3.

5. Florence Howe and Helen Bass, eds., *No More Masks! An Anthology of Poems by Women* (New York: Doubleday, 1973); *The World Split Open: Four Centuries of Women Poets in England and America* (New York: Random, 1974).

6. The manuscript of this poem is in the Berg Collection of the New York Public Library.

7. See, for example, Rukeyser, *Willard Gibbs* (New York: Doubleday, 1942); *The Traces of Thomas Hariot* (New York: Random, 1971); and *One Life* [a biographical poem on Wendell Wilkie] (New York: Simon and Schuster, 1957).

8. Teasdale, quoted in *Mirror of the Heart*, ed. William Drake (New York: Macmillan, 1984), xxxi.

9. See Betty Friedan, *The Feminine Mystique* (New York: Norton, 1963).

10. Margaret Atwood, "Unfinished Woman," *New York Times Book Review*, 11 June 1978, 42.

11. Auden, foreword to *A Change of World* (New Haven, Conn.: Yale University Press, 1951).

12. Rich, in *The Diamond Cutters and Other Poems* (New York: Harper, 1955), 89–90.

13. Rich, "Split at the Root," in *Blood, Bread, and Poetry* (New York: Norton, 1986), 120, 117.

14. Rich, in *Snapshots of a Daughter in Law: Poems 1954–1962* (New York: Norton, 1962), 59.

15. Rich, *The Will to Change: Poems 1969–1970* (New York: Norton, 1970), 50.

16. Rich, *Diving into the Wreck: Poems 1971–1972* (New York: Norton, 1972).

17. Rich, *Twenty-one Love Poems* (1976), published with *The Dream of a Common Language* (New York: Norton, 1978); *A Wild Patience Has Taken Me This Far* (New York: Norton, 1981); *Your Native Land, Your Life* (New York: Norton, 1986).

18. Rich, "Blood, Bread, and Poetry: The Location of the Poet (1984)," in *Blood, Bread, and Poetry*, 180.

19. For discussion of the feminist critical debate, see Elaine Showalter, ed., *Feminist Criticism: Essays on Women, Literature, and Theory* (New York: Pantheon, 1985); Elizabeth Abel, ed., *Writing and Sexual Difference* (Chicago: University of Chicago Press, 1982); and Alicia Ostriker, *Stealing the Language: The Emergence of Women's Poetry in America* (Boston: Beacon, 1986).

20. Ostriker, *Stealing the Language*, 8.

21. Vendler, *The Music of What Happens: Poems, Poets, Critics* (Cambridge: Harvard University Press, 1988), 301, 300, 369.

22. Gilbert and Gubar, *Shakespeare's Sisters: Feminist Essays on Women Poets* (Bloomington: Indiana University Press, 1979).

23. Gilbert and Gubar, eds., *The Norton Anthology of Literature by Women* (New York: Norton, 1985), 1977.

24. For a discussion of Bogan's problem, see Elizabeth Frank, *Louise Bogan: A Portrait* (New York: Knopf, 1985), 77.

25. Bishop, quoted in *American Poetry Observed: Poets on Their Work*, ed. Joe David Bellamy (Urbana: University of Illinois Press, 1984), 56.

26. The Feminist Press is located in New York City; the Alice James Poetry Collective is in Cambridge, Massachusetts; Crossing Press is in Trumansburg, New York; Women in Literature, Inc., is in Reno, Nevada; Kitchen Table: Women of Color Press is in Latham, New York; Sinister Wisdom is in Berkeley, California. For a more complete listing of both presses and periodicals that are primarily devoted to the publication of work by and about women, see the

International Directory of Little Magazines and Small Presses, ed. Len Fulton (Paradise, Calif.: Dustbooks, 1988).

27. Kizer, *Yin* (Brockport, N.Y.: BOA Editions, 1984).

28. Kizer, *Knock Upon Silence* (New York: Doubleday, 1965).

29. Kumin, *Halfway* (New York: Holt, 1961).

30. Brooks, *Annie Allen* (New York: Harper, 1949).

31. Brooks, *A Street in Bronzeville* (New York: Harper, 1945), 5.

32. Brooks, *Primer for Blacks* (Chicago: Brooks Press, 1980).

33. Quoted in *Contemporary Literary Criticism* 14 (Detroit: Gale, 1980), 7; Bellamy, *American Poetry Observed*, 5.

34. Ai, *Killing Floor* (Boston: Houghton-Mifflin, 1973), 7.

35. Lorde, "Age, Race, Class, and Sex: Women Redefining Difference," in *Sister Outsider* (Trumansburg, N.Y.: Crossing Press, 1984), 114.

36. Lorde, "Eye to Eye: Black Women, Hatred, and Anger," in *Sister Outsider*, 145–75.

37. Lorde, *The New York Head Shop and Museum* (New York: Norton, 1975).

38. Walker, *The Color Purple* (New York: Harcourt, 1982).

39. Walker, *Good Night, Willie Lee, I'll See You in the Morning* (New York: Dial, 1979), 23.

40. See, for example, Hacker, *Love, Death, and the Changing of the Seasons* (New York: Arbor, 1986); Broumas, *Pastoral Jazz* (Port Townsend, Wash.: Copper Canyon, 1983); Miller, *American Odalisque* (Port Townsend, Wash.: Copper Canyon, 1987).

41. Peacock, *Raw Heaven* (New York: Random, 1984).

42. Salter, *The Unfinished Painting* (New York: Knopf, 1988).

43. See, for example, Olds, "A Student's Memoir of Muriel Rukeyser," *Poetry East* 16/17 (Spring/Summer 1985), 49–69.

44. Olds, *Satan Says* (Pittsburgh: University of Pittsburgh Press, 1980); *The Dead and the Living* (New York: Knopf, 1984); *The Gold Cell* (New York: Knopf, 1987). These editions hereafter cited in text.

45. See, for example, Amy Hoffman, "Retrospective Review of Sharon Olds," in *Poetry East* 25 (Spring 1988): 138–43.

46. This gentleman prefers to remain anonymous.

10

American Poetry: 1970–1990

JONATHAN HOLDEN

Poetry, more than ever, is harnessed by and subordinate to its criticism.

—*The Reaper*

In his essay "The Specialization of Poetry," published in the *Hudson Review* in 1975, Wendell Berry described in somewhat invidious terms the situation of American poetry ten years ago, and he offered some prescriptions for its maladies, prescriptions which in retrospect seem to be foreshadowings of events which, indeed, took place.

> Because of the proliferation of so-called protest poetry, and the widespread involvement of poets in public issues, after about 1964 it became possible to suppose that . . . the effort of many poets to speak out against public outrage might recover some of the lost estate of poetry. . . . But the political "involvement" of poets appears, now, to have subsided, leaving the "effective range and influence" of poetry no larger than before. . . . Poetry remains a specialized art, its range and influence so constricted that poets have very nearly become their own audience.[1]

Using quotations from interviews with poets as evidence, Berry then accused the specialist poet of disregard for "the issues of traditional form" and suggested that the contemporary poet-specialist has cultivated a poetry of sensibility. He issued the following warning: "The danger may not be so much in the over cultivation of sensibility as in its *exclusive* cultivation. Sensibility becomes the inescapable stock in trade of the isolated poet who is increasingly cut off from both song and story because the nature of these is communal. . . . I find it impossible to believe that song can come from or lead to a sense of isolation. . . . But even more suggestive of the specialization of contemporary poets is their estrangement from story telling."[2] Berry's conclusion summed up his assessment of the situation of poetry in the following cautionary terms: "There is in reality no such choice as Yeats's 'Perfection of the life, or of the work.' The decision to sacrifice either one of them for the sake of the other becomes ultimately the fatal disease of both. . . . The *use* of life to perfect work is an evil of the specialized intellect. It makes of the most humane of disciplines an exploitive industry."[3]

Although Berry's polemic in the passage above is an extreme one— issuing from the same mind which would abolish not only the automobile but technology in general—his description of American poetry as an "industry" contains more than a grain of truth. Indeed, it is essential to acknowledge the "industrial" nature of American poetry since the mid-sixties, and also the reasons behind it, if one is to appreciate adequately the main trends in American poetry since the seventies; for the issues underlying American poetry since about 1976 are the immediate result— or reaction to—the situation of poetry during the late sixties and early seventies.

Partly because of the reaction against the elitist, eastern-based New Critical hegemony carrying out the programs of T. S. Eliot, but also partly because, as colleges and universities expanded to keep pace with demographic trends, higher education in America became democratized as it never had been before, the sixties saw a democratization of poetry (and of high culture in general) the scale of which is accurately measured by Berry's word "industry." Virtually all the main trends in poetry during the late sixties and early seventies—stylistic as well as institutional—can be in part or else entirely attributed to "democratization." With the establishment of the National Endowment for the Arts in the late sixties, for the first time ever in the history of American letters poets could get financial backing from sources other than conservative English departments or from foundations whose generosity had been directed mainly to the service of conservative, elitist aesthetics. Starting in the late sixties a whole generation of young poets, using the fanciful formulas pioneered by Kenneth Koch and laid out in his book *Wishes, Lies and Dreams*, served as a sort of domestic Peace Corps in the NEA-funded Poets-in-the-Schools programs—programs which, in an attempt to interest young people in poetry, encouraged a kind of poetry which could almost be regarded as "oral-formulaic." But the popularization of high culture had its cost, most memorably remarked in Jacques Barzun's infamous and bitter little dictum: "College is a place where artificial pearls are synthesized for real swine." Poets-in-the-Schools, while humanizing poetry for children, propagated the sentimental and inaccurate notion that poetry could become a body of knowledge available to people who didn't necessarily read very much or very well.

Another of the more notable symptoms of the democratization of poetry was that, for a while at least, the most prominent American poetry vortex shifted from Boston and New York to the Midwest, revolving around such figures as Robert Bly and James Wright. Because of the proliferation of creative writing workshops in colleges and universities during the sixties—workshops pioneered at the University of Iowa under the direction of Paul Engle—a vortex that was in origin midwestern spread copies of itself throughout the United States. For the first time ever, American poetry became decentralized, and this decentralization appears to be permanent, at least so long as creative-writing pedagogy is supported by American colleges and universities. The two most prominent poetic modes that flowered between 1960 and the mid-seventies, Confessional poetry and Deep Image poetry, were likewise part and parcel of American poetry's democratization and industrialization. The kinds of anguished personal experience—divorce, insanity, alienation— that the Confessionals wrote about were subjects open to *everybody* and didn't require research or recondite cultural initiation. Similarly, almost by definition, the "archetypal" dream materials that were the subject matter of poems in the Deep Image mode were not only ahistorical but were also open, literally, to everybody, regardless of intellect, caste, education, or geography. Meanwhile, partly because of available funding but also because of the democratized, *non*literary character of much poetry in the late sixties and early seventies, the institution of the poetry reading flourished on college campuses as perhaps it never had before.

Since 1976, most of the prominent events, both in the evolution of poetic styles and in the criticism of poetry in America, can be considered elements of a vehement but perhaps inevitable backlash to the liberal democratization of poetry which had, as Berry suggests, been going on since 1964—a reaction signaled most emphatically by Robert Pinsky's book-length critical essay *The Situation of Poetry* (1976) and by Daniel Halpern's *The American Poetry Anthology* (1976). Both books were representative of a set of new and interrelated developments in American poetry. If these developments had any one thing in common it was that they were characterized by an increased self-consciousness about poetic artifice and poetic epistemology, a self-consciousness which—except for

M. L. Rosenthal's important study *The New Poets* (1967), in which the term *Confessional poetry* was invented—had been notably absent during the sixties and early seventies; for the very nature of the Confessional and Deep Image modes, when they held sway in the late sixties and early seventies, had militated against the self-conscious display of craft or rhetorical calculation. Both Pinsky's book and the poems in the Halpern anthology expressed dissatisfaction with the prevailing poetic decorum and signaled the restoration to respectability of a wide variety of poetic modes which, under the hegemony of Eliot and the New Critics and, later, in the antiintellectual counterrevolution of the late sixties, had been relegated to a marginal status in the evolving milieu of American poetry.

Although Pinsky's essay was closely reasoned, urbane in its tone, and almost scholarly in its rhetoric, without the shrillness of the famous Imagist manifestos, it was, in effect, a manifesto. It was overtly opinionated. It chided Robert Bly for a "more-imagistic-than-thou" attitude; and it pointed out, in a tone that was both troubled and amused, how stock had become the vocabulary of the Deep Image poem:

> One of the most contemporary strains in contemporary poetry is often interior, submerged, free-playing, elusive, more fresh than earnest, more eager to surprise than to tell. The "surrealist" diction associated with such writing sometimes suggests, not a realm beyond surface reality, but a *particular* reality, hermetically primitive, based on a new poetic diction: "breath," "snow," "future," "blood," "silence," "eats," "water," and most of all "light" doing the wildly unexpected. . . . This is a kind of one-of-the-guys surrealism.[4]

Pinsky's main thrust was to remind the reader of the artificiality of poetic conventions, that the apparent spontaneity of Deep Image and Romantic poems was really a highly evolved period style, a set of mannerisms— that indeed the very nature of language renders the presentation of "immediate" experience impossible:

> Modern poetry was created by writers born about a hundred years ago. The premises of their work included a mistrust of abstraction and statement, a desire to escape the blatantly conventional aspects of form, and an ambition to grasp the fluid, absolutely particular life of the physical world by using the static, general medium of language. These premises are paradoxical, or at least peculiar, in themselves. . . .
>
> Or, they once seemed peculiar. These special, perhaps even tormented premises and ways of writing have become a tradition: a climate of implicit expectation and tacit knowledge.[5]

Pinsky's allegation that the poetry he was criticizing was founded on a fraudulent epistemology was, perhaps, overdrawn; but his suggested antidote to Imagism as an exhausted period style—that poetic language could and should admit more abstract discourse—seemed to prophesy, or at least to acknowledge and to ratify, trends which were already taking place, some of which could already be discerned among the poems in Halpern's anthology: the "meditative" poetry of a writer like Robert Hass, the narrative realism of poets like Gary Gildner or Frank Bidart, the formalism of a poet like Marilyn Hacker, the wit of a poet like William Matthews, all under forty years of age when the Halpern anthology was published.

Indeed, one of the most significant symptoms of the increasing self-consciousness among poets and their readers which we observe around 1976 is that this year marks, approximately, the beginning of a large outpouring of excellent practical criticism much like the outpouring which accompanied the advent of Modernism in 1913. Why such an outburst at this time? Probably because of the very "industrialization" of creative writing which Berry had complained about; for in the dozens of creative writing programs which had sprung up in imitation of the Iowa Writers Workshop as its graduates spread out like missionaries through the American colleges and universities, as American creative writing reached an "industrial" scale, the pressure upon young writers to master or to imitate the style of the moment grew correspondingly more acute. It grew in direct proportion to the number of competing writers and the degree of the institutionalization of poetry. To attack the dominant mode of the moment was tantamount to attacking an institution.

Perhaps the most intelligent and telling attack on the outgoing Deep Image period style was by Paul Breslin, in his essay "How to Read the New Contemporary Poem," published in the *American Scholar* in 1978. Breslin had delivered a rather more acerbic version of this essay in 1977 at the Modern Language Association Convention under the title "Nihilistic Decorum in Contemporary American Poetry," opening with the complaint that a "narrow and dull decorum" had spread over most American poetry.

A similarly important critical survey of contemporary American poetry was Stanley Plumly's two-part essay "Chapter and Verse," published in 1978 in the *American Poetry Review*. During the late sixties and early seventies, in reaction to the genteel, ironic, metered, "late-Modernist" poetry of the late fifties—a mode epitomized in the first edition (1957) of *New Poets of England and America*—"free verse" had become virtually the *lingua franca* of poetic discourse. But it wasn't until Plumly's essay that the prevailing fashion of free verse was given any theoretical justification. Plumly, a highly accomplished poet himself, characterized the typical free-verse poem as a "prose lyric," a type of poem relying on the rhetoric of "voice" instead of the silent rhetoric of the "image."[6] The primacy of voice in Plumly's aesthetic reflected three aspects of the contemporary tradition in 1977: (1) the popularity, already waning but still significant, of the poetry reading, in which the poet's voice was actually present before an audience; (2) the beginning of a shift in fashion, away from the "narrow and dull" decorum of the Deep Image lyric impugned by Breslin, toward a poetic milieu which would tolerate and even encourage a greater diversity of modes, including the narrative— a mode in which the existence of a storytelling voice would seem to have always been inherently necessary; and (3) a restoration of the dignity of individual personality in poetry. Whereas the Jungian epistemology of Deep Image poetry had encouraged the cultivation by poets of a generic, archetypal persona speaking for all humanity for all time, the narrative, free-verse, conversation-poem that was the "prose lyric" had, by definition, to be spoken by a particular individual from a particular historical moment.

What is perhaps more significant, Plumly's justification for free verse as specially adaptable for individual "voice" constituted the most convincing denial yet formulated for the implicit justification of free verse in Deep Image poetry, which had assumed that a poetry whose content issued directly from the unconscious could never admit to too much conscious craft and prosodic artifice. Deep Image verse *had* to look spontaneous, primitive, crude. Plumly's essay was the first attempt by a poet to argue the case for free verse on the grounds of its application toward sophisticated, civilized intentions, on the grounds of its potential *urbanity*. In this respect, Plumly's essay, like Pinsky's *The Situation of Poetry*, foreshadowed many of the major developments in American poetry that have occurred since 1977.

Of the cultural and poetic developments begun in the late sixties and early seventies, only one continued to gain momentum, both critical and creative, after 1976. This was the creation, begun by Adrienne Rich, of a distinct "women's" poetic tradition, a creation signaled by her groundbreaking essay/lecture "When We Dead Awaken," published first in

College English (October 1972) and reprinted in William Heyen's anthology *American Poets in 1976* (1976), but signaled more emphatically by Rich's National Book Award-winning poetry collection *Diving into the Wreck* (1973). It was in 1976, however, that this emerging tradition was given its first thorough critical definition, by the poet/critic Suzanne Juhasz, in her study *Naked and Fiery Forms: Modern American Poetry by Women*. Whereas critical approaches such as Plumly's and Pinsky's were reactionary, Juhasz's study—as revolutionary a manifesto as Pinsky's *The Situation of Poetry* was a conservative one—proposed an aesthetic for what she perceived, accurately as it turns out, to be an emerging women's tradition in American poetry, a tradition availing itself of the spirit of "liberation" which had characterized so much of the political rhetoric of liberals and radicals during the late sixties and the early seventies:

> The new tradition exists: wrought slowly through the century with pain and daring, it daily encounters and confronts a growing audience. No one style or form defines it, yet certain qualities do characterize the poetry of contemporary women poets: a voice that is open, intimate, particular, involved, engaged, committed. It is a poetry whose poet speaks as a woman, so that the form of her poem is an extension of herself. A poetry that seeks to affect actively its audience. A poetry that is real, because the voice that speaks is as real as the poet can be about herself. . . . A poetry that is revolutionary, because, both "naked and fiery," it touches, and [in the words of Nikki Giovanni] "touching was and still is and will always / be the true / revolution."[7]

Ten years later, in her short essay "American Poetry, Now Shaped by Women," Alicia Ostriker would write:

> There is reason to believe that American women poets writing in the last 25 years constitute a literary movement comparable to Romanticism or modernism in our literary past and that their work is destined not only to enter the mainstream but to change the stream's future course. To be sure, the idea of "women's poetry" is still distressing in some quarters, as is the whole notion of a female literary tradition. . . . The belief that true poetry is genderless—which is a disguised form of believing that true poetry is masculine—fails to recognize that writers necessarily articulate gendered experience just as they necessarily articulate the spirit of a nationality, an age, a language.[8]

Like Juhasz, Ostriker proposed that women's poetry is characterized by its intimate and direct contact with its audience: "The best women writers tend to be intimate rather than remote, passionate rather than distant, and to defy divisions between emotion and intellect, private and public, life and art, writer and reader. . . . If poetry written by contemporary women demands that we read as participants, it may help us discover not only more of what it means to be a woman but more of what it means to be human."[9]

Meanwhile, although the sixties were over, the poetry "industry" in 1976 was still expanding. The Associated Writing Programs (AWP), founded in 1967 by R. V. Cassill, grew steadily in influence and membership, providing guidance to the hundreds of creative writing programs being started up in colleges and universities. In 1975, AWP instituted its award series book competition in fiction and poetry. By 1984, *The AWP Catalogue of Writing Programs* contained descriptions for 279 writing programs in the United States and Canada.

The growth of creative writing pedagogy and the numbers of talented graduates from the burgeoning creative writing programs resulted in the creation of publishing opportunities other than the new AWP award series. The Walt Whitman Award, the Princeton Poetry Series, and the Houghton Mifflin Poetry Series were all instituted in 1976; and 1977 saw the founding of the Elliston Award (for the best collection published by a small press). In the September/October 1977 issue of *Coda*, a headline reported, with some alarm, "Editors deluged by submissions." In 1979, with the help of a massive grant by the author James Michener and the administrative skill of the poet/editor Daniel Halpern, the National Poetry Series was instituted. By the mid-eighties, probably more good poetry was being written and published in America than in any country at any time in human history. Indeed, America was perhaps the only country in history in which hundreds of people could earn a living as poets by teaching creative writing in universities at a professor's salary while traveling regularly to give poetry readings at other universities. Not only was the quality of much of this poetry very high, but, for reasons which I have already suggested, the kinds of poems being written and published were various, constituting an aesthetic pluralism.

Although the drift of American poetry has been, as I have already suggested, in a conservative direction, its main and central strand has been its "realist" component, continuing the liberal, humanistic, and egalitarian cultural projects of the late sixties and early seventies; and within this strand, the now fully emerged "women's" poetic tradition has been the most vital. The reason for this is simple. Realism, as a glance at the work of such American early modern classics as *Babbitt* and

Winesburg, Ohio, would suggest, has always derived its impetus and force from the act of exposure of uncomfortable and inadequately acknowledged truths underlying various forms of official complacency. This is why, for the last fifteen years, much of the important Realist fiction in America has been written by women. Except when writing about odd corners of experience such as the Vietnam War, many male fiction writers in America, lacking material crying for exposure, have had to content themselves with fabulation and formal experiment; by contrast, the details of life as a female in America had never been, until recently, thoroughly held to the light from a female point of view.

The dichotomy between men's and women's writing, glaringly obvious in the domain of serious fiction, is also apparent in slightly different form in the differences that have evolved between male and female poetry in America. Although "realistic" in setting and characterization, much American male poetry tends to be what Wendell Berry labels a poetry of "sensibility." By contrast, much female poetry, though often anguished and passionate, attempts to deal realistically with questions of history, ideology, and social and personal responsibility—to deal with ideas rather than "feelings" in an attempt to reveal, almost analytically, connections between the subjective life of an individual female and the objective political, economic, and personal facts which determine her situation.

Paradigmatic of this type of poetry at its best might be Sharon Olds's important collection *The Dead and the Living*, a book which was both the Lamont Poetry Selection for 1983 and a National Book Critics Circle Award winner. The confessional poems which comprise the strongest half of the book, poems replete with gritty journalistic detail, expose almost relentlessly the links between Olds's ostensibly safe, comfortable bourgeois life as a mother on the one hand and various unpleasant historical facts—the Holocaust, wars waged by male governments, imperialism, and oppression—on the other. The book is energized by Olds's agonized sense of responsibility at her *female* role as a bearer of children into a world in which, all too easily, they could find themselves being either victims or oppressors. By alternating between public events and poems about domestic, private life, Olds dramatizes how her own body—exemplary of the female body in its potentiality for birth—is located at the very nexus of history, of past and future, of public and private, of the dead and of the living, how as a mother one is drawn not just theoretically into history but into it *bodily*—that there is no shelter from it or from one's responsibility in it. Thus, in "Rite of Passage," Olds is able to be horrified by her own son as a first grader:

As the guests arrive at my son's party
they gather in the living room—
short men in first grade

. . . .
        They clear their
throats a lot, a room of small bankers,
they fold their arms and frown. *I could beat you*
up, a seven says to a six,

. . . .
We could easily kill a two year old,
he [Olds's son] says in his clear voice. The other
men agree, they clear their throats
like Generals, they relax and get down to
playing war, celebrating my son's life.[10]

The insistence on exploring the nature and degree of one's responsibility to the world and one's personal and historical connections with it supplies the driving impulse behind the work of two other very important American women poets writing today: Carolyn Forché, whose *The Country Between Us* (1981) tries to repair the disrelation between felt individual life in America and American oppression in Central America; and Carolyn Kizer, whose *Yin*, winner of the 1985 Pulitzer Prize, forges a passionate female mythology in which marriage, children, and generational continuity are celebrated. Two of the most ambitious poems in *Yin*, "The Copulating Gods" and "Semele Recycled," propose, in complementary ways, a modern mythology of gender. "The Copulating Gods," assuming the sexual superiority of women (and poets) to men (and critics), portrays human religion as issuing from an eternal female principle so powerful and pervasive that it drives males to invent compensatory male sky-gods such as Jupiter. In this way God, who is female, allows Herself out of a kind of *noblesse oblige* to be invented in male manifestations, by men, just as poets allow their work to be explicated by critics. The poem is addressed to a "you" who is male, but whose sexuality issues ultimately from the female principle which dominates the universe:

             Come, kiss!
Come, swoon again, we who invented dying
And the whole alchemy of resurrection.
They will concoct a scripture explaining this.[11]

The poem's vision of the complementary and mutually dependent natures of "male" and "female" (critic and poet) is more than a joke or some clever paradox: it is the most lyric and yet rigorously developed proposal of how both genders may accommodate one another that any contemporary poet, including Adrienne Rich, has put forth.

In American male poetry since 1976, the most vital strand of the new "realism" has, like poetry in the women's tradition, derived its impetus from acts of exposure—exposure not of veiled truths about gender and power but of the hidden costs of middle-class comfort in American society. Philip Levine had been publishing such poems for years—poems evincing explicitly a sociopolitical conscience in a historical context. But perhaps as a reaction against the oddly fraudulent opulence of American middle-class life in the early eighties—as if America were reenacting one hundred years later a Gilded Age political style—a number of American poets younger than Levine were writing poems which eloquently took up the task of exposure.

Foremost among these poets has been C. K. Williams, whose fourth and strongest collection, *Tar*, tries repeatedly to come to terms with disturbing social and economic facts, asking how prosperous members of the American middle class can reconcile their comfort and prerogatives with the blatant suffering and exploitation that immediately surround them. Williams focuses on the discrepancy between privileged and poor, which, particularly in cities (where most of Williams's poems are set), has been enlarged to glaring proportions by the Reagan administration's policies during the early eighties. This discrepancy is also explored in Denis Johnson's *The Incognito Lounge*. In a poem called, significantly, "In the Light of Other Lives," he writes:

> It's raining and the street lights on the wet
> streets are like regurgitated lights,
> but the ambulance's ruby element
> can move among our rooms without a care
> so that we who generally sleep
> where it is black awaken in a red
> light of other lives.[12]

The vast majority of male American Realism however, has not been political but as is the nature of much Realism, regional, a poetry of local color: Sydney Lea writing about New Hampshire, Brendan Galvin writing about Cape Cod, Stephen Dunn and Louis Simpson writing about eastern suburban life, Ted Kooser writing about small-town Nebraska life, the late Richard Hugo (1923–1982) writing about Montana and the Pacific Northwest, Philip Booth writing out of the severity of Maine, and Philip Schultz capturing the daily nightmare of felt life in New York City.

Brendan Galvin and Richard Hugo represent rural, local-color regionalism at its best. They celebrate, through rich description, vanishing ways of life, ways of life which in America are being all but obliterated by housing developments, malls, and freeways. The more marginal such local cultures become, the more elegiacally they are celebrated. Galvin's celebration of the lives of Cape Cod fishermen and Hugo's celebration of the backward lives in economically depressed, dilapidated, western towns by-passed by freeways are examples of a nostalgic thematic which came into prominence in English language poetry with Wordsworth and which would appear to constitute an inevitable by-product of the development of industrial and postindustrial society.

As might be expected, however, the geographical region richest in local color has remained the South. The most influential Realist, writing in the tradition of America's first official poet laureate, Robert Penn Warren, has proved to be Dave Smith, whose ancestral ground is the tidewater region of Virginia. *Roundhouse Voices*, Smith's new and selected poems published in 1985, is deeply and authentically Southern— Faulknerian in its oral quality, a layered assemblage of stories told by a medley of voices who together comprise an insistent, sad, stubborn gossip issuing from the mind not so much of a single individual as of a place, a mythic community. As Smith puts it in "The Colors of Our Age: Pink and Black":

> Out here, supper waiting, I watch my son
> slip off, jacketed, time, place,
> ancestors of no consequence to him,
>
> . . . .
> For him, we are the irrelevance of age.
> Who, then, will tell him of wars,
> of faces that gather in his face
> like shadows?[13]

The most strident publication backing Realism and, as an aspect of Realism, narrative poetry was a little magazine called the *Reaper*, started in 1981 by Robert McDowell and Mark Jarman at Indiana State University in Evansville. The *Reaper* introduced itself with a manifesto which proclaimed:

> Navel gazers and mannerists, their time is running out. Their poems, too long even when they are short, full of embarrassing lines that "context" is supposed to justify, confirm the suspicion that our poets just aren't listening to their language anymore . . . inaccuracy, bathos, sentimentality, posturing, evasion—wither at the sound of *The Reaper's* whetstone singing. . . . . The poems collected here in issue number one, unmannered, tell stories *which their imagery serves.*[14]

The *Reaper,* like Pinsky, was intent on exposing literary manners which had gone stale. Whereas Pinsky's proposed antidote to empty manners was the admission of more abstract statement into poetic discourse, the *Reaper's* antidote was more narration. Narrative could serve as a reminder to poets that in order to make a good poem one must have a valid occasion to write about, an occasion urgent and dramatic enough to be the springboard for a story.

The poet whom the *Reaper* showcased as exemplary of the power of narrative was Jared Carter, whose poems such as "The Gleaner" and "The Shriving" transplanted to a midwestern setting verse stories which were altogether the equal of early Frost poems. Meanwhile, other poets, perhaps out of weariness with lyric decorum, with its narrow focus on the poet's "inner life" and with what Wendell Berry had called its "estrangement from story telling," began to experiment with narration. Louis Simpson adopted an urbane, omniscient, Chekhovian storytelling voice in order to write in verse stories about characters other than himself. Perhaps the most celebrated storyteller in the later eighties was C. K. Williams. In poems such as "Tar" and "The Gas Station," Williams invented a long poetic line that enabled him to speak poems in a storytelling voice, to incorporate all the digressions necessary in artful storytelling while retaining some of the relentless forward movement and intensity of lyric.

Realism is perhaps by nature democratic and egalitarian—*low* mimetic, to borrow Northrop Frye's useful distinction. Since 1976, American Realism in poetry has, in every sense, been "middle of the road." Its formal characteristics—free verse, vernacular diction—are natural to it. They evolved almost inevitably from Whitman. Of the two main developments in American poetry since 1976, one of them—the most prominent—has been, as I have already suggested, reactionary, toward the political Right, and has manifested itself mainly in the formulation of a conservative poetic style which has come to be known as the New Formalism, a style which itself constitutes an implicit ideological statement. The other main development, Language poetry, is radical, using literary and also High-Theoretical Criticism as a springboard for the criticism of bourgeois, "capitalist" culture. Like the political Left itself, this style is a marginal one. As these two styles, the New Formalism and Language poetry, developed in the early eighties, it was as if their differences reflected divisions evolving in the socioeconomic structure of America itself under the Reagan administration.

The New Formalism accomplished the partial gentrification of American poetry, as the latest members of the old elite—the genteel interests which, in the late fifties, in the height of Eliot's hegemony, had guided the tradition—attempted to get back what had been theirs. Symptomatic of this restoration of the old system of influence might, perhaps, be the assumption in 1983 of James Merrill to the office of judge for the Yale Younger Poets Series, replacing the late Richard Hugo. The literary journal created by Hilton Kramer as the main publishing organ of the New Formalism, the *New Criterion*, by appropriating the name of the famous journal once edited by T. S. Eliot, very pointedly allied itself with Eliot's conservative "Tory" values.

The New Formalism retrieved the genteel strand of ironic, fixed-form, Late Modernist poetry which had reigned in the forties and fifties, a strand epitomized, perhaps, by the vintage work of Richard Wilbur. But whereas Late Modernist poetry, conceived under the spell of Eliot and influenced heavily by Eliot's rediscovery of the English Metaphysicals, had been "metaphysical" itself—constructed around philosophical paradoxes and employing extended metaphors whose legitimacy derived from comparison to metaphysical conceits—the poems of one of the first New Formalist poets to gain a reputation, Brad Leithauser (an early recipient of a MacArthur fellowship), dealt with such issues as the poet's adjustment to the practice of law and the social and sexual dynamics of tennis classes: it was poetry by the rich, about the minor worries of the rich, a sort of expensive, very tasteful, interior decoration. Other younger poets working in a formalist vein included Molly Peacock, William Logan, Judith Moffett, Gjertrud Schnackenberg, and Timothy Steele. Richard Wilbur had given formalism its most memorable dictum in his famous metaphor which held that rhyme and meter were necessary in order to contain the pent-up energy of content in the same sense that the power of a "genie" was derived from the pressure of its captivity in a bottle. The New Formalism, as practiced by its more successful adherents such as Leithauser and Vikram Seth, produced elegant bottles without genies in them.

One of the most spectacular productions of the New Formalists was an entire novel (307 pages) in verse, *The Golden Gate*, by Vikram Seth, published in 1986. In the same year a new anthology, entitled *Strong Measures: Contemporary American Poetry in Traditional Forms*, edited by Philip Dacey and David Jauss, was published. By 1986, the New Formalism had indeed grown into a full-fledged institution, with its own journal and its own anthology.

Meanwhile, developments on the Left were analyzed in the first issue of the *Reaper* in a short essay entitled "Navigating the Flood." The essay began:

> In November, 1979, *The Reaper* attended After the Flood, a symposium at the Folger Shakespeare Library in Washington D.C. where panelists Harold Bloom, Richard Howard, John Hollander, Donald Davie, Marjorie Perloff, and Stanley Plumly scrutinized the state of contemporary American poetry and its criticism. During the presentation, group discussions and informal chats, the dominant emerging perspective seemed *not* to include the poem, but only ways of talking about the poem. . . . John Hollander implied that a poem in its very form is a critical text that comments on itself. And Harold Bloom typified the symposium's spirit by quoting, and misreading, Oscar Wilde: "*The only civilized form of autobiography*—I know no more adequate characterization of the highest criticism." It was remarkable to discover how little the panelists actually disagreed. Since then *The Reaper* has come to a few conclusions about the symposium topic. 1. Poetry, more than ever, is harnessed by and subordinate to its criticism. . . . 2. Critics are creating an exclusive audience for poetry, which consists only of themselves and the poets they promote. . . . 3. When critics cease with explanations and turn to examples, more often than not what they like is not good: they try to invent surprises where no surprise exists. . . . At the symposium, Ashbery was the one poet deferred to, analyzed, airbrushed, fawned over, and lovingly chided by every panelist. . . . However, as became clear at the symposium, contemporary critics are not satisfied with their role. . . . *The Reaper's* third conclusion is linked to the first and is illustrated by the critics' desire to celebrate the activity of talking about poems—not the art itself. [15]

The *Reaper's* report then goes on to detail the response of the symposium to two poems of that type which has come to be called "meditative": "Wet Casements," by John Ashbery, and Robert Hass's "Meditation at Lagunitas." As if following the directive by Robert Pinsky in *The Situation of Poetry* for admission of more abstract discourse into poems—more "telling" and less "showing"—these poems abandon the strategy of the dramatic lyric in favor of discursive abstract speculation. The *Reaper* suggests that these poems were written, in effect, for critics: "The critic who is interested primarily in developing a new program for reading can always babble on from the cloying camp of pre-digested theories. What counts is the evasive text which gives the critic the opportunity to invent substance where little exists. Poets who practice this sort of writing hide in their work and lend themselves to abstract theorization." The *Reaper* essay concludes: "Poetry must be written that casts a cold eye on criticism. . . . Are the poems extolled by critics like Harold Bloom, Richard Howard, Stanley Plumly, et al., good poems, or merely grist for critical mills? Poetry and criticism are two different things. It is time to remember that the poem comes first."[16]

It is now nine years since the symposium and six years since the *Reaper* essay was published, and that essay has proved prophetic. Ashbery is perhaps the most critically acclaimed poet of our moment, and Hass is perhaps the most critically acclaimed poet of the generation following Ashbery. Both have been recipients of MacArthur fellowships. Wallace Stevens, whose meditative later poems are models for Ashbery and Hass, has replaced Eliot at the head of the Modernist canon; and various strands of High-Theoretical Criticism—reader-response theory and Derridean theory, with their "suspicious" approaches to interpretation of texts— have replaced the old New Criticism. Like the New Criticism, these recent approaches have developed their own specialized jargon and place heavy emphasis upon close reading of "texts"; but unlike the New Criticism, they have refused to take for granted any reliable relation between words and what they might signify. Stevens's approach to language—his poetic demonstrations of the ways in which language predetermines how we view the world instead of describing already known phenomena—has turned out to be almost tailor-made for critics interested in applying fashionable theory to current poetry. Thus, in a critical study of Wallace Stevens and William Carlos Williams, *The Transparent Lyric* (1984), the critic David Walker was able to propose that the protagonist of many of the poems of Stevens and Williams is not the "speaker" of their poems but the reader: "I propose to call this kind of poem the transparent lyric: in replacing the lyric speaker with the reader as the center of dramatic attention, the poem itself becomes a transparent medium through which the reader is led to see the world in a particular way." Later, Walker writes:

The transparent lyric may be defined as a poem whose rhetoric establishes its own incompleteness; it is present not as completed discourse but as a structure that invites the reader to project himself or herself into its world, and thus to verify it as contiguous with reality. In imitating the process of thinking, of confronting the world and responding to it, the poem engages the reader in a different way from poetry grounded in an expressive theory of art, and thus requires a different kind of criticism.[17]

Such an aesthetic, proposed here by a *critic* but implicitly imputed to our poets, recapitulates in slightly more precise terms than the *Reaper* essay does the way in which the current critical climate has attempted to empower critical interpretation with some of the prerogatives of the creative artist. Walker offers the interpreter of a text a blank check and a rationale for using the text of a poem for *any* purpose whatever. A poem, in Walker's eyes, is thus apparently a sort of ur-text which a critic—the privileged party in literary discourse—can actually complete.

Walker's description of the "transparent lyric" could even more easily apply to the poetry of John Ashbery than to Stevens or to Williams. Ashbery's poetry seems tailor-made for High-Theoretical treatment. Consider, for example, the following treatment by Charles Altieri, in *Self and Sensibility in Contemporary American Poetry* (1984), of Ashbery's "No Way of Knowing": "For Ashbery the mind stands toward its own knowing in the condition of infinite regressiveness that Derrida shows is the dilemma inherent in trying to know about the language we use in describing our knowledge . . . for Ashbery the problematics of relation are not primarily of sign and signified but of act to other acts as the mind tries to identify secure resting places."[18] This passage may sound convoluted; but a glance at the Ashbery poem in question makes it apparent that discourse like Altieri's is the only means of approaching Ashbery linguistically. Most Ashbery poems cannot be explicated by traditional, New Critical techniques.

This same assumption of a shift in poetic authority from poets to critics informs the most comprehensive current study of contemporary American poetry, Altieri's *Self and Sensibility in Contemporary American Poetry*. As the end of Altieri's study puts it: "Poetry's obligations remain constant, requiring us to hold contemporary poets to the highest standards developed by our cultural heritage. Without such *critical pressure* [my italics] we may hasten a day when that heritage is in fact as irrelevant as it is often claimed to be. For we will no longer recognize ourselves as capable of sharing the desires it cultivates and the powers it provides."[19] Although the word "it" in the last sentence above is used equivocally, the equivocation appears to be deliberate: "it" can refer to "our cultural heritage," or to "critical pressure," or to both. Altieri's implication is obvious: critics, not poets, are custodians and interpreters for all of us of "our cultural heritage."

This very issue—whether critical discourse is privileged over poetic discourse—is at the heart of Hank Lazer's recent essay "The Crisis in Poetry." Lazer opens his essay with a quotation by Louis Simpson from Simpson's address "What Is a Poet," delivered at the eleventh Alabama Symposium (18 October 1984):

> For twenty years American poets have not discussed the nature of poetry. There has not been the exchange there used to be . . . perhaps because arguing over poetry seems trivial when we are living under the shadow of nuclear annihilation. Another reason is the ascendency of criticism. If poets do not speak for themselves others will speak for them, and when poets vacated the platform critics rushed to take their place. The poets have been willing to see this happen —they are workers and not given to abstract thinking. They believe that the best literary criticism and the only kind that's likely to last is a poem.[20]

Lazer then reviews a variety of recent critical books about poetry, giving special attention to "Charles Bernstein's essays [*Content's Dream: Essays 1975–1980*, 1985], for they challenge many current views about style, ideology, reading, and our relationship to language and the production of meaning," and he dismisses such practical criticism as Peter Stitt's: "Stitt proposes at the outset to write good old humanism, with sincerity and respect, and with its attendant hostility to 'theory,' its lack of interest in questions about the nature of language, or representation. . . . For Stitt to convince us of the validity of his position, he needs to offer some consideration of the relation between the poem (or words) and 'the external truth of the world,' the latter, for me, being hard to imagine as existing *apart* from language." Later, Lazer makes a statement which is especially revealing in the light of the *Reaper* essay: "Thus Altieri may be right to suggest that 'speculative criticism now attracts much of the audience and the energy the last decade devoted to poetry.' "[21]

Both Lazer and Altieri pick on contemporary poetry for its allegedly "diminished" status not because contemporary American poetry is weak—it has never been stronger—but because it is not interested in what *they* are. The most flagrant omission by both of them is any mention of why the issues which so interest them have conventionally been handled most comfortably in prose rather than verse. Should Wittgenstein's *Tractatus* have been set in verse? Or Marx's *Capital?* Or Hegel? Many American poets have read and understood these books. But they have chosen not to apply Continental philosophy or Deconstructionist theory to the art of poetic composition, for much the same reason that a good orthopedic surgeon would know better, when playing tennis, than to try (or even want) to analyze the physical mechanics involved in producing each stroke. Poets are, as Simpson so deftly put it, "workers."

A second and more disturbing omission by Lazer—a de facto omission in Altieri's *Self and Sensibility* as well—is that poems are never discussed as if they were about people's lives. Critics such as these would appear to lead lives in which they did *nothing* except read, in which the only experience which meant anything to them was "textual"—the opposite, perhaps, of "good old humanism." In this respect, their approach to poetry has much in common with that of the so-called Language poets, of whom Charles Bernstein himself may be the most provocative theorist/practitioner. As Marjorie Perloff, who has for some years now been America's most faithful and intelligent chronicler of avant-garde literature, put it in her essay "The Word as Such: L=A=N=G=U=A=G=E Poetry in the Eighties" (*American Poetry Review*, May/June 1984): "For Olsen and Creeley, 'Form is never more than an extension of content.' For the Language poet, this aphorism becomes: 'Theory is never more than the extension of practice.' "[22]

The premises of Language poetry follow from the assumption that, as Perloff put it: "poetic discourse is . . . not the expression of words of an individual speaking subject, but the creation of that subject by the particular set of discourses (cultural, social, historical) in which he or she functions." In other words, language is prior to experience: the nature of the signifier determines the nature of the signified. Such an assumption is a logical and only a modest step beyond David Walker's assignment to the *reader* of the role of protagonist in poetic discourse: if language, as Bernstein argues, "exists in a matrix of social and historical relations that are more significant to the formation of an individual than any personal qualities of the life or voice of the author," then language itself is the "protagonist" not merely of poetic discourse but of *all* discourse, for the assumptions of Language poetry abolish distinctions between genres. As Perloff put it: "Whatever the generic category, the important distinction to be made is not between 'story' and 'prose poem' or 'story' and 'essay' but, as Charles Bernstein points out, between 'different

contexts of reading and different readerships'. . . . To read such . . .
texts as [Lyn] Hejinian's *My Life* or [Lydia] Boris's *Story*, is to become
aware of what Language poets call 'the rights of the signifier.' "[23] The
Language poetry movement is thus politically radical in that one of its
aims is to expose, in the words of Bernstein, "the optical illusion of reality
in capitalist thought." Like the criticism of Lazer, it bases its authority
not on sympathy with but on almost total disaffection from mainstream
American life, from (to borrow Simpson's telling analogy) "the workers,"
whom such critics—"vanguards" of an aesthetic "proletariat"—presume
to guide, all in the best interests of our cultural heritage.

The mainstream of American poetry, however—what Altieri calls "the
dominant mode" and what Bernstein dismisses as "official verse cul-
ture"—has continued to be, whether narrative or meditative, in a Realist
mode that is essentially egalitarian, university-based, middle-class, and
written in free verse that has, by and large, vastly improved since the
sixties, evolving into a flexible medley of older prosodies so rich in echoes
that it bears out Eliot's famous dictum that "no verse is ever really free."
The strong poems which make up this mainstream also bear out Louis
Simpson's reminder that, for our poets, "the best literary criticism and
the only kind that's likely to last is a poem": Patricia Goedicke's Symbolist
poem "Mahler in the Living Room," C. K. Williams's "From My Win-
dow," Stephen Dunn's "The Routine Things Around the House," Tess
Gallagher's "Each Bird Waking," Linda Gregg's "Whole and Without
Blessing," William Matthews's "In Memory of the Utah Stars," Jorie
Graham's "Two Paintings by Gustav Klimt," Brendan Galvin's "Seals in
the Inner Harbor," Carolyn Forché's "The Colonel," Sydney Lea's "The
Feud," Philip Booth's *Before Sleep,* Sharon Olds's *The Dead and the
Living,* Robert Pinsky's "History of My Heart," Philip Schultz's "Deep
Within The Ravine," Wendell Berry's "The Barn," and so on. Ten years
after Halpern's anthology, *The Morrow Anthology of Younger American
Poets* and *New American Poets of the 80s*—volumes which might almost
be considered sequels to the Halpern anthology because many of the
poets featured in them had first appeared in Halpern's book—display
the depth and strength of the mainstream, "centrist," Realist mode.

Flanking this mainstream Realism there is, on the Right, a small
but disproportionately influential and wealthy elite sympathetic to such
modes as the New Formalism; and there is, on the Left—bred out of the
same boom in higher education that had turned American poetry into an
"industry"—a small but well-entrenched, disaffected set not of poet/

critics but of "critic/poets," completing the pluralistic milieu which the astute critic, James E. B. Breslin, in his *From Modern to Contemporary* (1983), urbanely referred to in his concluding chapter title as "Our Town."

Notes

1. Berry, "The Specialization of Poetry," *Hudson Review* 28, no. 1 (Spring 1975): 12, 16.

2. Ibid., 22–23.

3. Ibid., 27.

4. Pinsky, *The Situation of Poetry: Contemporary Poetry and Its Tradiions* (Princeton, N. J.: Princeton University Press, 1976), 162–63.

5. Ibid., 3.

6. Plumly, "Chapter and Verse," *American Poetry Review* 7 (January/February 1978): 21–32.

7. Juhasz, *Naked and Fiery Forms: Modern American Poetry by Women* (New York: Harper, 1976), 205.

8. Ostriker, "American Poetry, Now Shaped by Women," *New York Times Book Review*, 9 March 1986, 28.

9. Ibid., 30.

10. Olds, *The Dead and The Living* (New York: Knopf, 1984), 66.

11. Kizer, *Yin* (Brockport, N.Y.: BOA Editions, 1984), 20.

12. Johnson, *The Incognito Lounge* (New York: Random, 1982), 47.

13. Smith, *Roundhouse Voices: New and Selected Poems* (New York: Harper, 1985), 91.

14. Editorial, *Reaper* 1 (1981): 3.

15. "Navigating the Flood," *Reaper* 1 (1981): 52–54.

16. Ibid., 56.

17. Walker, *The Transparent Lyric* (Princeton, N.J.: Princeton University Press, 1984) xii, 18.

18. Altieri, *Self and Sensibility in Contemporary American Poetry* (New York: Cambridge University Press, 1984), 240.

19. Ibid., 212–13.

20. Lazer, "Criticism and the Crisis in American Poetry," *Missouri Review* 9, no. 6 (1985–86): 201.

21. Ibid., 202, 215.

22. Perloff, "The World as Such: L=A=N=G=U=A=G=E Poetry in the Eighties," *American Poetry Review* 13, no. 3 (May/June 1984): 18.

23. Ibid., 18.

Selected Bibliography   Notes on Contributors   Index

Selected Bibliography

Poetry

AI [Florence Ai Ogawa] (1947–). *Cruelty* (1973), *Killing Floor* (1979), *Sin* (1986).

AIKEN, CONRAD (1889–1973). *Earth Triumphant* (1914), *Senlin: A Biography* (1918), *Priapus and the Pool* (1922), *Selected Poems* (1929, rev. ed. 1935), *Preludes for Memnan* (1931), *Brownstone Eclogues* (1942), *Collected Poems* (1953, rev. ed. 1970), *Selected Poems* (1961).

ASHBERY, JOHN (1927–). *Some Trees* (1956), *The Tennis Court Oath* (1962), *Rivers and Mountains* (1966), *The Double Dream of Spring* (1970), *Three Poems* (1972), *Self-Portrait in a Convex Mirror* (1975), *Houseboat Days* (1977), *As We Know* (1979), *Shadow Train* (1981), *A Wave* (1984), *Selected Poems* (1985), *April Galleons* (1987).

AUDEN, W. H. (1907–73). *Poems* (1930), *The Orators* (1932), *On This Island* (1936), *Selected Poems* (1938), *Another Time* (1940), *The Age of Anxiety* (1947), *Nones* (1952), *The Shield of Achilles* (1955), *Homage to Clio* (1960), *Collected Shorter Poems* (1966), *Collected Longer Poems* (1966), *City Without Walls* (1969), *Collected Poems* (1976).

BARAKA, IMAMU AMIRI [Leroi Jones] (1934–). *Preface to a Twenty Volume Suicide Note* (1960), *The Dead Lecturer* (1965), *Black Art* (1966), *Black Magic: Poetry 1961–1967* (1969), *It's Nation Time* (1970), *Selected Poetry of Amiri Baraka—Leroi Jones* (1979).

BARLOW, JOEL (1754–1812). *Visions of Columbus* (1787), *The Columbiad* (1807).

BERRY, WENDELL (1934–). *November Twenty-six Nineteen Hundred Sixty-three* (1964), *Openings: Poems* (1968), *Forming: A Handbook* (1970), *The Country of Marriage* (1973), *Clearing* (1977), *The Wheel* (1981), *Collected Poems* (1985), *Home Economics* (1987).

BERRYMAN, JOHN (1914–72). *The Dispossessed* (1948), *Homage to Mistress Bradstreet* (1956), *77 Dream Songs* (1964), *His Toy, His Dream, His Rest* (1968), *Short Poems* (1968), *The Dream Songs* (1969), *Love and Fame* (1970), *Delusions, Etc.* (1972), *Recovery* (1973), *Henry's Fate and Other Poems* (1977).

BIDART, FRANK (1939–). *Golden State* (1973), *The Book of the Body* (1977), *The Sacrifice* (1983).

BISHOP, ELIZABETH (1911–79). *North and South* (1946), *North and South—A Cold Spring* (1955), *Questions of Travel* (1965), *The Complete Poems* (1969), *Geography III* (1976), *The Complete Poems, 1927–1979* (1983).

BLACKBURN, PAUL (1926–71). *The Cities* (1967), *Early Selected y Mas: Collected Poems, 1949–1961* (1972), *Collected Poems* (1983).

277

BLACKMUR, R. P. (1904–65). *Jordan's Delight* (1937), *The Second World* (1942), *The Good European* (1947), *Poems of R. P. Blackmur* (1977).

BLY, ROBERT (1926–). *Silence in the Snowy Fields* (1962), *The Light Around the Body* (1967), *Sleepers Joining Hands* (1973), *The Morning Glory* (1975), *This Body Is Made of Camphor and Gopherwood* (1977), *This Tree Will Be Here for a Thousand Years* (1979), *The Man in the Black Coat Turns* (1981), *Loving a Woman of Two Worlds* (1985), *Selected Poems* (1986).

BOGAN, LOUISE (1897–1970). *Body of This Death* (1923), *Dark Summer* (1929), *The Sleeping Fury* (1937), *Poems and New Poems* (1941), *Collected Poems: 1923–1953* (1954), *The Blue Estuaries: Poems 1923–1975*.

BRADSTREET, ANNE (ca. 1612–72). *The Tenth Muse* (1650).

BROOKS, GWENDOLYN (1917–). *A Street in Bronzeville* (1945), *Annie Allen* (1949), *Bronzeville Boys and Girls* (1956), *Selected Poems* (1963), *In the Mecca* (1968), *Riot* (1969), *Family Pictures* (1970), *To Disembark* (1981).

BROWN, STERLING (1901–). *Southern Road* (1932), *The Collected Poems of Sterling Brown* (1980).

BRYANT, WILLIAM CULLEN (1794–1878). *The Embargo* (1809); *Poems* (1840).

CARRUTH, HAYDEN (1921–). *The Crow and the Heart* (1959), *Journey to a Known Place* (1961), *For You* (1970), *From Snow, from Rock, from Chaos* (1973), *Dark World* (1974), *The Bloomingdale Papers* (1974), *Brothers, I Loved You All* (1978), *The Sleeping Beauty* (1982), *If You Call This Cry a Song* (1983), *Asphalt Georgics* (1985), *Selected Poetry* (1985).

CLIFTON, LUCILLE (1936–). *Good Times* (1969), *Good News about the Earth* (1972), *All Us Come Cross the Water* (1973), *The Times They Used To Be* (1974), *An Ordinary Woman* (1974), *The Boy Who Didn't Believe in Spring* (1978), *Two-Headed Woman* (1980), *Lucky Stone* (1986).

CORSO, GREGORY (1930–). *The Vestal Lady on Brattle* (1955), *Gasoline* (1958), *The Happy Birthday of Death* (1960), *Long Live Man* (1962), *Elegiac Feeling American* (1970), *Earth Egg* (1974), *Herald of the Autochthonic Spirit* (1981).

COWLEY, MALCOLM (1898–1989). *Blue Juanita* (1929), *The Dry Season* (1941), *Blue Juanita: Collected Poems* (1968).

CRANE, HART (1899–1933). *White Buildings* (1926), *The Bridge* (1930), *Collected Poems* (1933), *Complete Poems and Selected Letters and Prose* (1966).

CREELEY, ROBERT (1926–). *For Love: Poems 1950–1960* (1962), *A Day Book* (1972), *Selected Poems* (1976), *Hello* (1978), *Later* (1979), *The Collected Poems of Robert Creeley, 1945–1975* (1982), *Mirrors* (1983), *Memory Gardens* (1986).

CULLEN, COUNTEE (1903–46). *Color* (1925), *Copper Sun* (1927), *The Black Christ* (1929), *The Medea* (1935), *On These I Stand* (1947).

CUMMINGS, E. E. (1894–1962). *Tulips and Chimneys* (1923), *&* (1925), *is 5* (1926), *Vi Va* (1931), *no thanks* (1935), *Collected Poems* (1938), *50 Poems* (1940), *XAIPE: 71 Poems* (1940), *100 Selected Poems* (1959), *Complete Poems* (1972).

DICKEY, JAMES (1923–). *Into the Stone and Other Poems* (1960), *Drowning with Others* (1962), *Helmets* (1964), *Buckdancer's Choice* (1965), *Poems 1957– 1967* (1967), *The Eyebeaters, Blood, Victory, Madness, Buckhead and*

Mercy (1970), *The Zodiac* (1976), *The Strength of Fields* (1979), *Puella* (1982).

DICKINSON, EMILY (1830–86). *Poems* (1890); *Complete Poems* (1960).

DOOLITTLE, HILDA [H. D.] (1886–1961). *Sea Garden* (1916), *Hymen* (1921), *Heliodora and Other Poems* (1924), *Collected Poems* (1924), *Red Roses for Bronze* (1931), *The Walls Do Not Fall* (1944), *Tribute to the Angels* (1945), *The Flowering of the Rod* (1946), *Selected Poems* (1957), *Hermetic Definitions* (1972), *Collected Poems: 1912–1944* (1982).

DOVE, RITA (1952–). *The Yellow House on the Corner* (1980); *Museum* (1983); *Thomas and Beulah* (1986).

DUGAN, ALAN (1923–). *Poems* (1961), *Poems 2* (1963), *Poems 3* (1967), *Collected Poems* (1969), *Poems 4* (1974), *New and Collected Poems: 1961–1983* (1983).

DUNCAN, ROBERT (1919–). *Caesar's Gate* (1955), *The Opening in the Field* (1960), *Roots and Branches* (1964), *Bending the Bow* (1968), *Groundwork: Before the War* (1984).

EBERHART, RICHARD (1904–). *A Bravery of Earth* (1930), *Reading the Spirit* (1936), *Song and Idea* (1940), *Poems: New and Selected* (1944), *Undercliff: Poems 1946–1953* (1953), *Great Praises* (1957), *Collected Poems: 1930–1960* (1960), *The Quarry* (1964), *Selected Poems: 1930–1965* (1965), *Shifts of Being* (1968), *Fields of Grace* (1972), *Collected Poems: 1930–1976* (1976), *Ways of Light: Poems 1972–1980* (1980), *The Long Reach: New and Uncollected Poems, 1948–1983* (1984).

ELIOT, T. S. (1888–1965). *Prufrock and Other Observations* (1917), *Poems* (1919), *Ara Vos Prec* (1920), *The Wasteland* (1922), *Ash Wednesday* (1930), *Collected Poems: 1909–1935* (1936), *Four Quartets* (1943), *The Complete Poems and Plays* (1952), *Collected Poems: 1909–1962* (1963).

FEARING, KENNETH (1902–61). *Collected Poems* (1940); *Stranger at Coney Island and Other Poems* (1948); *New and Selected Poems* (1956).

FERLINGHETTI, LAWRENCE (1919–). *A Coney Island of the Mind* (1958), *Starting from San Francisco* (1961), *The Secret Meaning of Things* (1969), *Open Eye, Open Heart* (1973), *Who Are We Now?* (1976), *Landscapes of Living and Dying* (1979), *Endless Life: Selected Poems* (1981), *Over All the Obscene Boundaries* (1984).

FROST, ROBERT (1874–1963). *A Boy's Will* (1913), *North of Boston* (1919), *Mountain Interval* (1916), *New Hampshire* (1923), *West-Running Brook* (1928), *A Further Range* (1936), *Collected Poems* (1939), *A Witness Tree* (1942), *A Masque of Reason* (1945), *A Masque of Mercy* (1947), *Steeple Bush* (1947), *In the Clearing* (1962), *The Poetry of Robert Frost* (1969).

GINSBERG, ALLEN (1926–). *Howl and Other Poems* (1956), *Kaddish and Other Poems* (1961), *Reality Sandwiches* (1963), *Planet News: 1961–1967* (1968), *The Fall of America: Poems of These States* (1973), *Mind Breaths: Poems 1972–1977* (1978), *Plutonium Ode: Poems 1977–1980* (1982), *Collected Poems: 1947–1980* (1984).

GIOVANNI, NIKKI (1943–). *Black Feeling, Black Talk* (1968), *Spin a Soft Black Song* (1970), *My House* (1972), *The Women and the Men* (1975).

HACKER, MARILYN (1942–). *Presentation Piece* (1973), *Separations* (1976), *Tak-*

ing Notice (1980), *Assumptions* (1985), *Love and Death and The Changing of the Seasons* (1986).

HALL, DONALD (1928–). *Exiles and Marriages* (1955), *The Dark Houses* (1958), *A Roof of Tiger Lilies* (1964), *The Alligator Bride: Poems New and Selected* (1969), *The Yellow Room: Love Poems* (1971), *The Town of Hill* (1975), *Kicking the Leaves* (1978), *The Happy Man* (1986), *The One Day* (1988).

HARPER, MICHAEL (1938–). *Dear John, Dear Coltrane* (1970), *History Is Your Own Heartbeat* (1971), *Song: I Want a Witness* (1972), *Debridement* (1973), *Nightmare Begins Responsibility* (1975), *Images of Kin: New and Selected Poems* (1977), *Healing Song for the Inner Ear* (1984).

HASS, ROBERT (1940–). *Field Guide* (1973), *Praise* (1979), *Human Wishes* (1989).

HAYDEN, ROBERT (1913–80). *Heart-Shape in the Dust* (1940), *Figures of Time* (1955), *Selected Poems* (1966), *Words in the Mourning Time* (1970), *The Night-Blooming Cereus* (1972), *Angle of Ascent: New and Selected Poems* (1975), *American Journal* (1980).

HECHT, ANTHONY (1923–). *A Summoning of Stones* (1954), *The Hard Hours* (1967), *Millions of Strange Shadows* (1977), *The Venetian Vespers* (1979).

HOWARD, RICHARD (1929–). *Quantities* (1962), *The Damages* (1967), *Untitled Subjects* (1969), *Findings* (1971), *Two-Part Inventions* (1974), *Fellow Feelings* (1976), *Misgivings* (1979), *Where on Earth Is God* (1983), *Lining Up* (1984), *No Traveller* (1989).

HUGHES, LANGSTON (1902–67). *The Weary Blues* (1926), *Fine Clothes to the Jew* (1927), *Dear Lovely Death* (1931), *The Dream Keeper and Other Poems* (1932), *A New Song* (1938), *Shakespeare in Harlem* (1942), *Jim Crow's Last Stand* (1943), *Lament for Dark Peoples* (1944), *Fields of Wonder* (1947), *One Way Ticket* (1949), *Montage of a Dream Deferred* (1951), *Selected Poems* (1959), *The Panther and the Lash* (1967).

HUGO, RICHARD (1923–82). *A Run of Jacks* (1961), *Death of the Kapowsin Tavern* (1965), *Good Luck in Cracked Italian* (1969), *The Lady in Kicking Horse Reservoir* (1973), *What Thou Lovest Well, Remains American* (1975), *31 Letters and 13 Dreams* (1977), *Selected Poems* (1979), *White Center* (1980), *The Right Madness on Skye* (1980), *Making Certain It Goes On: Collected Poems* (1983).

IGNATOW, DAVID (1914–). *Poems* (1948), *The Gentle Weight Lifter* (1955), *Say Pardon* (1962), *Figures of the Human* (1964), *Rescue the Dead* (1968), *Poems: 1934–1969* (1970), *Facing the Tree: New Poems* (1975), *Selected Poems* (1975), *Tread the Dark* (1978), *Whisper to the Earth* (1981), *Leaving the Door Open* (1984), *New and Collected Poems: 1970–1985* (1986).

JARRELL, RANDALL (1914–65). *Blood for a Stranger* (1942), *Little Friend, Little Friend* (1945), *Losses* (1948), *The Seven-League Crutches* (1951), *Selected Poems* (1955), *The Woman at the Washington Zoo* (1960), *Selected Poems* (1964), *The Lost World: New Poems* (1965), *The Complete Poems* (1969).

JEFFERS, ROBINSON (1887–1962). *Tamar and Other Poems* (1924), *Roan Stallion* (1925), *The Woman at Point Sur* (1928), *Cawder and Other Poems* (1928), *Dear Judas and Other Poems* (1929), *Solstice and Other Poems* (1935), *Selected Poetry* (1938), *Be Angry at the Sun* (1941), *The Double Axe and Other Poems* (1948), *The Beginning of the End* (1963), *Selected Poems* (1965).

JOHNSON, JAMES WELDON (1871–1938). *Fifty Years and Other Poems* (1917), *God's Trombones* (1927).

JORDAN, JUNE (1936–). *Some Changes* (1971), *Things That I Do in the Dark: Selected Poetry* (1977, rev. ed. 1981), *Passion: New Poems 1977–1980* (1980).

JUSTICE, DONALD (1925–). *The Summer Anniversaries* (1960), *Night Light* (1967), *Departures* (1973), *Selected Poems* (1979), *The Sunset Maker* (1987).

KAUFMAN, BOB (1925–85). *Solitudes Crowded with Loneliness* (1965), *The Ancient Rain* (1981).

KEES, WELDON (1914–55). *Collected Poems* (1962).

KINNELL, GALWAY (1927–). *What a Kingdom It Was* (1960), *Flower Herding on Mount Monadnock* (1964), *Body Rags* (1968), *The Book of Nightmares* (1971), *The Avenue Bearing the Initial of Christ into the New World: Poems 1946–1964* (1974), *Mortal Acts, Mortal Words* (1980), *Selected Poems* (1982), *The Past* (1985).

KIZER, CAROLYN (1925–). *The Ungrateful Garden* (1961), *Knock upon Silence* (1965). *Midnight Was My Cry: New and Selected Poems* (1971), *Mermaids in the Basement: Poems for Women* (1984), *Yin* (1984), *The Nearness of You* (1986).

KNIGHT, ETHERIDGE (1931–). *Poems from Prison* (1968), *Belly Song and Other Poems* (1973), *Born of a Woman: New and Selected Poems* (1980), *The Essential Etheridge Knight* (1986).

KUMIN, MAXINE (1925–). *Halfway* (1961), *The Privilege* (1965), *The Nightmare Factory* (1969), *Up Country* (1972), *House, Bridge, Fountain, Gate* (1975), *The Retrieval System* (1978), *Our Ground Time Here Will Be Brief: New and Selected Poems* (1982), *The Long Approach* (1985).

KUNITZ, STANLEY (1905–). *Intellectual Things* (1930), *Passport to the War* (1944), *Selected Poems: 1928–1958* (1958), *The Testing Tree* (1971), *The Poems of Stanley Kunitz: 1928–1978* (1979), *Next-to-Last Things* (1985).

LANIER, SIDNEY (1842–81). *Poems of Sidney Lanier* (1920).

LEVERTOV, DENISE (1923–). *With Eyes at the Back of Our Heads* (1959), *Ladder* (1961), *O Taste and See* (1964), *The Sorrow Dance* (1967), *Relearning the Alphabet* (1970), *To Stay Alive* (1971), *Footprints* (1972), *The Freeing of the Dust* (1975), *Life in the Forest* (1978), *Collected Earlier Poems: 1940–1960* (1980), *Candles in Babylon* (1982), *Poems: 1940–1967* (1983), *Oblique Prayers* (1984), *Breathing the Water* (1987), *Poems: 1968–1972* (1987).

LEVINE, PHILIP (1928–). *On the Edge* (1963), *Not This Pig* (1968), *Red Dust* (1971), *They Feed They Lion* (1972), *1933* (1974), *The Names of the Lost* (1976), *Ashes: Poems Old and New* (1979), *7 Years from Somewhere* (1979), *One for the Rose* (1981), *Selected Poems* (1984), *Sweet Will* (1985), *A Walk with Tom Jefferson* (1988).

LOGAN, JOHN (1923–89). *Cycle for Mother Cabrini* (1955), *Ghosts of the Heart* (1960), *Spring of the Thief* (1963), *The Zig-Zag Walk* (1969), *The Anonymous Lover* (1973), *The Bridge of Change* (1980), *Only the Dreamer Can Change the Dream: Selected Poems* (1981), *Collected Poems* (1989).

LORDE, AUDRE (1934–). *Cables to Rage* (1970), *From a Land Where Other People Live* (1973), *New York Head Shop and Museum* (1975), *Coal* (1976), *The Black Unicorn* (1978), *Chosen Poems: Old and New* (1982).

LOWELL, AMY (1874–1925). *A Dome of Many-Coloured Glass* (1912), *Sword Blades and Poppy Seed* (1914); *Can Grande's Castle* (1918), *What's O'clock* (1925), *East Wind* (1926), *Complete Poetical Works of Amy Lowell* (1955).

LOWELL, ROBERT (1917–77). *Lord Weary's Castle* (1946), *The Mills of the Kavanaughs* (1951), *Life Studies* (1959), *For the Union Dead* (1964), *Near the Ocean* (1967), *Notebook* (1969, rev. ed. 1970), *For Lizzie and Harriet* (1973), *The Dolphin* (1973), *History* (1973), *Selected Poems* (1976), *Day by Day* (1977).

McKAY, CLAUDE (1890–1945). *Songs of Jamaica* (1912), *Constab Ballads* (1912), *Spring in New Hampshire* (1920), *Harlem Shadows* (1922), *Selected Poems* (1953).

MACLEISH, ARCHIBALD (1892–1982). *Street of the Moon* (1926), *New Found Land* (1930), *Conquistador* (1932), *Poems: 1924–1932* (1933), *America Was Promises* (1939), *Collected Poems* (1953, rev. ed. 1963), *The Human Season: Selected Poems, 1926–1972* (1972).

MASTERS, EDGAR LEE (1868–1950). *Spoon River Anthology* (1915), *The New Spoon River* (1929).

MEREDITH, WILLIAM (1919–). *Love Letter from an Impossible Land* (1944), *Ships and Other Figures* (1948), *The Open Sea and Other Poems* (1958), *The Wreck of the Thresher and Other Poems* (1964), *Earth Walk: New and Selected Poems* (1970), *Hazard, The Painter* (1973), *The Cheer* (1980), *Partial Accounts: Selected and New Poems* (1987).

MERRILL, JAMES (1926–). *First Poems* (1951), *The Country of a Thousand Years of Peace* (1959), *Water Street* (1962), *Nights and Days* (1966), *The Fire Screen* (1969), *Braving the Elements* (1972), *Divine Comedies* (1976), *From the First Nine: Poems 1946–1976* (1982), *The Changing Light at Sandover* (1982), *Late Settings* (1985).

MERWIN, W. S. (1927–). *A Mask for Janus* (1952), *The Dancing Bears* (1954), *Green with Beasts* (1956), *The Drunk in the Furnace* (1960), *The Moving Target* (1963), *The Lice* (1967), *The Carrier of Ladders* (1970), *Writings to an Unfinished Accompaniment* (1973), *The Compass Flower* (1977), *Opening the Hand* (1983), *Selected Poems* (1988), *The Rain in the Trees* (1988).

MILLAY, EDNA ST. VINCENT (1892–1950). *Renascence and Other Poems* (1917), *The Harp Weaver and Other Poems* (1923), *The Buck in the Snow* (1928), *Conversation at Midnight* (1937), *Collected Sonnets* (1941), *Collected Lyrics* (1943), *Mine the Harvest* (1954), *Collected Poems* (1956).

MOORE, MARIANNE (1887–1972). *Poems* (1921), *Observations* (1924), *Selected Poems* (1935), *The Pangolin* (1936), *What Are Years?* (1941), *Nevertheless* (1944), *Collected Poems* (1951), *Complete Poems* (1967, rev. ed. 1980).

O'HARA, FRANK (1926–66). *Meditations in an Emergency* (1957), *Second Avenue* (1960), *Odes* (1960), *Lunch Poems* (1964), *The Collected Poems of Frank O'Hara* (1971), *The Selected Poems of Frank O'Hara* (1974), *Poems Retrieved* (1977).

OLSON, CHARLES (1910–70). *The Maximus Poems* (1960), *The Distances* (1960), *The Maximus Poems IV, V, and VI* (1968), *Archaeologist of Morning: The Collected Poems Outside the Maximus Series* (1971), *The Maximus Poems: Volume Three* (1975), *The Maximus Poems* (1983), *The Collected Poems* (1986).

OPPEN, GEORGE (1908–84). *Discrete Series* (1939), *The Materials* (1962), *This Is Which* (1965), *Of Being Numerous* (1968), *Seascape: Needle's Eye* (1973), *Collected Poems* (1976), *Primitive* (1978).

OSTRIKER, ALICIA (1940–). *The Mother/Child Papers* (1980), *A Woman under the Surface* (1982).

PATCHEN, KENNETH (1911–72). *Before the Brave* (1936), *First Will and Testament* (1939), *The Dark Kingdom* (1942), *Cloth of the Tempest* (1943), *Pictures of Life and Death* (1947), *Selected Poems* (1958), *Love Poems* (1964), *Collected Poems* (1968), *In Quest of Candlelighters* (1972).

PLATH, SYLVIA (1932–63). *The Colossus* (1962), *Ariel* (1966), *Crossing the Water* (1971), *Winter Trees* (1972), *Collected Poems* (1981).

POUND, EZRA (1885–1972). *Ripostes* (1912), *Lustra* (1916), *Hugh Selwyn Mauberley* (1920), *Personae: Collected Poems* (1926, rev. ed. 1949), *Draft of XVI Cantos* (1925), *The Pisan Cantos* (1948), *The Cantos* (1948, expanded eds. 1965, 1971).

RAKOSI, CARL (1903–). *Selected Poems* (1941), *Amulet* (1967), *Ere-Voice* (1971), *Ex-Cranium, Night* (1975).

RANSOM, JOHN CROWE (1888–1974). *Chills and Fever* (1924), *Grace after Meat* (1924), *Two Gentlemen in Bonds* (1927), *Selected Poems* (1995, rev. eds. 1963, 1969).

RANDALL, DUDLEY (1914–). *Cities Burning* (1968), *Love You* (1970).

REED, ISHMAEL (1938–). *catechism of d neoamerican hoodoo church* (1970), *Conjure: Selected Poems, 1963–1970* (1972), *Chattanooga* (1973).

REXROTH, KENNETH (1905–84). *In What Hour* (1940), *The Phoenix and the Tortoise* (1944), *The Signature of All Things* (1949), *The Dragon and the Unicorn* (1952), *The Homestead Called Damascus* (1963), *Collected Shorter Poems* (1966), *Collected Longer Poems* (1968), *New Poems* (1974), *Selected Poems* (1985).

REZNIKOFF, CHARLES (1894–1976). *Rhythms* (1918), *Poems* (1919), *Five Groups of Verse* (1927), *Going To and Fro and Walking Up and Down* (1941), *By the Waters of Manhattan: Selected Verse* (1962), *By the Well of Living and Seeing: New and Selected Poems* (1974), *Holocaust* (1975), *Poems 1918–1936* (1976), *Poems 1937–1975* (1977), *Testimony* (1978).

RICH, ADRIENNE (1929–). *A Change of World* (1951), *The Diamond Cutters* (1955), *Snapshots of a Daughter-in-Law* (1963), *Necessities of Life* (1966), *Leaflets* (1969), *The Will to Change* (1971), *Diving into the Wreck* (1973), *Poems: Selected and New, 1950–1974* (1975), *The Dream of a Common Language* (1978), *A Wild Patience Has Taken Me This Far* (1981), *The Fact of a Doorframe: Poems Selected and New, 1950–1984* (1985).

ROBINSON, EDWIN ARLINGTON (1869–1935). *The Children of the Night* (1897), *Captain Craig* (1902), *The Town by the River* (1910), *Man Against the Sky* (1916), *Collected Poems* (1937).

ROETHKE, THEODORE (1908–63). *Open House* (1941), *The Lost Son and Other Poems* (1948), *Praise to the End!* (1951), *The Waking: Poems 1933–1953* (1953), *Words for the Wind: The Collected Verse of Theodore Roethke* (1958), *The Far Field* (1964), *Collected Poems* (1966).

RUKEYSER, MURIEL (1913–80). *Theory of Flight* (1935), *U.S.I.* (1938), *Beast in View* (1944), *The Green Wave* (1948), *Selected Poems* (1951), *Body of Waking* (1958), *Waterlily Fire: Poems 1932–1962* (1962), *The Speed of*

Darkness (1968), *Breaking Open* (1973), *The Gates* (1976), *Outer Banks* (1980), *Collected Poems* (1982).

SANCHEZ, SONIA (1935–). *Homecoming* (1969); *We a BaddDD People* (1970); *Homegirls & Handgrenades* (1984).

SANDBURG, CARL (1878–1967). *Chicago Poems* (1916), *Cornhuskers* (1918), *Smoke and Steel* (1920), *The People, Yes* (1936), *Complete Poems* (1950, rev. ed. 1970).

SCHWARTZ, DELMORE (1913–66). *In Dreams Begin Responsibilities* (1938), *Genesis I* (1943), *Vaudeville for a Princess* (1950), *Selected Poems: Summer Knowledge* (1959), *The Last and Lost Poems of Delmore Schwartz* (1979).

SEXTON, ANNE (1928–74). *To Bedlam and Part Way Back* (1960), *All My Pretty Ones* (1962), *Live or Die* (1966), *Love Poems* (1967), *Transformations* (1971), *The Book of Folly* (1972), *The Death Notebooks* (1974), *Anne Sexton: The Complete Poems* (1981).

SHAPIRO, KARL (1913–). *Person, Place, and Thing* (1942), *V-Letter and Other Poems* (1944), *Essay on Rime* (1947), *The Trial of a Poet* (1947), *Poems: 1940–1953* (1953), *Poems of a Jew* (1958), *The Bourgeois Poet* (1964), *Selected Poems* (1968), *The White-haired Lover* (1968), *Adult Bookstore* (1976), *Collected Poems: 1940–1977* (1978), *Love and War, Art and God* (1984), *Selected Poems* (1988).

SIMIC, CHARLES (1938–). *What the Grass Says* (1967), *Somewhere among us a Stone Is Taking Notes* (1968), *Dismantling the Silence* (1971), *Return to a Place Lit by a Glass of Milk* (1974), *Charon's Cosmology* (1977), *Classic Ballroom Dances* (1980), *Austerities* (1982), *Selected Poems* (1985), *Unending Blues* (1986).

SIMPSON, LOUIS (1923–). *The Arrivistes* (1949), *Good News of Death and Other Poems* (1955), *A Dream of Governors* (1959), *At the End of the Open Road* (1963), *Selected Poems* (1965), *Adventures of the Letter I* (1971), *Searching for the Ox* (1976), *Caviare at the Funeral* (1980), *The Best Hour of the Night* (1983), *People Live Here: Selected Poems 1949–1983* (1983), *Collected Poems* (1988).

SNODGRASS, W. D. (1926–). *Heart's Needle* (1959), *After Experience* (1968), *The Führer Bunker: A Cycle of Poems* (1977), *Selected Poems* (1987).

SNYDER, GARY (1930–). *Myths and Texts* (1960), *The Back Country* (1968), *Regarding Wave* (1970), *Turtle Island* (1975), *Axe Handles* (1983).

STAFFORD, WILLIAM (1914–). *West of Your City* (1961), *Traveling Through the Dark* (1962), *The Rescued Year* (1966), *Allegiances* (1970), *Someday, Maybe* (1973), *Stories That Could Be True: New and Collected Poems* (1977), *A Glass Face in the Rain* (1982), *An Oregon Message* (1987), *Places Where There Aren't Any People* (1988).

STEIN, GERTRUDE (1874–1946). *Poems and Other Creative Writings: Tender Buttons* (1914), *The Unpublished Works of Gertrude Stein* (8 vols., 1951–58).

STEVENS, WALLACE (1879–1955). *Harmonium* (1923, rev. ed. 1931), *Ideas of Order* (1936), *Owl's Clover* (1936), *The Man with the Blue Guitar* (1937), *Parts of a World* (1942), *Transport to Summer* (1947), *The Auroras of Autumn* (1950), *Selected Poems* (1953), *Collected Poems* (1954), *Opus Posthumous* (1957), *The Palm at the End of the Mind* (1971).

STRAND, MARK (1934–). *Sleeping with One Eye Open* (1964), *Reasons for Moving* (1968), *Darker* (1970), *The Story of Our Lives* (1973), *The Late Hour* (1978), *The Monument* (1978), *Selected Poems* (1980), *The Night Book* (1985).

SWENSON, MAY (1919–). *Another Animal* (1954), *A Cage of Spines* (1958), *To Mix with Time: New and Selected Poems* (1963), *Half Sun, Half Sleep: New Poems* (1967), *Iconographs* (1970), *New and Selected Things Taking Place* (1978).

TATE, ALLEN (1899–1979). *Mr. Pope and Other Poems* (1928), *Poems: 1928–1931* (1932), *The Mediterranean and Other Poems* (1936), *The Winter Sea* (1944), *Poems, 1922–1947* (1948), *The Swimmers and Other Selected Poems* (1970), *Collected Poems* (1977).

TOLSON, MELVIN (1898–1966). *Libretto for the Republic of Liberia* (1953), *Harlem Gallery* (1965).

TOOMER, JEAN (1894–1967). *Cane* (1923).

WALKER, ALICE (1944–). *Revolutionary Petunias and Other Poems* (1973), *Goodnight, Willie Lee, I'll See You in the Morning* (1984), *Horses Make a Landscape Look More Beautiful* (1984).

WARREN, ROBERT PENN (1905–89). *Thirty-Six Poems* (1936), *Eleven Poems on the Same Theme* (1942), *Selected Poems* (1944), *Promises* (1957), *You, Emperors and Others* (1960), *Selected Poems: New and Old* (1966), *Incarnations* (1968), *Audubon: A Vision* (1969), *Or Else* (1974), *Selected Poems: 1923–1975* (1976), *Now and Then* (1978), *Being Here* (1980), *Rumor Verified* (1981), *Selected Poems: 1923–1985* (1985).

WILBUR, RICHARD (1921–). *The Beautiful Changes and Other Poems* (1947), *Ceremony and Other Poems* (1950), *Things of This World: Poems* (1956), *Advice to a Prophet and Other Poems* (1961), *The Poems of Richard Wilbur* (1965), *Walking to Sleep: New Poems and Translations* (1969), *The Mind Reader: New Poems* (1976), *Collected Poems* (1988).

WILLIAMS, C. K. (1936–). *Lies* (1969), *I Am the Bitter Name* (1972), *With Ignorance* (1977), *Tar* (1983), *Flesh and Blood* (1987).

WILLIAMS, WILLIAM CARLOS (1883–1963). *Al Que Quiere!* (1917), *Spring and All* (1923), *The Complete Collected Poems: 1906–1938* (1938), *Paterson, Book I* (1946), *Paterson, Book II* (1948), *Paterson, Book III* (1949), *Selected Poems* (1949, rev. ed. 1963), *The Collected Later Poems* (1950, rev. ed. 1963), *The Collected Earlier Poems* (1951), *Paterson, Book IV* (1951), *The Desert Music* (1954), *Journey to Love* (1955), *Paterson, Book V* (1958), *Pictures from Breughel* (1962), *Paterson* (1963), *Selected Poems* (1985), *Complete Poems* (2 vols. 1986–88).

WINTERS, YVOR (1900–68). *The Proof* (1930), *Before Disaster* (1934), *Poems* (1940), *The Giant Weapon* (1943), *Collected Poems* (1952, rev. ed. 1960), *The Brink of Darkness* (1965), *Early Poems* (1966), *The Poems of Yvor Winters* (1980).

WRIGHT, JAMES (1927–80). *The Green Wall* (1957), *St. Judas* (1959), *The Branch Will Not Break* (1963), *Shall We Gather at the River* (1968), *Collected Poems* (1971), *Two Citizens* (1973), *To a Blossoming Pear Tree* (1977), *This Journey* (1982).

WRIGHT, JAY (1935–). *The Home-Coming Singer* (1971); *Soothsayers and Omens*

(1976); *Dimensions of History* (1976); *The Double Invention of Komo* (1980), *Selected Poems of Jay Wright* (1987).

YOUNG, AL (1939–). *Dancing* (1969); *The Song Turning Back into Itself* (1971), *The Blues Don't Change: New and Selected Poems* (1982), *Sitting Pretty* (1986).

ZUKOFSKY, LOUIS (1904–78). *Some Time* (1956), *A, 1–12* (1959), *All: The Collected Short Poems 1923–1958* (1965), *All: The Collected Short Poems 1956–1964* (1966), *A, 13–21* (1969), *A: Complete Version* (1978).

Criticism and Poetics

ALLEN, DONALD M., and WARREN TALLMAN. *The Poetics of the New American Poetry* (1973).

ALLEN, PAULA GUNN, ed. *The Sacred Hoop: Recovering the Feminine in American Indian Traditions* (1986).

ALTIERI, CHARLES. *Enlarging the Temple: New Directions in American Poetry in the 1960's* (1979), *Self and Sensibility in Contemporary Poetry* (1984).

AUDEN, W. H. *The Dyer's Hand* (1962).

BLACKMUR, R. P. *The Double Agent* (1935), *Language as Gesture* (1952).

BLOOM, HAROLD. *The Anxiety of Influence: A Theory of Poetry* (1975).

BLY, ROBERT. *Leaping Poetry: An Idea with Poems and Translations* (1975).

BOGAN, LOUISE. *Achievement in American Poetry* (1951).

BROOKS, CLEANTH. *The Well-Wrought Urn* (1947).

DAVIE, DONALD. *Ezra Pound: The Poet as Sculptor* (1964).

DuPLESSIS, RACHEL BLAU, ed. *Writing Beyond the Ending: Narrative Strategies of Twentieth-Century Women Writers* (1985).

ELIOT, T. S. *The Sacred Wood* (1920), *Selected Prose* (1953).

FROST, ROBERT. *Selected Prose* (1964).

FRYE, NORTHROP. *Anatomy of Criticism* (1973).

GILBERT, SANDRA, and SUSAN GUBAR, eds. *Shakespeare's Sisters, Feminist Essays on Women Poets* (1979), *The Madwoman in the Attic: The Woman Writer and the Nineteenth Century Literary Imagination* (1979).

HARTMAN, CHARLES O. *Free Verse: An Essay on Prosody* (1980).

HASS, ROBERT. *Twentieth Century Pleasures* (1984).

HELLER, MICHAEL. *Conviction's Net of Branches: Essays on the Objectivist Poets and Poetry* (1985).

HENDERSON, STEPHEN. *Understanding the New Black Poetry* (1972).

HOLDEN, JONATHAN. *The Rhetoric of the Contemporary Lyric* (1980), *Style and Authenticity in Postmodern Poetry* (1986).

HOWARD, RICHARD. *Alone with America: Essays on the Art of Poetry in the United States Since 1950* (1969, rev. ed. 1980).

JARRELL, RANDALL. *Poetry and the Age* (1953), *A Sad Heart at the Supermarket* (1962), *The Third Book of Criticism* (1969).

JUHASZ, SUZANNE, ed. *Naked and Fiery Forms: Modern Poetry by Women* (1976).

KENNER, HUGH. *The Pound Era* (1972), *A Homemade World: American Modernist Writers* (1975).

LEVERTOV, DENISE. *The Poet in the World* (1973), *Light Up the Cave* (1981).
OLSON, CHARLES. *Selected Writings of Charles Olson* (1962).
OSTRIKER, ALICIA. *Stealing the Language: The Emergence of Women's Poetry in America* (1986).
PERLOFF, MARJORIE. *The Poetics of Indeterminacy: Rimbaud to Cage* (1981).
PINKSY, ROBERT. *The Situation of Poetry* (1976).
POUND, EZRA. *ABC of Reading* (1934), *Guide to Kulchur* (1938).
REXROTH, KENNETH. *Assay* (1962), *American Poetry in the Twentieth Century* (1971).
RICH, ADRIENNE. *On Lies, Secrets, and Silence: Selected Prose 1966–1978* (1979).
RICHARDS, I. A. *Principles of Literary Criticism* (1948).
SHOWALTER, ELAINE, ed. *The New Feminist Criticism* (1985).
STEVENS, WALLACE. *The Necessary Angel* (1951).
WALKER, DAVID. *The Transparent Lyric* (1984).
WILLIAMS, WILLIAM CARLOS. *In the American Grain* (1925), *Selected Essays* (1954).

Critical Histories

AARON, DANIEL. *Writers on the Left* (1977).
BAYM, MAX. *A History of Literary Aesthetics in America* (1973).
BRESLIN, JAMES E. B. *From Modern to Contemporary: American Poetry, 1945–1965* (1984).
CIARDI, JOHN. *Mid-Century American Poetry* (1950).
PEARCE, ROY HARVEY. *The Continuity of American Poetry* (1961, rev. ed. 1965).
SPILLER, ROBERT E., ed. *Literary History of the United States* (1969).
WAGGONER, HYATT. *American Poets from the Puritans to the Present* (1968).

Anthologies

ALLEN, DONALD. *The New American Poetry* (1960).
BERG, STEPHEN, and ROBERT MEZEY. *Naked Poetry: Recent American Poetry in Open Forms* (1969).
CARROLL, PAUL. *The Poem in Its Skin* (1968).
CHAPMAN, ABRAHAM. *Black Voices: An Anthology of Afro-American Literature* (1968), *New Black Voices: An Anthology of Contemporary Afro-American Literature* (1972).
ELLMAN, RICHARD, and ROBERT O'CLAIR. *The Norton Anthology of Modern Poetry* (1973).
GILBERT, SANDRA, and SUSAN GUBAR. *The Norton Anthology of Literature by Women* (1985).
GRAHN, JUDY. *Another Mother Tongue: Gay Words, Gay Worlds* (1986).
HALL, DONALD. *Contemporary American Poetry* (1962).
HALL, DONALD, ROBERT PACK, and LOUIS SIMPSON. *The New Poets of England and America* (1957).
HALPERN, DANIEL. *The American Poetry Anthology: Poets under Forty* (1975).

Howe, Florence, and Ellen Bass. *No More Masks!* (1973).

Lowenfels, Walter. *Where Is Vietnam? American Poets Respond* (1967).

Major, Clarence. *The New Black Poetry* (1969); *Swallow the Lake* (1970).

Meltzer, David. *The San Francisco Poets* (1971).

Myers, Jack, and Roger Weingarten. *New American Poets of the 80s* (1984); *New American Poets of the 90s* (1991).

Padgett, Ron, and David Shapiro. *An Anthology of New York Poets* (1970).

Poulin, A., Jr. *Contemporary American Poetry* (4th ed., 1985).

Rosenthal, M. L. *The New Poets: American and British Poetry since World War II* (1967).

Rothenberg, Jerome. *America: A Prophecy* (1974).

Smith, Barbara. *Home Girls: A Black Feminist Anthology* (1983).

Smith, Dave, and David Bottoms. *The Morrow Anthology of Younger American Poets* (1985).

Stedman, Edmund Clarence. *American Anthology* (1900).

Strand, Mark. *The Contemporary American Poets: American Poetry since 1940* (1969).

Notes on Contributors

KATE DANIELS is a professor of English at Louisiana State University and an editor of the poetry journal *Poetry East*. She is the author of two books of poetry from University of Pittsburgh Press, *The White Wave* and *The Niobe Poems*, and she is currently completing a study on the life and work of the poet Muriel Rukeyser, entitled *Muriel Rukeyser: A Life of Poetry*, forthcoming from Random House.

MARK DOTY has been a faculty member of Goddard College and Sarah Lawrence College and is currently a faculty member of the Vermont College MFA Program in Writing. He is the author of three books of poetry, the latest being *Bethlehem in Broad Daylight*. He has received fellowships from the Massachusetts Artists Foundation, the Vermont Council on the Arts, and the National Endowment for the Arts.

ED FOLSOM is a professor of English and American studies at the University of Iowa. He is coeditor of three books concerning American poetry, among them *Walt Whitman: The Measure of His Song*. He is also editor of the *Walt Whitman Quarterly Review* and has been an associate editor of the *Iowa Review*. He is a recipient of a National Endowment for the Humanities summer stipend and is currently completing work on a book entitled *Talking Back to Walt Whitman*.

MICHAEL HELLER is a faculty member of New York University's American Language Institute and an editor of *Origin* and *Pequod* journals. He has published four books of poetry, the most recent being *Knowledge*, a book of criticism, *Conviction's Net of Branches: Essays on the Objectivist Poets and Poetry*, and a novella, *Marble Snows*. He has received awards from the Poetry Society of America, the New York State CAPS grants, and the New School for Social Research.

EDWARD HIRSCH is a professor of English at the University of Houston. He is the author of three books of poetry, *For the Sleepwalkers*, *Wild Gratitude*, which won the National Book Critics Award, and *The Night Parade*. He has received awards from the National Endowment for the Arts, the Guggenheim Foundation, the Academy of American Poets, the Delmore Schwartz Prize from New York University, and the Texas Institute of Letters.

JONATHAN HOLDEN is a professor of English at Kansas State University, where he directs the creative writing program. He is the author of four books of poetry, the latest being *Against Paradise,* and four books of criticism, most recently *Style and Authenticity in Postmodern Poetry.* He has been awarded the Juniper Prize, the AWP Award in poetry, the Devins Award, and, among others, a National Endowment for the Arts Fellowship.

RICHARD JACKSON is a professor of English at the University of Tennessee at Chattanooga, where he edits the *Poetry Miscellany.* He is the author of two books of poetry, *A Part of the Story* and *Worlds Apart,* and a book of criticism, *Dismantling Time in Contemporary Poetry.* He is also the editor of the two-volume series of interviews with contemporary poets, *Acts of Mind,* and he has been awarded several fellowships to study translation in Yugoslavia.

ROGER MITCHELL is a professor of English at Indiana University, where he directs the Indiana University Summer Writers' Conference. He is the author of three volumes of poetry, *Letters from Siberia, Moving,* and *A Clear Space on a Cold Day.* He was for many years the poetry editor of the *Minnesota Review.*

JACK MYERS is a professor of English at Southern Methodist University. He is the author of five books of poetry, the latest being *Blindsided,* and has edited and coedited five books on and about poetry, including *The Longman Dictionary of Poetic Terms.* He has received two National Endowments for the Arts Fellowships, the Texas Institute of Letters Award, and a Yaddo Fellowship and was a 1985 winner of the National Poetry Series.

TIMOTHY SEIBLES teaches at the Episcopal School of Dallas. He is the author of two chapbooks of poetry and a full-length collection entitled *Body Moves.* In 1990 he was awarded a National Endowment for the Arts Fellowship. Currently he is completing work on a second collection of poems.

LESLIE ULLMAN is a professor of English and the director of creative writing at the University of Texas at El Paso and a member of the Vermont College MFA Program in Writing. She is the author of two books of poetry: *Natural Histories,* the 1979 Yale Series of Poetry winner, and *Dreams by No One's Daughter.* She has also received awards from the National Endowment for the Arts and the Great Lakes Association.

DAVID WOJAHN is a professor of English at Indiana University and a member of the Vermont College MFA Program in Writing. He is the author of three books of poetry, *Icehouse Lights,* the 1981 Yale Series of Poetry winner, *Glassworks,* and *Mystery Train.* He is an editor of the literary journal *Crazy Horse* and of the Pushcart Prize, and he has received the William Carlos Williams Book Award, a National Endowment for the Arts Fellowship, an Amy Lowell Travelling Fellowship, and a fellowship from the Fine Arts Work Center in Provincetown.

Index

Aaron, Daniel, 86
Abstract Expressionism, 146–47, 202
Adams, Leonie, 78
Ai (Ogawa), 245–46; *Killing Floor*, 185, 246; "Lesson, Lesson," 246; "The Mortician's Twelve-Year-Old Son," 185
Aiken, Conrad, 49
Allen, Donald, 191; *The New American Poetry, 1945–1960*, 191
Allen, Samuel, 187
Altieri, Charles, 199–200, 207, 270–71
American poetry: as amalgam, 5–6; canon of, 5, 16; content of, 4–5; history and sources of, 3, 6–7, 15–17, 17–20; language of, 2–3, 4–5, 16–17; pattern of, 1–2; and realism, 10–11; and tradition, 16–17, 21–22
American Scholar, 258
American Writers Congresses, 94, 95
Arensberg, Walter, 65
Armory Show, the (post-Impressionists), 46
Ashbery, John, 48, 201, 202–3, 269, 270; and Abstract Expressionism, 202; *Some Trees*, 147
Associated Writing Programs, 261
Auden, W. H., 95, 115–16; on Adrienne Rich, 233–34; "At the Grave of Henry James," 116; "The Dark Years," 116; "In Praise of Limestone," 115; "Journey to Iceland," 95; "A Note on Order," 115
AWP Catalogue of Writing Programs, The, 261

Baraka, Imamu Amiri. *See* Jones, Leroi
Barthelme, Donald, 195, 204
Barzun, Jacques, 255
Baym, Max, 131
Beats, the, 142–45, 177, 221; influence of jazz on, 177
Bernstein, Charles, 272–73; *Contents' Dream: Essays 1975–80*, 271
Berry, Wendell, 258, 262, 266; "The Specialization of Poetry," 254–56

Berryman, John, 111–12, 193, 194–95; and Anne Bradstreet, 21, 148; *Dream Songs*, 148, 194–95; *Homage to Mistress Bradstreet*, 21, 112, 148; *Sonnets*, 112; "Winter Landscape," 112
Bishop, Elizabeth, 114–15, 150–52, 214–15, 142; *A Cold Spring*, 150; "The Fish," 115; "The Imaginary Iceberg," 114; "Little Exercise," 115; "The Map," 115; "The Monument," 115; *West of Childhood: Poems 1960–1965*, 215
Black Arts movement, 183
Black literary aesthetic, 159–60, 171–72, 183–84; Allen on, 187; Cullen on, 167; and definition of an artist, 171; European influence on, 162; Hughes on, 167; jazz influence on, 176–77; origins, of 19–20
Black Mountain Review, 197
Black Mountain school, 140, 197, 201
Blackmur, R. P., 58, 71, 116
Blake, William, 74–75
Bloom, Harold, 268, 269
Bly, Robert, 204–7, 257; *Fifties*, 155, 204–5; *The Light Around the Body*, 207; *Silence in the Snowy Fields*, 207; "A Wrong Turning in American Poetry," 206
Bogan, Louise, 78, 79, 241–42
Bradley, F. H., 61–62
Bradstreet, Anne, 9–10, 20–21, 112
Breslin, James E. B., 132, 133; *From Modern to Contemporary*, 274
Breslin, Paul, 258
Bridgman, Robert, 48
Brooks, Gwendolyn, 114, 174–75, 219–20, 244–45; *Annie Allen*, 114, 175; "The Mother," 175, 244–45; "Primer for Blacks," 245; "A Song in the Front Yard," 175; *A Street in Bronzeville*, 114; "When You Have Forgotten Sunday: The Love Story," 174
Brooks, Van Wyck, 58

Brown, Sterling, 168–69; "Southern Road," 168; "Strong Men," 169; "When de Saints Go Ma'chin' Home," 169

Calinescu, Matei, 27, 28
Captivity narratives, 20–21
Ciardi, John: *Mid-Century American Poets*, 136
Civil rights movement, 181–82
Coda, 261
Coleridge, Samuel Taylor, 119
Communism. *See* Marxism
Confessional poetry, 193–97, 256–57; John Berryman, 194–95; in the fifties, 147–55; Robert Lowell, 193–94; Sylvia Plath, 195–97; Anne Sexton, 195–97
Contact, 89
Contemporary Literature, 92
Cooper, Jane, 12
Coover, Robert: *The Public Burning*, 134
Corso, Gregory, 144–45
Cowley, Malcolm, 86
Crane, Hart, 72–73, 74–78, 85–86; "Ave Maria," 78; *The Bridge*, 7–8, 77–78; "The Broken Tower," 73; "For the Marriage of Faustus and Helen," 76; "General Aims and Theories," 74–75; "Proem," 78; "To Brooklyn Bridge," 77–78; "Voyages," 74, 75; *White Buildings*, 74, 75
Creative writing programs, 256, 258, 261
Creeley, Robert, 140–41, 197–98, 272; *For Love*, 141; on New Criticism, 131–32; "Return," 126
Criterion, 59, 62
Cullen, Countee, 163–64, 167; "Heritage," 163–64; "That Bright Chimeric Beast," 164; "Yet Do I Marvel," 163
Cummings, E. E., 57, 70–71, 126; *The Enormous Room*, 70

Dacey, Philip: *Strong Measures: Contemporary Poetry in Traditional Forms*, 268
Davie, Donald, 103, 268
Deconstructionism, 269–71
Deep Image poetry, 203–10, 257, 259; Donald Hall, 209–10; Louis Simpson, 208–9; soft surrealism, 210–13; William Stafford, 209; James Wright, 207–8
DeMan, Paul: *Blindness and Insight*, 103

Dembo, L. S., 92
Derrida, Jacques, 269, 270
Dial, 26, 46, 51
Dickey, James, 216
Dickinson, Emily, 8, 10–12, 15
Doolittle, Hilda (H. D.), 30, 43–45, 103, 123–24; "Cities," 44; *The Flowering of the Rod*, 124; "Huntress," 44; and Imagism, 43; "Oread," 30; and Pound, 43; *Sea Garden*, 43–44; *The Walls Do Not Fall*, 124; "The Wind Sleepers," 44
Duffy, William, 204–5
Dugan, Alan, 213, 217, 218
Dunbar, Paul Laurence, 158–59; "The Party," 159
Duncan, Robert, 199, 200

Eady, Cornelius, 186; *Victims of the Latest Dance Craze*, 186
Eberhart, Richard, 119; "A Meditation," 119
Egoist, 51
Einstein, Albert, 27, 102, 106
Eliot, T. S., 28, 41–43, 55–56, 58–62, 104, 116–17; "Aunt Helen," 42; and the *Criterion*, 59; *Four Quartets*, 198–99; "Gerontion," 60; "Hugh Selwyn Mauberly," 94–95; "Little Gidding," 116–17; "The Love Song of J. Alfred Prufrock," 42, 43; "The Metaphysical Poets," 55–56; "Morning at the Window," 42; "Notes Towards the Definition of Culture," 106; and Pound, 106; *The Sacred Wood*, 59; "Tradition and the Individual Talent," 58–59; *The Waste Land*, 55–56, 60–61, 62, 65, 66, 76; and Williams, 66
Emerson, Ralph Waldo, 31, 46
Empson, William: *Seven Types of Ambiguity*, 59
Engle, Paul, 256
Everson, William (Brother Antoninus), 145
Expansional poets, 215–20

Fearing, Kenneth, 122
Feminism, 239–41. *See also* Women's movement
Fenollosa, Ernest, 38
Ferlinghetti, Lawrence: *A Coney Island of the Mind*, 144
Fifties, 155, 204–5
Fitzgerald, F. Scott, 58
Forbidden Planet, The, 135
Forche, Carolyn, 263

Foster, Richard, 142
Freeman, Joseph, 93
Free verse, 25–26, 28, 34–35, 37, 259
French surrealism, 205
Freud, Sigmund, 27, 36, 124
Frost, Robert, 34–37, 71–72, 108–10;
    "Directive," 109, 117; and Pound, 36–
    37; and Stevens, 72; "A Tuft of
    Flowers," 34–35
Fugitive, 62
Fugitives, the, 62–63, 87–88; "I'll Take
    My Stand," 63

Galvin, Brendan, 265
Gardner, Isabella, 214
Garland, Hamlin, 71
Gibbs, Barbara, 192
Gilbert, Sandra, 11, 240
Ginsberg, Allen, 142–44, 221; *Howl*,
    143–44; *Kaddish*, 143; on
    transcendence, 143
Giovanni, Nikki: "The True Import of
    Present Dialogue: Black vs. Negro,"
    182
Gold, Mike, 93
Golffing, Francis, 192
Great Depression, the (Black Tuesday),
    54, 85
Greenberg, Samuel, 77
Gregory, Horace, 113
Gubar, Susan: *Shakespeare's Sisters:
    Feminist Essays on Women Poets*, 240

Hall, Donald, 207; *Contemporary
    American Poetry*, 209; *New Poets of
    England and America*, 190
Halpern Daniel, 256, 257, 261, 273; *The
    American Poetry Anthology*, 256
Happenings, 202, 204
Harlem Renaissance, 56–57, 159–68,
    183; Cullen 163–64, 167; Hughes,
    165–67, 172; Johnson, 161, 163, 164–
    65; McKay, 161–62
Harper, Michael: *Nightmare Begins
    Responsibility*, 184
Hass, Robert: "Meditation at Lagunitas,"
    268
Hayden, Robert, 219
H. D. *See* Doolittle, Hilda
Hecht, Anthony, 214
Hejinian, Lynn: *My Life*, 273
Heller, Joseph: *Catch 22*, 221
Heyen, William: *American Poets in
    1976*, 260
Hitler, Adolf, 94, 98
Hoffman, Frederick, 56

Hollander, John, 268
Hope, Francis, 54
Hough, Graham, 33
Howard, Richard, 214, 216, 268, 269
Howe, Irving, 32–33, 99
Hudgins, Andrew, 15
Hudson Review, 254
Hughes, Langston, 165–67, 172, 176–77;
    aesthetic of, 165–66, 176–77; "Dream
    Boogie," 176–77; "Harlem Sweeties,"
    172; "I Dream a World," 166; *Montage
    of a Dream Deferred*, 176, 177;
    "Mother to Son," 166; "The Negro
    Artist and the Racial Mountain," 167;
    "The Negro Speaks of Rivers," 166;
    Shakespeare in Harlem, 172; "The
    Weary Blues," 165
Hugo, Richard, 217–18, 265

Imagism, 30, 37, 38–39, 43, 44, 106
Industrial revolution, 27
Iowa, University of: Writers Workshop,
    256, 258
Ironic surrealism, 213

Jarman, Mark, 265
Jarrell, Randall, 108–11, 131; "The Age
    of Criticism," 104, 106, 111, 131; on
    critics, 137; *90° North*, 110, 137; "The
    Orient Express," 111; "The Other
    Frost," 108; on Robert Lowell, 152;
    Selected Poems, 137; "The Truth," 137
Jauss, David, 268. *See also* Dacey,
    Philip
Jazz Age, the, 58
Jeffers, Robinson, 88–89, 122, 124;
    "Original Sin," 122; "Their Beauty Has
    More Meaning," 122
Johnson, Denis: "In the Light of Other
    Lives," 264
Johnson, Georgia Douglas, 164;
    "Common Dust," 165
Johnson, James Weldon, 161; "Go Down
    Death (A Funeral Sermon)," 161
Jones, LeRoi (Imamu Amiri Baraka),
    178–80; *The Dead Lecturer*, 179; "I
    Substitute for the Dead Lecturer,"
    180; "Way Out West," 178–79
Jordan, June: "Newport Jazz Festival,"
    185; on Whitman, 15
Joyce, James: *Ulysses*, 62
Juhasz, Suzanne, 260
Jung, Carl, 205, 259
Justice, Donald, 8–9

Kaufman, Bob, 180–81; "Battle Report," 180–81
Keats, John, 105
Kees, Weldon, 138–39; "Round," 138–39; "The Umbrella," 139
Kelly, Robert, 203
Kenner, Hugh, 69, 91; "Oppen, Zukofsky, and the Poem as Lens," 90
Kermode, Frank, 31
Kierkegaard, Søren, 115
Kinnell, Galway, 211; "The Bear," 211
Kizer, Carolyn, 215, 243–44, 263–64; "The Copulating Gods," 263–64; "Pro Femina," 243–44
Knight, Etheridge, 183
Koch, Kenneth, 255
Kramer, Hilton, 267
Krutch, Joseph Wood, 93
Kumin, Maxine, 218–19, 244
Kunitz, Stanley, 119–20, 138, 148–49

Language poetry, 267, 272–73
Lanier, Sidney, 15
Lazer, Hank, 271, 272, 273; "The Crisis in Poetry," 271
Lee, Don L. (Haki R. Madhubuti), 182–83, 185–86; "a poem to complement other poems," 182; "Rainforest," 186
Leithauser, Brad, 267
Lensing, George, 203
Levertov, Denise, 141–42, 197, 198–99; "Illustrious Ancestors," 141; "Some Notes on Organic Form" 199
Levine, Philip, 264
Lewis, C. D., 95
Lieberman, Laurence: "The Expansional Poet: A Return to Personality," 215
Lindsay, Vachel, 25, 26, 49
Little Review, 46
Locke, Alain, 171
Lorde, Audre, 246–47; "Love Poem," 247
Lowell, Amy, 38, 78
Lowell, Robert, 113–14, 152–55, 193–94; "Inauguration Day: January 1953," 135; Life Studies, 152–55, 194; "Memories of West Street and Lepke," 134; The Mills of the Kavanaughs, 152, 153; on the prose memoir, 154; "Sailing Home from Rapallo," 155

Maas, Willard, 225
McAlmon, Robert, 68
McCarthy trials, 134

McDowell, Robert, 265
McKay, Claude, 161–62, 171; "If We Must Die," 162; "The White House," 162
MacLeish, Archibald, 55, 72
Madhubuti, Haki R. See Lee, Don L.
Mariani, Paul, 85, 96
Marxism, 27, 86, 87, 92–93, 94, 95, 230
Masters, Edgar Lee, 25, 26, 49–50; "Judge Somers," 50; Spoon River Anthology, 49–50
Melville, Herman, 18; "The Temeraire," 7
Merrill, James, 214
Mersmann, James: Out of the Vietnam Vortex: A Study of Poets and Poetry Against the War, 220
Merwin, W. S., 18, 211–12
Michener, James, 261
Miles, Josephine, 98
Millay, Edna St. Vincent, 57, 79
Miller, J. Hillis, 67–68
Modernism, 25–29, 32–33, 54–55, 58–59, 84; and Imagism, 30
Monroe, Harriet, 34, 89, 90
Moore, Marianne, 65–67, 69–70; "Poetry," 67
Moran, Ronald, 203
Morrow Anthology of Younger Poets (ed. Dave Smith), 273
Mussolini, Benito, 40, 89, 100, 123

National Endowment for the Arts, 255
National woman suffrage movement, 57
Naturalism, 34, 36
New American Poetry, 1945–1960, The (ed. Donald Allen), 191, 210
New American Poets of the 80s (eds. Myers and Weingarten), 273
New Criterion, 267
New Criticism, the, 98, 128; the end of, 131, 132
New Formalism, the, 266–67, 273
New Journalism, the, 204
New Masses, 87, 93, 94
New Poets of England and America, (ed. Donald Hall), 190, 209, 259
New York School, 145–47, 200–203; John Ashbery, 202–3; Kenneth Koch, 201; Frank O'Hara, 202; Peter Schjeldahl, 201; James Schuyler, 201
Niedecker, Lorine, 90
Nietzsche, Friedrich, 27
No More Masks! (ed. Bass), 227

Objectivism, 90–93
O'Hara, Frank, 145–47, 201–2; *Lunch Poems*, 202; "Personism," 201, 202
Olds, Sharon, 249–51, 262–63; "The Connoisseuse of Slugs," 250–51; "First Sex," 249–50; "Love in Blood Time," 250, 448–49; "Rite of Passage," 263; "What If God," 249
Olson, Charles, 125, 139–40, 197, 198
Open form, 140. *See also* Projectivism
Oppen, George, 90, 91, 92, 93
Organic form, 140, 272
Origin, 197
Ostriker, Alicia, 239–40; "American Poetry, Now Shaped by Women," 260–61
Others, 51

Padgett, Ron, 201
Paris Review, 119–20
Partisan Review, 94
Patchen, Kenneth, 125
Peacock, Molly, 248–49
Perloff, Marjorie, 272–73
"Personism," 201, 202
Phillips, William, 94
Pinsky, Robert, 266; *The Situation of Poetry*, 256–58
Plath, Sylvia, 195–97
Plumly, Stanley, 258–59, 260
Poetry: A Magazine of Verse, 38, 75, 89
Poets-in-the-Schools programs, 201, 255
Pop Art, 204
Post-Impressionism, 46
Poulin, A. J., 220
Pound, Ezra, 16, 36–41, 58, 59, 89, 122–23; Chinese translation, 29, 123, 40; and Eliot, 41, 58, 59; and Frost, 36–37; and H. D., 43; "Homage to Sextus Propertius," 40; "Hugh Selwyn Mauberly," 32, 40, 54–55, 60; and Imagism, 38–40; Mussolini, 40, 89, 123; *Pisan Cantos*, 123; and *Poetry*, 37; "The River Merchant's Wife: A Letter," 29; "Salutation," 29; on Whitman, 16; and Williams, 45
Prohibition amendment, 56
Projectivism, 139–40. *See also* Black Mountain School
Protest poetry, 220–22

Rahv, Philip, 94
Rakosi, Carl, 90, 91, 92, 99
Ransom, John Crowe, 62–64, 87–88; on

criticism, 131; *I'll Take My Stand*, 63. *See also* Fugitives, the,
Realism, 93, 264–66
Reaper, 254, 265–66, 268–69
"Red Wheelbarrow, The," 30–31
Reed, John, 87
Rexroth, Kenneth, 95, 121–22, 142, 143; "Climbing Milestone Mountain, August 22, 1937," 121; on *Howl*, 143
Reznikoff, Charles, 90, 91, 92
Rich, Adrienne, 9–11, 216–17, 233–38, 240, 260; on bisexuality 11; "The Burning of Paper Instead of Children," 236–37; critical reception of, 233–34; *Diving into the Wreck: Poems 1971–1972*, 237–38, 260; domestic life of, 234–35; "Incipience," 238; influence of, 9–11; "Love in the Museum," 234; "Prospective Immigrants Please Note," 235–36; "Shooting Script," 236; "A Valediction Forbidding Mourning," 237; *The Will to Change*, 236
Richards, I. A., 56, 59
Rimbaud, Arthur, 67
Robinson, Edwin Arlington, 33–34; *King Jasper*, 34–35; "Richard Cory," 33–34
Roethke, Theodore, 117–19, 149–50, 215–16; "A Field of Light," 118; *The Lost Son and Other Poems*, 118
Rosenberg, Julius and Ethel, *134*
Rosenfeld, Paul, 66, 94
Rosenthal, M. L., 143, 153
Rukeyser, Muriel, 95, 120–21, 217, 224–33; "Ajanta," 120; "Along History," 228; "Käthe Kollwitz," 230, 232; "Myth," 229; *Night Music*, 95; "Nine Poems for the Unborn Child," 229; politics of, 230; as predecessor of women's movement, 224–25; "Rational Man," 231; on sexuality, 228–29, 231–32; "The Speed of Darkness," 228–29; "To Enter That Rhythm Where the Self Is Lost," 226
Russian revolution, 86–87. *See also* Marxism

Sacco and Vanzetti, 56, 121
Salter, Mary Jo, 249
Sandburg, Carl, 25, 49–51, 93; *Chicago Poems*, 50; "Halsted Street Car," 50–51; "Soup," 51
San Francisco poets, the, 142, 221
Sarton, May, 98
Schjeldahl, Peter, 201
Schuyler, James, 201

Schwartz, Delmore, 98, 102, 103, 104, 107–8, 121; "The Isolation of Modern Poetry," 103; "The Literary Dictatorship of T. S. Eliot," 104; "Present Moment," 108; on Roethke, 149
Scopes trial, 63
Seidel, Emil, 50
Seth, Vikram, 268
Sewanee Review, 113
Sexton, Anne, 195–96, 197
Shapiro, Karl, 125–26; on Randall Jarrell, 137
Simpson, Louis, 208–9; "What is a Poet?" 271
Sixties, (ed. Robert Bly), 205, 206
Slave narratives, 19–20
Smith, Dave, 265
Snodgrass, W. D., 193–94
Snyder, Gary, 145, 199
Soft surrealism, 210–13
Sontag, Susan, 204
Spanish surrealism, 203, 205, 206, 208
Spender, Stephen, 95
Stafford, William, 205, 209, 210, 215
Stalin, Josef, 94, 95
Stanza-paragraph, 170
Stein, Gertrude, 46–48; The Autobiography of Alice B. Toklas, 48; "Lifting Belly," 48; "A Red Hat," 47
Stevens, Wallace, 72–74, 95–96, 102, 103–4, 269; "Anecdote of the Jar," 74; "Esthétique du Mal," 104; "Fabliau of Florida," 29–30; Harmonium, 51, 74
Stieglitz, Alfred, 46, 66
Stitt, Peter, 271
Strand, Mark, 210, 212–13
Surrealism, 205, 210–13
Symbolism, 103

Tate, Allen, 64–65, 102, 103, 105–6, 116; on the fifties, 135
Taylor, Clyde, 178
Teasdale, Sara, 78, 79, 232
Thompson, Virgil, 47, 48
Tolson, Melvin B., 96, 172–74; "Dark Symphony," 172–74
Toomer, Jean, 57, 96
Traherne, Thomas, 128

Trilling, Lionel, 27
Trotsky, Leon, 94

Universities: and poetry, 256, 258, 261

Van Doren, Mark, 111
Vanzetti. See Sacco and Vanzetti
Vendler, Helen, 240–41
Victorian era, 27, 28, 31
Vietnam War, 192, 206, 220, 221, 262

Wakoski, Diane, 210
Wald, Alan, 94
Walker, Alice: "On Stripping Bark from Myself," 247
Walker, David, 269, 272; The Transparent Lyric, 269–70
Walker, Margaret: For My People, 170–71; "For My People," 170; "Molly Means," 170; stanza-paragraph, 170
Warren, Robert Penn, 112–13, 138
Watts, Emily Stipes, 19
Wheatley, Phillis, 19–20
Whitman, Walt, 1, 11–17, 20, 22, 77
Wilbur, Richard, 127–28, 136–37, 213, 267
Williams, C. K., 264
Williams, William Carlos, 6–7, 30–31, 45–46, 65–69, 85, 88, 89, 90, 106–07; "The Red Wheelbarrow," 30–31
Winters, Yvor, 102, 105, 109, 113
Women's movement, 9–12, 19, 224–44; definition of, 239–41; equal rights, 248; feminist presses, 243; polarities of, 242
Women's poetic tradition, formalists in, 248–49, 266–67
Woolf, Virginia, 26, 32
World War I, 29, 31, 40, 54
Wright, James, 205, 207–8, 256
Writers Workshop, 256, 258, 261
Wylie, Elinor, 78, 79

Yale Review, 103, 215
Yeats, William Butler, 98, 100, 103, 111, 117, 125, 225

Zen Buddhism, 145
Zola, Emile, 33, 34, 93
Zukofsky, Louis, 90, 91, 92, 95, 96
Zweig, Paul: "The New Surrealism," 210